AFRICAN AMERICAN LITERATURE IN TRANSITION, 1800–1830

African American literature in the years between 1800 and 1830 emerged from significant transitions in the cultural, technological, and political circulation of ideas. Transformations included increased numbers of Black organizations, shifts in the physical mobility of Black peoples, expanded circulation of abolitionist and Black newsprint as well as greater production of Black authored texts and images. The perpetuation of slavery in the early American republic meant that many people of African descent conveyed experiences of bondage or promoted abolition in complex ways, relying on a diverse array of print and illustrative forms. Accordingly, this volume takes a thematic approach to African American literature from 1800 to 1830, exploring Black organizational life before 1830, movement and mobility in African American literature, and print culture in circulation, illustration, and the narrative form.

JASMINE NICHOLE COBB is the Bacca Foundation Associate Professor of African & African American Studies and of Art, Art History and Visual Studies at Duke University. She is the author of *Picture Freedom: Remaking Black Visuality in the Early Nineteenth Century* (2015). She teaches courses on Black visual culture and representation. Cobb earned a PhD from the University of Pennsylvania and is a recipient of the American Fellowship from the American Association of University Women (AAUW).

AFRICAN AMERICAN LITERATURE IN TRANSITION

Editor Joycelyn K. Moody, The University of Texas at San Antonio

Associate Editor Cassander Smith, The University of Alabama

Across 17 authoritative volumes and featuring over 200 of today's foremost literary critics and social historians, African American Literature in Transition offers a critical and comprehensive revisionary analysis of creative expression by people of African descent. Reading transtemporally from the origins of "African American literature" by the first peoples calling themselves "African Americans," this series foregrounds change, and examines pivotal moments, years, decades, and centuries in African American literature and culture. While collectively analyzing both far-reaching and flash-forward transitions within four centuries, the multi-volume series replaces conventional historical periodization in African American scholastic and literary anthologies with a framework that contextualizes shifts, changes, and transformations in African American literature, culture, politics, and history.

Books in the series

African American Literature in Transition, 1800–1830 edited by JASMINE NICHOLE COBB

African American Literature in Transition, 1830–1850 edited by BENJAMIN FAGAN

African American Literature in Transition, 1850–1865 edited by TERESA ZACKODNIK

African American Literature in Transition, 1865–1880 edited by ERIC GARDNER

African American Literature in Transition, 1900–1910 edited by SHIRLEY MOODY-TURNER

African American Literature in Transition, 1960–1970 edited by SHELLY EVERSLEY

AFRICAN AMERICAN LITERATURE IN TRANSITION, 1800–1830

EDITED BY

JASMINE NICHOLE COBB

Duke University

CAMBRIDGE
UNIVERSITY PRESS

University Printing House, Cambridge CB2 8BS, United Kingdom

One Liberty Plaza, 20th Floor, New York, NY 10006, USA

477 Williamstown Road, Port Melbourne, VIC 3207, Australia

314–321, 3rd Floor, Plot 3, Splendor Forum, Jasola District Centre, New Delhi – 110025, India

79 Anson Road, #06–04/06, Singapore 079906

Cambridge University Press is part of the University of Cambridge.

It furthers the University's mission by disseminating knowledge in the pursuit of education, learning, and research at the highest international levels of excellence.

www.cambridge.org
Information on this title: www.cambridge.org/9781108429078
DOI: 10.1017/9781108632003

First published 2021

Printed in the United Kingdom by TJ Books Limited, Padstow Cornwall

A catalogue record for this publication is available from the British Library.

Library of Congress Cataloging-in-Publication Data
NAMES: Cobb, Jasmine Nichole, editor.
TITLE: African American literature in transition, 1800–1830 / edited by Jasmine Nichole Cobb, Duke Trinity College.
DESCRIPTION: Cambridge ; New York : Cambridge University Press, 2021. | SERIES: African American literature in transition ; 2 | Includes bibliographic references and index. |
IDENTIFIERS: LCCN 2020045817 (print) | LCCN 2020045818 (ebook) | ISBN 9781108429078 (hardback) | ISBN 9781108454421 (paperback) | ISBN 9781108632003 (epub)
SUBJECTS: LCSH: American literature–African American authors–History and criticism. | African Americans–Intellectual life–19th century. | African Americans in literature.
CLASSIFICATION: LCC PS153.N5 A33645 2021 (print) | LCC PS153.N5 (ebook) | DDC 810.8/89607309034–dc23
LC record available at https://lccn.loc.gov/2020045817
LC ebook record available at https://lccn.loc.gov/2020045818

ISBN 978-1-108-42907-8 Hardback

Contents

List of Figures *page* vii
List of Contributors ix
General Editor's Preface xi
Chronology xiii

Introduction: African American Writing Out of Bounds, 1800–1830 1
Jasmine Nichole Cobb

PART I BLACK ORGANIZATIONAL LIFE BEFORE 1830 15

1 Race, Writing, and Eschatological Hope, 1800–1830 19
Maurice Wallace

2 Daniel Coker, David Walker, and the Politics of Dialogue with Whites in Early Nineteenth-Century African American Literature 44
William L. Andrews

3 Black Entrepreneurship, Economic Self-Determination and Early Print in Antebellum Brooklyn 71
Prithi Kanakamedala

PART II MOVEMENT AND MOBILITY IN AFRICAN AMERICAN LITERATURE 91

4 Early African American Literature and the British Empire, 1808–1835 95
Joseph Rezek

5 Robert Roberts's *The House Servant's Directory* and the Performance of Stability in African American Print, 1800–1830 119
Britt Rusert

6 Dream Visions in Early Black Autobiography; Or, Why Frederick Douglass Doesn't Dream 146
Bryan Sinche

PART III PRINT CULTURE IN CIRCULATION 167

7 Reading, Black Feminism, and the Press around 1827 171
Teresa Zackodnik

8 "Theresa" and the Early Transatlantic Mixed-Race Heroine: Black Solidarity in *Freedom's Journal* 202
Brigitte Fielder

9 Redemption, the Historical Imagination, and Early Black Biographical Writing 227
Stefan M. Wheelock

PART IV ILLUSTRATION AND THE NARRATIVE FORM 255

10 Theorizing Vision and Selfhood in Early Black Writing and Art 259
Sarah Blackwood

11 Embodying Activism, Bearing Witness: The Portraits of Early African American Ministers in Philadelphia 288
Aston Gonzalez

12 Visual Insubordination within Early African American Portraiture and Illustrated Books 316
Martha J. Cutter

Index 344

Figures

5.1 Excerpt from Robert Roberts's *The House Servant's Directory* in the August 10, 1829 issue of *The Lynchburg Virginian.* *page* 120
10.1 Joshua Johnson, *Mary Ann Jewins Burnett,* oil on canvas, *c.*1812. 272
10.2 Joshua Johnson, *James McCormick Family*, oil on canvas, *c.*1804–1824. 275
10.3 Joshua Johnson, *Rebecca Myring Everette and Her Children,* oil on canvas, 1818. 276
10.4 Joshua Johnson, *Emma Von Name,* oil on canvas, *c.*1805. 279
11.1 Anonymous, [*Portrait of Richard Allen*], *c.*1784. 291
11.2 Anonymous, *Rev. Richard Allen, founder of the American Methodist Episcopal Church, in the United States of America, 1779*, c.1813. 292
11.3 John Boyd, *The Rev. Richard Allen, Bishop of the First African Methodist Episcopal Church, in the U. States*, 1823. 296
11.4 W.R. Jones and John Boyd, *The Revd. Absalom Jones, Rector of St. Thomas's African Episcopal Church in the City of Philad*, 1823. 298
11.5 W.R. Jones and B. Tanner, *Revd. John Gloucester, Late pastor of the First African Presbyterian Church in Philadelphia*, 1823. 303
11.6 Robert Tiller, *Revd. Jeremiah Gloucester, Late pastor of the Second African Presbyterian Church in Philadelphia.* 306
12.1 *Slave Torture* in *The Anti-Slavery Almanac* vol. 1.3 (1838). 320
12.2 Membership Certificate from the New-Jersey Society Promoting the Abolition of Slavery, 1839. 322
12.3 Patrick Reason, *Am I Not a Man and a Brother* (1839). 322

12.4 Frontispiece of *Life and Adventures of Robert, the Hermit of Massachusetts Who Has Lived 14 Years in a Cave, Secluded from Human Society Comprising, an Account of his Birth, Parentage, Sufferings, and Providential Escape from Unjust and Cruel Bondage in Early Life, and His Reasons for Becoming a Recluse*, 1829. 324
12.5 Frontispiece of Charles Edwards Lester and Peter Wheeler, *Chains and Freedom; or, The Life and Adventures of Peter Wheeler, a Colored Man Yet Living*, 1839. 329
12.6 Illustration from Moses Roper, *A Narrative of the Adventures and Escape*, 1838. 331
12.7 Frontispiece portrait from Moses Roper, *A Narrative of the Adventures and Escape of Moses Roper from American Slavery, with a Portrait*, 1840. 333
12.8 "My Heart is Almost Broken," from Henry Bibb's *Narrative* (1849, 2nd edition). 334
12.9 Frontispiece and title page to some versions of Henry Bibb's *Narrative* (1849, 2nd edition) with double portrait. 336

Contributors

JASMINE NICHOLE COBB, Duke University.

MAURICE WALLACE, Rutgers University.

WILLIAM L. ANDREWS, University of North Carolina, Chapel Hill.

PRITHI KANAKAMEDALA, Bronx Community College of the City University of New York.

JOSEPH REZEK, Boston University.

BRITT RUSERT, University of Massachusetts, Amherst.

BRYAN SINCHE, University of Hartford.

TERESA ZACKODNIK, University of Alberta.

BRIGITTE FIELDER, University of Wisconsin-Madison.

STEFAN M. WHEELOCK, George Mason University.

SARAH BLACKWOOD, Pace University.

ASTON GONZALEZ, Salisbury University.

MARTHA J. CUTTER, University of Connecticut.

Preface
African American Literature in Transition

Joycelyn K. Moody, General Editor

When I accepted the invitation to act as Series Editor for African American Literature in Transition, Barack Obama had several months more to serve as President of the United States. The US was in a time of tremendous transition, we knew, but the extent of the impact of the coming election and its outcomes on the lives of African Americans, we had yet to learn. In the years since, dozens of today's foremost literary critics and social historians have traced across this authoritative multi-volume series revisionary analyses of creative expression by peoples of the African diaspora. Reading transtemporally, African American Literature in Transition foregrounds change, and examines pivotal moments and eras in African American history and historiography, literature and culture, art and ideology. The contributors explore four centuries of far-reaching as well as flash-forward transitions, to replace conventional literary periodization with a framework that contextualizes shifts, changes, and transformations affecting African American people.

Taken singly or together, the more than 200 chapters of the series provide not customary synopses of African American literature but unprecedented, detailed analyses – each expansive, in-depth, engaging. Every contributor finds their perfect pitch. Where contributors are musicians, then, to quote John Lovell, Jr.'s *Black Song: The Forge and the Flame*, "music raise[s] both performer and audience far above routine emotion; the elderly throw away their sticks and dance."

The central aim of African American Literature in Transition is to reorient readers' expectations of the literary critical and appreciative experience. The series emphasizes the importance of reading intertextually, transhistorically, and interdisciplinarily. In this way, we foster readers' comprehension of ways in which legal cases such as the *Dred Scott* Decision and *Plessy* v. *Ferguson*, for example, were forecast in David Walker's 1829 *Appeal to the Colored Citizens of the World* and have reappeared in *Solitary: My Story of Transformation and Hope*, by Albert

1804 The Haitian Revolution (commenced in 1791) concludes on January 1 with Haiti's independence.
New Jersey passes "An Act for the Gradual Abolition of Slavery," becoming the last Northern state to commit to gradual emancipation. Eight free states and eight slave states are now divided by the Mason-Dixon line.

1805 Venture Smith dies in Connecticut.

1807 First African Presbyterian Church is founded in Philadelphia and receives its charter two years later.
Abolition of the transatlantic slave trade in Britain.
Federal legislation signed by Thomas Jefferson to abolish the transatlantic slave trade takes effect on January 1.

1809 Orations on January 2 commemorate the abolition of the international slave trade. Published examples include Henry Sipkins's *An Oration on the Abolition of the Slave Trade*; William Hamilton's *An Address to the New York African Society, for the Mutual Relief, Delivered In the Universalist Church, January 2, 1809*; and Joseph Sidney's *An Oration Commemorative of the Abolition of the Slave Trade in the United States; Delivered before the Wilberforce Philanthropic Association. In the City of New-York on the Second of January, 1809*.
The *Long Island Star* commences publication.

1810 The Brooklyn African Woolman Benevolent Society is established.
The Blind African Slave; Or, Memoirs of Boyrereau Brinch, Nicknamed Jeffrey Brace, is published in St. Albans, Vermont.

1812 Martin R. Delany is born in Charles Town, West Virginia.
The War of 1812 between the United States and Britain begins.
Transatlantic merchant Paul Cuffee publishes his pro-emigration pamphlet, *A Brief Account of the Settlement and Present Situation of the Colony of Sierra Leone*.

1813 Harriet Jacobs is thought to be born in Edenton, North Carolina.
Philadelphian James Forten is almost certainly the anonymous author of *Letters from A Man of Colour, on a Late Bill before the Senate of Pennsylvania*.

1814 William Wells Brown is thought to be born in Kentucky.
The United States wins the War of 1812.
Peter Croger opens the African School in Brooklyn.

1816 Henry Highland Garnet is born in New Market, Maryland.
The African Methodist Episcopal (AME) Church is founded by Richard Allen, who serves as its first bishop.
The American Colonization Society is established to promote Black repatriation to Africa.
William Henry Brown opens the African Company in New York City

1817 Victor Séjour is born in New Orleans, Louisiana.
New York State passes a law stating slavery will end on July 4, 1827, following its Gradual Emancipation Law in 1799.
The AME Book Concern is instituted as the first Black publishing house.
Zilpha Elaw attends her first camp meeting.

1818 Frederick Douglass is born in Talbot County, Maryland, and Elizabeth Keckley is born in Dinwiddie, Virginia.
The Haitian government begins offering Black Americans paid passage to induce immigration to Haiti; the founding of the Haytian Emigration Society of Coloured People
Black Brooklynites found the Brooklyn African Methodist Episcopalian Church.
Jarena Lee begins holding prayer meetings in her own home.

1819 Jarena Lee becomes the first woman whom Richard Allen authorizes to preach in the AME church.
Zilpha Elaw attends a second camp meeting where she is inspired to address the congregation and formally recognizes her call to preach.

1820 The Missouri Compromise takes effect. Missouri is admitted as a slave state while Maine is admitted as a free state.

1821 Lucy Terry dies in Sunderland, Vermont.
The American Colonization Society obtains the land to establish the privately-owned colony later named Liberia.
Brown moves his theater company and renames it African Grove Theatre

1822 James Monroe Whitfield is born in New Hampshire.
Denmark Vesey's slave revolt is foiled in Charleston, South Carolina.

1823 William Henry Brown writes and stages *The Drama of King Shotaway* with his Black theater company, the African Company, at the African Grove Theatre in New York City.
Julia A. J. Foote is born in Schenectady, New York.

1824 A petition to establish the Second African Presbyterian Church in Philadelphia is granted.
The Haitian Emigration Society is founded in Philadelphia.

1825 Frances Harper is born in Baltimore, Maryland, and Harriet Wilson is born in Milford, New Hampshire.
Harriet Jacobs arrives at the Norcom plantation.
The *Life of William Grimes, Runaway Slave* is published in New York as one of the first book-length, self-penned US slave narratives; Venture Smith's shorter narrative was dictated and published in 1798.
William Grimes's *The Life of William Grimes, the Runaway Slave, Written by Himself* is published and will be republished in 1855.

1826 Sojourner Truth escapes from slavery in New York.

1827 Slavery ends in New York State.
Freedom's Journal, the first Black periodical in the United States, is launched in New York City by owners Samuel Cornish and John Brown Russwurm.
The Society of Young Ladies is formed in Lynn, Massachusetts.

1828 The Reading Room Society for young Black men of Philadelphia is founded.
Zilpha Elaw begins preaching in the slave-holding South.

1829 *Freedom's Journal* prints its final issue.
The first edition of David Walker's *Appeal, in Four Articles; Together with a Preamble, to the Colored Citizens of the World* is published in pamphlet format in Boston. He publishes a second and third, final, edition in 1830.
George Moses Horton's first collection of poetry, *The Hope of Liberty*, is published in Raleigh, North Carolina.

1830 David Walker dies in Boston, Massachusetts.
Congress passes the Indian Removal Act.
Race riots take place in Cincinnati, Ohio, leading to substantial Black emigration.
The National Negro Convention Movement begins at a meeting in Philadelphia.
Census records indicate a United States population of 12,866,020 including a Black population of 2,328,842 (319,599 of whom were free).

1831 The *Liberator* begins publication on January 1 in Boston with William Lloyd Garrison as the editor.
Black women of Philadelphia begin the Female Literary Society.
Maria W. Stewart publishes *Religion and the Pure Principles of Morality* in Boston.

1832 Maria Stewart gives a public address to the Afric-American Female Intelligence Society in Boston.

1833 American Anti-Slavery Society Convention meets in Philadelphia on December 4.

Introduction
African American Writing Out of Bounds, 1800–1830

Jasmine Nichole Cobb

African American Literature in Transition, volume 2 (AALT), chronicles and interprets authors, texts, and cultural transitions of the years between 1800 and 1830. Divided into four parts, this volume takes up well-known figures but explores their themes in ways that reveal transformations that made their literary production possible. African American literature of the early national period was produced on the run, amid slavery's penchant for backbreaking labor and before the widespread organization of US abolition. African American authors of this period were not writing with the support of a highly organized "Black public sphere," such as the one that emerged by 1830, so much as they were creating those institutions with the intellectual labor and cultural production that is the subject of this volume. Chapters here examine transformations in the ways people of African descent thought of themselves and about whiteness, in addition to their ruminations on slavery, justice, and national belonging.

The quest for freedom is a driving force of African American literature produced in the thirty-year period between 1800 and 1830. These three decades are not only unique for marking the turn of the nineteenth century, but also for how they entail simultaneous progress and setbacks for people of African descent moving out of the chains of slavery. Still more than thirty years before the abolition of slavery in 1865, this period encompassed legislative efforts in individual states to slowly emancipate unfree people of African descent in the northern states east of the Mississippi River. For example, New Jersey was the last state in the North to pass such a law – its Act for the Gradual Abolition of Slavery – in 1804. However, by this date, states including Massachusetts, Vermont, Pennsylvania, and New York were already limiting the years of servitude placed on bondspersons at birth. New York's 1799 law emancipated unfree children born after July 4, 1799, with men set free by the age of 28 and women at age 25; the New York legislature eventually replaced this system with the 1817 law that decreed New York slavery would end on

July 4, 1827. Although many of these laws focused on recompense for whites instead of Blacks, such edicts contributed to a climate of national discourse about the condition of Black people in the United States. Taken as a whole, gradual emancipation laws made this thirty-year period one of judicial confrontations, where people petitioned the courts and public opinion on Black people's rights to assemble, to move across state lines, to develop literacy, and to see themselves as other than "slaves." Whereas, however, this period was also bookended by Fugitive Slave Acts in 1793 and 1850, legislation whereby the federal government demanded that even non-slave-owning citizens participate in the maintenance of slavery by returning runaways, this period vacillated on the status of Black people. Would they ever be free from slavery? Would free Blacks ever count as citizens?

This volume contends that the material conditions of the years between 1800 and 1830 rendered Black authors and much of African American literature "out of bounds." Contributors engage literature by people of African descent outside of slavery's fetters, or Black cultural producers creating work deemed untoward, or literatures developed outside the covers of bound books. Given the constant undulation between pro-abolition and pro-slavery agendas, even in northern regions, the idea of Black literature was plagued not only by prohibitions on literacy and circumscription on Black people's mobility, but also by ambivalence about what in fact would have been acceptable public discourse for people of African descent. This volume explores African American literature that elided the suppression of African American thought by directly confronting the urgencies of the moment, especially themes related to the pursuit and the experience of freedom. Transitions in the social, political, and cultural conditions of the decades in question, show themselves in literary production at the turn of the nineteenth century.

Legal and extralegal routes to emancipation shaped the early decades of the nineteenth century. By the early 1800s, most states north of the Mason-Dixon line were home to noticeable communities of free African Americans. Although free Blacks were small in proportion to other demographics recorded on the US census, the visual impact of Black free people – with their separate churches, their public celebrations, and their sheer distinction from the enslaved – made Black freedom robust in the minds of whites in the evolving republic.[1] Although some African Americans paid for their freedom, sued for their freedom, or petitioned courts when their owners broke laws requiring the registration of human property,[2] extralegal means of obtaining freedom were significant to the establishment of free communities. Organized maneuvering via the Underground Railroad, for example, contributed to the increase in free Black populations and their diversity in the North. This network of Black and white abolitionists, as well as Quakers, organized "stations" and donated money to help fugitive free people journey from southern states to the North and sometimes as far as Canada. It also provided a means by which Black abolitionists could support the cause, in addition to organizing meetings and publishing prose that formed the burgeoning US antislavery movement that bloomed after 1830. However, the Underground Railroad was not the only means of extralegal escape from bondage as most fugitives from slavery were individuals who absconded on their own and without an organized network of help. Historian John Hope Franklin points to the strenuous efforts of Black runaways of the South who "ran away each year into the woods, swamps, hills, backcountry, towns, and cities of the South."[3] Newspapers such as the *Pennsylvania Gazette* (1728) and the *South Carolina Gazette* (1732) advertised runaway notices for Black fugitives in Pennsylvania, for instance, who departed from owners and were thought to reside in free Black communities. Blacks who absconded from slavery both in the North and in the South, summarily, sought refuge in various regions. By any means available to them, people of African descent were getting out of the binds of slavery and the period 1800 to 1830 was shaped by their actions.

So what did African Americans write about between 1800 and 1830? Exits from slavery and the burgeoning national discourse about the peculiar institution corresponded to the increasing popularity of the slave narrative. Scholar of African American literature William Andrews explains that these texts "chronicle the evolution of white supremacy in the South" and that, as autobiography, slave narratives indicate the ways in which people of African descent managed "to bequeath a literary legacy of enormous collective significance to the South and the United States."[4] This genre was firmly established by the turn of the nineteenth century and became increasingly popular over time, with more than one hundred autobiographies by enslaved persons published between 1745 and 1865.[5] Eight narratives were published between 1800 and 1830, including George White's *A Brief Account of the Life, Experience, Travels, and Gospel Labours of George White, an African: Written by Himself, and Revised by a Friend* (1810) and William Grimes's *Life of William Grimes, the Runaway Slave, Written by Himself* (1825). Narratives of this period might be considered among those that "attempt to re-member the African self, to articulate an African character outside Africa, to transcend or otherwise come to terms with written materials such as "A Narrative of the Proceedings of the Black People During the Late Awful Calamity in Philadelphia" and all of the writing that supported the establishment of the first separate Black church, Mother Bethel AME in Philadelphia, Pennsylvania.

Black religion and the establishment of separate institutions required extensive writing. People of African descent established their own churches, and these buildings served as spiritual homes and places for political organizing, as well as educational institutions. Ministers like Jones and Allen engaged in publication as members of a community of Black religious figures who produced a number of important writings that emerged from the exclusion of Black people – barred from churches and fraternal organizations – who started their own institutions. In addition to churches, these religious figureheads established mutual aid societies to bury their dead, feed their poor, and educate children as well as adults. African American organizations including the Freemasons, the AME Church, mutual benefit groups, and others produced literature and print documents that exist as archival records and tell about the cultural transitions of the early nineteenth century. For Chapter 3, Prithi Kanakamedala asks us to think about the formation of Black institutions and the reliance on print as robust connections employed by working free Blacks, and not just elites. I lay out the meaning and significance of Black organizational life at this time in the introduction to Part I.

Black literature at the turn of the nineteenth century had also contemplated international affairs. For Chapter 4, Joseph Rezek shows that early Black writers made particular use of England as a trope for exploring exit from the United States – writers like Paul Cuffee and Prince Saunders. In addition to these, other Black writers openly considered emigration to Africa, as well as to Haiti and Mexico in writing penned before 1830. Their concerns were not only domestic in nature; as people of African descent in Saint-Domingue revolted against slavery in 1789, many African American writers vigorously considered resistance and the formation of an independent Haiti in 1804. In fact, resistance and the organized suppression of the slave trade in the Atlantic world provided fodder for much literature. The Act for the Abolition of the Slave Trade, passed by the British Parliament in 1807, followed by the US Act Prohibiting the Importation of Slaves, ratified in 1808, meant increased publication of tracts and treatises considering the expediency of abolition. While a common concern for the plight of international Black peoples invigorated discussions about citizenship, abolition, and emigration in the Black community, whites also mobilized their own groups to contemplate many of these same themes. African Americans faced the ambiguous motives of the American Colonization Society, founded primarily by whites in 1816 to support the emigration of African Americans "back" to Africa.

Black thinkers who wrote about the flight from captivity or contemplated slavery's immorality were also working without the organized network of the US antislavery movement. Although a growing abolitionist sentiment was transatlantic, interracial, and gender-diverse by the nineteenth century, the widespread institutionalization of US activism was not solidified until 1833 with the founding of the American Anti-Slavery Society (AAS). Prior to this establishment, individual local organizations, such as the New England Anti-Slavery Society founded in Boston (1832) or the Female Association for Promoting the Manufacture and Use of Free Cotton established in Philadelphia (1829), provided the means of organized antislavery activism.[11] Thus, the propaganda dispersed by the AAS, such as the weekly *National Anti-Slavery Standard* (1840), the *Slave's Friend* children's magazine (1836), and the monthly *Antislavery Record* (1835), emerged after more than eighty years of African American literature.[12] These publications inherently reflect the imprint of Black thought in the eighteenth and nineteenth centuries. Accordingly, *AALT* is not simply about the external forces and transformations that developed African American literature but is also expressly about the changes and developments ignited by Black cultural producers who transformed US literature, writ large.

Nonetheless, antislavery writing is a key place for mining literature by African American women. Northern Black women were key contributors to what historian Erica Ball describes as "conduct writing," literature produced by African Americans that "associated middle-class ideals about respectable conduct with antislavery politics and race consciousness" to make free Blacks "living refutations of proslavery doctrine."[13] Much of this content would be published after 1830 in venues such as the "Ladies' Department" of the *Liberator* or in the pages of the *Freedom's Journal.* Such a timeline suggests that editorial control by men, both Black and white, might have suppressed Black women's published writing in the decades before 1830.

But Black women were essential to the production and expansion of African American literary culture before 1830, and the richness of their work often exists in ephemeral materials and private writings. The life of Sarah Mapps Douglass, the elite Black woman, abolitionist and teacher of Philadelphia, exemplifies the breadth of literary engagement that characterized the lives of some Black women before 1830. Douglass was teacher areas of the humanities. It balances the treatment of literary materials produced by people of African descent *as* literature with the analysis of those materials as an archive in the making during the time period. This entails both the acts of self-making and the acts of image-making that defined the work of Black literary production at the turn of the nineteenth century. Chapters in *AALT* volume two consider the texts produced during the period but also the cultural and life transitions that impacted the authors and their works.

In addition to other early volumes in the *African American Literature in Transition* series, "Out of Bounds" complements work that explores Black literary production in the early decades of the nineteenth century. Since the turn of the twenty-first century, with works such as Elizabeth McHenry's *Forgotten Readers: Recovering the Lost History of African American Literary Societies* (2002), scholarship on African American literature has sought to diversify the angles or approaches through which we engage the experience of Black writing. Expanding our approach to literature has also meant expanding our approach to who counts as a writer. In particular, Black feminist scholars have paid close attention to work produced by Black women, including Joycelyn Moody's (2001) examination of spiritual narratives, P. Gabrielle Foreman's (2009) review of writing conventions and Katherine Clay Bassard's (2010) exploration of women and the Bible.[20] Thinking critically about readers of any era means thinking about audiences for literature, and, influenced by McHenry's text, scholars have also thought deeply about the production and location of African American literature in the nineteenth century such as with Eric Gardner's (2010) concern for material outside of newspapers or Laura Cohen and Jason Stein's (2012) edited volume.[21]

Volume two of *AALT* approaches the study of literature in this period by examining works across mediums. Contributors to this volume draw upon organizational records, pamphlets, speeches, and personal letters, in addition to books, paintings and drawings to fill out a picture of early African American writing. They limn an archive of early Black portraiture as well as slave narratives to discern transitions in African American literature at the turn of the nineteenth century, such as Martha J. Cutter's Chapter 12 on transitions in frontispiece portraits. Along these lines, books matter and the circulation of manuscripts and the rhetorical tropes that facilitate that movement are taken up in Chapters 5 and 6 (Rusert and Sinche). This text follows Gardner's charge to expand conceptions of Black literature beyond bound books (such as the slave narrative) and beyond the subjects of "slavery and the move from slavery."[22]

While I maintain the question of slavery and freedom was the defining issue of the period, chapters in this volume demonstrate the multivalent approach nineteenth-century African Americans took to this issue. Cultural producers of this period contemplated nationalism, patriotism, and self-determination. Their writings took up slavery and abolition, not only through works that recounted the bondsperson's experience, but also in those detailing the tribulations of Blacks who enslaved other Blacks, for example, taken up in Stefan Wheelock's examination of Venture Smith in Chapter 9. Likewise, in paintings of Black sitters as well as white, turn-of-the-century people of African descent illustrated the period's racial disparities. Chapters in this volume reveal a multi-generational tradition of Black literature already in motion by 1800, documented in diverse literary ephemera such as orations and petitions, and also captured in illustrations and public celebrations.

Overall, *AALT* volume two reflects my intentions and preferences as editor, namely my interests in free Blacks and Black freedom. Whereas both these themes were scarce in the period 1800–1830, subjects and literary materials investigated in this volume take curious approaches that focus on the "out of bounds" or the ways in which people of African descent and their cultural products acted outside the dictates of early nineteenth-century norms. Expanding upon African American literature in the early nineteenth century necessarily means an exploration of concerns for home, citizenship, nationhood, as well as questions about Atlantic exchanges, Black people outside the United States and religious community. To document a burgeoning bureaucracy or publicize American damnation was a radical and unwelcomed act. Similar to other volumes in the *AALT* series, an array of cultural transitions of the period variously helped and hindered the development of African American literature. Contributors to this particular volume represent the fields of literature, but also history, art history and African American studies. They are scholars with diverse aesthetic, intellectual and philosophical approaches to the period, working in universities in the United States or Great Britain.

Notes

1 Jasmine Nichole Cobb, *Picture Freedom: Remaking Black Visuality in the Early Nineteenth Century* (New York: New York University Press, 2015).

2 Edlie L. Wong, *Neither Fugitive nor Free: Atlantic Slavery, Freedom Suits, and the Legal Culture of Travel* (New York: New York University Press, 2009).

3 John Hope Franklin and Loren Schweninger, *Runaway Slaves: Rebels on the Plantation* (Oxford: Oxford University Press, 2000), 367.
4 http://docsouth.unc.edu/neh/intro.html
5 http://docsouth.unc.edu/neh/chronautobio.html
6 Joycelyn Moody, "African American Women and the United States Slave Narrative," in *The Cambridge Companion to African American Women's Literature*, ed. Angelyn Mitchell and Danille K. Taylor (Cambridge: Cambridge University Press 2009), 112.
7 John Ernest, "Introduction," in *The Oxford Handbook of the African American Slave Narrative* (Oxford: Oxford University Press, 2014), 6.
8 David Waldstreicher. *Notes on the State of Virginia: With Related Documents* (New York: Palgrave, 2002).
9 William M. Banks, *Black Intellectuals: A Race and Responsibility in American Life* (New York: W.W. Norton & Company, 1998), 6–10.
10 Richard Newman, Patrick Rael, and Phillip Lapsansky, eds., *Pamphlets of Protest: An Anthology of Early African American Protest Literature, 1790–1860* (New York: Routledge, 2001), 8.
11 Jean Fagan Yellin and John C. Van Horne, eds., *The Abolitionist Sisterhood: Women's Political Culture in Antebellum America* (Ithaca, NY: Cornell University Press, 1994), xv.
12 For more on the publications produced by the American Antislavery Society see Christopher D. Geist, "The 'Slave's Friend': An Abolitionist Magazine for Children," *American Periodicals* 9 (1999), 27–35.
13 Erica Ball, *To Live an Antislavery Life: Personal Politics and the Antebellum Black Middle Class* (Augusta, GA: University of Georgia Press, 2012), 13.
14 Mia E. Bay, Farah J. Griffin, Martha S. Jones, and Barbara D. Savage, *Toward an Intellectual History of Black Women* (Chapel Hill: University of North Carolina Press, 2015), 82.
15 Jasmine Nichole Cobb, "'Forget Me Not': Free Black Women and Sentimentality," *MELUS: Multi-Ethnic Literature of the United States* 40: no. 3 (Fall 2015): 28–46.
16 Dorothy Sterling, ed., *We Are Your Sisters: Black Women in the Nineteenth Century* (New York: W.W. Norton 1984): 127.
17 Sarah Moore Grimkè. *Letters to Sarah Douglass*. 1844. (Chicago: University of Chicago Press).
18 Farah Jasmine Griffin, *Beloved Sisters and Loving Friends: Letters from Rebecca Primus of Royal Oak, Maryland, and Addie Brown of Hartford, Connecticut, 1854–1868* (New York: One World, The Ballantine Publishing Group, 1999), 4.
19 Audrey Fisch, ed., *The Cambridge Companion to the African American Slave Narrative* (Cambridge: Cambridge University Press, 2007); Maryemma Graham and Jerry W. Ward, Jr., eds., *Cambridge History of African American Literature* (Cambridge: Cambridge University Press, 2011); John Cullen Gruesser and Hanna Wallinger, eds., *Loopholes and Retreats: African American Writers and the Nineteenth Century* (Wien: Lit; London: distributed in the UK by Global Book Marketing, 2009).

20 Katherine Clay Bassard, *Transforming Scriptures: African American Women Writers and the Bible* (Athens, GA: University of Georgia Press, 2010); Pier Gabrielle Foreman, *Activist Sentiments: Reading Black Women in the Nineteenth Century* (Urbana: University of Illinois Press, 2009); Joycelyn Moody, *Sentimental Confessions: Spiritual Narratives of Nineteenth-Century African American Women* (Athens, GA: University of Georgia Press, 2001).

21 Lara Langer Cohen and Jordan Alexander Stein, eds., *Early African American Print Culture* (Philadelphia: University of Pennsylvania Press, 2012); Eric Gardner, *Unexpected Places: Relocating Nineteenth-Century African American Literature* (Jackson: University of Mississippi Press, 2010); Elizabeth McHenry, *Forgotten Readers: Recovering the Lost History of African American Literary Societies* (Durham, NC: Duke University Press, 2002).

22 Gardner, *Unexpected Places*, 7.

PART I

Black Organizational Life before 1830

The three chapters in Part I, "Black Organizational Life before 1830," explore institutional transformations that supported Black literature of the period, focusing on church, print, and labor as key sites that supported the production of African American literature. Whereas opportunities to lead churches, print outlets, and labor organizations were male dominated, the chapters in this section also prioritize the efforts of men in the production of early African American literature. For more detail on the significance and presence of Black women in literature of this period, scholars should turn toward schooling as the expansion of educational institutions represents an important transition in African American literary culture in the early 1800s. "Many African Americans yearned to become literate, to have access to the news and ideas," according to historian Heather Williams, even among enslaved communities in the South.[1] Black women were at the helm of schools for infants, children and young adults that were also growing in prominence during this period. Emma Lapsansky cites ten schools that anchored Philadelphia's free Black community, alongside fourteen churches, before the Civil War.[2] The presence of these spaces was not uncontested. Scholars here acknowledge the danger associated with Black literacy in the south, but free Black northerners also faced persecution when seeking formal education and conditions worsened approaching 1830. "White resistance" to Black education responded to various currents, including "gradual emancipation, the transformation of abolitionism, and African American calls for citizenship [which] combusted in 1831 to ignite white opposition to Black higher education."[3] Sarah Harris of Connecticut saw her chance at education evoke violence and legal prosecution for her would-be teacher Prudence Crandall, the white woman abolitionist and educator willing to admit an African American pupil in 1832. Because Black women were studying in school environments and preparing to teach future generations of

African American children and adults, their literary experiences of reading and writing (even if not publishing) are foundational to understanding transitions in early nineteenth-century African American literature.

Alongside education, evolutions in the organized practice of Black religion are key in these early decades of the nineteenth century. Historian Martha Jones explains the impact of a momentous "public culture" anchored by "African American religious denominations – Methodist, Baptist, Presbyterian, Congregationalist, and Episcopalian" with their "governing bodies" that helped advance the interests of African Americans.[4] For example, in Philadelphia, the establishment of a separate Black church, Mother Bethel AME in 1794, ignited the creation of a network of Black churches and a number of publications that supported Black Christian practice. Similarly, reverend Thomas Paul founded "Boston's African Baptist Church, a spiritual, intellectual, and political focal point of the Black community," housed at the African Meeting House on the north side of Beacon Hill.[5] Paul's credits include officiating the wedding of Maria and James Stewart, establishing the African Baptist Church in 1805, along with Scipio Dalton, and helping to establish the Abyssinian Baptist Church of New York City in 1808. These churches emerged like many others, out of a widespread refusal among free Blacks to tolerate racism and segregated pews in predominantly white churches. For Chapter 1, Maurice Wallace examines Black preachers and African American literature to reveal the writing lives of Black religious thinkers. Wallace examines texts by Black clergy active between 1800 and 1830, to include Richard Allen, Absalom Jones, Peter Spencer, and Jarena Lee, as well as David Walker, in order to think seriously about these notable religious actors as authors. The work of these figures represents the physical transformation of religious institutions, including the establishment of church structures and their norms of governance regarding women preachers. Through their writing, Allen and others also construct the intellectual history driving the organization of Black religious practice in an era of emancipations.

Innovations in print were essential to the transmission of information in this era before the publication of Black newspapers. African Americans issuing public statements in print largely focused on pamphlets. This medium, "something between a broadside and a book" – served as a place for essays, information, and proceedings that were more accessible than books and more substantive than broadsides: "between the 1790s and 1860s, Black writers produced hundreds of pamphlets."[6] For early nineteenth-century Black writers, pamphleteering entailed many appeals. These items cost much less to produce than books; pamphlets could be written and published quickly while an issue was fresh in the public mind, and they were versatile, taking many forms, from argumentative essays to personal narratives to fictionalized dialogues. For Chapter 2, William L. Andrews discusses the introduction of the slave's voice into pamphlet literature as well as slavery narratives where master and slave address one another, directly. Reading texts by Reverend Daniel Coker of Baltimore and the esteemed Benjamin Banneker, Andrews also takes up transitions in pamphlet publication and circulation.

While churches and print material represent cornerstones in the archive of African American intellectual production of the early nineteenth century, they can also suggest that literate elites and religious clergy were the drivers of Black institutional activity. Chapter 3 examines the establishment of Black organizations and businesses among other echelons of free people. Turning to Brooklyn, New York and deviating from a focus on Black elites, Prithi Kanakamedala explores efforts among Black laborers to define themselves and re-delineate, in radical ways, the structures that anchored their communities –namely schools and labor organizations. She reveals how this community built self-determined institutions between 1800 and 1830, knowing that abolition in New York State in 1827 would not usher equality. Their efforts, according to Kanakamedala, created vital networks of resistance between Brooklyn, Manhattan, Boston, Philadelphia, and beyond. This chapter explores the ways in which a hostile mainstream press, patronizing white audiences specifically, also published materials that were in service of the efforts of free Black Brooklynites.

Notes

1 Heather Andrea Williams, *Self-Taught: African American Education in Slavery and Freedom* (Chapel Hill: University of North Carolina Press, 2009), 12.
2 Emma Jones Lapsansky, "'Since They Got Those Separate Churches': Afro-Americans and Racism in Jacksonian Philadelphia," *American Quarterly* 32: no. 1 (Spring, 1980): 59.
3 Hilary J. Moss, *Schooling Citizens: The Struggle for African American Education in Antebellum America* (Chicago: University of Chicago Press, 2010), 19.
4 Martha Jones, *All Bound up Together: The Woman Question in African American Public Culture, 1830–1900* (Chapel Hill, NC: University of North Carolina Press, 2007), 16.

of liberationist thought and feeling stretching over two continents. As Graham Russell Hodges has written, "In Nova Scotia and Sierra Leone, loyalist African Americans established a radical fusion of Christianity, republicanism, and black nationalism while in exile." Hodges explains, "When disenchanted blacks in Nova Scotia migrated to Sierra Leone in 1791 [*sic*], they perceived their [exodus], which was widely discussed around the Atlantic basin, as fulfillment of biblical prophecies. Word of this new black nationalism reached New York . . . "[9]

In New York, an emergent African Methodist community, inspired by so much praise of Black life and religious liberty reported in Sierra Leone, set in motion what Hodges characterizes as an overlooked "third revolution" in the United States, one swift to reach African Americans in Virginia, Delaware, Maryland, New Jersey, and Pennsylvania.[10] Before the nineteenth century was fully underway, it seems, Methodism, the church of Francis Asbury, John Wesley, Charles Wesley, and George Whitefield, had stoked the Black religious imagination and captured its liberationist zeal like no other denomination before it. Committed politically to the cause of antislavery as early as 1782, when it formally excluded slaveholders from its brotherhood, the numbers of Black devotees to Methodism soon swelled to levels unseen in early American religious history. Methodism's sympathy was not to last, however. As Black membership in the Methodist Church increased, white sympathy, Hodges writes, "cooled."[11] Still, the liberationist fires exciting this third revolution were not to be extinguished.

Not a few men of mark, including Richard Allen, Absolom Jones, Paul Cuffee, Peter Williams, Lemuel Haynes, and George White, emerged out of this early Methodist liberationist movement as prolific clergy whose sermons and other writings continue to hold an important place in the African American culture. In their oratory, essays, letters, and life writings, they give voice to a transition in early African American letters that emphasized political theology and Black representational politics. This is to say that, however worthwhile the formal excavations of Wheatley, Lucy Terry, Jupiter Hammon, George Moses Horton and other early Black American writers might be for the first- and second-stage revivalist influences that shaped these figures' poetic production, this is only half the work of African American religious criticism before 1830. The other half considers the parallel influence of Black ecclesial thought, in particular, on the emergence of an independent Black literature. As Bruce underscores, the separation of Black churches from white ecclesial control not only "encouraged a more autonomous group identity," but "pointed to an autonomy understood within longer traditions of public discourse" as well.[12] As US slavery continued unabated and the intolerable conditions circumscribing Black religious life in white settings intensified, African American believers appealed to a separate if parallel literature, counterposing the deeper entrenchments of white Protestants into slavery's necessary fictions of African inhumanity. Put more succinctly, while independent African American churches came to represent "the kinds of things black men and women could do if given a chance," as Bruce argues, so did the formation of a tradition of African American letters.[13] Between 1800 and 1830, African American literature did not merely give voice to new emancipatory theological currents; it became *the* voice of a distilled Black liberation theology in literary-inflected sermons, speeches, and first-person narratives. Among the works reflecting this double helix of Black religious and literary history are two little-known spiritual autobiographies: *A Brief Account of the Life, Experiences, Travels and Gospel Labors of George White, an African*, by George White (1810), and *The Life, History and Unparalleled Sufferings of John Jea, the African Preacher*, by John Jea (1811).

"*Having now, no other master but him*": Bondage, Freedom and the Political Economy of Conversion

Admittedly, neither White nor Jea is an obvious starting-point for this chapter's limning of the power of Black organizational life – namely, the force of Black Methodism in America before 1830 – on the discursive production of early African American literature. Neither *A Brief Account of the Life, Experiences, Travels and Gospel Labors of George White* nor *The Life, History and Unparalleled Sufferings of John Jea* could be said by anyone to belong to that effort in any obvious way. Although literary historian William L. Andrews reminds us that White "was the first slave narrator to compose and write down his life on his own,"[14] and Henry Louis Gates has pointed out that Jea was "one of the few, if not the only black poet before this century who published both an autobiography and a work of imaginative literature,"[15] still White and Jea have gotten scarce attention in Black literary and religious history, Andrews and Gates notwithstanding.[16] But White and Jea, I submit, are considerably more significant than the sparse real estate devoted to them in scholarship on African American literature. Hodges is provocation enough: "The two works must be considered in the evolution of the black American intellectual tradition," he

> The last master I was sold to, I ran from to the house of God, and was baptized unbeknown to him; and when the minister made it known to him, he was like a man that had lost his reason ... My master then beat me most cruelly, and threatened to beat the minister over the head with a cane. He then took me before the magistrates, who examined me, and inquired what I knew about God and the Lord Jesus Christ. Upon this I made a public acknowledgement before [them] that God, for Christ's sake, had pardoned my sins and blotted out all mine iniquities, through our Lord Jesus Christ, whereby *he was become by defense and deliverer* ... On hearing this, the magistrates told me *I was free from my master, and at liberty to leave him* ...[27]

Religion, it seems, is the great emancipator. And liberty, much more than an embodied achievement only; the "liberty to leave" follows not so much from the will or authority of the magistrates as from "spiritual law of liberty," Jea is swift to point out.[28] This spiritualizing of the concrete conditions defining slavery and freedom, and appeal to a poetics of Christian irony (according to which the first ends last and the last, first, for instance) subtends the emancipatory departure of White and Jea from their predecessors' (Wheatley, Hammon, Terry, Horton) theological sensibilities.

There are few illustrations of an early Black liberation theology more patently or economically portrayed than in the interchanging senses of terms such as *bondage*, *freedom*, *liberty*, and *deliverance* enlivening the confessional character of Jea's text. Captivity giving way to confession, Jea attributes his rescue from the slave's wretched estate to "a great deliverance I experienced, being released from the bondage of sin and [S]atan, and delivered from the misery in which I was."[29] So close are the facts and feelings of Jea's "great deliverance" from slavery to the revivalist conversion event that one wonders whether the double voice of liberation and doxology represents their accord in the always-already racial unthought of the Methodist imagination, or their conflict, the one striving with the other to establish the ground of Black freedom.[30] In White, too, a confluence of spiritual and material meaning hints at a new emancipatory politics of Black religious expression. Although there is no disputing Hodges's claim that "White does not mention in his autobiography ... the swirling controversies in [White's] New York over abolition and the slave trade, [or] the unceasing irritants of slavecatching, clandestine slave sales, [or] the denial of black civil rights,"[31] the suggestion of a chiasmus-making corollary to White's judgment on "the slavery of sin," could have escaped no one's notice. Nor the antislavery signifyin(g) obtaining to his

"Having now, no other master but [God]."[32] Who could imagine even so restrained a pronouncement as this among the Virgilian pieties of Wheatley or Hammon?

Not uniquely do George White's *A Brief Account of the Life, Travels and Gospel Labours of George White, An African*, and John Jea's *The Life, History, and Unparalleled Sufferings of John Jea, the African Preacher* give voice, soft and loud, to an emergent political theology in African American letters between 1800 and 1830. It is, however, according to the purposive nature of spiritual autobiography in the Puritan and post-Puritan age that White and Jea not only verify the contested humanity of the African by way of "literally writing themselves into being," as Henry Louis Gates famously put it,[33] but also instantiate belief in a new American reformation, *Black*, by way of narrativizing themselves into representative Christian personhood. These materials represent a transition to a new Christian morality. Not coincidentally, the conversion drama encoding it is a distinctively Methodist one in intellectual and print history. It is to the flourishing of literary and print culture within Methodism's discrete adaptation to the independent Black church movement that we now turn.

Religion, Print and Power: *Freedom's Journal*, 1827–1829

By now, it should be clear that an ideological insurgency, a radical new Black self-determination, established the Black church in America. Ultimately, though, the autonomous Black church was but a sign of that insurgency, not its sum – a tributary, not the ocean-end of the revolutionary struggle to independent Black voice and power. If White and Jea index the written beginnings of early Black liberationist thought at the end of the nineteenth century's first decade, then the popularization of the hopes of Black liberation sentiment in spiritual and "ministerial" autobiography may be owed to the radical politics of Christian faith and Black nationalism reflected in the many pages of the earliest-known independent Black newspaper in the United States, *Freedom's Journal*.[34] Between 1827 and 1829, *Freedom's Journal* helped establish the Black liberationist project as an irrevocable aspect of print culture in the United States and its wide-ranging circulation. Robert Levine offers that like later Black press, *Freedom's Journal* participated in one of the "boldest interventions into US public culture" in this period: it facilitated the introduction of "a black nationalist voice ... into discussions about section, race, and nation."[35] Following this trajectory, Levine argues, "we regard the black public, particularly as developed and publicized by its recent newspapers as constitutive part of a public sphere." *Freedom's Journal* did exactly this, fashioning new space for the circulation of African American letters within the Black public sphere through material means decidedly Methodist in orientation if not exactly in origin.

That *Freedom's Journal* was founded in the free Black community of New York City is no minor historical detail. There, Methodism achieved a sturdy foothold among free Blacks. "Spurning institutions they associated with slavery, blacks flooded into the rising Methodist denomination," writes Hodges. With scant ties to colonial slavery and many of its clergy holding defiantly to an antislavery position, "[t]he church of John and Charles Wesley appealed to ambitious, intelligent, young African Americans."[36] By the start of the new century, with the sale of slaves prohibited in the state since 1785 and gradual emancipation a legislative directive in 1799, New York realized a thriving African Methodist community among whom abided not only George White and John Jea, but Reverend Peter Williams, Sr., a prominent member of New York's Methodist society and, in 1791, a founder of the independent African Methodist Episcopal Zion Church; and Reverend Peter Williams, Jr., founder of the second Black Episcopal congregation in the United States, St. Philip's African Church, and co-founder of *Freedom's Journal*.

While *Freedom's Journal* was not officially a Methodist organ, Black Methodism's deep reach into African American political thought between 1800 and 1830 could scarcely escape the paper's pages. Much more than the prospect of Williams's direct influence on *Freedom Journal*'s objective to promote literacy and African American uplift, Methodism's increasing reliance on "words and books," like so many other Protestant denominations in the United States, including, especially, high church groups like Anglicans and Presbyterians, likely helped to advance a belief shared by the founders of *Freedom's Journal* in the power of print to elevate African Americans.[37] In a "Prospectus" appearing in *Freedom Journal*'s inaugural edition, editors Samuel E. Cornish and John B. Russwurm declared, "Experience has taught us that the Press is the most convenient and economical method by which [community improvement] is to be obtained."[38] If, by 1827, "the Press" had become the preferred medium of a new Black antebellum self-determination, according to which African American radicals and reformists like Cornish and Russwurm might, at last, "plead [their] own cause" as the editors insisted their paper was intent upon doing ("Too long have others spoken for us"), then *Freedom's Journal* would help leverage racial uplift by attaching Black nationalist imaginings, formerly sketched in religious orations and antislavery speech-making, to print's social and religious power. *Freedom's Journal* offered Black writers "a forum through which important rhetorical and literary texts could be disseminated to a wide audience."[39] Again,

> *Freedom's Journal* published poems, essays, sermons and orations by African Americans that would be otherwise available to only a limited audience, such as those present at a lecture or speech, or those persons having access to essays published in pamphlet form. The publication in *Freedom's Journal* of speeches delivered in various cities connected geographically separated African Americans, giving readers a sense that they were part of a community with common interests and goals. These texts could also serve as models for those were becoming empowered to speak for themselves.[40]

As surely as *Freedom's Journal* helped coalesce Black people into "a [*national*] community with common interests and goals," its expansive circulation also *depended* on established networks and "underground channels."[41] In short order, it had subscription agents in ten states from Maine to North Carolina, and in places as distant as Liverpool, Waterloo, and Port-au-Prince. As Jacqueline Bacon reminds us, for example, "African American sailors from the North had developed contacts in the South, creating underground channels for the distribution of antislavery information and texts."[42] Perhaps more or less reliably, *Freedom's Journal* was disseminated by "runaways, itinerant laborers, *churches and other religious organizations*," Bacon maintains.[43] No doubt the fields and flows of Black cultural and institutional life created and maintained by Black church networks, specifically, helped carry *Freedom's Journal* along, North, South, and abroad.

The interstate and international reach of Black organizational life in the antebellum period, however, not only carried *Freedom's Journal* over a surprisingly diffuse geography, but *Freedom's Journal* itself was a cultural carrier of Black liberationist thought and practice. Cultural institutions including African American Methodism, Prince Hall freemasonry, Free African benevolence societies, and Black abolitionist groups like Boston's Massachusetts General Colored Association helped circulate the periodical. With print "promising to link together the disparate and scattered black communities of the early republic," according to Levine, *Freedom's Journal* introduced early Black "poems, essays, [and transcribed] sermons and orations" into the orbit of its associational ties.[44] Among the various figures appearing in *Freedom's Journal*, Phillis Wheatley's poetry, a sketch of the life of Paul Cuffee, verse by the slave-poet George Moses Horton, and an open letter by Richard Allen condemning the actions and attitudes of the American Colonization Society stand out.[45] However, given this chapter's concern for the deep-seated sway of Methodist theology, in particular, upon the religiously-inflected origins of African American literature and its material conditions of possibility in New York City, that Wheatley and Horton, to say nothing of Allen, had important Methodist connections comes as no shock.[46] Nor do those associated with the author of the signal work of Black political theology before 1830, *Walker's Appeal, in Four Articles; Together with a Preamble, to the Colored Citizens of the United States* (1829). David Walker's easy circulation of *Freedom's Journal* as one of its fourteen authorized subscription agents was surely supported by active participation in the May Street Methodist Church and the African Masonic Lodge in 1820s Boston.

David Walker's Traveling Shoes: Approaching *Walker's Appeal ... To the Colored Citizens of United States*

Thanks to the scrupulous research of early American historian Peter P. Hinks, a great many details about David Walker's life and career compose a portrait of him as notable as that of any of his Black Boston contemporaries. Though finding a public career as antislavery activist in Boston, Walker was born near (perhaps in) Wilmington, North Carolina. His mother was a free woman in 1796; his father, reportedly, enslaved. Himself a freeman, his standing following the condition of his mother as North Carolina law and custom directed, Walker spent his young adulthood in Charleston, South Carolina, it seems, where, importantly, he got on with what may have been today's Emanuel (or Mother) AME Church, if not by direct membership, then by society with the thousands of Black Methodists in Charleston who took their independence from the white Methodist church coincidentally with Walker's coming of age there.[47] In his religious and political thought, Charleston was formative to Walker's radical antislavery convictions. Specifically, Hinks submits that "[i]n Charleston, Walker may have concluded that an independent church with its own system of biblical interpretation was the single greatest threat to white authority because of the degree to which it upheld a vision of black autonomy, solidarity, and mission."[48] There, coming and going among those lately plotting the 1822 slave uprising that would deliver Denmark Vesey to his execution, Walker "was convinced that Christianity and the Bible were antislavery and that they justified aggressive actions against enslavement and oppression."[49] Taking a deeply theological view on slavery and freedom (much as George White and John Jea had in earlier years), Walker just as surely came to know the value of the independence of Black churches, Methodist ones in particular, for the actualization of his growing antislavery hopes. That "[t]he best-informed whites all concluded that the existence of the African Church was essential to the development of the [Vesey] plot, both ideologically and organizationally" suggests an agency of the early Black church so critically consequential to Black eschatological hope and duty that even outsiders recognized its obvious sway.[50] Still, Walker was not long for Charleston after 1822.

Quitting Charleston for Savannah, possibly, and Philadelphia, almost certainly, Walker pushed further north, landing in Boston in 1825. In Boston he fell in among the Black Methodists and local freemasons. Although Hinks stresses Walker's membership in Boston's African Masonic Lodge as an important source of Black nationalist sociality and Christian congress, suggesting "[t]he relationships David Walker formed in the African Lodge were some of the most central ones of his life in Boston," Hinks does not deny the weight of "other significant events and institutions of the Boston black community" in reinforcing Walker's Black liberationist views.[51] It is "likely," Hinks adds, "that [Walker] had ... a deep commitment to the black Methodist church" in Boston, too.[52] Casting his lot with the May Street Methodist Church, organized under the charismatic antislavery leadership of Rev. Samuel Snowden, a Southerner and ex-slave, Walker proved his denominational loyalty, even though, by now, Baptists enjoyed the greater public visibility in Boston's free Black society. Who knows but that Snowden and the May Street Methodist Church were well ready for Walker and *Freedom's Journal* when he signed on as a Boston subscription agent sometime before the paper's inaugural issue.

Walker remained a dedicated agent to *Freedom's Journal* for the full length of its print life and showed the greater commitment to its cause and mission by extending his service to the short-lived *Rights of All* newspaper which succeeded *Freedom's Journal* in 1829. In his role as agent, Walker embodied a certain cultural ideal, one harmonious with the migratory reflexes that brought Walker and many other free Blacks living in the South to Philadelphia, New York, and points further north. As an "Authorized Agent," Walker helped to set *Freedom's Journal* in literal circulation. Exactly where his passage North ended, *Freedom's Journal* took on the material form of Walker's, and every bondsman's, will to free circulation. Levine's article "Circulating the Nation: David Walker, the Missouri Compromise and the Rise of the Black Press" highlights this very surrogacy of the paper's reach for the migrants. As Levine suggests, it "is not so much the content of the various editorials and articles that appeared in [*Freedom's Journal*]."[53] Rather, it is the close material relationship between the wider circulation of *Freedom's Journal* and the fact of early African American literature as an extension of a Black liberation struggle represented, to no small degree, in the paper's traveling pages.

With its stated devotion to "the improvement of the colored populations"[54] broadly expressed, and its undeclared but still-yet evident determination to distill out of many what Bruce calls "a potent black voice,"[55] one that might speak self-determinatively to the slavery and colonization debates in the public sphere, *Freedom's Journal* offered its subscribers an alternative discursive community for the times. To some extent, its editors could not but understand the evolution of that voice in terms of literary achievement. They had a "sense of the importance of a black literary voice and its distinctive role in American society," Bruce writes.[56] That voice, they believed, testified to the lie of African inferiority, "encouraging literary culture and literary achievement as part of the effort to improve free black society while [simultaneously] responding to that society's traducers."[57] Against this backdrop, *Freedom's Journal* published what Bruce has distinguished as "one of the first lengthy pieces of fiction by a black American."[58] Run in four installments over two months in 1828, "Theresa – A Haytien Tale" fictionalized events surrounding the Haitian Revolution with a Black heroine, Theresa. Its author uncertain, the story's publication set the editors' Black nationalist sympathies in undeniable relief. Though, generally, *Freedom's Journal* failed to grasp the limits of tethering its uplift ambitions to a deeply flawed respectability behavioralism, its publication of works like "Theresa – A Haytien Tale," on the other hand, aimed to direct Black literature away from the temptations of belletristic display (that might suffice to prove Blacks' capacity for high culture) toward sometimes radical racial ends. As a figure for the intersectional politics of *Freedom's Journal* by way of which *Freedom's Journal* at once encouraged and cultivated an activist Black literary voice before 1830, one destined to extend earlier liberationist sensibilities to American print culture, David Walker, it seems, had few peers.

In "Circulating the Nation," Levine recalls remarks made by Walker to a meeting of friends of *Freedom's Journal* at Boston's (African Methodist) Ebenezer Church in 1828, in which he outlined "the disadvantages under which the people of Colour [*sic*] labor under," one account of the meeting went, concluding it was because of "the neglect of literature" that so many difficulties yet prevailed.[59] All along, Walker took the editors' belief in the practical value of literature to the designs of Black uplift (not an unproblematic construction in Walker's speech and in the paper generally)[60] as having great importance to *Freedom's Journal* and the organizational mission to which Walker believed a newly formed General Colored Association (GCA) should dedicate itself: "form[ing] ourselves into a general body" in order to "protect, aid and assist each other" as nation. In language that could not but recall Walker's Methodist devotion, he called on GCA to reactivate its support of *Freedom's Journal* and thereby "facilitate our salvation." Making his case this way, Walker appealed to the God of Augustinian theodicy "who ever had, and will, repay every nation according to its works."[61] Religious pieties aside, as early as its second issue, the paper's literary purposes were in evidence. In its second number, it extolled the "honour" Phillis Wheatley brought on the name and character of African Americans in the new century, for example, reprinting extracts from Wheatley's "On the Death of J. C., an Infant" and "An Hymn to the Morning" for its readers.[62] But it was the "material fact of the newspaper itself," Levine argues, not its poetic or narrative extracts (such as they were) nor its various homages to figures like Wheatley that supported Walker's further hope of reconciling the "unorganized condition" worrying Black life, generally, and Black Bostonians, in particular. In his words and work, Walker cast *Freedom's Journal* – "the material fact" of it – as a vital auxiliary to "unit[ing] the colored population, so far, through the United States . . . as may be practicable and expedient."[63]

If Walker and the coterie of Black men who pledged to help revivify enthusiasm for the first African American newspaper and expand its circulation "regarded print, rather than oratory, as promising to link together the disparate and scattered black communities of the early republic," as Levine maintains, then the "expedient" accomplishment of those objectives would require the availability of systems of formal and informal sociality, networks of collegiality, and proven pathways of communication and travel.[64] Put another way, if, as an authorized agent of *Freedom's Journal*, Walker was "entrusted to [help] achieve the goal of building the paper's circulation," naturally his church and Masonic memberships afforded his efforts the resources of a liberal network of new prospects, many, by virtue of church and lodge affiliation, already inclined to sympathize with the paper's activist aims.[65] Rather than view *Freedom's Journal* in the light of its organizing or educative instrumentalities only, where wider readerships are not only preexistent but created whole-cloth by the newly literate, however, let us view it (and its key importance to the future past of African American literature) in the light of its pregnant symbolism.

Although *Freedom's Journal*'s dissemination over eleven states and three foreign countries stood in for "a model of the circulatory freedom" coveted by enslaved and free Black people alike,[66] it was set flowing against a tide of competing print and commercial interests as well. It was not only oratory the paper's editors aimed to harness in print, as Levine posits so discerningly; it was its interference in the traffic of Black bodies in early national print culture. Runaway slave advertisements in "circulars, newspapers, broadsides and handbills," belonged to the shadow archive *Freedom's Journal* countervailed.[67] No such ads appeared anywhere in *Freedoms Journal.* Because of their ubiquity in other print and press sources from the Revolutionary period until the close of the Civil War, their nonexistence in *Freedom's Journal* made for so stark a contrast with contemporaneous printing practices that to think of *Freedom's Journal* as enacting resistance in its "material fact" (Levine) hardly overstates things. By way of its *circulation* (as against its material fact), it accomplished something more radical still: it conducted its own form of fugitivity, circulating across so diffuse a geography as to become, in this way, its own self-authorizing paper pass. More than a traveling paper, though, *Freedom's Journal* came to be an alternate form of paper currency by the time it ceased publication in 1829, its end urgently opening the door for Walker's *Appeal.*

"Are We Men?": Politics, Poetics and the Past Future of African American Literature

Appearing in the waning months in 1829, David Walker's *Appeal* was nothing if not a sign and prophecy of what was to come in African American public life and letters after 1830. As much a Jeremiah-call to the "Coloured Citizens of the World, But in Particular, and Very Expressly, to Those of the United States of America," *Appeal* was also, in a way, a climax of antislavery feeling borne by Black Methodist fervor. Although many writers before and after Walker succeeded in integrating political and religious discourses into a distinctive African American vocality, none, I argue, was quite so zealous as Walker. Heroic as Walker's labors sound to Black radical sympathies, however, zeal cuts two ways.

That Walker's *Appeal* was published in pamphlet form ought not mislead the contemporary critic/reader. Walker's consequence to African American literature is hardly diminished by that early form. It would be anachronistic to think so. With the newspaper, the pamphlet was the most important print type in shaping republican citizenship. The book as we know it today had yet to attain democratic import in 1829.[68] The material form of Walker's *Appeal*, then, insinuated his call for the violent overthrow of the slave system within the nation-building logic and tradition of the American Revolution. And yet Walker's jeremiad was equally informed by a tradition of classical and biblical interpretation intent upon a view of Black life in the United States as the effect of Europe's monstrous interruption of an erstwhile history of African nobility, genius, and accomplishment. Bruce explains that "Walker drew heavily on the ideas of ancient African greatness" much like his contemporaries writing to "*Freedom's Journal* [who] ... described 'the sons of Africa or of Ham, among whom learning originated, and was carried thence into Greece, where it was improved upon and refined.'" Bruce goes on:

> [Walker] drew on a still older tradition with a double-edged use of Egyptian history, likening the slavery of Africans in America to that of Israel in Egypt ... Echoing earlier generations, he compared the histories of Europe and Africa to relativize the concept of barbarism, saying that European history revealed a people who acted "more like devils than accountable men.[69]

That Bruce somewhat misunderstands Walker's nascent Afrocentrism as having "played a part in thinking about African American since ... the nineteenth century" matters significantly less here than his more accurate, if later, observation that in *Appeal* Walker annexed African American "traditions of moral superiority going back ... even to Wheatley, achieving a directness that ... went far beyond his predecessors."[70] Walker's stance was not only more direct than any Black writer dared before him, with its talk of "tyrants and devils" vindictively "hurl[ed] into atoms [to] make way for his people," it was approaching apocalyptic.[71] Nat Turner's Rebellion in 1831, with all its Armageddon incentive, all but actualized Walker's words ("Can [white] Americans escape God Almighty?" Walker baited) not many months after.[72] Whether Walker's *Appeal* could have inspired Turner's deadly revolt, or merely indexed the intensity of fiery antislavery fervor felt by persons enslaved and free in the slaveholding states entering upon the middle decades of the nineteenth century, Walker's call-to-arms did not fail to circulate far and wide, through the North and the South. Its influence on the antislavery future of the nineteenth century, on the Black print culture of pamphlets, broadsides and newspapers to come (e.g., *Liberator*, *North Star*) have only begun to be appreciated. This is to say nothing of the political fever Walker's *Appeal* surely helped to induce, which, but a generation later, eventuated in war.

Still, it cannot be overlooked that Walker's *Appeal* follows a decidedly masculinist, if not finally conservative, trajectory of Black liberation struggle, theology and social thought. Article IV puts the gendered conditions of fight and freedom in striking evidence:

> They (the whites) know well, if we are *men* – and there is a secret monitor in their hearts which tells them we are – they know, I say, if we *are* men, and see them treating us in the manner they do, that there can be nothing in our hearts but death alone, for them, notwithstanding we may appear cheerful, when we see them murdering our dear mothers and wives, because we cannot help ourselves. Man, in all ages and all nations of the earth, is the same. Man is a peculiar creature – he is the image of his God, though he may be subjected to the most wretched condition upon earth ...[73]

If Walker revealed that his faith issued from a vaguely muscular form of Christianity in Article II (recall God who "*hurl[s]* tyrants and devil into atoms"), then the gendered conditions of his wider liberation politics are disclosed in Article IV. Here Walker discloses an antagonistic homosociality between Black and white "*men*," the former vexed by the latter's injury to "our dear mothers and wives," real and symbolic. Men, it seems, are as "peculiar" as creaturely man is from the rest of God's created works.

Appeal's masculinist instincts are nowhere more forcefully revealed, however, than in the emphatic conclusion of Article 1. "Are we MEN!! – I ask you, O my brethren! are [*sic*] we MEN?" Walker implores his readers. Or yet again, in Article IV: "O! coloured men!! O! coloured men!!! O! coloured men!!!! Look!! look!!!" Not only does Walker's implied audience, addressed in contradistinction of "our wives ... our mothers ... our fathers and dear little children," betray resolutely gendered presuppositions about *Appeal*'s readership and Walker's sociology of revolution, but knowledge of Walker's membership in the strictly fraternal Prince Hall Masonic lodge in Boston resists any more charitable reading of *Appeal*'s gendered grammars. Those who would secure the free Black future *Appeal* prophesies are, in sex and striving, men. That African American literary history from 1800 to 1830 has privileged men writers, then, hardly surprises. Where Black women's writing, specifically, is concerned, the period stretching from Phillis Wheatley and Lucy Terry in the eighteenth century to Ann Plato, Zilpha Elaw, and Julia Foote in the nineteenth century is a deep and yawning gulf. Somewhere within that gulf African American women writers have been mostly lost to public or professional memory, drowned out by the insistently patriarchal voices, one can only assume, of early race men who even now clamor for critical attention.[74]

Whatever the case, this much is not to be denied: Between 1800 and 1830, the evolution of African American literature was one with the ongoing development of a public Black voice set on speaking its own liberatory hopes, imagining its own racial eschatology in the United States and, occasionally, abroad. While it is certain that the seeds of that inchoate Black liberation theology were present in Black religion's earliest sensibilities in the New World, in the "hush arbor" preachments of slave religion prior to the institutionalization of Black Protestantism in denominationally-identified churches, a more powerful liberation theology and a new ecclesial network helping to sustain and disseminate it came forcefully into being in this period. More accurately, the period gave rise to a Black Methodist literary legacy and a publication imperative, from the spiritual autobiographies of George White and John Jea to the founding of *Freedom's Journal* and David Walker's *Appeal.* The significance of these figures exceeds their own unique histories and careers, however. They are stand-ins for others, too, whose prayers and prophecies for a free future, documented in verse and speech and story, went missing long ago or, unluckily, unrecorded. The extant works are crucial, then, to Black cultural and literary history between 1800 and 1830 as they offer up the strongest evidence available of the doubly political, religious, and ethical authority African American letters commanded concerning Black freedom decades before the Civil War. Lincoln's vexed Emancipation Proclamation notwithstanding, Black freedom, it would seem, was in the hands (and hearts) of faith-filled, freedom-loving Black folks first and early. Early Black print in America is the proof of it.

Notes

1 This term belongs to Joanna Brooks. See Joanna Brooks, *American Lazarus: Religion and the Rise of African-American and Native American Literatures* (New York: Oxford University Press, 2003), 24.

2 Ibid., 21.

3 Ibid., 24.

4 In fact, it could be said, credibly – and somewhat reversing Brooks – that in the Second Great Awakening period theology, church polity, and denominationalism did not so much leave their consequences on "communities of color" as those communities shaped and helped to sustain the fire of American religious fervor.

5 Benjamin Mays, *The Negro's God as Reflected in His Literature* (Boston, MA: Chapman & Grimes, 1938), 14, 1.

6 Ibid., 2. Emphasis added.

7 Exodus 20:2 NIV.
8 Dickson Bruce, *The Origins of African American Literature, 1680–1865* (Charlottesville, VA: University Press of Virginia, 2001), 63.
9 Graham Russell Hodges, ed. , *Black Itinerants of the Gospel: The Narratives of John Jea and George White* (Madison, WI: Madison House, 1993), 4. Although Hodge's introduction to this volume establishes 1791 as the year of the Nova Scotian "hegira," other reliable sources set the date of that monumental colonization event in 1792.
10 Ibid., 1.
11 Ibid., 7.
12 Bruce, *Origins of African American Literature*, 102–103.
13 Ibid, 104.
14 William L. Andrews, *To Tell a Free Story: The First Century of Afro-American Autobiography, 1760–1865* (Urbana: University of Illinois Press, 1986), 48.
15 Henry Louis Gates, Jr., *The Signifying Monkey: A Theory of African-American Literary Criticism* (New York: Oxford University Press, 1988), 158.
16 Other notable exceptions include chapters on Jea and/or White by David Kazanjian, Joycelyn Moody, Yolanda Pierce, and John Salliant. See David Kazanjian, "Mercantile Exchanges, Mercantilist Enclosures: Racial Capitalism in the Black Mariner Narratives of Venture Smith and John Jea," *CR: The New Centennial Review*, 3, no. 1 (2003): 147–178; Joycelyn Moody, "'I hadn't joined church yet, and I wasn't scared of anybody': Violence and Homosociality in Early Black Men's Christian Narratives," *a/b: Auto/Biography Studies*, 27, no. 1 (Summer 2012): 153–182; Yolanda Pierce, *Hell without Fires: Slavery, Christianity and the Antebellum Spiritual Narrative* (Gainesville: University Press of Florida, 2005); John Salliant, "Travelling in Old and New Worlds with John Jea, the African Preacher, 1773–1816," *Journal of American Studies*, 33, no. 3 (December 1999): 473–490.
17 Hodges, *Black Itinerants of the Gospel*, 35.
18 Writes Philip Gould, "By the end of the eighteenth century . . . the demonstration of one's religious conversion and Christian feeling was an important convention of the slave narrative. This development registers the institutional and cultural forces shaping the very meaning in the writings of 'liberty' and 'slavery.'" Philip Gould, "The Rise, Development, and Circulation of the Slave Narrative," in *The Cambridge Companion to the African American Slave Narrative*, ed. Audrey Fisch (Cambridge MA: Cambridge University Press, 2007), 15–16.
19 Marcella Grendler, Andrew Leiter, and Jill Sexton, eds. *Guide to Religious Content in Slave Narratives. Documenting the American South* (Chapel Hill: University of North Carolina), http://docsouth.unc.edu/neh/religiouscontent.html. *Guide* is a convenient online archive of Christian themes, practices and events found in the slave narratives belonging to the DocSouth digital collection at UNC.
20 Ibid.
21 Ibid.

22 George White, *A Brief Account of the Life, Experiences, Travels and Gospel Labors of George White, An African* (New York: John C. Totten, 1810) in Hodges, *Black Itinerants of the Gospel*, 52. Emphasis added. Subsequent references are to this edition and pages cited parenthetically in the text above.

23 Venture Smith, *A Narrative of the Life and Adventures of Venture, a Native of Africa: But Resident above Sixty Years in the United States of America. Related by Himself* (New London, CT: C. Holt, 1798), http://docsouth.unc.edu/neh/venture/menu.html. Ottobah Cugoano, "Narrative of the Enslavement of Ottobah Cugoano, a Native of Africa; Published by Himself on the Year 1787," in *The Negro's Memorial; or, Abolitionist's Catechism; by an Abolitionist*, Thomas Fisher (London: The Author, 1825), http://docsouth.unc.edu/neh/cugoano/cugoano.html.

24 John Jea, *The Life, History, and Unparalleled Sufferings of John Jea, the African Preacher, Written by Himself* (Portsea England, 1811) in Hodges, *Black Itinerants of the Gospel*, 89. Emphasis added. Subsequent references are to this edition and pages cited parenthetically in the text above.

25 Ibid., 92.

26 Ibid., 91.

27 Ibid., 111, emphasis added.

28 Ibid.

29 Ibid., 100.

30 Although one may locate the common conventions of *Puritan* conversion most famously in Edmund Morgan's *Visible Saints: The History of a Puritan Idea* (1963), Daniel Shea's *Spiritual Autobiography in Early America* (1963) and Patricia Caldwell's *The Puritan Conversion Narrative: The Beginnings of American Expression* (1983), the ever closer similarities obtaining between *Methodist* conversion and the event of Black freedom are forcefully evident in the rhetorical resonance created by the likes of Sampson Stanifort, a "twenty-five-year-old soldier in the English army" who was "converted in a Methodist revival" in 1743. On his conversion, Stanifort proclaimed, "My chains fell off; my heart was free." Stanifort's autobiography is representative of "a great bulk of conversion literature" in the history of early Methodism. For a systematic treatment of Stanifort and the Methodist conversion narrative, see D. Bruce Hindmarsh, "'My chains fell off, my heart was free': Early Methodist Conversion Narrative in England" *Church History* 68, no. 4 (December 1999): 910–929. By the "always-already racial unthought of the Puritan imagination," I mean to recall that arresting observation of Saidiya Hartman: "On one hand, the slave is the foundation of the national order, and, on the other, the slave occupies the position of the unthought." To imagine the slave "in the position of the unthought" is not to imagine the slave absent so much as it is to imagine the slave as a spectrality, an unaccounted for un(der)thought. Saidiya V. Hartman and Frank Wilderson III, "The Position of the Unthought," *Qui Parle* 13, no. 2 (2003): 184–185.

31 Hodges, *Black Itinerants of the Gospel*, 18.

32 White, *Brief Account*, 53.

33 Gates, Jr. *The Signifying Monkey* 144.
34 William L. Andrews, "The Politics of African-American Ministerial Autobiography from Reconstruction to the 1920s," in *African-American Christianity: Essays in History*, ed. Paul E. Johnson, (Berkeley: University of California Press, 1994), 111–133.
35 Robert Levine, "Circulating the Nation," in The Black Press: New Literary and Historical Essays, ed. Todd Vogel (New Brunswick, NJ: Rutgers University Press, 2001), 29. Levine has David Walker's voice specifically in mind. I take Walker's voice to be indexical of the tone of Black religious discourse in the acme years of the Second Great Awakening.
36 Hodges, *Black Itinerants of the Gospel*, 4.
37 Hodges, *Black Itinerants of the Gospel*, 23. The repeated efforts of the untutored George White to gain licensure as a Methodist minister is one index of the Methodist hierarchy. White returned to the licensing board five times before successfully demonstrating literacy sufficient enough to earn a license as a local preacher and, in 1815, an ordained deacon. On White's trials within Methodism, see Hodges, *Black Itinerants of the Gospel*, 10–18.
Although Peter Williams, credited as a co-founder of *Freedom's Journal*, and Samuel Cornish, one of the paper's founding co-editors, were Episcopalian and Presbyterian leaders, respectively, this fact does not diminish the Methodist movement's influence on the early politics of Black nationalism gaining force as *Freedom's Journal* was launched. According to Hodges, "Methodism . . . was already an umbrella for the aspirations of black nationalist denominations," ibid., 4. Prominent Black Methodists of the era included White, Jea, Paul Cuffee, Richard Allen, Daniel Coker, and Peter Williams, Sr.
38 Samuel E. Cornish and John B. Russwurm, "Prospectus," *Freedom's Journal* 1, no. 1, March 16, 1827.
39 Jacqueline Bacon, "The History of Freedom's Journal: A Study in Empowerment and Community," *Journal of African American History* 88, no. 1 (2003): 10.
40 Ibid., 10–11.
41 Ibid., 11, 8.
42 Ibid., 8.
43 Ibid. Emphasis added.
44 Levine, "Circulating the Nation," 18.
45 In each case, *Freedom's Journal* reprinted works previously published. For a discussion of Wheatley and Cuffee in *Freedom's Journal*, see Christopher Cameron, *To Plead Our Own Cause: African Americans in Massachusetts and the Making of the Anti-Slavery Movement* (Kent: Kent State University Press, 2014), 118–119. For a discussion of Allen's letter, see Levine, "Circulating the Nation," 30–31.
46 Allen was founder of the African Methodist Episcopal church. See Richard S. Newman, *Freedom's Prophet: Richard Allen, the AME Church, and the Black Founding Fathers* (New York: New York University. Press, 2009) for the fullest account of Allen's Methodist career.

Samuel J. Rogal referred to Wheatley's "loose ties" to Methodism in his article "Phillis Wheatley's Methodist Connection" *Black American Literature Forum* 21, no. 1/2 (Spring–Summer, 1987): 85–95. Rogal's characterization of Wheatley had largely to do with the extent to which Wheatley could be said to have expressed any "deep interest or concern for Methodist activities in Britain or North America." Still, Rogal goes on to say, "Phillis Wheatley must have known something about Methodism and Methodist activities in Great Britain," ibid., 90, 94 n.1. Although there remain questions about Wheatley's formal commitments to Methodism, the interest in Wheatley by British Methodists was substantive and formal. See, too, Mukhtar Ali Isani, "The Methodist Connection: New Variants on Some Phillis Wheatley Poems" *Early American Literature* 22, no. 1 (March 1987): 108–113.

Although there is too little evidence to prove that George Moses Horton had any direct affiliation with the Methodist movement, in his biographical sketch, "Life of George M. Horton: Colored Bard of North Carolina" (1845), Horton identifies the availability of "Wesley's old hymns" as a significant influence on his poetical formation. George M. Horton, "Life of George M. Horton: Colored Bard of North Carolina," in *The Poetical Works of George M. Horton, Colored Bard of North Carolina, To Which is Prefixed the Life of the Author* (Hillsborough, NC: D. Heartt, 1845), viii. http://docsouth.unc.edu/fpn/hortonlife/horton.html.

47 See Peter P. Hinks, *To Awaken My Afflicted Brethren: David Walker and the Problem of Antebellum Slave Resistance* (University Park: Pennsylvania State University Press, 1997). Hinks reports that in 1817 some 4,367 Black members of the predominantly white Charleston Methodist church seceded in hopes of forming an independent AME church.

Emanuel AME Church (also called Mother AME) is familiar to us as the scene of the 2015 massacre of nine church members by the hand of white supremacist and domestic terrorist Dylan Roof.

48 Ibid, 39.

49 Ibid.

50 Ibid., 37. "While black revolt in the Charleston of 1822 would have been possible without the AME church," Hinks goes on, "its organizational potential would have been severely curtailed." To my point, "David Walker could have been directly acquainted with this use of the church" (38).

51 Ibid., p. 73.

52 Ibid., p. 78.

53 Levine, "Circulating the Nation," 18.

54 The strapline "DEVOTED TO THE IMPROVEMENT OF THE COLORED POPULATION" appeared on the masthead of Freedom's Journal for the first time April 4, 1828, the beginning of the paper's second volume. It replaced the similarly reformist, but rather more explicitly nationalistic biblical strapline "RIGHTEOUSNESS EXALTETH A NATION" which ran for the entirety of the first 52-week volume.

55 Bruce, *Origins of African American Literature*, 166.

56 Ibid., 168.
57 Ibid.
58 Ibid., 172.
59 "Freedom's Journal," *Freedom's Journal* 2, no. 5, April 25, 1828: 38.
60 "[W]e shall consider it a part of our duty to recommend to our young readers, such authors as will not only enlarge their stock of useful knowledge, but will also serve to stimulate them to higher attainments in science," the editors wrote in the first number. That their higher objectives were ensnared in an early Black middle-class respectability politics is indisputable and a problematic issue for historians of Black print culture who would only valorize *Freedom's Journal* for its historical standing. "To Our Patrons," *Freedom's Journal* 1, no. 1 , March 16, 1827: 1. See, too, Elizabeth Stordeur Pryor *Colored Travelers: Mobility and the Fight for Citizenship before the Civil War* (Chapel Hill: University of North Carolina Press, 2016) on the "activist respectability" animating the work of otherwise radical black antislavery subjects including Cornish, Russwurm, and Walker.
61 David Walker, "Address Delivered before the General Colored Association by David Walker," *Freedom's Journal* 2, no. 38, December 19, 1828: 295.
62 *Freedom's Journal* 1, no. 2, March 23, 1827: 6.
63 Walker, "Address Delivered before the General Colored Association by David Walker," 295.
64 Levine, "Circulating the Nation," 18.
65 Ibid., 23.
66 Ibid., 29.
67 Pryor, *Colored Travelers*, 50.
68 For a summary of the history of the pamphlet in early America, see Robert G. Parkinson, "Print, the Press, and the American Revolution," in *Oxford Research Encyclopedia of American History*, ed. Jon Butler and Christopher Grasso (Oxford: Oxford University Press, 2015), http://americanhistory.oxfordre.com. Among literary historians, specifically, discussion of the cultural role and literary value accorded to pamphlets cannot avoid Michael Warner, *Letters of the Republic: Publication and the Public Sphere in Eighteenth-Century America* (Cambridge, MA: Harvard University Press, 1990).
69 Bruce, *Origins of African American Literature*, 180.
70 Ibid., 181. Walker's belief in what the late classicist Martin Bernal referred to as "the Afro-Asiatic roots" of the classical world are, more precisely than Bruce puts it, a reflex of Walker's Masonic mind. Black Freemasonry, and therefore this understanding of Black genius and the debt owed to African knowledge systems in antiquity, dates to the eighteenth century in the United States. See my chapter "'Are We Men': Prince Hall, Martin Delaney and the Masculine Ideal in Black Freemasonry" in *Constructing the Black Masculine: Identity and Ideality in African American Men's Literature and Culture, 1775–1995* (Durham, NC: Duke University Press, 2002), 53–81.

71 "O Americans! Americans!! I call God – I call angels – I call men, to witness, that your DESTRUCTION *is at hand,* and will be speedily consummated unless you REPENT." David Walker, *Walker's Appeal in Four Articles; Together with a Preamble, To the Coloured Citizens of the Word, but in Particular, and Most Expressly, Those of the United States of America, Written in Boston, State of Massachusetts, September 28, 1828* (Boston, MA: David Walker, 1830), 49. http://docsouth.unc.edu/nc/walker/walker.html.

72 Ibid.

73 Ibid. Emphasis Walker's.

74 For more, see Hazel Carby, *Race Men* (Cambridge MA: Harvard University Press, 1998).

CHAPTER 2

Daniel Coker, David Walker, and the Politics of Dialogue with Whites in Early Nineteenth-Century African American Literature

William L. Andrews

The Emergence of African American Pamphlets

Despite the enactment of laws effecting the gradual abolition of slavery in New England and most Mid-Atlantic states by 1810, hostility to free Black people, and also to antislavery advocates white as well as Black, persisted throughout the young Republic. In 1792, for instance, the Maryland House of Delegates officially condemned the state abolition society, coming within two votes of declaring it "subversive to the rights of our citizens."[1] By 1798, in the wake of official censure and repressive legislation against its activities, the Maryland abolition society had disbanded, having watched similar organizations collapse in Virginia and Delaware.[2] Free African American communities continued to plead their case for justice in the early years of the eighteenth century. They appealed to state and national lawmakers for justice by publishing petitions and pamphlets, as had white colonists several decades earlier when they called for redress from the British government for measures they felt were discriminatory and oppressive.[3] "Adaptable as an argumentative essay, a short narrative of events, or a bare-bones sketch of an organization's proceedings," African American pamphlets in the early Republic opened up opportunities for individual Black voices to be heard on an unprecedented scale and with a striking degree of candor and autonomy.[4] North and South, pioneering pamphlets, as well as petitions and addresses, served as "precursors" to African American periodical literature, whose origins are usually traced to the inaugural issue of the first African American newspaper, *Freedom's Journal*, which appeared on March 16, 1827, in New York City.[5]

Petitions and speeches published by some of the most respectable, eloquent, and diplomatic men of Black America had little success in convincing white politicians of the moral, social, and political imperative of addressing the horrors of American chattel slavery. Daniel Coker (1780–1846), a 30-year-old schoolteacher and minister from the free

Black elite of Baltimore, Maryland,[6] turned to pamphleteering in 1810 out of frustration over the failures of previously published African American abolitionist speeches and petitions. In *A Dialogue between a Virginian and an African Minister, Written by the Rev. Daniel Coker, a Descendant of Africa*, apparently Coker's first foray into the world of published letters, the self-described "Minister of the African Methodist Episcopal Church" announced: "The flagrant violation of the rights of humanity was set forth in an humble manner, by the Rev. Absalom Jones, and Mr. James Forten of Philadelphia, in their petition to congress at one of their sessions, held in Philadelphia, in behalf of their suffering brethren in captivity. But were their petitions granted? No."[7] If Black leaders such as Absalom Jones, head of Philadelphia's African Methodist Episcopal Church, and James Forten, a prominent Philadelphia businessman and civil rights champion, could not induce Congress in 1800 to modify the Fugitive Slave provision of 1794 and bring an end to the African slave trade,[8] what hope was there for further "humbly" submitted petitions of this kind? If legally-sanctioned appeals to ideals of reason and rights embedded in America's liberal tradition availed free African Americans nothing in lobbying for an end to slavery, what – or who – could move the slaveholder (and his northern allies) to action? Perhaps only the impassioned voice of the one who had suffered most from slavery, the slave himself.

The introduction of the voice of the slave into print reformist debates over slavery began in the late eighteenth century in the English-speaking world, when British publishers and New England printers acquainted a curious white readership with the lives and opinions of extraordinary African-born slaves, in particular James Albert Ukawsaw Gronniosaw (1770), Ottobah Cugoano (1787), Olaudah Equiano (1789), and Venture Smith (1798).[9] The large majority of the earliest-known slave narratives, however, demonstrated less explicit opposition to slavery as an institution than did Benjamin Banneker's famous 1791 letter to Thomas Jefferson, in which the Black Maryland almanac-maker and astronomer condemned the "fraud and violence" by which so many of his "brethren" toiled in the United States "under groaning captivity and cruel oppression."[10] Yet even Banneker (1731–1806) stopped short of demanding that the slaveholding author of the Declaration of Independence prove his devotion to freedom by liberating his own slaves. Declining "to presume to prescribe" the actions Jefferson and other US leaders should take to end "the injustice of a state of slavery," Banneker was content to provide Jefferson moral counsel: "Wean yourselves of those narrow prejudices" on which the enslavement of African Americans had been justified and "'put your soul in their souls' stead.'" Having recognized their spiritual equality with African Americans, Banneker's letter implied that European Americans like Jefferson, their "hearts ... enlarged with kindness and benevolence toward [the enslaved]," could be counted on to establish justice between the races.[11]

Two slave narratives of the early National era, Equiano's and Smith's, attacked slavery on moral and religious grounds. However, Equiano focused on the transatlantic slave trade to the West Indies, while Smith's indignation was confined largely to racism in Connecticut. Such piecemeal tactics allowed the vast southern slaveocracy to escape censure in the African American slave narrative until 1825, when the first account of the harrowing life of a southern slave came into print.[12] After the *Life of William Grimes, the Runaway Slave*, the narratives of fugitives from southern slavery came increasingly to the forefront of antislavery literature, intensifying sectional hostilities and providing additional excuses for the South to turn a deaf ear to protests against slavery emanating from the North. But during the quarter-century between the narratives of Equiano and Smith and of William Grimes, antislavery writers experimented with the idea that slaves and masters might still address each other through formalized literary dialogues, a genre that had already enabled differing religious, political, and intellectual points of view to engage each other in eighteenth-century North America.[13]

Adaptations of the literary dialogue to antislavery purposes stemmed from Thomas Tryon's *Friendly Advice to the Gentlemen-planters of the East and West Indies* (1684), in which a fictitious West Indian slave's discourse convinces his master that brutal treatment of the enslaved is inimical to Christianity. Although Tryon's text issues no explicit call for the abolition of slavery in Britain's American colonies, Samuel Hopkins's *Dialogue Concerning the Slavery of the Africans* (1776) does. The most noted American antislavery dialogue of the eighteenth century, Hopkins's text pits two white men, a slaveholder and an abolitionist, in a debate that concludes with the latter's call for an immediate, general emancipation. By the early nineteenth century, however, proslavery evangelicals in the United States had converted the dialogue format into defenses of slavery sometimes articulated by pious, Scripture-spouting fictive slaves themselves.[14]

One of the most uncompromising American denunciations of slavery, conducted mainly on a secular human-rights basis in a literary dialogue, appeared in *The Columbian Orator*, a widely-reprinted eloquence manual first published in Boston in 1797.[15] In 1831, Frederick Douglass, a 13-

year-old domestic slave in Baltimore, discovered "Dialogue Between a Master and Slave" in a used copy of *The Columbian Orator* and thrilled to the sharp retorts of the fearlessly frank slave depicted therein. "The slave was made to say some very smart as well as impressive things in reply to his master," Douglass recalled in his first autobiography, "things which had the desired though unexpected effect; for the conversation resulted in the voluntary emancipation of the slave on the part of the master."[16] Conjuring in his own inchoate imagination a vision of himself as a speaking subject, Douglass drew from this dialogue a reason to believe in a future of freedom: "The moral which I gained from the dialogue was the power of truth over the conscience of even a slaveholder."[17] A similar faith in "the power of truth" over "even a slaveholder" impelled Daniel Coker to pen his own remarkable literary experiment, in which a free Black minister converts a Virginia slaveholder into an exponent of "gradual emancipation" partly by invoking the personal narrative of an exemplary Christian slave.[18]

Coker's Dialogue between Minister and Slaver

If an untutored, enslaved Baltimore teenager like Frederick Douglass could find and be inspired by the "Dialogue Between a Master and Slave" in *The Columbian Orator*, it is certainly not a stretch to imagine Daniel Coker, fugitive slave, professional teacher, and organizer of Black churches in Baltimore, being spurred by the same text, or other contemporary dialogues both pro- and antislavery, to create a dialogue of his own. What is only sketched in the 750-word formal dialogue in *The Columbian Orator* is fleshed out and turned into a moral drama in Coker's forty-three-page pamphlet. Presiding over the exchange is a well-spoken free Black minister who hears every proslavery argument that his antagonist, a rather simple but comparatively open-minded Virginia slaveholder, can muster, and then patiently refutes each one. The interracial colloquy is conducted with great civility. The willingness of each interlocutor to question and challenge the other testifies to their tacitly agreed upon equality as partners in the discourse even though one is an "African" and the other a "Virginian." Although the "African minister" invites "Mr. C," a "gentleman" of unspecified race or color, to record the dialogue, one can hardly doubt that the minister is Coker's mouthpiece, invented to preach the author's gospel of freedom so compellingly that the Virginian does not demur when the minister triumphantly concludes, "I am happy that I have made a proselyte of you, to humanity."[19] The distinction between the "Minister of the

African Methodist Episcopal Church in Baltimore" in the dialogue's subtitle and the unnamed "African Minister" of the dialogue proper may have been Coker's way of protecting himself against charges of blasphemy against proslavery orthodoxy in the slave state of Maryland.

The unnamed Virginian of the *Dialogue* appears to be Coker's *beau ideal* of a well-informed, prosperous Christian paternalistic slaveholder. Addressing the Virginian with the utmost courtesy and temperate language, the African minister never castigates or rebukes the slaveholder during their dialogue. Coker allows the Virginian's own words to reveal how deceived he has been by self-interest and popular sophisms about the necessity of enslaving "uncivilized Africans" who, being "unacquainted with the arts of life," are therefore useful "only under the direction of others."[20] When the Virginian attempts to defend slavery by appealing to the Christian Scriptures, the minister quickly exposes the half-truths, misconceptions, and contradictions on which the slaver's biblical defense of human bondage rests. No fire-eating bigot, the white man promptly acknowledges the fallacies of his position. Moreover, the Virginian proves himself a man of feeling. Early in the dialogue he weeps as the minster reminds him of the suffering of slaves in coffles. Nor is the Virginian incorrigibly corrupt. The minister has little difficulty in getting his white interlocutor to declare himself "convinced that slavery is a great evil," although initially the white man asserts that emancipation would lead to "greater evils."[21] In a fashion reminiscent of the way Banneker approaches Jefferson in the latter's letter of appeal, Coker's minister seems motivated by a sense of moral obligation to disabuse the Virginian, who addresses the minister as "my dear friend," of his prejudices so he may escape his racial solipsism and moral myopia.[22] Coker's evident aim was to model for his white readership a slaveholder who would willingly defer to a marshaling of reason, moral appeal, and spiritual example from an antislavery, educated, free African American. A corollary purpose of the dialogue may have been to impress upon "African ministers" throughout the United States their peculiar responsibility not only to preach an antislavery message to their Black parishioners but to be prepared to speak truth to power as Black America's moral and spiritual tribunes to benighted but still redeemable white Christians like the Virginian.

When Banneker addressed his own Virginian, Thomas Jefferson, on behalf of those whom he claimed as "my brethren," Banneker argued his case on the grounds of natural law, "the rights of human nature," and, to a lesser extent, "the obligations of Christianity" to relieve "every part of the human race, from whatever burden or oppression they may unjustly labor under."[23] In his "answer" thanking Banneker for the letter and the almanac that accompanied it, Jefferson expressed a vague hope for "raising the condition" of "our black brethren" to "what it ought to be" without specifying what that improved "condition" should be or when the "raising" ought to occur.[24] Ignoring the admonitions Banneker made to him, Jefferson said nothing in his brief reply about the emancipation of slaves in the United States, his own or anyone else's.[25] When Jefferson forwarded Banneker's almanac to the Marquis de Condorcet, the Secretary of State made much of the almanac-maker's "moral eminence" as "a very worthy & respectable member of society."[26] But Jefferson perceived no connection between Banneker's individual achievements and the rights of the enslaved to join Banneker among the free citizenry of the United States. "He is a free man," Jefferson pointedly announced in introducing Banneker to Condorcet. But a singular free Black man's accomplishments apparently had no necessary moral or sociopolitical application to slaves as far as Jefferson was concerned.

What set Coker's rhetorical agenda apart from Banneker's – making the *Dialogue* a bolder advance on the color line than Banneker's letter – was Coker's refusal to rest his case against slavery and for emancipation solely on the arguments of the free "African minister." The minister would exhort the Virginian to endorse emancipation at least as a moral principle, as Banneker had pleaded with Jefferson. But as Coker knew, and as his minister-persona affirms toward the end of the *Dialogue*, a plan for emancipation had already been proposed by Jefferson himself. According to the minister, Jefferson's blueprint for "gradual emancipation" appears in his *Notes on the State of Virginia* (1787), which the minister recommends to the Virginian when the latter asks for a practicable means of abolishing slavery in the United States.[27] The issue, therefore, was not whether a white slaveholder might acquiesce to the idea that slavery was a "great evil." Like Jefferson in the *Notes*, Coker's Virginian grants slavery's moral indefensibility mid-way through the *Dialogue*. Censuring slavery, however, was little more than a precondition for the more radical and expansive vision of social justice that Coker aimed to articulate through his fictive Black and white interlocutors. In neither the *Notes* nor his response to Banneker's open letter did Jefferson commit to the principle, let alone the practice, of emancipation. Nor did he show any disposition to accept freed slaves in the United States as citizens in the country of their birth. To move his own Virginia slaveholder beyond Jefferson's sophistic, equivocal prevaricating about slavery, Coker also needed to move beyond Banneker's tempered lawyerly posture. He needed to introduce a new voice into the debate, that of the individual southern slave as unjustly suffering servant, a victim of hideous abuse and yet spiritually impregnable against slavery's brutalizing power.

The narrative of the unnamed slave emerges in the *Dialogue* as the capstone to the minister's argument that "the slave is a moral agent" and is therefore eminently deserving of humane treatment at the least and liberation in almost all cases.[28] Only after issuing a genuine offer of freedom, as the Virginian promises the minister he will do to all fifty-five of his slaves, and only after hearing one or more of those slaves decline liberty, as the minister grants a few slaves may also do, would the Virginian be "justified" in keeping someone enslaved.[29] But even under these circumstances, the minister insists, a slaveholder would still be under a solemn responsibility, that of "a faithful guardian" who provides his remaining slaves "a Christian education" and "a sufficiency of the necessaries of life."[30] The fact that so many slaveholders in Virginia rule their slaves "despotically," denying the basic needs of their physical bodies and their immortal souls, becomes the minister's most fervent antislavery claim in the *Dialogue*, which he substantiates by reading the words of "one of those sufferers, that I have been speaking of," namely the slave of a man determined to deprive his slaves of access to the Christian Gospel.[31]

Why are so many slaves "deprived of instruction in the doctrine, and duties of religion," in some cases by violence inflicted by "their wicked masters (so called)"?[32] The minister has a ready reply to his own rhetorical question. "Is it not too obvious, that those masters who try to keep their slaves from the means of [Christian] instruction, do it in order to keep them in a state of ignorance, lest they should become too wise to answer their [masters'] selfish purposes and too knowing to rest easy, and satisfied in their degraded situation?"[33] This oblique allusion to the potential of the Christian gospel to instill in the enslaved a restless resistance to the degradation of their condition is as close as Coker allows his African man of God to get to advocating outright non-compliance with slavery by the enslaved themselves. Hinting at the revolutionary implications of Christianity's radical equalitarianism lets Coker introduce an implicit argument for social and political egalitarianism in the United States that goes well beyond the antislavery, pro-emancipation points the Virginian easily grants earlier in the *Dialogue*. Only after advancing his incisive, though understated, explanation for why many masters keep their slaves "in a state of ignorance" regarding the Gospel does the minister focus on "a relation of the experiences of one of those sufferers," who, having heard and believed fully in the Christian Gospel, received the full brunt of his enslaver's retaliation.[34]

"In his own words": The Slave's Discourse

The unnamed slave's narrative in the *Dialogue* begins with a graphic account of violence done to a slave whose only offense is being a Christian whose enslaver objects to his publicly embracing his faith. "I am chained, and kept back from my public meetings" are the Christian slave's first words, which are key to his character and to his enslaver's outrage.[35] Though in most respects a pacifist, the slave practices non-violent defiance of his master in the name of his religious obligation to attend "public meetings" of the faithful, no doubt attended largely by persons of the slave's own color. If the narrator's enslaver is as suspicious as many other slaveholders (according to the African minister) about the subversive implications of such "meetings," however "public," and of the message, however Gospel-grounded, promulgated in them, it is not difficult to see why the angry slaver puts the Christian slave in chains. "I am chained in and out of the house for thirty and some times forty hours together, without the least nourishment, under the sun," the slave continues. As though such a punishment were not sufficient to discourage him from attempting more "public" demonstrations of his faith, "I am tied and stretched on the ground, as my blessed master [Jesus Christ] was, and suffer the owner of my body to cut my flesh, until pounds of blood, which came from my body, would congeal and cling to the soals [*sic*] of my shoes, and pave my way for several yards. When he would have satisfied his thirst in spilling my blood, he would turn from me to refresh himself with his bottle."[36]

This grisly scene of torture, compounded by the image of the degenerate, quasi-vampirish slaver, "thirsty" for blood and fortified by alcohol, is so appalling that Virginian interrupts the narrative with "Stop sir. Let that be concealed from a christian nation."[37] It is not hard to recognize the irony of the Virginian's solicitude for the tender feelings of a "christian nation" that would prefer to suppress testimony of this sort rather than have it be widely known. But when the tortured slave compares himself "staked and stretched on the ground" to "my blessed master" nailed and suspended from the cross, the narrative testifies plainly to the empowering relationship of the speaker to his salvific "blessed master," despite the violent abuse he must suffer from "the owner of my body."[38]

Refusing the Virginian's request for silence, the minister pauses the narrative of "my suffering brother's experience" only long enough to read the white man a prophetic warning from the Book of Isaiah: "*the Lord*" will "*punish the inhabitants of the earth for their iniquity*" at a time when "*the earth also shall disclose her blood, and shall no more cover her slain.*"[39] Having realized that attempting to silence the words of the enslaved torture victim is vain, "since I find from that scripture, it will ere long, be known," the Virginian reverses himself and asks the minister to resume "the experience of this negro."[40] The narrative immediately points to the slave's primary offense in his earthly master's eyes as well as the temptation the slaver issues to the slave in order to make the torture end. The slaver impiously demands that the slave "renounce my religion, and the God that made me." Contemplating "my blood running so free," the sufferer is prompted to envision even more inspiriting parallels between himself and Jesus Christ. Far from renouncing Christ, the slave's "heart could not help praising my Saviour, and thanking God that he had given me the privilege, and endowed me with fortitude sufficient to bear it." Without so much as a murmur in his enslaver's direction, the slave becomes "more fervent in prayer" to his God, an even clearer testimony to the genuineness of the slave's faith and unshakeable personal "fortitude." The final "diabolical stratagem" of the slaver, having "an iron collar riveted around my neck" before being "clapt in a field to labour," is designed "to put me to shame," "as though I was a deserter or was about to make an elopement [i.e., run away]."[41] The floggings and attempted humiliations aimed at reducing the slave to the dishonored status of "a malefactor" might "shame" a person who lacked the narrator's empowering identification with his God. But to this man of indomitable faith, every indignity and form of abuse only remind him of his "dear Lord and Master," who "had commanded me to bear my cross, and take his yoke upon me."[42] As a result, instead of fear or hopelessness, "my soul, my heart was elevated." Thus, a narrative of extreme tribulation ends on a note of spiritual triumph: "I thought I could have flown, and I went to work with more submission, and with more apparent love than I had done heretofore."[43]

The Virginian's Response to the Slave's Narrative

Twenty-first century readers may find the Virginian's response to the narrative almost anti-climactic. He is not moved to reflect on the magnitude of the slave's Christian fortitude or his dedication to his faith in spite of the extreme persecution visited on him by the sadistic slaver. Nor does the Virginian ponder, outwardly at least, the spiritual threat looming before those, like himself, who risk the wrath of Isaiah's God for the "iniquity" of slave owning. Perhaps uneasiness over the guilt he might accrue should he retain as his slaves those who refuse an offer of liberty is what prompts him to assure the minister that after freeing all his slaves who accept the offer, he will treat those who "should think proper to stay with me . . . as well as my own children."[44] It is unclear whether Coker intended his reader to question the Virginian's implicit paternalistic equation of the freed Negro with a white child. What does seem clear is Coker's desire to portray the spiritually enlightened slave as a moral inspiration to the Virginian. Entering the dialogue, the slaveholder maintains that his slaves are his property, no more, no less. After conversing with the free Black minister, the Virginian concedes that enslaving Black people is wrong, but he still doubts that freeing them would do them or American society any good. Only after hearing the first-person narrative of the Christian slave is the Virginian moved to realize that the enslaved under his control have as much claim to his beneficence as his own offspring. When the slaveholder acknowledges this, he completes a process, overseen by the minister from the outset of the *Dialogue*, that leads the Virginian from first regarding his slaves as property, to viewing them as a troublesome social problem, to finally recognizing their claim to an intimate human connection to himself. By listening to the slave's own words, Coker's white reader gains insight into the depth of an individual slave's religious faith and moral courage, which speak powerfully to his dignity and humanity.

Forty years before Harriet Beecher Stowe's creation of Uncle Tom in 1852, whose story of egregious bodily suffering and exemplary spiritual "submission" and "apparent love" stimulated an unprecedented sentimental identification of whites in the North with slaves in the South, Daniel Coker yoked extreme white perversity with idealized Black spirituality for purposes similar to Stowe's. Both writers embodied singular redemptive Christian faith in a southern slave. What the Virginian learns to do after hearing the slave's narrative is what Banneker asks of Jefferson: "as Job proposed to his friends, 'put your soul in their souls' stead,' thus shall your hearts be enlarged with kindness and benevolence towards them."[45] More urgently and explicitly than Banneker's letter, Coker's *Dialogue*, especially the narrative of the Christian slave, exploits the individual voice of sentiment and soul, as well as the public language of reason and political rights, to break through the racial suspicions, anxieties, and fears that permeate Jefferson's *Notes*. Banneker leaves Jefferson to decide what he can or should do to right the incalculable wrongs of slavery. Coker's more assertive minister leads the Virginian to free his own slaves, embracing abolition strongly enough to announce, "if I had my will, there should not be a slave in the United States."[46] Aware that Jefferson seemed to have a will but refused to seize a way to abolition, Coker portrays his Virginian also perplexed as to "how this could be brought about."[47] But markedly unlike Jefferson, the Virginian wants to find an answer, which is why he asks his free Black "dear friend": "Pray let me hear your ideas on this matter."

A Dialogue Between a Virginian and an African Minister concludes with a discussion, led by the minister, of how best to effect gradual emancipation throughout the country. The minister quotes from a Maryland antislavery writer, John Parrish, whose *Remarks on the Slavery of the Black People* (1806) cites approvingly Jefferson's plan in the *Notes* for the "gradual emancipation" of the slaves.[48] The African minister, quoting Parrish (who quotes Jefferson), admits that "the immediate liberation of all the slaves, may be attended with some difficulty."[49] However, quoting Parrish's invocation of Jefferson, Coker's minister adds that by "fixing a period, after which none should be born slaves in the United States; and the coloured children to be free at a certain age ... in due time, a gradual emancipation would take place."[50] By marshaling the gradual emancipation proposals of Parrish and Jefferson, two respected contemporary southern intellectuals, Coker gives his Virginian ample precedent and justification for endorsing the gradual abolition of slavery too, which the Virginian does by stating that such a way of ending slavery "ought to be done."[51]

What Coker's African minister does not mention is the support both Parrish and Jefferson express for the colonization of all emancipated slaves beyond the borders of the United States. In the *Notes*, Jefferson is vague about where freed African American slaves should be deported, but he is emphatic about one thing: "When freed, he [the slave] is to be removed beyond the reach of mixture."[52] Parrish also rejects any notion that European Americans and African Americans could share the blessings of a common liberty. Congress should set aside "a tract within the western wilderness (where there are millions of acres likely to continue many ages unoccupied) for the colonization of those who are already free."[53] Slaveholders should be incentivized to emancipate their slaves "on condition of their so removing" to the same "western wilderness."[54] Parrish's racial anxieties about emancipated former slaves did not lead him to adopt Jefferson's conviction that race war between whites and freed Blacks was inevitable unless the latter were deported. But both white men found the probability of race-mixing between whites and freed Blacks sufficiently repugnant that they predicated their emancipation schemes on assurances that neither plan would promote "unnatural connexions" that would lead inevitably to the Black subaltern's "staining the blood of his master."[55]

White dread of race-mixing articulated by the likes of Jefferson and Parrish could be readily exploited by anyone, North or South, who, in the name of defending the American experiment, argued that slavery provided the strongest bulwark against social disorder, a repulsive symptom of which would be the creation of "a mungrel breed" by freeing the enslaved.[56] Taking this issue seriously, Coker has his Virginian object early in the *Dialogue* to emancipation because it would inevitably lead to "an unnatural mixture of blood."[57] In perhaps the most puzzlingly ambiguous phase of the *Dialogue*, the African minister espouses an attitude toward race-mixing that sounds consistent with the segregationist views of Jefferson and Parrish. The minister does not deny that race-mixing is "unnatural," nor does he reprove the Virginian for his obvious disparagement of mixed-race people when he speculates gloomily on the long-term product of emancipation: "our posterity at length would all be mulattoes." The minister agrees that America must not become a "mulatto" nation: "This, I confess, would be a very alarming circumstance."[58] However, the minister refuses to adopt the Virginian's alarmism.

As far as African Americans are concerned, the sight of "black men with white wives" is "a rare thing indeed," according to the minister. Black males in these liaisons "are generally of the lowest class, and are despised by their own people," presumably because most Black people think that having a white wife, instead of augmenting a Black husband's social status, only depreciates it.[59] Besides earning well-deserved social opprobrium, interracial marriages also contradict the will of God. "To perpetuate the distinction of colour," the minister explains, "Divine Providence" has "implanted" into people of both colors "a natural aversion and disgust" towards the other.[60] Who are most to blame for defying God's providential design to keep the races separate? White men "of high rank," who "profess abhorrence to such connections," but who "have been first in the transgression."[61] Thus, ironically, it is whites, not Blacks, who are responsible for "daily enhancing the number" of mulattoes in America "in a way, truly disgraceful to both colours."[62] More importantly, such "disgraceful" behavior is primarily attributable to slaveholders and the supremely unnatural institution of slavery: "Fathers will have their own children for slaves; men will possess their own brothers and sisters for property, and leave them to their heirs, or sell them to strangers for life; and youths will have their own grey headed uncles and aunts for slaves."[63] This line of argument lets Coker blame slaveholding for the social "evil" of race-mixing. Abolish slavery, goes the drift of the minister's argument, and the country would be rescued from a "mulatto" future.

Coker is depicted as light complexioned in extant portraits. That light complexion may have cost him the leadership of the African Methodist Episcopal Church.[64] Having the African minister speak so derogatorily of mixed-race people suggests two decisions the author may have made in creating the *Dialogue.* First, he may have felt that concessions to white anxieties about race-mixing were necessary in order to reinforce the fundamental thesis of the *Dialogue* – that emancipation would cure many "evils" in America, including a proliferating mixed-race population. Second, Coker may not have been clear in his own mind about how or to what extent white and Black people would or could interact socially, economically, and politically in a post-slavery America. This uncertainty may be one reason why Coker's dialogue goes no farther than Jefferson or Parrish in imagining an America in which former slaves and former slavers could live, work, and interact together as free and equal partners. The closest thing to an answer Coker ever gave to these questions came in 1820 when he abandoned the United States for Liberia aboard a ship sponsored by the American Colonization Society. In letters appended to the brief journal of his voyage published in 1820, the minister-turned-missionary urged African Americans to join him in Africa where "you may do much better than you can possibly do in America."[65] Daniel Coker lived out the rest of his days in Freetown, Sierra Leone.

David Walker's Appeal for Dialogue

During the first three decades of the nineteenth century, it was not unusual to hear prominent southern statesmen proclaim their abhorrence of slavery, particularly after the bloody slave revolt in San Domingo in 1791 that created Haiti, the first independent Black nation in the Americas.[66] In 1820 Representative John Tyler of Virginia spoke for many in the southern camp during the Missouri controversy when he called slavery "a dark cloud" that threatened "to increase in its darkness over one particular portion of this land till its horrors shall burst upon it" in violence and tragedy.[67] Nevertheless, conflating the moral menace of slavery and the social and physical danger of the freed slave to the white South let most southern leaders condemn slavery as an evil and defend it in the next breath as a necessary evil. Like Jefferson, former President James Madison favored a "gradual" end to slavery contingent on the permanent removal of the freed population from the United States. Without the protection of distance, white southerners could never feel safe, Madison asserted in 1819, from the "jealousies and hostilities," "vindictive recollections," and "predatory propensities" of freed Negroes.[68] Increasingly in the 1820s, slaveholders fearful of either racial violence or rampant miscegenation in the wake of emancipation, gradual or otherwise, touted colonization as the best means of ensuring that freed people of African descent would not stay in the United States long enough to disturb what Madison called "existing and probably unalterable prejudices" on the part of whites against Black people.[69]

To a proud, free Black man like Boston's David Walker, the true indignity of the colonization scheme lay in the power it gave to slave-owners to deny their slaves access to the only liberating dialogue they were likely to hear in the South – that is, the words of free African Americans, perhaps even the written words of Banneker, Coker, or Walker himself. In his furiously antislavery *Appeal*, which he published in Boston in 1829 and revised a year later, Walker predicted that "If the free are allowed to stay among the slaves, they will have intercourse together, and, of course, the free will learn the slaves *bad habits*, by teaching them that they are MEN, as well as other people, and certainly *ought* and *must* be FREE."[70] One reason why Walker, born and raised in Wilmington, North Carolina, migrated to Boston in the mid-1820s was that he knew there was no place in the South where a free Negro could say that slaves not only "ought" to be free but "*must*" be liberated – even if Black people had to "obtain our liberty by the crushing arm of power."[71] *Walker's Appeal* represents the third and probably the last effort by a free Black man from the antebellum South to engage slaveholders in a discourse about emancipation. Appealing to the white South's desire for self-preservation, if not justice, Walker's pamphlet warned America that it could have no peace without justice, no deliverance from the social cataclysm Jefferson most feared except by immediate emancipation.

Although patterned in obvious respects on the US Constitution, Walker's *Appeal* belongs to a tradition of African American jeremiad that in the antebellum era portrayed white America as a corrupt, arrogant, hypocritical, and oppressive Israel in desperate need of conversion from its national sin of slavery. Failure to purge itself of this evil would be an affront to God's justice and an invitation to divine judgment. "O Americans! Americans!!" Walker exhorts at the conclusion of Article III of his *Appeal*: "I call God – I call angels – I call men, to witness, that your DESTRUCTION *is at hand*, and will be speedily consummated unless you REPENT."[72] Later the *Appeal* invokes "the God of armies," "the God of battles," and the "God [who] will dash tyrants" as the power that will deliver African Americans from "your deplorable and wretched condition under the Christians of America."[73] Hedging on explicitly inciting slaves to revolt, Walker does not call for wholesale violent retribution against southern whites. But he does maintain that slaves have both a political and spiritual right to rise up:

> The man who would not fight under our Lord and Master Jesus Christ, in the glorious and heavenly cause of freedom and of God – to be delivered from the most wretched, abject and servile slavery, that ever a people was afflicted with since the foundation of the world, to the present day – ought to be kept with all of his children or family, in slavery, or in chains, to be butchered by his *cruel enemies.*[74]

This unprecedentedly "militant abolitionism" qualified Walker for the title of "father of black nationalist theory in America," making him a key precursor to twentieth-century heroes such as Paul Robeson and Malcolm X.[75]

Walker's melding of a theology of divine deliverance and a philosophy of this-world rights had its intellectual roots in the thought of men like Banneker and Coker, who strove in their writing to keep the spiritual and the secular in a mutually reinforcing dialogue. Walker's distinctive contribution to the African American dialogic tradition of Banneker and Coker stems from the urgent, sometimes strident, but consistently prophetic voice that permeates the *Appeal* and endows it with a sense of apocalyptic mission. The emotionally volatile, overwhelmingly personal quality of Walker's voice – entreating, ridiculing, accusing, goading, threatening, raging in alternating address to Black people and white people – turned what might have seemed disjointed blustery rhetoric into a moral and political peroration strong enough to move the slaveocracy to the severest efforts it had yet undertaken to suppress African American print discourse in the South.[76]

Although the slaveocracy refused to hear anything in Walker's *Appeal* except a death threat, to his African American readership Walker propounds "a great work for you to do": "You have to prove to the Americans and the world, that we are MEN, and not *brutes*, as we have been represented, and by millions treated."[77] Such a proof required that racist sentiment be traced to its sources and then answered candidly and without apology. Brutal representations of Black people, Walker contends, were nowhere more damningly displayed than in Jefferson's *Notes on the State of Virginia*. Unlike Banneker, who tries respectfully to reason with Jefferson as an intellectual equal, Walker treats the *Notes* with undisguised contempt as though its author has personally insulted him and Black people worldwide. Walker quotes as particularly offensive Jefferson's observation in the

Notes that "it is not their [Black people's] *condition* then, but *nature*, which has produced the distinction," that is, the notion of mental distinction that justified whites' enslavement of Blacks.[78] After surveying biblical and ancient history for parallels to the barbarity of the "*white Christians of America,*" and finding none, Walker concludes, "The whites have always been an unjust, jealous, unmerciful, avaricious and blood-thirsty set of beings, always seeking after power and authority."[79] Whether in Greece, Rome, Gaul, Spain, Britain, or Europe, "we see them acting more like devils than accountable men."[80] Christianizing whites only made them more "enlightened and sensible" about the most efficient ways to practice their "hellish cruelties" upon people of color.[81] His history lesson completed, Walker pronounces,

> I therefore, in the name and fear of the Lord God of Heaven and of earth, divested of prejudice either on the side of my colour or that of the whites, advance my suspicion of them, whether they are *as good by nature* as we are or not. Their actions, since they were known as a people, have been the reverse.[82]

Walker's choice of the phrase "advance my suspicion of them" constitutes a direct, mocking parody of another famous passage in the *Notes*, where, ironically, Jefferson tries to back away from the imputation to Black people of natural inferiority that he advances in the following notorious observation, singled out by Walker: "I advance it therefore as a suspicion only that the blacks, whether originally a distinct race, or made distinct by time and circumstances, are inferior to the whites in the endowments both of body and mind."[83] Refusing to accept this statement as a sign that Jefferson might be, in Banneker's words, "well disposed towards us,"[84] Walker expropriates Jefferson's language of "suspicion only" to expose it for what it was – a pretense of open-mindedness that barely concealed a disposition to judge by appearances after calling them indicators of "nature." Placing whites under the same "suspicion" and, "divested of prejudices" (particularly the presumption that Christian whites are "enlightened"), Walker proceeds to judge white "nature" on the basis of historical evidence. The accumulated testimony of Europe's "avaricious and blood-thirsty" past becomes a devastating demolition of Jefferson's self-exempting "suspicions" and of white America's jerry-built notions of racial "nature."

Walker's sarcastic parody of Jefferson constitutes an early instance of African American literary signifying on a canonical white American text.[85] Walker invokes and repurposes Jefferson's suspicion about African American endowments in order to push beyond "body and mind" to the heart and soul of the issue of racial "nature." The historical record Walker amasses argues that "since they were known as a people" white behavior has been "the reverse" of any contention that they are "as good by nature" as Blacks. How natural, then, to characterize whites (repeatedly in the *Appeal*) as "our *natural enemies*," since "they, themselves, (and not us) render themselves our natural enemies, by treating us so cruel."[86]

Given the manifold ways the whites' historical behavior demonstrated their being the "natural enemies" of Blacks, Walker likely was tempted to attribute to inherent irreconcilable racial differences the extreme moral disparities and explosive political antagonism separating the two races. The racial conflagration Walker warns whites to beware would have seemed more inevitable and necessary had he insisted on whites' natural moral inferiority to Blacks. However, Walker rejects such a confident interpretation of white racial nature even as he asserts the natural rights of Blacks to rise up in revolution against white tyranny and oppression. Whites had indisputably "act[ed] more like devils than accountable men," despite having received "the essence of the gospel" centuries ago, as "the Ethiopians have not." Nevertheless, Walker was not prepared to level more than a tentative judgment: "I do indeed suspect them [American whites], but this, as I before observed, is shut up with the Lord, we cannot tell, it will be proved in succeeding generations."[87]

Walker's unwillingness to play God with white America, his reserving of final judgment about essential nature out of respect for as yet undisclosed evidence from ongoing history, provides an important commentary on Jefferson's final posture in the *Notes* regarding the question of the natural inferiority of Black people. Just as Jefferson had his "suspicions" about Black "endowments both of body and mind," so Walker "suspected" white endowments of the heart and conscience. The difference between the two men, however, lies in the kind of relationship to the racial other that each author recommends to his readers. Based simply on his "suspicions" about people of African descent, Jefferson insists that there could be no hope of association, let alone mutuality, between white and Black Americans, especially after emancipation. By contrast, although Walker's suspicions of the moral corruption of whites seem to have been at least as deep as Jefferson's doubts about Black intellectual capacity, the author of the *Appeal* does not conclude that absolute segregation or race war was the only solution to the problem of slavery and white racism in America.

"I should like to see the whites repent peradventure God may have mercy on them," Walker announces early in his text.[88] He does not conclude the last article of the *Appeal* before offering more than once a way out for white Americans, summed up in this final plea:

> I speak Americans for your good. We must and shall be free I say, in spite of you. You may do your best to keep us in wretchedness and misery, to enrich you and your children; but God will deliver us from under you. And wo, wo, will be to you if we have to obtain our freedom by fighting. Throw away your fears and prejudices then, and enlighten us and treat us like men, and we will like you more than we do now hate you,*[89] and tell us now no more about colonization, for America is as much our country, as it is yours.– Treat us like men, and there is no danger but we will all live in peace and happiness together.[90]

A few lines later, Walker adds, "there is not a doubt in my mind, but that the whole of the past will be sunk into oblivion, and we yet, under God, will become a united and happy people. The whites say it is impossible, but remember that nothing is impossible with God."[91]

David Walker's Vision

Despite his righteous excoriation of white Americans for the historically unprecedented atrocity of chattel slavery, Walker's evangelical appeal for moral regeneration among both whites and Blacks, probably heightened by millennial fervor in the 1820s, testifies to the author's faith in the idea that racial justice and comity could still be restored to America.[92] Notwithstanding his disgust over the sham and shame of the United States and his profound distrust of whites, Walker does not rule out a future in which the American dream, as Walker envisions it, could be realized. White Americans had to abolish slavery and disabuse themselves of the notion that free Blacks or freed slaves would ever agree to be deported from the land of their birth to faraway colonies created by whites. Unlike Coker, whose African minister skirts the colonizationist agenda of gradual emancipation proponents like Jefferson and Parrish, Walker sharply attacks the racism, hypocrisy, and greed underlying the colonizationists' motives. The miscegenation anxieties that Coker's African minister tries so self-deprecatingly to quell in the Virginian, Walker brushes aside contemptuously in the *Appeal*:

> I would not give a *pinch of snuff* to be married to any white person I ever saw in all the days of my life. And I do say it, that the black man, or man of colour, who will leave his own colour (provided he can get one, who is good for any thing) and marry a white woman, to be a double slave to her, just because she is *white,* ought to be treated by her as he surely will be, viz: as a NIGER!!!![93]

Walker advises white Americans, instead of obsessing over their "fears and prejudices" about intermixing with inferior Blacks, to open their eyes to the moral superiority of a race of people who, proud to be "not like you," reject whiteness as a standard of beauty as well as behavior.[94] Because Walker believed that whites were still capable of hearing his message and responding positively to it, he entitled his manifesto an "appeal." From a quasi-legal standpoint, the *Appeal* represents Walker's call for a new hearing in the national court of public opinion. No doubt he felt his was the final call that white America could expect before the cataclysm he prophesied should white America fail to repent of slaveholding. Still, Walker's *Appeal* was just that: an appeal, not a verdict.

Although Walker made significant advances beyond the posture and recommendations for reform adopted by Banneker and Coker, the *Appeal* offers little in the way of specifics about the social, economic, and political ideals and practices that would govern the "united and happy people" of Walker's post-slavery America. Beyond an end to slavery and the advent of non-exploitative relationships between whites and Blacks, Walker says little about how his equalitarian ideal could be translated into sociopolitical reality. He appears to have believed, with many other early nineteenth-century evangelicals, that reform proceeds from "individual repentance, reformation, and activism," with African Americans having a particularly important, though vaguely stated, role in the transforming of American life.[95] Regardless of what Walker's social, economic, or political goals may have been for America, he makes clear that nothing could be accomplished without an affirmation by white Americans of their commonality, as human beings and as citizens of the putatively United States, with Black Americans.[96] Such an affirmation had to involve more than the granting of freedom to Black Americans, since, according to the Declaration of Independence (which Walker cites at the end of the *Appeal*), all men, including African Americans, had been endowed with that natural right in the first place. Beyond and in addition to the abolition of slavery as the political cornerstone of the "happy country" he envisions, Walker demands that white Americans "make a national acknowledgment to us for the wrongs they have inflicted on us."[97] The *Appeal* does not clarify whether the "national acknowldgement" for past injustices that Walker had in mind was a form of reparations, and if so, whether it was to be confined to words or extended to more substantive measures.

Walker's outlook was considerably more visionary, even idealistic, than that of his African American predecessors. Only Walker envisions at the end of the *Appeal* a national – not just a *Black* nationalist – dream of a permanently "united" America whose pursuit of happiness seems assured provided slavery is ended. On that ground, "if the whites will listen," Walker offers his country the framework for a healing dialogue. In response, he received from the North as well as the South, from white abolitionists as well as southern slaveholders, widespread condemnation from all but the most radical antislavery leaders.[98] Undaunted, Walker rushed into print a second and third reprinting of his *Appeal*, convinced that all the South's vigilance and repression would not prevent his pamphlet from finding its way into the slave quarters. His mysterious death, on June 28, 1830, only heightened suspicions among Walker's fellow Blacks that the slaveholding power in the United States would never engage in genuine dialogue with African Americans about an end to slavery and racial injustice.

Thoughts on life and death were central to the *Appeal.* "I count my life not dear unto me," Walker wrote, "for what is the use of living, when in fact I am dead."[99] Speaking of himself as a dead man may have been Walker's way of acknowledging his possible assassination once the white South and its henchmen in the North realized that the only way to deter such appeals for freedom was to silence those who delivered them. In declaring his own death, Walker also affirms his existential identification with the slaves whom he exhorts in the *Appeal*, who from the moment they were born had been socially dead because the institution of chattel slavery denied them not only the status of personhood but also the kinship bonds, communal identity, and social legitimacy that define the vital relationships of individuals in a society.[100] Speaking, as it were, from the social grave to which all African Americans had been consigned in the United States, Walker nevertheless maintains his faith "that I am in the hand of God" and thus "ready to be offered at any moment."[101] Despite the prospect of martyrdom, the "God of the Blacks" remained the ultimate arbiter of his fate.[102] As an individual Black man his fate might be death, but as a prophetic voice of Black people, he foresaw a new life for Black Americans in freedom.

Walker's brand of militant African American Christianity offered Coker's African minister's "suffering brother" in slavery a dramatic alternative to Coker's version of the relationship that bound God to Blacks and whites. The slave in Coker's *Dialogue* understands God as a heavenly "Lord and Master" who "had commanded me to bear my cross, and take his yoke upon me" as a "privilege" of Christian service and a guarantee of salvation in the next world.[103] At best, conversion sacralizes the slave's yoke. At worst, it endows the slave with enough self-discipline and fortitude to return to his work "with more submission, and with more apparent love than [he] had done heretofore." Although the "love" that sustains the slave is due to his heavenly "Lord and Master" and not to his "diabolical" white enslaver, the slave gives no indication that he longs for a secular justice to match his spiritual justification. All signs in his narrative point to the reverse. It falls to the African minister to wield the slave's narrative so as to induce the Virginian to feel worse about the slave's suffering than the slave seems to feel about it himself. Because Christianity for the slave requires nothing more of him than service to his spiritual Master by patiently enduring his earthly one, it is up to the minister to exhort the Virginian to feel more responsibility to right the injustices of slavery in *this* world than the slave himself ever asks of him. This divergence between the apolitical Christianity of the slave and the politicized Christianity espoused by the African minister is another problematic feature of Coker's *Dialogue*. By the end of the *Dialogue* one could argue that the minister and the unnamed slave share less common ground on issues of social justice and religious duty than do the minister and the Virginian. At the same time that the dialogue in Coker's text builds a bond between the Black minister and the white southern slaveholder, that same dialogue calls attention to the distance between the slave and both the free Black and white interlocutors.

In contrast, Walker's concept of the relationship among God, whites, and Blacks postulates a congruence and reciprocity between the interests of free Blacks and slaves, between whites and Blacks, and between human and divine responsibilities in both this world and the next: "God has commenced a course of exposition among the Americans" that demands a response from both Blacks and whites.[104] Whites, whether southern or northern, must rid themselves of their presumptions of superiority to people of color and accept the imperative need for individual and collective repentance. No one, neither the slave nor the free person, neither the slaveholding southerner nor the racist northerner, was exempt from God's demand for an America cleansed of the sin of slavery. "The God of justice and of armies" who "will surely go before you" assigns to Black Americans the central role in the redemption of America.[105] "We must exert ourselves to the full" through collective preparation (education and mutual aid) and social activism (resistance to colonization and insistence on immediate emancipation).[106] Organized and united "under God," Black Americans will realize their special global destiny as a people: the evangelization of the entire world and "the *entire emancipation of your enslaved brethren all over the world.*"[107] The moral initiative to appeal for change and the political determination to bring it about are equally and mutually necessary to ultimate freedom. This Walker makes explicit in his assurance that "it is the will of the Lord that our greatest happiness shall consist in working for the salvation of our whole body."[108] In the deliberately double meaning of "salvation," both political and religious, for both this world and the next, Walker's *Appeal* brings to bold fruition an idea only incipient in the dialogic experiments of Banneker and Coker, that recognizing and following Black, not white, moral and spiritual leadership was the only hope for a slavery-corrupted America.

Notes

1 Ira Berlin, *Slaves without Masters* (New York: Pantheon, 1974), 81.

2 Berlin, *Slaves without Masters*, 83–84.

3 In "A Narrative of the Interesting Origins and (Somewhat) Surprising Developments of African American Print Culture," *American Literary History* 17, no. 4 (Winter, 2005): 714–740, Frances Smith Foster discusses the range of publications, many sponsored by the "Afro-Protestant Church," with particular emphasis on the Afro-Protestant periodical press, that constitutes "early African-American print culture." Foster notes that denouncing slavery, prejudice, and social injustice was only part of the multi-faceted mission of eighteenth- and early nineteenth-century African American print culture, which was also dedicated to "creating and nurturing . . . individual and communal agendas" on behalf of Black Americans in various locales (720).

4 Richard Newman, Patrick Rael, and Philip Lapsansky, eds., *Pamphlets of Protest* (New York: Routledge, 2001), 2–4, 6–8.

5 Foster, "A Narrative," 736.

6 For biographical information on Daniel Coker, see Berlin, *Slaves*, 281–282; Josephus R. Coan, "Daniel Coker: Nineteenth-Century Black Church Organizer, Educator, and Missionary," *Journal of the Interdenominational Theological Seminary* 1 (1975): 17–31; Betty Thomas, "Coker, Daniel," *Dictionary of American Negro Biography*, eds. Rayford W. Logan and Michael R. Winston (New York: W. W. Norton, 1982); and Mary F. Corey, "Daniel Coker," *African American National Biography*, eds. Henry Louis Gates Jr. and Evelyn Brooks Higginbotham. *Oxford African American Studies Center*, www.oxfordaasc.com.libproxy.lib.unc.edu/article/opr/t0001/e0123.

7 Daniel Coker, *A Dialogue Between a Virginian and an African Minister, Written by the Rev. Daniel Coker, a Descendant of Africa . . . Minister of the African Methodist Episcopal Church in Baltimore* (Baltimore: The Author, 1810), 14. This pamphlet is reprinted in Newman, Rael, and Lapsansky, *Pamphlets of Protest*.

8 Absalom Jones, et al., "Petition of the People of Colour, free men, within the City and Suburbs of Philadelphia" (1799) and "Letter from James Forten to Honourable George Thatcher, Member of Congress," in John Parrish, *Remarks on the Slavery of the Black People; Addressed to the Citizens of the United States, Particularly to those who are in Legislative or Executive Stations in the General or State Governments* (Philadelphia, PA: The Author, 1806), 49–52.

9 *A Narrative of the Most Remarkable Particulars in the Life of James Albert Ukawsaw Gronniosaw, an African Prince* (1770), Cugoano's *Thoughts and Sentiments on the Evil and Wicked Traffic of the Slavery and Commerce of the Human Species* (1787), *and The Interesting Narrative of the Life of Olaudah Equiano, or Gustavus Vassa, the African* (1789) appear in *Pioneers of the Black Atlantic*, eds. Henry Louis Gates Jr., and William L. Andrews (Washington, DC: Civitas, 1998). A facsimile of *A Narrative of the Life and Adventures of Venture, a Native of Africa* (1798) appears in Chandler B. Saint and George A. Krimsky, *Making Freedom: The Extraordinary Life of Venture Smith* (Middletown, CT: Wesleyan University Press, 2009).

10 *Copy of a Letter from Benjamin Banneker, to the Secretary of State, with His Answer* (Philadelphia, PA: Daniel Lawrence, 1792), 8. Further quotations from this letter are taken from this edition. For scholarship on the exchange between Banneker and Jefferson, see the rhetorical analysis of Angela G. Ray, "'In My Own Hand Writing': Benjamin Banneker Addresses the Slaveholder of Monticello," *Rhetoric & Public Affairs* 1: 3 (fall 1998): 387–405; and the historical perspective of William L. Andrews, "Benjamin Banneker's Revision of Thomas Jefferson: Conscience Versus Science in the Early American Antislavery Debate," in *Genius in Bondage*, eds. Vincent Carretta and Philip Gould (Lexington: University Press of Kentucky, 2001), 218–241.

11 Ibid., 8.

12 See William Grimes, *Life of William Grimes, the Runaway Slave*, eds. William L. Andrews and Regina E. Mason (1825; New York: Oxford University Press, 2008) and the discussion of Grimes's *Life* in Andrews, *To Tell a Free Story: The First Century of Afro-American Autobiography, 1760–1865* (Urbana: University of Illinois Press, 1986), 77–81.

13 Texts in which the word "dialogue" or a synonym for it appear in the title numbered in the thousands in eighteenth-century England. See Kevin L. Cope, "Seminal Disseminations: Dialogue, Domestic Directions, and the Sudden Construction of Character," *Compendious Conversations*, ed. Kevin L. Cope (Frankfurt: Peter Lang, 1992), 167. During this time a wide variety of genres, including dialogues of the dead, verse dialogues, satiric dialogues, and philosophical dialogues, gained popular audiences (Frederick M. Keener, *English Dialogues of the Dead* (New York: Columbia University Press, 1973); K.J.H. Berland, "Didactic, Catecheticall, or Obstetricious? Socrates and Eighteenth-Century Dialogue," Cope, *Compendious Conversations*, 93–94). From the late seventeenth century, literary dialogues, some as short as broadsides, others in pamphlet form, addressed contemporary issues in the North American colonies and the early United States. In 1671 John Eliot's *Indian Dialogues*, which put

arguments for Christianity in the mouth of converted Indians, constituted an early American experiment in interracial dialogue. Topics for discussion in later years included religious matters, e.g., *Dialogue between a minister and Billy, a young parishioner, on the subject of Singing Praises to God* (Danbury, 1794); moral instruction, e.g., *Dialogue between an uncle and his kinsman* (Boston, 1764) and *A dialogue between death and a lady* (Boston, 1775); and politics, e.g., *A Dialogue between a southern delegate and his spouse, on his return from the grand Continental congress* (New York, 1774) and *A Dialogue between the devil, and George III* (Boston, 1782).

14 Thomas Tryon, *Friendly Advice to the Gentlemen-planters of the East and West Indies* (London: Andrew Sowle, 1684); Samuel Hopkins, *A Dialogue Concerning the Slavery of the Africans* (Norwich, CT: Judah P. Spooner, 1776); Dickson D. Bruce Jr., *The Origins of African American Literature, 1680–1865* (Charlottesville, VA: University Press of Virginia, 2001), 22–24, 112–118.

15 "Dialogue Between a Master and Slave," in *The Columbian Orator*, ed. Caleb Bingham, (Boston: Manning and Loring, 1797).

16 *Narrative of the Life of Frederick Douglass, An American Slave* (Boston: Anti-Slavery Office, 1845), 39.

17 Ibid., 40.

18 Coker, *A Dialogue*, 38.

19 Ibid.

20 Ibid., 26.

21 Ibid.

22 Ibid., 38.

23 *Copy of a Letter from Benjamin Banneker*, 6, 5.

24 Ibid., 11.

25 Ibid.

26 Jefferson to Condorcet, 30 August 1791. "Founders Online," United States National Archives, https://founders.archives.gov/documents/Jefferson/01-22-02-0092.

27 Thomas Jefferson, *Notes on the State of Virginia* (Philadelphia, PA: The Author, 1788), Query XIV, 146–147; Coker, *A Dialogue*, 28.

28 Coker, *A Dialogue*, 33.

29 Ibid., 31.

30 Ibid.

31 Ibid., 34.

32 Ibid., 33.

33 Ibid., 34.

34 Ibid.

35 Ibid.

36 Ibid., 34–35.

37 Ibid., 35.

38 Ibid., 34.

39 Ibid., 35.

40 Ibid.

41 Ibid., 35–36.
42 Ibid.
43 Ibid. Although what Coker intended by the word "'apparent'" cannot be ascertained, from the context the word is likely to signify manifest, clearly visible, or obvious. The type of Christian Coker embodies in the suffering slave is so filled with "love," despite all the hateful treatment he has received, that it is apparent to anyone who observes him.
44 Ibid.
45 *Copy of a Letter from Benjamin Banneker*, 8.
46 Coker, *A Dialogue*, 37.
47 Ibid.
48 Ibid., 37–38. John Parrish, *Remarks on the Slavery of the Black People* (Philadelphia, PA: The Author, 1806),41. Parrish contends that "no just law" can legitimize slavery. "It is against the essence of the Constitution, and very contrary to the nature and spirit of Christianity" (31).
49 Coker, *A Dialogue*, 37.
50 Ibid., 37–38; Parrish, *Remarks*, 41.
51 Coker, *A Dialogue*, 38.
52 Jefferson, *Notes*, 154.
53 Parrish, *Remarks*, 43.
54 Ibid., 44.
55 Ibid., 43; Jefferson's prophesy of race war appears in *Notes*, Query 18, 173–174.
56 Larry E. Tise, *ProSlavery: A History of the Defense of Slavery in America, 1701–1840* (Athens: University of Georgia Press, 1987), 231–232.
57 Coker, *A Dialogue*, 28.
58 Ibid.
59 Ibid.
60 Ibid.
61 Ibid., 29. Given the fact that the rumors about Jefferson's relationship to Sally Hemings had been in wide circulation by the time of the *Dialogue*, the likelihood is strong that Coker alludes to Jefferson in this remark.
62 Ibid.
63 Ibid., 30.
64 At the founding conference of the African Methodist Episcopal denomination in April 1816, Coker was declared the first AME bishop, but he declined the office, after "many, who described themselves as 'pure blacks,' objected to Coker's leadership. They complained that Coker, born of an English indentured servant mother and an enslaved Black father, was too 'light' in complexion" to lead an 'African connexion.'" James Oliver Horton and Lois E. Horton, *In Hope of Liberty: Culture, Community and Protest among Northern Free Blacks, 1700–1860* (New York: Oxford University Press, 1997), 141. See the portrait of Coker in Daniel A. Payne, *History of the African Methodist Episcopal Church*, ed. C. S. Smith (Nashville, TN: A.M.E. Sunday-School Union, 1891), 90. http://docsouth.unc.edu/church/payne/ill1.html

65 Daniel Coker, *Journal of Daniel Coker, A Descendant of Africa* (Baltimore, MD: The Author, 1820), 44.

66 For a list of prominent Virginians who spoke of the evils of slavery, see Richard Beale Davis, *Intellectual Life in Jefferson's Virginia* (Chapel Hill: University of North Carolina Press, 1964), 414–415. For the impact of the San Domingo revolt on antebellum writers, see Eric J. Sundquist, *To Wake the Nations: Race in the Making of American Literature* (Cambridge, MA: Harvard University Press, 1993), 31–36.

67 Beverly B. Munford, *Virginia's Attitude toward Slavery and Secession.* (Richmond, VA: L. H. Jenkins, 1909), 87.

68 James Madison to Robert J. Evans, 15 June 1819, Founders Online. https://founders.archives.gov/documents/Madison/04-01-02-0421.

69 Madison to Evans; Winthrop D. Jordan, *White Over Black: American Attitudes toward the Negro, 1550–1812.* (Chapel Hill: University of North Carolina Press, 1968), 566–569; David Brion Davis, *The Problem of Slavery in the Age of Emancipation* (New York: Vintage, 2014), 83–166.

70 David Walker, *Walker's Appeal, in Four Articles; Together with a Preamble, to the Coloured Citizens of the World* (Boston, MA: The Author, 1830), 52. See Peter P. Hinks's scholarly edition of *Walker's Appeal* (University Park: Pennsylvania State University Press, 2000).

71 Ibid., 79. The most extensive study of Walker's life and work is Peter P. Hinks, *To Awaken My Afflicted Brethren: David Walker and the Problem of Antebellum Resistance* (University Park: Pennsylvania State University Press, 1997). See also Donald M. Jacobs, ed., *Courage and Conscience: Black and White Abolitionists in Boston* (Bloomington, IN: Indiana University Press, 1993). An early biographical sketch written by a Walker contemporary, Henry Highland Garnet, appeared in *Walker's Appeal, with a Brief Sketch of His Life* (New York: J.H. Tobitt, 1848).

72 Walker, *Walker's Appeal*, 49.

73 Ibid., 73, 78, 81, 23.

74 Ibid., 15.

75 Sterling Stuckey, *Slave Culture* (New York: Oxford University Press, 1987), 120.

76 In response to the *Appeal*, Georgia and Louisiana passed new repressive laws against the circulation of abolitionist literature among the slaves. The legislatures of Mississippi, Virginia, and Louisiana went into special session to respond to what they perceived as a crisis (Stuckey, 136–137). In February 1830 four Black men were arrested in New Orleans on charges of circulating the *Appeal*. Rumors circulated about a white cabal that had offered a 1,000-dollar reward for the murder of David Walker (Horton and Horton, 173).

77 Walker, *Walker's Appeal*, 35.

78 Ibid., 18.

79 Ibid., 17, 20.

80 Ibid., 20.

81 Ibid., 21.

82 Ibid.
83 Jefferson, *Notes*, 153.
84 *Copy of a Letter from Benjamin Banneker*, 4.
85 For the theory of "signifying" as a mode of literary parody and ironic reinterpretation, see Henry Louis Gates Jr., *The Signifying Monkey* (New York: Oxford University Press, 1987).
86 Walker, *Walker's Appeal*, 26, 70.
87 Ibid., 21.
88 Ibid., 24.
89 At the asterisk in this quotation, Walker added the following footnote to his text: "You are not astonished at my saying we hate you, for if we are men, we cannot but hate you, while you are treating us like dogs" (70).
90 Ibid., 79.
91 Ibid., 80.
92 Hinks, ed., *Walker's Appeal*, xxxii–xxxiv; Wilson Moses aligns Walker's opposition to the colonization scheme and his hope for American reform with the African American majority's "intense commitment to the United States, its culture, and its people" during the antebellum era. Wilson Moses, *The Golden Age of Black Nationalism, 1850–1924* (New York: Oxford University Press, 1978), 45.
93 Ibid., 11.
94 Ibid., 21. Walker testifies to his faith in the discernment of Black people, once they have divested themselves of false white models, when he predicts that "if ever the world becomes Christianized, (which must certainly take place before long) it will be through the means, under God of the *Blacks.*"
95 Hinks, ed., *Walker's Appeal*, xxxiv.
96 Walker "was willing to see Americans, black and white, as 'one people,' provided that blacks had significant influence in determining the direction of the country, provided America ceased being a 'white' country" (Stuckey, 131).
97 Walker, *Walker's Appeal*, 80.
98 For Black and white abolitionists' reactions to Walker, see Hinks, ed., *Walker's Appeal*, xli–xliv.
99 Walker, *Walker's Appeal*, 81.
100 Orlando Patterson, *Slavery and Social Death* (Cambridge, MA: Harvard University Press, 1982), 5–8.
101 Walker, *Walker's Appeal*, 81.
102 Ibid., 21.
103 Coker, *A Dialogue*, 35–36.
104 Walker, *Walker's Appeal*, 61.
105 Ibid., 12.
106 Ibid., 70.
107 Ibid., 21, 34.
108 Ibid., 34–35.

CHAPTER 3

Black Entrepreneurship, Economic Self-Determination and Early Print in Antebellum Brooklyn

Prithi Kanakamedala

New York's gradual emancipation era, from 1799 to 1827, upheld slaveholders' economic interests and did little to improve the economic, political, and social needs of people of African descent, both enslaved and free. In Brooklyn, New York, its free Black community members – among them Peter Croger (?–1848), a whitewasher; Benjamin Croger (1789–1853), also a whitewasher; and Henry C. Thompson (?–?), a blacking manufacturer – struggled to secure work that reflected the true extent of their talents and capabilities. As racism restricted them to a limited labor market, they worked low-wage menial jobs, which forced them to live on or below the poverty line. City directories and newspaper advertisements, starting in 1809 and running throughout the antebellum period, reveal that Black Brooklynites, like their neighbors in the separate city of Manhattan, worked as whitewashers, boot blacks, blacksmiths, dock workers, and laborers. Despite this struggle for a wider variety of jobs that might have showcased greater skill and perhaps earned higher wages, members of Brooklyn's small but significant free Black community radically organized their labor to serve in an additional public capacity as grassroots organizational officers, educators, church elders, and community leaders.

Between 1810 and 1831, Black Brooklynites sought crucial local print forms including newspaper advertisements, notices, and pamphlets, to ensure their self-determination and public service were publicly recorded, publicized, and recognized. Print gave voice to their labor and participation in civic life, even as they were denied voice by state and nation, and print presented powerful articulations of their own self-defined liberation. This self-definition was necessary, especially in Brooklyn, where African Americans were almost exclusively working class and that community relied on itself to create its own institutions without the assistance of a Black elite, white philanthropists, or already existing organizations.

If the hyperlocal focus on Brooklyn for this chapter seems parochial, it is important to note that Brooklyn was a separate municipality until the consolidation of New York in 1898. It had its own peculiar history that created both opportunities and significant challenges to its free Black community, and within these material realities, ordinary people of color found ways to support their humanity and to create larger antislavery networks through protest and print. With a focus on the borough's history of antislavery activism and print culture, this chapter examines the lives and labor of Peter Croger, his younger brother Benjamin Croger, and their neighbor Henry C. Thompson. Thereby, we explore African American self-determination and selfhood in public life and print in Brooklyn, as it transformed from town to city in the first half of the nineteenth century.

Labor and Print in Antebellum Brooklyn

In 1800, Brooklyn was just one of six agricultural towns in Kings County, and it lay directly across the East River from rapidly urbanizing Manhattan. Just one year prior, New York State took its first steps toward dismantling slavery and became the second-to-last northern state to do so. Vermont, Pennsylvania, Massachusetts, New Hampshire, Connecticut, and Rhode Island had already abolished slavery prior to, during, or in the immediate aftermath of the American Revolution. During New York's gradual emancipation era, slavery declined in Manhattan for a variety of economic, political, and religious reasons, and the city quickly reestablished itself as a vital mercantile and financial port city in the Atlantic world. This was not the case in neighboring Kings County. Brooklyn, with its close proximity to Manhattan, was perhaps the most developed of Kings County's six towns with ropewalks, churches, a distillery, a print shop, and one circulating newspaper. In 1816, the village of Brooklyn, comprising about one square mile, was created within the town of the same name to reflect its slow urban development on Long Island's northwestern tip. But the majority of Kings County still remained distinctly agricultural. In fact, some outer areas, such as Flatlands, heavily relied on its agrarian economy through the 1880s. This agrarianism meant that while slavery atrophied in other urban centers in the North in the 1790s and early 1800s, their numbers actually strengthened in Kings County where enslaved labor was crucial in sustaining the area's agricultural fortunes. With slavery in higher numbers than any other county in New York State, one historian coined Kings County a "slave-holding capital."[1]

The economic consequences of slavery's slow demise in Kings County had a devastating impact on Brooklyn's growing free Black community. Black Brooklynites were distinctly working class. There was no equivalent of the wealthy Forten family of Philadelphia or the Lyons family of Manhattan, and they did not receive assistance from white-led antislavery organizations such as Manhattan's New-York Manumission Society in the creation of their independent institutions. Peter Croger founded the Brooklyn African Woolman Benevolent Society, the town's first mutual aid organization, in 1810; he founded the first African school explicitly dedicated to educating the village's Black community in 1815; he served as church elder at the Brooklyn African Methodist Episcopal (AME) Church, the town's first Black-led church established in 1818; and meanwhile Croger worked in Brooklyn as a whitewasher, a contractor, or day laborer who mixed and applied a whitewash paint compound of slated lime and water to fences, barns, gates, walls, and ceilings. His brother, Benjamin Croger, co-founded the Brooklyn African Woolman Benevolent Society and the church, and also worked in Brooklyn as a whitewasher. Henry C. Thompson, who later joined the mutual aid organization and expanded Brooklyn's African School, also became an early land investor in Weeksville, the second-largest independent and self-determined free Black community in antebellum America, founded in 1838. Thompson worked in Brooklyn as a blacking manufacturer.[2] Many of the professions available to them correlated to work previously done by enslaved laborers. As enslaved workers, people of African descent worked as carpenters, shoemakers, millers, weavers, seamstresses, candle makers, chimney and fireplace cleaners, tool menders, and cooks in Brooklyn. During gradual emancipation and in the post-emancipation decades, while a few New Yorkers and Brooklynites worked as professional educators, or in the specific case of James McCune Smith, a doctor, the majority of African Americans were documented in census records and city directories as blacksmiths, whitewashers, boot blacks, carpenters, tailors, and tobacconists.[3]

The Crogers and Thompson lived and worked in Brooklyn from approximately 1805, when it was only a modest town of 5,740 residents, of which 300 were free Black men, women, and children. The town quadrupled in size by the 1830s and was fast emerging as the third largest city in the United States by their death in the 1850s. During this time, the town established the arteries of urban infrastructure: roads were expanded, farmland was parceled off and sold as lots to private investors, residents established banks, churches, schools, and literary societies. And at each stage, Black Brooklynites were almost exclusively denied participation in the development of their town. Within this urban context and expansion, Brooklyn's free Black community created spaces that allowed for self-determined dialogue, intellectual activity, and political action. They placed a school advertisement in the notices section of the town's main newspaper, the *Long Island Star*, and published the proceedings of an anti-colonization protest that also appeared in the news section of the same newspaper. Together, these items, along with a pamphlet featuring the constitution of a Black-led local mutual aid society, reveal print as an important driver of Black organizational life in Brooklyn and beyond. While paper fueled communication within organizations, the business of Black organizational life provided material for print culture.

Remarkably, given the absence of a Black press, Black Brooklynites relied exclusively on the town's local white printers to convey and record their work. The AME Church did not commence publishing operations until 1817 in Philadelphia, and *Freedom's Journal*, the nation's first anti-slavery and Black newspaper did not appear in print until March 1827 in Manhattan. In doing so, the print culture of early Brooklyn reflected its contemporary politics in which the tension between white supremacy and Black self-determination occupied the same intimate streets and print spaces. There were only three white printers with their own print shops in Brooklyn from 1800 to 1830 – Thomas Kirk, Erastus Worthington, and Christian Brown – and their production was dwarfed in comparison to Manhattan's output. But rapid technological changes in print culture including the printing press, papermaking, and bookbinding meant materials could be printed quickly and cheaply, and they had the ability to reach a wide audience. Brooklyn's free Black community took advantage of these print changes to create a more inclusive, democratic narrative. In print, Black Brooklynites challenged racist assumptions about their intellectual capacity. So often essentialized, objectified, and subjected to intense scrutiny by their white neighbors, the range of self-created formal and informal labor undertaken by Black Brooklynites not only expanded their roles within the town, its depiction in print simultaneously offered powerful written, rather than visual, arguments of their right to be seen as citizens and neighbors of equal standing by demonstrating, articulating, and naming their skills, talents and capabilities as Americans.[4] The rest of the chapter follows the print chronology of this culminating activism.

A Newspaper Advertisement for the African School

People of African descent in cities such as Boston, Philadelphia, New York, and later Brooklyn, had long presented powerful articulations of their struggle and liberation in print in which they were determined to speak for themselves. "[African American print culture] became a primary tool in constructing African America," as Frances Smith Foster asserts, "in ensuring the protections and progress of the 'race' or the 'nation' not only in defending themselves from libelous or ignorant attacks by other Americans but even more for reconstructing individual and group definitions and for advocating behaviors and philosophies that were positive and purposeful."[5] This print era long preceded the African American slave autobiographies, including works such as Frederick Douglass's *Narrative of the Life of Frederick Douglass* (1845), Henry Bibb's *Narrative of the Life and Adventures of Henry* Bibb (1849), and Harriet Jacobs's *Incidents in the Life of a Slave* Girl (1861), that have since become the center of antebellum American historiography and the American literary canon.[6] From the late eighteenth century to the early nineteenth century, Black-led cultural production included the printing of lectures, meeting minutes, constitutional by-laws, sermons, and the recorded resolutions of both state and national Black conventions in the form of pamphlets, broadsides, petitions, and newspapers. This plethora of material included Phillis Wheatley's work beginning in 1773, African American petitions to the Massachusetts legislature in 1773 and 1777, Richard Allen and Absalom Jones's *Narrative of the Proceedings of Black people, during the late awful calamity in Philadelphia* in 1793, Prince Hall's *Charge Delivered to the brethren of the African Lodge* in 1797, and the *Oration on the Abolition of the Slave Trade in the United States, delivered at the African Asbury Church, in the City of New York* in 1814.[7] A little over a year later, on January 18, 1815, Peter Croger placed an advertisement for his African school in the *Long Island Star*, Brooklyn's local newspaper.[8]

Nestled between a membership advertisement for the town's Panharmonic Society and a tax demand on all carriage transportation, the notice for Croger's African School featured on the penultimate page of the four-page *Long Island Star*. The small, five-line notice read:

> African School
> A DAY and Evening SCHOOL is now opened
> at the house of *Peter Croger*, in James
> Street, Brooklyn, where those who wish may be
> taught the common branches of education

"African" laid claim to the organization's right to self-naming and to ancestral solidarity, rather than operating as a geographic marker, and its political intent resonated with the naming of several other Black-led contemporary organizations in Manhattan and Brooklyn, including the New York African Society for Mutual Relief, New York African Marine Fund, African Methodist Episcopal Zion Church, New-York African Clarkson Association, and New York's African schools.[9]

Peter Croger opened Brooklyn's first school for the education of African American adults and children at his home on James Street in 1815 (The area was subsequently razed entirely, and its history lost when construction of the Brooklyn Bridge began in 1869). By this time, residents of African, Dutch, and English descent were joined by a gradual influx of Irish immigrants. Together, they occupied the same narrow streets and spaces in Brooklyn – the notion of segregated neighborhoods did not exist – and the town's racial tensions are evident through its institution-building and local print publications. The African School had been founded out of necessity as emancipation held no promise of equality. Croger's desire, therefore, to see his school advertised in print in the town's main newspaper was certainly part convenience, but the notice was largely a revolutionary act. While no evidence exists today of how many students were impacted by the grassroots school, its existence was significant. The ability to read, write, and help others gain literacy was a means of liberation for the free Black community in Brooklyn and beyond as they fought widespread oppression.

Croger set up the African School at a time when slavery still had no end date in New York state. According to its Gradual Emancipation Act (1799), anyone born to an enslaved mother after July 4, 1799, would be free at the age of twenty-eight if male, or twenty-five if female. Anyone born before that date was enslaved for life. The law maximized slaveholding profits and guaranteed an enslaved person worked during their prime years, if they even survived that long. The *Long Island Star* newspaper reflected these economic priorities and white anxieties about slavery's demise. Founded in 1809 by Irish-born Thomas Kirk, the *Long Island Star*, despite its title, focused primarily on Brooklyn and Kings County. As the first issue of the publication announced, it was created to reflect Brooklyn's "growing prosperity and increasing population."[10] Kirk, who had begun his print career in Manhattan, moved to Brooklyn when the city became overcrowded and therefore became one of the town's earliest printers. The *Long Island Star* was actually his second newspaper venture in Brooklyn. His first, the *Courier and New York and Long Island Advertiser*, began in 1809 and folded within twelve months as it became increasingly clear Brooklynites wanted a newspaper that focused on the town's expanding commercial activity.[11] From its print commencement, the newspaper frequently featured advertisements for runaways or freedom seekers. In a six-month period taken from 1815, the newspaper featured seven runaway slave advertisements. The advertisements included a notice for a 20-year-old Black man from north Williamsburg, Long Island; a 20-year-old male from the remote, agricultural area of south Gravesend; and a 19-year-old teenager from Shelter Island, Long Island.[12] One year later, the newspaper advertised the sale of "several slaves" around twenty-one years of age, just across the small creek that connected Brooklyn to Newtown, Long Island (today the modern day borough of Queens).[13]

Opportunities for Brooklyn's free Black community to participate in their growing town's literacy initiatives looked bleak. In 1816, when white trustees of the town's first public school announced its opening at Kirk's print shop and stated the institution was only able to accommodate thirty to forty students, they concluded that "it may be understood that no colored children will be received."[14] It was commercially lucrative for Kirk to print both the outcomes of grassroots building by the town's free Black community alongside the enslavement of other Black people in his newspaper. But it also revealed a great deal about Brooklyn's pervasive racism, the limits of gradual emancipation, and the power of white printers who denied Black residents access to education and literacy. These printers held significant power and influence, and their ability to control literacy and literary activity in Brooklyn should not be underestimated. From its founding in 1809 to 1831, the *Long Island Star* was run by a series of white printers based in the village of Brooklyn, including Kirk, Alden Spooner, and Erastus Washington. Spooner actually served two separate terms and became the newspaper's longest serving editor until it ceased publication in 1863.[15] As one-person operations, these men acted sequentially as printer, publisher, and editor, and exclusively controlled each aspect. With the help of an assistant, the printer laid down the letters in metal guides, edited the entries, and oversaw the newspaper's business operations. This expensive and risky business model, common in Brooklyn and Manhattan in the early antebellum period, meant that publications often folded quickly and would simply relaunch under new leadership, or a new publication would take its place.[16] The political power of these print businessmen within Brooklyn was intensified by a lack of competition. Manhattan, in contrast, had eleven circulating newspapers to Brooklyn's one from 1800 to 1815, none of which were explicitly antislavery, but which certainly had differing sympathies to slavery's gradual abolition in New York.[17]

Despite widespread racism and hostility, Black Brooklynites placed several advertisements for educational opportunities for free people of color in the *Long Island Star*. These forms of print activism were a precedent to the advertising for Black-led schools that followed in the post-emancipation years and in later, friendlier print venues such as *Freedom's Journal*, *The Colored American*, *The Liberator*, the *North Star*, and other antislavery publications and the Black press where such advertisements fostered the creation of an antislavery network. In Brooklyn, not only was the act of establishing the African school in 1815 radical in itself (even the African school system in Manhattan, with the financial backing of the white-led New-York Manumission Society, was relatively shielded from potential racial violence), but by pursuing advertising in otherwise unwelcome print spaces, Brooklyn's antislavery pioneers forced white supremacists to acknowledge their labor and community building. Croger's notice for the African School ran for three weeks in the *Long Island Star* and therefore ensured his leadership received attention from a wide readership including his neighbors within the town and beyond. By this time, the Croger brothers had already established the town's first mutual aid society, and the school was an expansion of their self-determined community labor.

Constitution of the Brooklyn African Woolman Benevolent Society

In 1810, brothers Peter and Benjamin Croger, together with their neighbor Joseph Smith, established the town's first mutual aid organization called the Brooklyn African Woolman Benevolent Society. Its name paid respect to New Jersey Quaker and itinerant preacher John Woolman (1720–1772), a white early antislavery pioneer who "roamed throughout the [northern and southern] colonies [throughout the 1750s] trying to convince his co-religionists of the sin of slaveholding."[18] Mutual aid societies, like the African Woolman Benevolent Society, were vital economic and cultural spaces that fostered close kinship ties beyond blood relations. In the absence of insurance policies, they protected and ensured the family of a deceased member would not be forced into poverty or to live in the town's almshouse or on the streets.[19] The Brooklyn organization was formed just two years after free Black men in Manhattan formed the New York African Society for Mutual Relief in 1808, which held similar objectives, and the two mutual aid societies represented a local network of self-care and economic self-reliance. As many of these benevolent organizations predated other key institutions in Black organizational life, they were often instrumental in the founding of independent Black churches in their towns and cities.

The Brooklyn African Woolman Benevolent Society first appeared in print nine years after its founding, and the organization paid 75 cents (around 14 dollars with inflation) for the notice's inclusion in the *Long Island Star*. It was not an insignificant amount of money given that the working wages for a Black man totaled approximately 250 dollars per annum or 21 dollars per month. Their newspaper notice on December 29, 1819, was sandwiched between an advertisement for vendor contract bids for the Brooklyn Navy Yard and a local business advertising the sale of a large assortment of single- and double-barrel guns, but it stood out partly because of the large font size in the advertisement header. The otherwise small, ten-line notice read:

> **Brooklyn African Woolman Benevolent Society**
>
> The Anniversary of this Society will be celebrated on Saturday next, being New Years day. The members are invited to attend at Mrs Benton's Inn, corner of Fulton and Middagh-streets, at 10 o'clock, am where a procession will be formed and move through some of the principal streets to the African Church at which place an oration and other exercises are expected. The *New-York African Wilberforce Society* will join the procession.
>
> PETER CROGER, President

The society's procession was part of a larger, growing protest tradition in the North, and the decision to print its route held political significance. In neighboring Manhattan, both the New York African Society for Mutual Relief and the New York African Wilberforce Society began marching through the city's streets to mark the abolition of the slave trade in 1808. In Boston, Black men marched annually from 1808 until the 1820s through the city's streets and ended at the African church.[20] In Brooklyn, the organization intended to march through the village's main streets as part of their anniversary celebrations and to end the procession at the AME church established by the Crogers just one year earlier in 1818.[21] Methodism was an old and respected faith in Kings County. In 1794, residents established the First Methodist Church of Brooklyn, or Sands Street Methodist. It was one of only three churches in Brooklyn for much of the late eighteenth century and turn of the nineteenth century. The church congregation included people of European descent, African descent, and Native Americans. However, protest took root at the church when African Americans renounced their membership after being forced to listen to the pro-slavery views of the church's pastor Alexander M'Caine. The departure of Brooklyn's Black community from Sands Street Methodist, where Thomas Kirk of the *Long Island Star* acted as a class elder and trustee from 1807, coincided with major religious reforms elsewhere.

In 1816, the same year that the village of Brooklyn was incorporated, Richard Allen formed the independent AME denomination. Just one year later, Peter and Benjamin Croger came together with their neighbors to discuss fundraising for an AME Church building in the village of Brooklyn. On February 7, 1818, its free Black community opened the AME Church on High Street. While they waited for a pastor from Philadelphia, Allen ordained several of the founders, including the Crogers, who served as church leaders. For the African Woolman Benevolent Society's anniversary, against the backdrop of Brooklyn's streets – a great number of which are still named after its wealthy white landowners and slaveholders – the organization would proudly and publicly display their radical activism by marching from their headquarters to the AME Church. The public formation of spectacle and politics by people of color was antithetical to New York's historic colonial slave laws, which had forbidden Black people from gathering in groups larger than three, or for the few hours of freedom that the Election Day and Pinkster festivals afforded them.[22]

By the time the Brooklyn African Woolman Benevolent Society marched through Brooklyn's streets, the town awaited absolute emancipation. In 1817, New York state passed its final emancipation law which stated slavery would be abolished on July 4, 1827, thereby giving an end date for those who had been born before July 4, 1799, and for whom the initial gradual emancipation law did not apply. But enslaved African Americans did not wait for freedom to be granted. Many seized their freedom by running away, negotiating with their slaveholder, or working with a member of the free Black community to purchase and then emancipate them. Amongst the chaos of freedom and unfreedom during gradual emancipation, Brooklyn's free Black community created organizations such as the African Woolman Benevolent Society to secure their civil rights. At a time when freedom was fragile and the threat of kidnapping loomed large, the organization's aim to "alleviate [community] distresses" represented a radical pursuit of freedom and prepared the community for the emancipation moment in the small town of Brooklyn as long as members "compl[ied] with these articles [of behavior]."[23] In nineteenth-century Brooklyn, like other cities in the United States, African Americans bore the burden of having to demonstrate their readiness for citizenship not yet guaranteed by law. Under that hypervisibility, Black Brooklynites monitored and policed their own behavior to challenge racist views that they were unable or unprepared to participate in a democratic society.

It was not until 1820, a decade after the Brooklyn African Woolman Benevolent Society's founding, that Erastus Worthington, while serving as the third publisher of the *Long Island Star*, printed the Benevolent Society's constitution in pamphlet form.[24] It is entirely likely the Crogers chose Worthington because the Benevolent Society had advertised numerous times in the *Long Island Star* under his proprietorship and most likely had a professional relationship with him. But Brooklyn had two printers at that time, Worthington and the *Long Island Star's* first publisher Thomas Kirk. Worthington was fast building a reputation for printing pamphlets that reflected Brooklyn's growing infrastructure. By 1820, Brooklyn was growing faster than Manhattan, and the population continued to double in every decade until the Civil War when it emerged as the third largest city in the United States. Worthington published the reports of a number of social reform organizations including the constitution of the Kings County Society, which supported local manufactures, and the annual reports of the Long Island Bible Society. He also controlled other literacy activities in Brooklyn, owned a bookstore and circulating library, and later served as postmaster for the town. A young Walt Whitman trained with Worthington until his death in 1831.[25] But in choosing to work with Worthington over Kirk, the officers of the African Woolman Benevolent Society ensured their achievements were part of the town's historical narrative of social reform while rejecting Kirk's racism outright.

When the organization's constitution was printed in 1820, the Brooklyn African Woolman Benevolent Society had already enjoyed an unusual longevity for a Black-led mutual aid organization. Many of these societies in the early republic and antebellum period eventually dissolved due to financial difficulties or the high demands made on voluntary officers who were already stretched too thin in their communities. As historian Craig S. Wilder notes, "as one dominant association fell, another rose at the center of Black public life."[26] The decision to print the constitution a decade after being established suggests that officers such as the Croger brothers held a firm belief that the pamphlet legitimized their organization in print even if it was marginalized in public political life. In the absence of either a Black press or a sympathetic white one, they pursued their own print initiative in pamphlet form so that it would act as a record of their achievements and labor. As Richard S. Newman, Patrick Rael, and Phil Lapsansky note, "it is important to emphasize [. . .] how significant early Black pamphleteers were to the freedom struggle."[27] In doing so, they joined a longer print protest tradition dating from the pamphleteers of the English Civil War (1642–1651), to the patriots of the American Revolution (1775–1783), to the Republicans of the French Revolution (1789–1799).[28]

In pamphlet form, the printed constitution was a brief twelve pages and measured seven inches by four inches, small enough, presumably, to be carried to meetings. The binding suggests that this publication was not intended for posterity, but the form's versatility was key. As historians note, "neither books (which until the 1830s and a revolution in binding techniques remained expensive) nor broadsides (one page posters that did not treat matters in any extended way), provided [the pamphlet's] ideal combination."[29] The cover played with a range of typefaces and fonts as was typical of pamphlets at that time, while the rest of the double-sided document lays out its constitution in a single font. The language of the African Woolman Benevolent Society's constitution echoed the radical nature of other contemporary mutual aid societies like the New York African Society for Mutual Relief. In both constitutions, the officers articulate their struggles (namely, the African Society for Mutual Relief calls them "extreme exigencies" and the Benevolent Society labels them "occasional distresses"), then they lay out the need to organize and mobilize ("distinguished by the name" and "uniting ourselves in a body"), and finally they place a great deal of emphasis on behavior and respectability.[30] The Brooklyn African Woolman Benevolent Society's objective stated:

> The reflection upon the various vicissitudes to which mankind are continually exposed, has been productive of various means to alleviate their distresses – provision is made for almost every species of wretchedness – the afflicted, the widow and the orphan generally, have a source to look for relief, and we, the subscribers, do conclude, that the most efficient method of securing ourselves from the extreme exigencies to which we are liable to be reduced, is, by uniting ourselves in a body, for the purpose of raising a fund for the relief of its members; consequently, we have associated ourselves, under the name and stile of the *Brooklyn African Woolman Benevolent Society*, with the pleasing hope of ameliorating the occasional distresses of each other by our mutual endeavors.[31]

On January 28, 1831, New York state formally granted the African Woolman Benevolent Society its articles of incorporation. The organization was officially part of Brooklyn's social reform movement, which also included sweeping changes in education, temperance, and spiritual perfection. However, like a great deal of African American ephemera, and despite its historic impact on Brooklyn, the story of the African Woolman Benevolent Society's printed constitution is one of erasure and recovery. The small pamphlet was lost in the archives for almost a century until an archivist rediscovered it within the collections of the New-York Historical Society.[32] Yet its very existence reminds us of the ways in which Brooklyn's free Black community created self-determined spaces in print culture and sought to independently publish their grassroots work.

The contemporary impact of the newspaper notices and pamphlet was evident in the larger print culture that emerged from Brooklyn as it urbanized. In 1822, twelve years before the town incorporated as a city, the Brooklyn directory commenced regular publication.[33] The directory listed the town's institutions and its residents with an emphasis on male homeowners or Head of Household, therefore only offering a partial glimpse into the complex racial, class, and gender composition of Brooklyn at that time. Boarders, renters, and almshouse residents are not listed at all, while Black women faced complete erasure from this type of historical record. Historians acknowledge that these archival scraps, particularly from 1800 to 1820, tend to privilege men of color over women, when people of color are recorded at all, and this chapter regrettably compounds the same problem.

The city directory laid out the village's boundaries, listed the town's masonic lodges, churches, the navy yard, and the post office, and it also named the town's officers, firemen, county militia, and school trustees. Although Brooklyn had not yet gained a reputation as the "City of Churches," the directory shows that the town already housed a disproportionate number of churches to residents. The AME Church listing shows that Peter and Benjamin Croger served as preachers and class leaders. In the second part of the publication, which took up the bulk of the directory, residents were listed alphabetically by last name. For Brooklyn's white residents, their last name was usually followed by their profession and then a residential address. For residents of color, like the Crogers, their presence in the directory was hypervisible. An asterisk accompanied their last name to indicate they were residents of color, followed by their residential address, while the occupation was removed entirely. The city directory reflected, to some extent, the print plan led by Black Brooklynites, which recorded their community work and public labor even as it erased their everyday free labor. But the impact of decades of the Black presence in print did lead to a significant development in New

York and African American print culture: the creation of an independent, Black-led press.

In 1827, just three months before New York's Emancipation Day, *Freedom's Journal* commenced publication in Manhattan with the powerful and self-determined opening "too long have others spoken for us."[34] What followed was a print manifesto of struggles and themes that had reverberated across northern cities including Brooklyn in the prior decades – education, community empowerment, the legacy of slavery, Black-led businesses and organizations, and the rights of citizenship. As Jacqueline Bacon notes, "generations of leaders had laid the groundwork for the periodical by building community institutions, demonstrating the power of rhetoric in forming a national consciousness, and asserting the right to determine their own destinies."[35] Black Brooklynites like the Crogers had already articulated many of these debates, and their community labor made a groundbreaking newspaper like *Freedom's Journal* possible even if Brooklyn's antislavery pioneers and their early organizations received no mention in the publication. By then, Black Brooklynites had successfully established a mutual aid society (1810), a private and later public school (1815, 1827), and the AME Church in Brooklyn (1818). All of these institutions became essential organizational pillars to Black lives and spaces for racial justice in Brooklyn as they had for communities in Boston, Philadelphia, and New York.

When slavery finally ended in New York on July 4, 1827, it had little economic impact on the everyday labor of free Black Brooklynites such as Henry C. Thompson, Peter Croger, and Benjamin Croger and certainly did not afford them social mobility. But as the 1820s drew to a close, these Brooklynites expanded their leadership roles once again and continued to engage in other forms of labor. Less than three months after state emancipation, the African School opened at African Hall, a larger site "under the immediate direction of the African Woolman Benevolent Society." Black Brooklynite Henry C. Thompson advertised the school in the *Long Island Star* and served as both president of the African Woolman Benevolent Society and a trustee at the African School.[36] With the success of the African School, Black Brooklynites expanded access to literacy across Kings County. By the 1840s, Brooklyn had three African schools, one in Brooklyn, a second in Weeksville, and a third in Williamsburg. These institutions were important places for fostering literacy and attracting a new generation of abolitionists who also served as educators, including Maria Stewart, William J. Wilson, Junius C. Morel, and Willis Hodges. In 1855, the Brooklyn Board of Education took over the African school system across the city and renamed the long-standing African School as Colored School No. 1. With a change in leadership, Black Brooklynites lost more than the naming of their schools. Students of color were often affected by overcrowding and a lack of resources, and African American educators complained of receiving insufficient support from the city. These problems persisted until integration of the public school system in the late nineteenth century.[37]

Anti-Colonization Protest in Print

In 1829, less than half a mile from Peter and Benjamin Crogers' homes, Christian Brown's print shop released the broadside "Brooklyn Boblashun!"[38] It was part of a long print tradition in the early republic that had begun in Boston and quickly gained currency in Philadelphia, New York, and even London. As historian Shane White indicates, "what limits whites would impose on African Americans as they attempted to establish their own right to public urban space were worked out piecemeal," and with the Bobalition print "they were left with an image of the city's Blacks as less than human, as objects of derision, and, most important, as a group who were getting ideas beyond their station."[39]

"Brooklyn Boblashun!" contained all the characteristic features of the Bobalition print: caricatures of Black identity, mockery of emancipation, and belittling of the literacy capacity of African Americans. Written by a "Long Island Niger" and featuring a wood engraving of a Black dandy, the print's crude racism offers a glimpse into how white Brooklynites' perception of the emancipation moment was to ultimately regard it as meaningless. It mocked the kind of social mobility and dignity that the Crogers and other Black Brooklynites sought through their labor and public roles in the community. A paucity of evidence makes it difficult to say where the broadside was displayed in Brooklyn but given its dimensions of twelve inches by seventeen inches, it is likely copies were placed in the windows of businesses throughout the town. And it is almost certain given Brooklyn's small population of approximately 12,400 people in 1830, the intimacy of the village, and the proximity of the print shop to the Crogers' home, that Black Brooklynites would have encountered the racist broadside.

The Bobalition print was just one visual manifestation of a larger anti-Black hostility prevalent in the early nineteenth century. The colonization movement sought to undo the decades of community building that free Black communities had struggled to establish. Supporters of the colonization movement, mostly landed white men in positions of influence, did not see African Americans as fellow Americans. Instead, they formally organized through the American Colonization Society, founded in 1816, and argued that the United States would never rid itself of racism and slavery. "What shall we do with the free people of color? What can we do for their happiness consistently with our own?" asked Robert Finley, the organization's founder, in *Thoughts on Colonization of Free Blacks*.[40] Their solution was to ultimately rid the United States of people of African descent. They fundraised through the main organization and local auxiliaries including one in Brooklyn where the president of the Brooklyn Savings Bank, one of the earliest financial institutions in the town, also served as the local chapter's president. The funds were used to support deportation schemes to the colony of Monrovia on the west coast of Africa while concurrently strengthening slaveholding interests in the United States.[41]

But free Black communities led waves of anti-colonization protests across the North, beginning in Philadelphia as early as January 1817. Two years after the publication of the "Brooklyn Boblashun," the Croger brothers, Thompson, and their neighbors led Brooklyn's anti-colonization protest, declaring their right to stay on American soil. On June 3, 1831, activists gathered at the African Hall on Nassau Street, a small wooden building which also served as the headquarters of the Brooklyn African Woolman Benevolent Society. Their address was reprinted in the *Long Island Star*, by now the largest circulating newspaper in Brooklyn. They stated:

> Resolved unanimously, That the call of this meeting be approved of; and that the colored citizens of this village have, with friendly feelings, taken into consideration the objects of the American Colonization Society, together with all of its auxiliary movements, preparatory for our removal to the coast of Africa; and we view them as wholly gratuitous, not called for by us, and not essential to the real welfare of our race. That we know of no other country that we can justly claim, or demand our rights as citizens, whether civil or political, but in the United States of America, our native soil. And, that was shall be active in our endeavors to convince the members of the Colonization Society, and the public generally, that we are *men*, that we are *brethren*, that we are *countrymen* and *fellow-citizens*; and demand an equal share of protection from our Federal Government with any other class of citizens in the community.[42]

Brooklyn's antislavery activists echoed the rhetoric of David Walker's *Appeal* and boldly announced their right to be seen in print and public life.[43] They pioneered a form of antislavery activism that demanded the right to the city and the ability to occupy the same public spaces and streets as white Brooklynites. In this newspaper article there was no mention of their day jobs – they did not speak as whitewashers, blacking manufacturers, and laborers – rather, these Brooklynites renamed their labor as community builders and citizens. They took advantage of print technologies, long before the abolitionists, to call for an immediate end to slavery's legacy and to create local and regional antislavery networks.

That fall in 1831, Black Brooklynites joined delegates in Philadelphia from all over the North for a national convention. It signaled the beginning of an ambitious reform movement led by African Americans, among them Brooklynites. Their organized labor and activism had a profound effect on a young William Lloyd Garrison, who would emerge as one of the more familiar faces of the radical abolitionist movement. In the 1820s, Garrison believed that slavery was morally reprehensible but also saw a potentially positive outcome in colonization schemes. In 1831, though white, he attended the Black National Convention and published *Thoughts on African Colonization* the following year. The pamphlet comprehensively laid out a series of arguments as to why the American Colonization Society was repugnant and their activities amounted to nothing more than federally backed deportation schemes. Garrison printed scores of Black-led anti-colonization protests including the Brooklyn protest held just two years prior to publication.[44] Black activism in politics and print was transformational for Garrison, who declared that of "the whole number of subscribers to the [antislavery newspaper] *Liberator*, only about one-fourth are white. The paper, then, belongs emphatically to the people of color – it is their organ . . . "[45]

Black activists in Brooklyn and beyond had spent decades ensuring print platforms accurately captured their intellectual work and community labor where city directories and census records had relatively failed. Recovering these early print scraps – a newspaper advertisement, a constitution, and a news item – not only raises the visibility of the pioneering grassroots organizing that emerged from early free Black communities in Brooklyn and beyond but also demonstrates the ways in which the power of print intersected with their work. They seized their own freedom through various forms of activism and used print culture to radically define the possibilities of their labor.

Notes

1 Harold X. Connolly, *A Ghetto Grows in Brooklyn* (New York: New York University Press, 1977), 5. For Brooklyn's reliance on enslaved labor during gradual emancipation, see Craig Steven Wilder, *A Covenant with Color: Race*

and Social Power in Brooklyn (New York: Columbia University Press, 2000), 21–51.

2 Prithi Kanakamedala, curator, *Brooklyn Abolitionists* exhibit, Brooklyn Historical Society, Brooklyn, NY, 2014–2018; Judith Wellman, *Brooklyn's Promised Land: The Free Black Community of Weeksville, New York* (New York: New York University Press, 2014), 13–14.

3 For more on African American labor in New York's early republic, see Leslie M. Harris, *In the Shadow of Slavery: African Americans in New York City, 1626–1863* (Chicago: University of Chicago Press, 2003), 96–105; Leslie M. Alexander, *African or American? Black Identity and Political Activism in New York City, 1784–1861* (Urbana: University of Illinois Press, 2008), 43–50.

4 For further discussion on verbal rather than visual lexicon use in antebellum northern free Black communities, see Jasmine Nichole Cobb, *Picture Freedom: Remaking Black Visuality in the Early Nineteenth Century* (New York: New York University Press, 2016), 148–192.

5 Frances Smith Foster, "A Narrative of the Interesting Origins and (Somewhat) Surprising Developments of African-American Print Culture," *American Literary History* 17, no. 4 (Winter 2005): 716.

6 Frederick Douglass, *Narrative of the Life of Frederick Douglass, an American Slave* (Boston, MA: Published at the Anti-Slavery Office, 1845); Henry Bibb, *Narrative of the Life and Adventures of Henry Bibb, an American slave* (New York: published by the author, 1849); Harriet Jacobs, *Incidents in the Life of a Slave Girl: written by herself* (Boston, MA: published for the author, 1861).

7 Phillis Wheatley, *Poems on Various Subjects, Religious, and Moral* (London: 1773); Petitions of African Americans to Massachusetts General Court to Abolish Slavery, 1773, 1777 from William Cooper Nell, *The Colored Patriots of the American Revolution* (Boston, MA: 1855), 40–41, 47–48; Richard Allen and Absalom Jones, *Narrative of the Proceedings of Black people, during the late awful calamity in Philadelphia, in the year 1793* (Philadelphia: 1794); Prince Hall, *A Charge Delivered to the African Lodge, June 24, 1797, at Menotomy* (1797); Joseph Sidney, *An Oration, Commemoration of the Abolition of the Slave Trade in the United States: Delivered in the African Asbury Church, in the City of New York, on the First of January, 1814* (New York: Printed for the Author, 1814).

8 "African School," *Long Island Star*, January 18, 1815.

9 Craig Steven Wilder, *In the Company of Black Men: The African Influence on African American Culture in New York City* (New York: New York University Press, 2001), 4.

10 "An Address to the Inhabitants of Long-Island," *Long Island Star*, June 8, 1809.

11 "Thomas Kirk: A Pioneer Publisher and Bookseller," *The Publishers' Weekly*, no. 89 (March 2, 1889): 364.

12 *Long Island Star*, Jan. 4, 1815, March 15, 1815, June 7, 1815, June 14, 1815, June 21, 1815, June 28, 1815, July 5, 1815.

13 *Long Island Star*, March 6, 1816, March 13, 1816.

14 "District School," *Long Island Star*, May 8, 1816.

15 Henry Reed Stiles, *A History of the City of Brooklyn: including the old towns of Brooklyn, Bushwick, and Williamsburgh* Vol I (1867; repr. Carlisle, MA: Applewood Books, 2009), 380, 385, 391; Ralph Foster Weld, *Brooklyn Village 1816–1834* (1938; New York: AMS Press, 1970), 133–134.

16 Steven Carl Smith, *An Empire of Print: The New York Publishing Trade in the Early American Republic* (University Park: The Pennsylvania State University Press, 2017), 20–25.

17 For a list of newspapers, see Michael Emery and Thorin Tritter, "Newspapers," *Encyclopedia of New York City* 2nd ed. (New Haven: Yale University Press, 2010), 893–906.

18 Manisha Sinha, *The Slave's Cause: A History of Abolition* (New Haven: Yale University Press, 2017), 19.

19 Wilder, *In the Company of Black Men*, 1.

20 Wilder, *In the Company of Black Men*, 92. See also Mitch Kachun, *Festivals of Freedom: Memory and Meaning in African American Emancipation Celebrations, 1808–1915* (Amherst and Boston: University of Massachusetts Press, 2006), 42– 50.

21 "Brooklyn African Woolman Benevolent Society," *Long Island Star*, December 29, 1819.

22 Montgomerie's Act: An Act for the more effectual preventing and punishing the conspiracy and insurrection of negro and other slaves and for better regulating them, 1730; Shane White, "'It was a Proud Day': African Americans, Festivals, and Parades in the North, 1741–1834," *Journal of American History* 81, no. 1 (1994): 13-50.

23 Brooklyn African Woolman Benevolent Society, *Constitution of the African Woolman Benevolent Society* (Brooklyn: Printed by E. Worthington, 1820), 20.

24 *Constitution of the African Woolman Benevolent Society.*

25 *Constitution of the Kings County Society for Promoting Agriculture and Domestic Manufactures* (Brooklyn, NY: Printed by Erastus Washington, 1819); *A Tour from the City of New York, to Detroit, in the Michigan Territory* (Brooklyn, NY: Printed by Erastus Washington, 1819); *The fifth annual report of the Long-Island Bible Society* (Brooklyn, NY: Printed by Erastus Washington, 1820); *Proceedings of the board of commissioners of the United States' Naval Fraternal Association* (Brooklyn, NY: Printed by E. Worthington, 1820).

26 Wilder, *In the Company of Black Men*, 104. See also Table 4.1 "Select African Voluntary Associations, 1784–1865," 74–76.

27 Richard Newman, Patrick Rael, and Phillip Lapsansky, *Pamphlets of Protest: An Anthology of Early African-American Protest Literature* (New York: Routledge, 2000), 11.

28 Newman, Rael, and Lapsansky, *Pamphlets of Protest*, 3.

29 Newman, Rael, and Lapsansky, *Pamphlets of* Protest, 2.

30 New York African Society for Mutual Relief, *The Constitution of the New York African Society for Mutual Relief* (New York: Printed by R. Sears, 1838), 1.

31 *Constitution of the African Woolman Benevolent Society*, 1.
32 Craig Steven Wilder, "The Rise and Influence of the New York African Society for Mutual Relief, 1808–1865," *Afro-Americans in New York Life and History* 22 (July 1998): 7–17; Sandra Shoiock Roff, "The Brooklyn African Woolman Benevolent Society Rediscovered," *Afro-Americans in New York Life and History* 10 (1986): 55–63.
33 Alden Spooner, *Spooner's Brooklyn Directory, for the Year 1822* (Brooklyn, NY: Published by Alden Spooner, at the Office of the Long-Island Star. No. 60 Fulton-Street, 1822).
34 *Freedom's Journal*, March 16, 1827.
35 Jacqueline Bacon, *Freedom's Journal: The First African-American Newspaper* (Lanham, MD: Lexington Books, 2007), 41.
36 "To the Public," *Long Island Star*, October 4, 1827.
37 Wilder, *Covenant with Color*, 70–75.
38 Long Island Niger, *Brooklyn boblashun! Hurore for Jackson* (Brooklyn, NY: Printed and sold, wholesale and retail, at Christian Brown printshop, 211 Water Street, 1829).
39 Shane White, "It was a proud day," 34, 35; see also Marcus Wood, *Black Milk: Imagining Slavery in the Visual Cultures of Brazil and America* (New York: Oxford University Press, 2013), 75–82; Cobb, *Picture Freedom*, 182–184.
40 Robert Finley, *Thoughts on Colonization of Free Blacks* (Washington, 1816), 1.
41 Craig Steven Wilder, *Ebony and Ivy: Race, Slavery, and the Troubled Histories of America's Universities* (New York: Bloomsbury Press, 2013), 247–280; Harris, *In the Shadow of Slavery*, 134–145.
42 *Long Island Star*, June 8, 1831.
43 David Walker, *Walker's Appeal, in four articles; together with a preamble to the colored citizens of the world, but in particular, and very expressly to those of the United States of America* (Boston, MA: D. Walker, 1830).
44 William Lloyd Garrison, *Thoughts on African Colonization, or an impartial exhibition of the doctrines, principles, and purposes of the American Colonization Society together with the resolutions, addresses, and remonstrances of the people of color* (Boston, MA: Garrison and Knapp, 1832). For more on Garrison's evolving views in the late 1820s, see Sinha, *The Slave's Cause*, 217–230.
45 Francis and Wendell P. Garrison, *William Lloyd Garrison, 1805–1879*, volume I (Boston and New York: Houghton, Mifflin, and Company), 432.

PART II

Movement and Mobility in African American Literature

Scholars contributing to Part II advance our knowledge of the movements associated with Black people and Black texts. In the decades from 1800 to 1830, legal statutes and slave revolts impacted the mobility of African American people and the flows of Black literary texts. These decades are peculiar even as they are bookended by landmark decisions – namely the Fugitive Slave Act of 1793 and the Fugitive Slave Act of 1850. Both statutes emboldened slave owners and catchers to pursue fugitive free Blacks in northern states and border territories, thus endangering free-born people of African descent as well. President George Washington never stopped pursuing Ona Judge, who absconded from his home in 1796, on her own, and moved into Philadelphia's community of free-born and fugitive free Blacks.[1] Likewise, the second fugitive slave law only added to the danger Harriet Jacobs faced in freedom, remaining on the run in the North even as she began to contemplate publication in the 1850s.[2] Yet, along with individuals who fled, readers familiar with Gabriel Prosser's attempt to march on Richmond in 1800 or with the German Coast Uprising in 1811 Louisiana and Denmark Vesey's 1822 plan for revolt in Charleston, South Carolina, know that these laws did not deter resistance to slavery. These efforts at insurrection prove a growing sentiment across the south, of which Nat Turner's 1831 rebellion is a mere part. In this period, events such as the Louisiana Purchase in 1803, which expanded the nation toward the west, and the Missouri Compromise in 1820 – admitting Maine as a free state and Missouri as a slave state – indicate that there was no more pressing issue of this period than the issue of slavery. With more than 85 percent of Black people in the United States still enslaved by 1830, despite the spread of gradual abolition laws throughout the northern states, the incendiary writing of this period should be read alongside the violent attempts to overthrow slavery and the slave revolts that would have been of particular interest to African American thinkers. Writing is an important corollary to Black resistance, including the literary acts of northern whites who petitioned states, such as Pennsylvania, to limit the migration of Black people into the state and to impose curfews on Black people already living in the counties.[3] Accordingly, chapters in this section explore movement or mobility to consider the ways in which the opportunity to travel across state and national boundaries, or the denial of this mobility, also shaped early African American literature.

In Chapter 4, Joseph Rezek reminds us that national currents in early African American literature were intertwined with international transitions in slavery and abolition. Rezek cites the 1807 Act Prohibiting Importation of Slaves in US federal law as well as Britain's Act for the Abolition of the Slave Trade, along with the 1816 formation of the American Colonization Society, as trends that inspired penchant for internationalism in early African American literature. Rezek examines the transatlantic movement of texts and ideas in this global political climate, approaching the Black Atlantic in the early nineteenth century and among writers who continued to look to Britain's example of abolition but also the perpetuation of slavery in the West Indies. His chapter reveals the movement of Black bodies and the laws that impacted those flows as having an identifiable impact on Black writing of the period.

However, the movement of Black texts was also shaped by the mobility of Black bodies, and not just the political fervor of the times. Rhetorical critic Jacqueline Bacon argues that the discovery of Walker's pamphlet "in Virginia, Louisiana, and Georgia, in the possession of slaves as well as free African Americans," indicates a large network for circulating Black print that would have included "runaways, itinerant laborers, longshoremen, sailors, and churches and other religious organizations" as well as northern bondspersons.[4] In a conversant manner, for Chapter 5, Britt Rusert explores the first commercially produced book written by an African American, Robert Roberts's *House Servants Directory*. Published in 1827, Roberts's text moved throughout the North and found audiences in the South well into the 1830s. While texts such as David Walker's *Appeal* were considered dangerous for their ability to incite insurrection, and even made reading dangerous for southern Black people, the *House Servants Directory* found audiences throughout the region and reveals transitions in mobility for texts. Rusert reveals sentiments about African American (im)mobility as written into the narrative and movement of African American literature.

Issues of movement and mobility in this period also shaped literature penned after 1830, and especially shaped the literary lives of Black women. Not until 1846 (and in England) would Zilpha Elaw get to publish

Memoirs of the Life, Religious Experience, Ministerial Travels, and Labours of Mrs. Elaw, though matrimony forced her to leave Pennsylvania for New Jersey, where she began her call to evangelism in 1819. Similarly, marriage moved Jarena Lee to the suburbs of Philadelphia in 1818, and her husband's death brought her back to the urban center in 1819, where Richard Allen authorized her call to preach. Both Elaw and Lee were "moved" in the spiritual sense while their mobility – in marriage and itinerancy – was impacted by the men in their lives. The 1839 publication of her *Life and Religious Experience of Jarena Lee, a Colored Lady: Giving an Account of the Call to Preach the Gospel* details experiences that took shape early in the century. For Chapter 6, Bryan Sinche discusses Lee, along with George White and Boyrereau Brinch, to think through the dream vision as a rhetorical trope in African American autobiography. Sinche lays out this tool as one that enables the mobility of Black-authored texts and the engagement of themes outside of the goals and protocols of the abolitionist movement. Accordingly, dreams show up during this period, such as Sojourner Truth's 1828 daydreams that Sinche describes, but also in later texts, such as Harriet Jacobs' *Incidents in the Life of a Slave Girl* (1860). In the lives of Black women, we come to see dreams as compulsive, tethered to movements that connect African American literatures from the nineteenth through the twentieth century.

Notes

1 Erica Armstrong Dunbar, *Never Caught: The Washingtons' Relentless Pursuit of Their Runaway Slave, Ona Judge* (New York: Simon and Schuster, 2017).
2 https://docsouth.unc.edu/fpn/jacobs/bio.html.
3 Jasmine Nichole Cobb, "Black Women and the *Liberator*," *African American Literature in Transition*, vol. 3, Benjamin Fagan, ed.
4 Jacqueline Bacon, *Freedom's Journal: The First African American Newspaper* (New York: Lexington Books, 2007), 53.

CHAPTER 4

Early African American Literature and the British Empire, 1808–1835

Joseph Rezek

As early African American writers in New York, Philadelphia, and Boston, worked tirelessly to promote freedom and to improve the lives of their brethren at home, they also kept apace of events that affected enslaved Africans and their descendants in the British Empire, from London to Jamaica to Canada to Sierra Leone. The fate of Black people under British rule was of particular interest to Black abolitionist men William Miller, Peter Williams, Jr., William Hamilton, Absalom Jones, Richard Allen, Paul Cuffee, Prince Saunders, John Russwurm, William Whipper, and David Walker, whose orations, political pamphlets, and newspapers were published between 1808 and 1835. The near simultaneous abolition of the transatlantic slave trades in Britain and the United States within a year, in 1807 and 1808 respectively, proved an especially generative event, as numerous writers reflected upon the interconnected history of the Atlantic world and drew inspiration from British abolitionists like Thomas Clarkson, William Wilberforce, and William Cowper. By the 1820s, euphoria about the slave trade's abolition had given way to disappointment about its illegal continuation and had led to resistance to racist organizations such as the American Colonization Society (ACS). African American interest in the British Empire accordingly changed over time as the question of West Indian emancipation took center stage in London and as some African Americans considered emigrating to British colonial possessions. Following many scholars who have viewed early African American literature as Black Atlantic literature, as well as scholars who have emphasized the transatlantic nature of early abolitionism,[1] this chapter argues that Black writing of the early national United States must be understood outside the bounds of the US nation and in relation to the history of slavery in the British Empire.

The severing of US political ties after the American Revolution has made the British Empire perhaps the least studied geopolitical entity among those of primary concern for Black writing in the early nineteenth century.[2] However, African American authors concerned with Black activism and community formation in the North, with changing political agendas, and with fights for equality and celebrations for freedom, directly engaged British thinkers and abolitionist writers and considered the experiences of Black peoples living in England and throughout the British colonies. This chapter explores the ways in which Black writers hailed England as a land of freedom and abolitionism; engaged with popular English sentimental poetry; addressed enslaved Africans in the British West Indies through the language of sympathy or identification; and, in the context of the ACS, cultivated a discourse around voluntary emigration to the British possessions of Sierra Leone and Canada.

The texts considered here were part of a second wave of pamphlet literature following pioneering texts from the 1780s and 1790s by Prince Hall, John Marrant, Richard Allen, and Absalom Jones. Viewing them as a discrete archive complicates the idea that all pre-1830 pamphlets are part of the same "generation."[3] This group of texts helped African American literature transition from its earliest, primarily evangelical eighteenth-century stage to the mid-nineteenth century era of activism, abolition, and autobiography. And yet they necessarily reveal only the priorities of their authors, an elite group of free Black men dedicated to literacy as a means to citizenship and devoted to relatively conservative institutions such as African churches, educational societies, and abolitionist groups. This archive thus has significant limitations along the axes of gender and social status even though there would have been large groups of women and men reading these texts or listening to them being read aloud (in churches or at home). Indeed, while women were major players in the institutions out of which these documents emerged and shaped the politics of Black representation in this period, print was a radically circumscribed medium available only to those authors with access to the means and methods of publication. Maria W. Stewart's writings, also addressed in this chapter, are the exception that proves the rule. Nevertheless, the texts considered here deserve our close attention as publications written primarily for Black audiences and financed by Black institutions. Forged in direct opposition to the racism of the white-dominated public sphere, they are quintessential documents of what Joanna Brooks has called "the early black print counterpublic."[4] As Jasmine Nichole Cobb has argued, print culture "provided a medium for disseminating ideas about politics and helped characterize the development of national identity for Black people."[5] This chapter argues that a self-conscious, rhetorical engagement with the circum-Atlantic scope of the British Empire was a central component of that development.[6]

British Abolitionists and British Writing

New Year's Day orations written by African Americans to commemorate the abolition of the slave trade in Britain and the United States narrate powerful Black Atlantic histories of Africa and the transatlantic slave trade.[7] Deeply interested in the origins of the African diaspora, these orations also display textual, historical, interpersonal, and imagined ties to the British Empire. Consider the oration by Reverend William Miller, a founding member of the African Methodist Episcopal Church in New York. Published in New York following its delivery in that church on January 1, 1810, the oration asserts that the recent actions of the British Parliament weigh equally to the actions of the United States Congress. He thanks "the throne of grace, for having directed the councils of our legislature and the parliament of Great Britain, to the consideration of the deplorable and ignominious condition of Africans and their descendants."[8] While slavery had long united Euro-American empires in the shared pursuit of sin, violence, crime, and plunder, Miller frames the abolition of the slave trade as a transnational achievement directed towards a unified goal. "Dear land of our ancestors!" declared Absalom Jones in his 1808 oration on the slave trade, "Thou shalt no more be stained with the blood of thy children, shed by British and American hands: the ocean shall no more afford a refuge to their bodies, from impending slavery: nor shall the shores of the British West India islands, and of the United States, any more witness the anguish of families, by a public sale."[9] The negative inflection of such ostensibly celebratory declarations – lingering on "the deplorable and ignominious condition of Africans," the "anguish of families" – suggests just how difficult it was to congratulate the two empires for a limited antislavery gesture while the institution of slavery still raged. Indeed, Miller grants that some of his listeners in New York "may have been eye-witnesses" to the horrific atrocities of slavery in the West Indies.[10]

And yet, Black writers strategically honored the efforts and successes of British abolitionists. England had stood as a beacon of freedom since the Somerset case functionally outlawed slavery in the British Isles (in 1772) and the British government granted enslaved Americans their freedom if they enlisted to fight against the United States during the Revolution (in 1775). US writers commemorating the close of the slave trade celebrated more recent abolitionists for their actions. In 1814, abolitionist Russell Parrott wrote, "among the names whom the Deity selected as the accomplishers of the great work of abolition, stand those of Sharp, Clarkson,

Grégoire, Wilberforce," including among well-known British figures Henry Grégoire, the French defender of African equality.[11] William Hamilton's 1815 oration – a despairing and radical text written as the illegal slave trade continued – exalts Thomas Clarkson as a champion of liberty, implicitly substituting his name for a traditional founding father like George Washington:

> Our children should be taught in their little songs, to lisp the name of Clarkson: he labored in the field for the abolition of the slave trade, literally day and night, with very little time to refresh himself with sleep. Twenty years did Mr. Clarkson labour for the abolition of the slave trade. His labours were finally successful: too much cannot be said in his praise. In the British Parliament, long and hard was the struggle for the destruction of this trade: and it was shameful for Britain, who boasts so much of her strong attachment to liberty, and humanity, that the struggle should be so long.[12]

Hamilton issues congratulations with a dose of admonition, calling the parliamentary struggle "shameful for Britain." In choosing to invoke Britain's "strong attachment to liberty," he also escalates his critique of an emerging American civil religion grounded in revered documents like the Declaration of Independence. It was not Washington, not Jefferson, but Clarkson who successfully labored "day and night" in order to hold his nation (Britain, not the United States) accountable to the promise of liberty.

Later writers like Prince Saunders, the African American diplomat, educator, and historian of the Haitian Revolution, and radical abolitionist David Walker hailed British abolitionists as more dependable than their supposed allies in the United States. Amid early debates spurred on by the ACS, and around the time of the founding of the Haytian Emigration Society of Coloured People in 1818, Saunders pointed to English support for Haiti as evidence of that nation's long commitment to the antislavery cause. He argued that the prospects of Haiti produce "a universally deep and active interest in the minds of that numerous hosts of abolitionists in Great Britain, whom we trust to have the best interests of the descendants of Africa deeply at heart."[13] Over a decade later, while revising his anti-colonization polemic *David Walker's Appeal to the Colored Citizens of the World* for its third edition in 1830, Walker added two passages applauding the English as the "best" and "greatest" friends of his race. Although he does not mention English abolitionists by name, they are implicitly held up in contrast to ACS proponents Henry Clay and Elias Caldwell, whom he excoriates throughout his text. Despite his own aversion to emigration, Walker acknowledged the desire for expatriation: "If any of us see fit to go away, go to those who have been for many years, and are now our greatest earthly friends and benefactors – the English. If not so, go to our brethren, the Haytians, who, according to their word, are bound to protect and comfort us."[14] Like many of his associates, Walker kept track of the new Parliamentary struggle to abolish slavery in the West Indies. While Britain and the United States abolished the transatlantic slave trade in the same year, by the late 1820s it was clear that the British were far ahead on the question of emancipation. Walker, in another passage added to the third edition, declared:

> The English are the best friends the coloured people have upon earth. Though they have oppressed us a little and have colonies now in the West Indies, which oppress us *sorely*. – Yet notwithstanding they (the English) have done one hundred times more for the melioration of our condition, than all the other nations of the earth put together. The blacks cannot but respect the English as a nation, notwithstanding they have treated us a little cruel.
>
> There is no intelligent *black man* who knows anything, but esteems a real Englishman, let him see him in what part of the world he will.[15]

Walker's remarkably understated hesitation in praising the English derives from the great problem of colonial slavery, and he attempts to solve this apparent contradiction by separating the metropole from the empire's actions abroad. To do this he makes a cultural argument, suggesting that something has been inscribed within the English nationality (in a "real Englishman," or in Englishmen "as a nation") that deserves his gratitude and every colored person's esteem and friendship. In a somewhat elitist move, moreover, Walker connects his esteem for the English to being a knowledgeable man of the world (an "intelligent *black man*"). Inseparable from his esteem is a tension perhaps more fraught than his admission that the English have been "a little cruel" – between the unequal role of benefactor and the egalitarian role of friend. Do the English support people of color at a distance, or do they fight for amelioration hand in hand? Walker's ambivalence about white allies emerges here even in a moment of praise.

Early African American writers also borrowed from and engaged with British abolitionist literature. William Miller directly quotes lines of poetry from William Cowper, the British antislavery writer well known for the long romantic poem *The Task* (1785) and the abolitionist ballad "The Negro's Complaint" (1788). US abolitionist periodicals, including *Liberator*, and other publications reprinted the latter poem, which railed against the slave trade, and Maria Stewart appended it at the conclusion of

Productions of Mrs. Maria W. Stewart, published in 1835.[16] Writing in the ventriloquized voice of a slave, Cowper condemned Britain:

Men from England bought and sold me,
  Paid my price in paltry gold;
But though slave they have enroll'd me,
  Minds are never to be sold.[17]

The commentary on England supports Stewart's condemnation of all nations who decimated Africa, a theme reiterated throughout her work in lines such as "America, America, foul and indelible is thy stain! Dark and dismal is the cloud that hangs over thee, for thy cruel wrongs and injuries to the fallen sons of Africa."[18] Cowper's poem provides an implicit transatlantic context, genealogy, and contrast for those injuries. A footnote Stewart added to this stanza at the word "England" resonates with notes written by David Walker (Stewart's friend and colleague): "England had 800,000 slaves, and she has made them FREE! America has 2,250,000! and she HOLDS THEM FAST!"[19] With this note, Stewart declares that England has acted upon "the negro's complaint," and demands that America follow in her footsteps.

Cowper's poem "Charity" (1782) also appeared in Miller's sermon, which Miller used to admonish Europeans for their deep moral failure as otherwise "civilized people."[20] "[W]e are astonished to find [them] sanctioning a trade so disgraceful to the human species, and so foul a blot on the christian character," Miller writes. "How just this question put to European nations by the poet,"

Canst thou, and honored with a christian name,
Buy what is woman-born, and feel no shame?
Trade in the blood of innocence and plead
Expedience as a warrant for the deed![21]

Miller's chosen passage emphasizes the violation of the intimate tie between a mother and her newborn infant, whose "blood of innocence" represents the gruesome commodity slavers trade. While "Charity" argues that the violence of global commerce undermines English values such as "sacred liberty,"[22] Miller's adaptation focuses on the slave trade. He invokes "innocence" by reminding his audience that Africans are enslaved not for any fault of their own – such as crime, war, or debt – and by highlighting progeneration to indict the modern custom that declared the status of enslavement was inheritable from one's mother. Miller's quotation of an English poet in a sermon meant for his African brethren is as significant as that poet's encapsulation of the injustices both authors emphatically reject.

John Russwurm and Samuel Cornish, editors of *Freedom's Journal* (1827–1829), the earliest-known African American newspaper, printed many British abolitionist texts, including those by Cowper. One especially notable article in the paper hailed the abolitionist writings of Ottobah Cugoano and Olaudah Equiano, leaders of the campaign to abolish the slave trade in Britain. Cugoano's "work on the slave trade," the article declares, "discovered a sound and vigorous mind," while the "memoirs" of Equiano (who wrote "a petition for the suppression of the slave trade") were "read with great interest." The original article was based on Grégoire's *An Enquiry Concerning the Intellectual and Moral Faculties, and Literature of Negroes* (trans. Brooklyn, 1810), and named Cugoano, Equiano, Francis Williams, Ignatius Sancho, Phillis Wheatley, Job Ben Solomon, Benjamin Banneker, and Toussaint Louverture in a long list of Africans who "abundantly [refute] the assumption" that "blacks are inferior to the whites in intellectual powers."[23]

In addition to their interest in British abolitionists and abolitionist literature, early African American writers also engaged with many texts from the traditional canon of English poetry (which for the most part ignored slavery altogether), including John Milton and popular eighteenth-century poets of sensibility Robert Blair, Thomas Gray, and Edward Young. Given their focus on existential and corporeal suffering, Black writers were often drawn to the poetry of mourning and melancholy. As Elizabeth McHenry has argued, many African Americans believed that literary activity was "a component of citizenship and the responsibility of all free blacks in the North."[24] In "Lecture Delivered at the Franklin Hall," Stewart recognized that such activity was often a struggle: "[W]hat literary acquirement can be made, or useful knowledge derived, from either maps, books, or charts, by those who continually drudge from Monday morning until Sunday noon?"[25] Even so, standard works were often quoted without attribution and may have been as familiar to Black audiences as quotations from the Bible. In an 1828 address delivered before the Colored Reading Society, William Whipper announced it was "the golden age of Literature" and encouraged "knowledge of the ancient classics" as a way to "see the beauty and understand many of the illusions of our best English writers" – probably thinking of Milton's *Paradise Lost* (1674).[26] Preacher Lemuel Haynes chose Milton's climactic representation of original sin as an epigraph to his 1805 sermon on "Universal Salvation."[27] In 1814, Russell Parrott eulogized abolitionist Benjamin Rush by silently borrowing three lines from Robert Blair's famous and continually reprinted, melancholy poem "The Grave" (1743): "The good man's end was peace,"

Parrott quotes, "how calm his exit."[28] After lamenting the "drudge" of work that prevents Black people from reading literature, Stewart silently quotes from Thomas Gray's "Elegy Written in a Country Churchyard" (1751). "Owing to the disadvantages under which we labor," Stewart writes, "there are many flowers among us that are 'born to bloom unseen / And waste their fragrance on the desert air.'"[29] Stewart slightly modified these lines, suggesting that she drew on her memory, not a printed book, just as she would while quoting the Bible.[30] Gray's famous poem locates untold intellectual and artistic potential in the lives of everyday people, the "mute inglorious Milton[s]" who lay buried and forgotten in the church's cemetery. Stewart's allusion invests her brethren with such potential even as it likens their "disadvantage[d]" lives – "unseen" and "waste[d]" – to a kind of social death.

More contemporaneous poems on similar themes also resonated with abolitionists. While commemorating the abolition of the slave trade in the African Church of New York in 1809, Henry Johnson concluded his introduction to orator Henry Sipkins with lines from a recently published poem by James Montgomery – also called "The Grave." Two stanzas summoned the pain from which Africans would finally be released in a "world of liberty" yet to come.[31] In such a world, Johnson writes, "the poor African [will] no longer have to exclaim":

> I long to lay this painful head.
>   And aching heart, beneath the soil;
> To slumber in that dreamless bed,
>   From all my toil.
>
> For misery stole me at my birth.
>   And cast me naked on the wild,
> I perish, O my mother earth;
>   Take home thy child.[32]

Hardly a triumphant way to welcome Sipkins to the pulpit, these lines emphasize suffering, not deliverance. In the context of this occasion, casting misery as a thief who "stole me at my birth" reimagines the origin of the speaker's suffering – which in Montgomery's poem remains entirely vague – in the slave trade.[33]

A few writers directly rebuked some of the most respected poets of the English literary tradition. In his 1828 address, Whipper engaged with Edward Young's popular poem *Night Thoughts* (1742–1745), a favorite text of Equiano and Cugoano and one from which Haynes also borrowed lines.[34] Young's poem offered various extended reflections on pious subjects like sin, death, mourning, and salvation, one per night over a series of nights. Ambition is the subject of *Night VI*, which warns Young's readers against striving for worldly goals. Whipper encouraged an ambitious program of self-improvement and activism before the Colored Reading Society and critiqued Young even as he invoked his authority. "Fame, Ambition, rise! proclaim!" Whipper wrote, "and tear us from the chains of slavery! be alert, be free; and then forever rest."[35] After this exclamation, and with some self-consciousness, he continued:

> Yes, ambition is my theme, – that 'powerful source of good and ill.' What, in the language of our gloomy poet, 'proud world and vain.' O, Young! would to heaven, that I, like thee, could do justice to the object of my choice. O, could I, in some small degree, approach to that utility, which must ever, ever, ever belong to thy Night Thoughts![36]

Despite his supposed "utility," the "gloomy" Young remains inadequate for African Americans. A demurral from worldly ambition was something even genteel activists like Whipper needed to reject. "Ambition!" Young writes, in the original, "pow'rful source of good and ill! / . . . / By toys entangled, or in guilt bemir'd, / It turns a curse."[37] A few lines later Young voices the profoundly conservative, pro-slavery view that thoughts of salvation could compensate even for the state of bondage: "What slave unbless'd, who from to-morrow's dawn / Expects an empire? he forgets his chain, / And, thron'd in thought, his absent sceptre waves."[38] Although Whipper encouraged familiarity with the English canon, he emphatically rejected the complacency proposed by some English writers. He and his brethren would never forget their chains. Nor would they forget the chains of others.

Black Lives in the West Indies

Many Black writers encouraged a diasporic consciousness by asking their audiences to keep in mind Africans and their descendants living under British rule elsewhere in the Atlantic world. William Miller's 1810 sermon conjured scenes of violence and misery under slavery in the Caribbean, contrasting them to the conditions at home in New York, while acknowledging that some listeners may have experienced or seen such miseries first-hand:

> Picture to your imaginations the women enduring all the inclemency of the torrid zone, their bodies uncovered, and their young and tender offspring

> tied to their backs, digging two or three feet with a hoe in a soil that almost resists the powers of the pick-ax; and if there is the least cessation in their most servile labours, – O! sad communication! they are laid down and receive corporeal punishment with the cart-whip, the sight of which is sufficient to produce a despondency in the unhappy slaves.[39]

Miller emphasizes two kinds of witnessing, optical and sonic, the latter of which encompasses both oral and printed communications. "[C]ommunication!" is almost as important a theme in the passage as violence, as Miller mentions "accounts you may have received" and encourages his listeners to "picture to your imagination" the scenes he describes. The passage also emphasizes its own multi-layered communicative function: to be heard first, and then read and passed around as a pamphlet, and perhaps to be read aloud again. Both within and outside the bounds of the printed page, Miller encourages a sympathetic, imaginative identification with slaves in the West Indies; his sermon becomes another "account" that brings the suffering of distant Africans close to home. And yet as Miller also suggests, for those of his listeners who had lived in the West Indies, no command to the imagination was necessary.[40]

The West Indies had long served as a point of contrast for writers in the North. In 1797 Prince Hall reflected on "the daily insults" with which Black Bostonians routinely met. "'Twas said by a gentleman who saw that filthy behaviour in the common," Hall wrote, that "a slave in the West-Indies, on Sunday or holidays enjoys himself and friends without any molestation."[41] Caribbean slave society was understood as a limit case by which to measure cruelty and oppression. In his *Appeal*, Walker offered shocking statistics from Jamaica to support one of his many arguments about slavery's deleterious effects. "In some of the West India Islands," Walker writes, "and over a large part of South America, there are six or eight coloured persons for one white. Why do they not take possession of those places? Who hinders them?"[42] A long, exasperated note he added to the third edition offers "the one Island of Jamaica, as a specimen of our meanness." Walker writes:

> In that Island, there are three hundred and fifty thousand souls – of whom fifteen thousand are whites, the remainder, three hundred and thirty-five thousand are coloured people! and this Island is ruled by the white people!!!!!!!! (15,000) ruling and tyrannizing over 335,000 persons!!!!!!!! – O! coloured men!! O! coloured men!!! O! coloured men!!!! Look!! Look!!! At this!!!! And, tell me if we are not abject and servile enough, how long, O! how long my colour shall we be dupes and dogs to the cruel whites?[43]

Walker goes on to repeat the demographic information four more times with characteristic typographical emphasis, mingling anger and despair with a call for revolution. Walker's note reveals a tension between identifying with Black people in Jamaica – they are of "my colour" – and wanting to distance himself from them in deeply gendered terms as "abject and servile." His shame, however, betrays the strength of his diasporic affiliation. And by sharing these statistics and his frustration with his Black audiences, he aims to channel anger into action.

Walker may well have gotten his statistics from an 1827 article reprinted in *Freedom's Journal*; or, indeed, he may have supplied the article to the newspaper himself.[44] *Freedom's Journal* regularly provided information about the experience of slavery in the British Caribbean alongside reports of the progress of the new abolition movement which had begun in England in the mid-1820s.[45] By this period a diasporic identification with bondsmen and bondswomen in the West Indies had become almost inseparable from the prospect of their emancipation. One reprinted tale, "What does your Sugar Cost," highlighted British campaigns to boycott slave products by dramatizing a young woman's realization of how much blood was spilled so the English could sweeten their tea.[46] Reprinting articles from other sources was a common practice for all newspapers; editors Samuel Cornish and John Russwurm sometimes kept their readers informed by including voices and opinions with which they did not necessarily agree.[47] Indeed, reprinted articles could be informative despite clearly objectionable rhetoric, as in one hysterical screed they borrowed from the US periodical *The Christian Spectator*. "The Philanthropists who procured the abolition of the slave trade in Great Britain, have formed a Society for the mitigation and gradual abolition of slavery," the article warned. "Let the alarm then be continually sounded. The British slaves will soon be free citizens. Destruction awaits us, unless something effectual is done."[48] The writers of the original article feared that a contagious fever of emancipation would cause an insurrection in the United States: "Their slave population is in the immediate neighborhood of our own. They speak the same language. The intercourse is easy, constant, and unavoidable." Read against the grain, as no doubt Russwurm and Cornish intended, the article announces the inevitability of emancipation. It also projects an indelible image of the "easy, constant" commerce among enslaved populations in the Anglophone world.

The editors of *Freedom's Journal* also helped their readers navigate the progress of the new abolition movement by providing their own critical commentary on parliamentary debates. In a headnote to one London report, the editors protested that some proposed amelioration measures, such as abolishing the driving system or allowing slaves to hold property, "are little better than nominal." If this was "all that can possibly be done," the headnote reads, then "it would be as well to acknowledge that nothing at all can be done."[49] Some objectionable articles were reprinted without comment, including a parliamentary speech that scolded Jamaican colonial assemblies for thwarting antislavery legislation but proposed amelioration laws in order to appease them.[50] In contrast, one reprinted abolitionist polemic argued forcefully that West Indian slavery was antithetical to the values of "a free and religious nation like England." Reprinted from a genteel literary annual, *The Amulet: or Christian and Literary Remembrancer* (which also featured contributions by Samuel Taylor Coleridge, Felicia Hemans, John Clare, and many others), "Thoughts on British Colonial Slavery" was written by one D. Wilson, who proposed to "awaken the public conscience" to the suppressed fact that slavery itself is no better than the slave trade, a "fraudulent" and "fatal traffic." A breathless catalogue of abuses demands sympathy for "our fellow creatures, our brethren in blood" who are "treated as beasts of burden" for the sake of "blood stained revenue." His goal of establishing "the contrariety between the Christian Religion and West Indian Slavery" would have been very welcome to *Freedom's Journal* readership.[51]

The editors also participated in British abolitionism by sending their newspaper across the Atlantic. On November 9, 1827, Russwurm reprinted a letter of acknowledgment from Thomas Pringle, then secretary for The Society for the Mitigation and Gradual Abolition of Slavery; he also published some of Pringle's antislavery poetry.[52] A Scottish poet and former editor of the *South African Journal*, Pringle would later edit and publish *History of Mary Prince* (1831), a harrowing account of slavery in Bermuda, the Turks Islands, and Antigua and one of the earliest-known slave narratives written in English by a woman.[53] Russwurm reprinted Pringle's letter "merely ... to let our friends at home, know that the Abolitionists of Great Britain are yet alive to the interests and causes of our enslaved brethren." In the letter, Pringle wrote, "I have received through the medium of Mr. James Cropper, of Liverpool, several numbers of your able and meritorious Journal ... The committee have been much gratified by their perusal, and by their direction I now send you a set of the publications of this Society up to the present date ... I shall be glad to continue this reciprocal interchange."[54] As Jacqueline Bacon has argued, this letter from Britain is evidence of "an ongoing collaboration between reformers in the two nations in which African Americans played a significant role."[55] It also emphasizes the importance of print as a medium of "reciprocal exchange." Pringle conjures multiple scenes of reading, including the "perusal" of *Freedom's Journal* in Britain and his own hope that the editors will appreciate his publications. Reprinting the letter, then, not only informs *Freedom's Journal*'s readers that British abolitionists care for "our enslaved brethren," the reprint also demonstrates British abolitionists took care to earn the good opinion of African American editors and readers.

One significant article written expressly for the newspaper, entitled "Slavery in the West Indies," reveals multiple catalysts for a diasporic world view. The article, likely written by Russwurm, vividly refutes a New York newspaper editor's claim that people of color, and particularly slaves in Jamaica, are happy in the state of bondage. Russwurm calls this an "absurd attempt," the result of an "impaired mind," and critiques the author's evidence, drawn from southerners and books written by Jamaican planters. These sources are untrustworthy, "interested individuals" whose "revenue is exuded out of the flesh and blood of their fellow creatures." He counters with evidence of his own:

> [W]e have received a file of Jamaica papers, two of which contain eighty-five advertisements for run-away slaves; the majority of which are marked either on the shoulder or breast. We will extract one as a sample. – "Ran away from the Subscriber Bob, alias Robert Grant, answering to the following description; a congo, 5 feet 2 inches in height, apparently marked M.B. on the right breast with other marks on the shoulders and scars of punishment on the back, &c." If 85 cases of this kind, in two very small newspapers, are not sufficient to refute all that has been said or written, by Mr. C. and his correspondents, there is no reliance to be placed in facts and demonstrations.[56]

This presentation's accomplishments are threefold. As a factual record, the runaway slave advertisements – later a staple of abolitionist writing – demolish Mr. C's arguments. As "a file of Jamaica papers," the advertisements also provide a window into the hemispheric breadth of *Freedom Journal*'s network of correspondents, which attended even to "very small newspapers" in Jamaica. In itself, too, the record of the "congo" African's scarred and mutilated body brings home to the newspaper's readers a powerful image of one brother's distant suffering under Caribbean slavery. He is a representative of the "85 cases" contained in the file of papers, themselves indicative of thousands more, and a grim and galvanizing reminder that the agony of the diaspora transcended the boundaries of empire.

The Promise of Freedom in Sierra Leone and Canada

Some early African American writers looked to the British Empire for possible sites of immigration, both before and after the American Colonization Society began pushing its racist agenda. Soon after over one thousand "Black loyalists" who had joined the British during the Revolution settled in the Canadian province of Nova Scotia, the Sierra Leone Company funded their migration to the African colony in 1791.[57] Two of these loyalists, David George and Boston King, wrote about their immigration to Sierra Leone in the 1790s,[58] and reports circulated in the first decade of the century about the deportation of a group of Jamaican maroons along the same colonial route, first to Nova Scotia and then to Africa.[59] In 1810 William Miller signaled his approval of voluntary Black settlement in Sierra Leone. In a moment that Leslie M. Alexander has called a "turning point in Black political consciousness,"[60] Miller framed the colony as evidence of the improved state of Africa after the slave trade's abolition:

> This place is perhaps well known to a number of you by the name of Sereleon [*sic*]. Great encouragement has been given to it as a colony of Great Britain, which promises a numerous population; and besides the migration of a number of Missionaries there, a society has been lately established in England, consisting of the leading characters of that kingdom, for the identical purpose of civilizing and improving the continent of Africa.[61]

Miller's remarks participate in a long tradition, going back to Equiano, of linking Africa's liberation and improvement to its Christianization. They bring Sierra Leone settlers into a diasporic vision through a religiously inflected affiliative gesture. The colony may have been "well known" among Miller's listeners at least partly through printed accounts of its history in local newspapers such as the *New York Daily Advertiser*, or in Philadelphia reprints of the Sierra Leone Company's reports, or in imported books such as Robert Dallas's *The History of the Maroons* (1803) or Thomas Winterbottom's *An Account of the Native Africans in the Neighbourhood of Sierra Leone* (1803).[62] A map of the colony printed in Philadelphia in 1795 represented a large area between Freetown and Granvilletown as "Land Granted to the Settlers" – presumably for the purpose of "civilizing and improving the continent of Africa," as Miller describes it – but the same map also noted, in the mountains beyond the settlement's borders, a "Town of Runaway Slaves," thus raising the prospect of an alternative kind of community.[63]

Paul Cuffee, the prosperous transatlantic merchant of African and Native American descent, became the most prominent Black proponent of emigration following voyages to Sierra Leone, London, and New York in 1811 and 1812. Cuffee was an agent for the African Institution in London and found many allies in the free Black community in New York, including the Episcopal minister Peter Williams, Jr., son of the founder of the AME Zion Church in New York, who advocated immigration to Sierra Leone and Haiti in the 1810s.[64] Cuffee and Williams shared a printer, the Quaker abolitionist Samuel Wood, who issued Williams's 1808 oration about the slave trade and Cuffee's pro-emigration pamphlet, *A Brief Account of the Settlement and Present Situation of the Colony of Sierra Leone* (1812). Cuffee's pamphlet described the colony and its government by "British law,"[65] described his missionary and abolitionist activities among African tribes, and listed various prospects for education, worship, and work, including the cultivation of the land, shipping, and whaling. Cuffee advocated emigration with the hope it would be attractive to "all our brethren, who may come from the British colonies or from America."[66] The War of 1812 disrupted his efforts, but after the peace in 1815 he continued to promote this cause.

After Cuffee's untimely death in 1817, Williams wrote a passionate eulogy that framed the prospect of settlement in Sierra Leone as redemption in an apocalyptic world. "All around us is crumbling to ruin," he begins, "the whole world has become a Golgotha, in which there is scarcely left a spot whereon one can set his foot, without standing on the bones of our ancestors and brethren." In the rhetorical architecture of Williams's speech, Cuffee's hard work to establish a colony in Africa functions as an implicit means to carve out just such a spot. Williams hails Cuffee for his "active commiseration in behalf of his African brethren" and his remarkable success in a racist world, "subjected to all the disadvantages which unreasonable prejudice heaps upon that class of men." His death brings great sorrow – "Africa, unhappy, bereaved Africa, pours a deluge of tears" – and Williams invests Sierra Leone with a lasting hope and a millennial temporality. Cuffee "hoped that our curse would be converted into a blessing." This involved not only bringing Christianity to "benighted regions," but also providing the basic necessities of domestic life, such as Cuffee's wish "that a house should be built" on each family farm. This compassionate vision of a future for Africans "on the soil of their progenitors" contrasts not only to Williams's desolate depiction of the world as Golgatha (a "wide and still expanding empire of death") but also to his account of the absurd trans-imperial feud between the United States and

Great Britain that disrupted Cuffee's plans.[67] Rivalries born from the War of 1812 ultimately made it difficult to convince the United States government to support African American immigration to a British territory. Yet Cuffee would not limit his efforts to Black people in Britain. "[A]s a member of the whole, African family," Cuffee wrote, according to Williams, "My wish . . . is for the good of this people universally."[68]

In Williams's account of Cuffee's achievements and aspirations, Sierra Leone emerges as a beacon of hope for a self-determined African future. That Williams's oration was reprinted in York, England, as "proof," in the words of the "Preface to the English Edition," "that superior abilities do not attach more to a white than to a coloured skin," is a testament both to the power of his eulogy as a lasting piece of oratory and to the renown of its subject.[69] The ACS's proposed policy of forced migration, popularized in the 1820s, changed the conversation about the desirability of emigration, although many Black activists were still sympathetic to voluntary plans like Cuffee's. Ten years after his death, *Freedom's Journal* serialized Cuffee's memoirs in its first issues, motived by its readership's continuing interest in African emigration and also the desire to celebrate Cuffee's remarkable rise to wealth, prosperity, and international fame.[70] Sustained interest in Sierra Leone, eventually in contrast to a rejection of the ACS-backed colony of Liberia, suggests that writers of this period preferred Britain to the United States as an imperial sponsor.

Preference for such sponsorship culminated with support for the Wilberforce settlement in Canada. Named in honor of the great British abolitionist, Wilberforce was founded by African Americans from Cincinnati, Ohio, who left the city after a period of intense anti-Black hostility and especially after a racist mob attempted to destroy their community in August 1829. The ACS's insidious promise of a northern United States free of Black residents encouraged white violence against growing Black communities like Cincinnati's First Ward.[71] Many Black abolitionists came to support immigration to Canada as a viable alternative to African colonization because the idea of settlement originated from within the Black community and was thus an exercise of self-determination. Support for Wilberforce inspired two eloquent speeches by Williams and Richard Allen, the latter given at the first Colored Convention in Philadelphia in September, 1830, which convened specifically to discuss and raise funds for "a settlement in the province of Upper Canada, in order to afford a place of refuge."[72]

Williams took the occasion of his Fourth of July speech in St. Philip's Church in New York in 1830 to rail against the ACS and to re-direct Black patriotism in the service of expatriation. Anticipating Frederick Douglass's famous 1852 Speech, "What, to the American slave, is your Fourth of July," Williams wrote, "The festivities of this day serve but to impress upon the minds of reflecting men of colour a deeper sense of the cruelty, the injustice, and oppression of which they have been the victims." "We are natives of this country," he wrote, "we ask only to be treated as well as foreigners." The events in Cincinnati signaled yet again the unrelenting hostility of whites, which tragically drove "your brethren ... into exile." Wilberforce provided some hope; "God, in his good providence, has opened for such of us as may choose to leave these States an asylum in the neighboring British province of Canada ... The laws are good, and the same for the coloured man as the white man. A powerful sympathy prevails there in our behalf, instead of the prejudice where here oppresses us." The importance of free choice was paramount. While asking his listeners to contribute "a few shillings" toward helping the settlement, he stressed that it "has a peculiar claim upon our patronage, because it has originated among our own people." Exiled from the United States, the Black community of Wilberforce would retain their national home in the African diaspora. "Let [them] have the amount which is usually spent by our people in this city on the 4th of July," he wrote; "This is truly patriotic."[73] Equal legal rights in Canada and the "powerful sympathy" evident among British citizens made Canada seem like a hospitable environment.

At an address at the first Colored Convention, Allen echoed Williams's critique of colonization, his fury about recent violence against free Black communities, and his support for repatriation in Canada, "in a land where the laws and prejudices of society will have no effect in retarding their advancement to the summit of civil and religious improvement."[74] William Lloyd Garrison supported the settlement and printed a favorable report of his visit there in 1831 in the *Liberator*.[75] In the end Wilberforce was not an idyll of freedom; by the 1840s, Irish settlers had purchased lands there and driven the Black residents out.[76] But the Colored Conventions that the settlement inspired lived on, as P. Gabrielle Foreman has shown,[77] born in an initial moment of optimism about Canada that in the decades that followed continued to inspire African Americans in search of hospitable ground.

* * *

A regular dialogue with Britain continued throughout the nineteenth century, from annual celebrations of West Indian Emancipation beginning

August 1, 1834, to the transatlantic lecture tours of Frederick Douglass.[78] Many Black abolitionists continued to idealize England's historical commitment to freedom as US slavery spread in the antebellum period, ravaging thousands of lives in the wake of big cotton.[79] England, as an idea, or the colonies, as a lived reality (in Nova Scotia, or Canada, or Sierra Leone) never lived up to the idealizations found in some Black writing, especially as the British Empire spread with impunity around the globe. A fascination with expatriation continued for African Americans writing in the nineteenth and twentieth centuries – often with unmet expectations, just like their forebearers. Many authors have searched out intellectual and artistic community while traveling to England, Canada, Germany, France, or the Caribbean, including Martin Delaney, W. E. B. Dubois, Anna Julia Cooper, Zora Neale Hurston, Richard Wright, and James Baldwin. Countless others have been inspired by diasporic and transnational aesthetic and political affiliations. In the early nineteenth century, the attraction to Britain might ultimately be best understood as part of what Paul Gilroy has called "the politics of fulfillment," a distinctive ideology of the Black Atlantic which demands "bourgeois civil society live up to the promises of its own rhetoric."[80] In contrast to the "politics of transfiguration" – a more radical, utopian, counter-cultural component of Black Atlantic double consciousness – the politics of fulfillment promotes the Enlightenment values of "emancipation, autonomy, and citizenship."[81] Early nineteenth-century African Americans living and writing and leading their communities in the United States fought hard for those practical goals. Given the hostility they faced at home it is perhaps not surprising that they looked to a rival empire for them to be fulfilled.

Notes

1 Paul Gilroy, *The Black Atlantic: Modernity and Double Consciousness* (Cambridge, MA: Harvard University Press, 1993); Vincent Carretta and Philip Gould, eds., *Genius in Bondage: Literature of the Early Black Atlantic* (Lexington: University Press of Kentucky, 2001); Cedrick May, *Evangelism and Resistance in the Black Atlantic, 1760–1835* (Athens and London: University of Georgia Press, 2008); Joanna Brooks, *American Lazarus: Religion and the Rise of African-American and Native American Literatures* (New York: Oxford University Press, 2003); Dwight McBride, *Impossible Witnesses: Truth, Abolitionism, and Slave Testimony* (New York: Oxford University Press, 2003); Hugh Thomas, *The Slave Trade: The Story of the Atlantic Slave Trade, 1440–1870* (New York: Simon and Schuster, 1997); Manisha Sinha, *The Slave's Cause: A History of Abolition* (New Haven: Yale

University Press, 2016); Martha Schoolman, *Abolitionist Geographies* (Minneapolis and London: University of Minnesota Press, 2014); Jeffrey Kerr-Ritchie, *Rites of August First: Emancipation Day in the Black Atlantic World* (Baton Rouge: Louisiana State University Press, 2007).

2 England and the British Empire are addressed, but not fully considered, in the rich historiography on African American life in the northern United States in the half century after the Revolution. Leslie M. Alexander, *African or American? Black Identity and Political Activism in New York City, 1784–1861* (Champaign: University of Illinois Press, 2008); Patrick Rael, *Black Identity and Black Protest in the Antebellum North* (Chapel Hill: University of North Carolina Press, 2002); Jasmine N. Cobb, *Picture Freedom: Remaking Black Visuality in the Early Nineteenth Century* (New York: New York University Press, 2015); James Sidbury, *Becoming African in America: Race and Nation in the Early Black Atlantic* (New York: Oxford University Press, 2007); Ira Berlin, *The Making of African America: The Four Great Migrations* (New York: Penguin, 2010); Leonard Curry, *The Free Black in Urban America, 1800–1850: The Shadow of the Dream* (Chicago: University of Chicago Press, 1981); Gary Nash, *Forging Freedom: The Formation of Philadelphia's Black Community, 1720–1840* (Cambridge: Harvard University Press, 1988); Floyd J. Miller, *The Search for a Black Nationality: Black Emigration and Colonization, 1787–1863* (Champaign: University of Illinois Press, 1975); Jacqueline Bacon, *Freedom's Journal: The First African-American Newspaper* (Lanham, MD: Lexington Books, 2007); Sinha, *The Slave's Cause: A History of Abolition*; Joanne Pope Melish, *Disowning Slavery: Gradual Emancipation and "Race" in New England, 1780–1860* (Ithaca: Cornell University Press, 1998); Mitch Kachun, *Festivals of Freedom: Memory and Meaning in African American Emancipation Celebrations, 1808–1915* (Amherst: University of Massachusetts Press, 2003); Shane White, "'It Was a Proud Day': African Americans, Festivals, and Parades in the North, 1741–1834.," *Journal of American History*, June (1994): 13–50; William Gravely, "The Dialectic of Double-Consciousness in Black American Freedom Celebrations, 1808–1863," *Journal of Negro History*, no. Winter (1982): 302–17; Nikki Taylor, "Reconsidering the 'Forced' Exodus of 1829: Free Black Emigration from Cincinnati, Ohio to Wilberforce, Canada," *The Journal of African American History* 87, Summer (2002): 283–302; May, *Evangelism and Resistance in the Black Atlantic, 1760–1835*; Eddie S. Glaude, *Exodus! Religion, Race, and Nation in Early Nineteenth-Century Black America* (Chicago: University of Chicago Press, 2000).

3 Richard Newman, Patrick Rael, and Phillip Lapsansky, "Introduction," in *Pamphlets of Protest: An Anthology of Early African American Protest Literature, 1790–1860* (New York: Routledge, 2001), 8.

4 Joanna Brooks, "The Early American Public Sphere and the Emergence of a Black Print Counterpublic," *The William and Mary Quarterly* 53, no. 3 (2005): 67–92. See also Newman, Rael, and Lapsansky, eds., *Pamphlets of Protest.*

5 Cobb, *Picture Freedom: Remaking Black Visuality in the Early Nineteenth Century*, 156. See also Lara Langer Cohen and Jordan Alexander Stein, eds., *Early African American Print Culture* (Philadelphia: University of Pennsylvania Press, 2012).
6 In many ways Black writers participated in a transatlantic consciousness that shaped Anglo-American culture at large – grounded in the material, migratory, cultural, and political ties that continued to link English-speaking populations in the decades after US independence. Atlantic World historiography is vast and has only increased over the last decade. For an important discussion of such scholarship from an interdisciplinary perspective, see Eric Slauter, "History, Literature, and the Atlantic World," *Early American Literature* 43, no. 1 (2008): 153–186.
7 Joseph Rezek, "The Orations on the Abolition of the Slave Trade and the Uses of Print in the Early Black Atlantic," *Early American Literature* 45, no. 3 (2010): 655–682. These texts survive as part of the printed record of what William Gravely has called the first African American "freedom celebration." Gravely, "The Dialectic of Double-Consciousness."
8 Miller, *A Sermon on the Abolition of the Slave Trade, Delivered in the African Church*, 3.
9 Absalom Jones, "A Thanksgiving Sermon, Preached January 1, 1808 … On Account of the Abolition of the Slave Trade" (1808) in *Early Negro Writing, 1760–1837*, ed. Dorothy Porter (Baltimore: Black Classics Press, 1971), 338.
10 William Miller, *A Sermon on the Abolition of the Slave Trade, Delivered in the African Church* (New York, 1810), 10.
11 Russell Parrott, "An Oration on the Abolition of the Slave Trade" (1814), in *Early Negro Writing*, 387–388.
12 William Hamilton, "An Oration on the Abolition of the Slave Trade" (1815), in *Early Negro Writing*, 398.
13 Prince Saunders, *A Memoir Presented to the American Convention for Promoting the Abolition of Slavery* (Philadelphia, 1818), 16.
14 David Walker, *Walker's Appeal, In Four Articles; Together with A Preamble, to the Coloured Citizens of the World, but in Particular, and Very Expressly, to Those of The United States of America, Written in Boston, State of Massachusetts, September 28, 1829. Third and Last Edition, With Additional Notes, Corrections, Etc.* (Boston, 1830), 62–63.
15 Ibid., 47.
16 Marilyn Richardson, *Maria W. Stewart, America's First Black Woman Political Writer: Essays and Speeches* (Bloomington and Indianapolis: Indiana University Press, 1987), 75–76. Richardson does not attribute the poem to Cowper.
17 Ibid., 74.
18 Ibid., 39
19 Ibid., 75
20 Miller, *A Sermon on the Abolition of the Slave Trade, Delivered in the African Church*, 9.

21 Ibid., 10. Miller may have been familiar with *Charity* from reading it in excerpted form or in any of the half dozen editions of his *Poems* published in Salem, Philadelphia, Baltimore, or Boston since 1792. This passage appears on p. 133 of the Philadelphia edition (vol. 2, *Poems, by William Cowper* [Philadelphia: Robert Johnson, 1803]). Cowper was one of the most popular poets in the early national United States, and his poems, especially *The Task*, were available both in imported and dozens of reprinted editions.

22 William Cowper, *Poems*, vol. 2 (Philadelphia: R. Carr for Robert Johnson, 1803), 136.

23 *Freedom's Journal*, May 18, 1827.

24 Elizabeth McHenry, *Forgotten Readers: Recovering the Lost History of African American Literary Societies* (Durham: Duke University Press, 2002), 86.

25 Maria Stewart, "Lecture Delivered at the Franklin Hall" (1832), in *Maria W. Stewart*, ed. Richardson, 48.

26 William Whipper, "An Address Delivered in Wesley Church on the Evening of June 12, before the Colored Reading Society of Philadelphia, for Mental Improvement" (1828), in *Early Negro Writing*, 107.

27 Lemuel Haynes, "Universal Salvation, A Very Ancient Doctrine: With Some Account of the Life and Character of the Author. A Sermon, Delivered at Rutland, West Parish, Vermont, in the Year 1805" (1810) in *Early Negro Writing*, 450. Haynes also ended his sermon with quotations from Pope's *Messiah*.

28 Parrott, "An Oration on the Abolition of the Slave Trade," 389.

29 Stewart, "Lecture Delivered at the Franklin Hall," 48.

30 The original line from Gray reads "waste its sweetness on the desert air." Richardson (ed.), *Maria W. Stewart*, 127 n71.

31 Henry Johnson, "Introductory Address to Henry Sipkins" (1809), in *Early Negro Writing*, 366.

32 Ibid.

33 "The Grave" appeared in the American edition of *The Wanderer of Switzerland and Other Poems* (New York: Stansbury, 1807), 73–80. In 1809, Montgomery published an epic poem, *The West Indies*, commemorating the slave trade's abolition, but it would have been impossible for Johnson to know about that project at this time.

34 Haynes, "Universal Salvation," 452.

35 Whipper, "An Address Delivered in Wesley Church on the Evening of June 12" 117.

36 Ibid.

37 Edward Young, *Night Thoughts on Life, Death, and Immortality*, vol. 1 (Philadelphia: Benjamin Johnson, 1805), 165.

38 Ibid., 173.

39 Miller, *A Sermon on the Abolition of the Slave Trade, Delivered in the African Church*, 10–11.

40 Such listeners may not have been unlike Thomas Porter, an African from Jamaica who sued for his freedom in New York in 1812. *Constitution and Act of Incorporation of the Pennsylvania Society for Promoting the Abolition of*

Slavery, and for the Relief of Free Negroes, Unlawfully Held in Bondage, and for the Improving the Condition of the African Race (Philadelphia, 1820), 24. See Leslie Harris, *In the Shadow of Slavery: African Americans in New York City, 1626-1863* (Chicago: University of Chicago Press, 2002), for a discussion of the migration of Africans from the Caribbean to New York City.

41 Prince Hall, "A Charge, Delivered to the African Lodge, June 24, 1797, At Menotomy.," in *"Face Zion Forward": First Writers of the Black Atlantic, 1785–1798*, ed. Joanna Brooks and John Saillant (Boston: Benjamin Edes, 1797), 203, 204.

42 Walker, *Walker's Appeal*, 71–72.

43 Ibid.

44 *Freedom's Journal*, Dec. 7, 1827; the article estimates that Jamaica has an enslaved population of 336,253.

45 On the new British abolition movement, see Kenneth Morgan, *Slavery and the British Empire: From Africa to America* (London: Oxford University Press, 2007), 177–183; Thomas, *The Slave Trade: The Story of the Atlantic Slave Trade, 1440–1870*; Sinha, *The Slave's Cause: A History of Abolition*; Ronald Kent Richardson, *Moral Imperium: Afro-Caribbeans and the Transformation of British Rule, 1776-1838* (New York: Greenwood Press, 1987).

46 *Freedom's Journal*, August 17 and August 24, 1827.

47 Bacon, *Freedom's Journal: The First African-American Newspaper*, 71–96.

48 *Freedom's Journal*, March 23, 1827.

49 *Freedom's Journal*, September 19, 1828.

50 *Freedom's Journal*, November 21, 1828.

51 *Freedom's Journal* March 7, 1828.

52 I attribute this to Russwurm because by September 1827, Cornish had left the paper.

53 For more on Pringle, see Sara Salih, "Introduction," in *The History of Mary Prince: A West Indian Slave*, ed. Sara Salih (New York: Penguin, 2000), xxiii–xxv.

54 *Freedom's Journal*, November 9, 1827.

55 Bacon, *Freedom's Journal: The First African-American Newspaper*, 231–232.

56 *Freedom's Journal*, May 11, 1827.

57 Sidbury, *Becoming African in America: Race and Nation in the Early Black Atlantic*; Joanna Brooks and John Saillant, eds., *"Face Zion Forward": First Writers of the Black Atlantic, 1785–1798*.

58 David George, "An Account of the Life of Mr. David George, from Sierra Leone in Africa; Given by Himself in a Conversation with Brother Rippon of London, and Brother Pierce of Birmingham" (1793), in *"Face Zion Forward,"* 177–190; Boston King, "Memoirs of the Life of Boston King, a Black Preacher. Written by Himself, during His Residence at Kingswood-School" (1798), in *"Face Zion Forward,"* 209–232.

59 James D. Lockett, "The Deportation of the Maroons of Trelawny Town to Nova Scotia, Then Back to Africa," *Journal of Black Studies* 30, no. 1 (September 1999): 5–14.

60 Alexander, *African or American? Black Identity and Political Activism in New York City, 1784–1861*, 26.
61 Miller, *A Sermon on the Abolition of the Slave Trade, Delivered in the African Church*, 12.
62 *New York Daily Advertiser*, November 30, 1802. The year of their publication, New York booksellers advertised for sale the London editions of Robert Charles Dallas, *The History of the Maroons; from Their Origin to the Establishment of Their Chief Tribe at Sierra Leone*, 2 vols. (London, 1803); Thomas Winterbottom, *An Account of the Native Africans in the Neighborhood of Sierra Leone*, 2 vols. (London, 1803). Thomas Dobson of Philadelphia reprinted many reports of the Sierra Leone Company in the 1790s. A letter from David George was reprinted in *Substance of the Report of the Court of Directors of the Sierra Leone Company, Delivered to The General Court of Proprietors* (Philadelphia, 1795), 22–23.
63 *Substance of the Report of the Court of Directors of the Sierra Leone Company*, n.p.
64 Alexander, *African or American? Black Identity and Political Activism in New York City, 1784–1861*, 38–40; Rosalind Cobb Wiggins, *Captain Paul Cuffe's Logs and Letters, 1808-1817: A Black Quaker's "Voice from within the Veil"* (Washington, DC: Howard University Press, 1996); Peter Williams, Jr., *A Discourse Delivered on the Death of Capt. Paul Cuffee, Before the New-York African Institution, in the African Methodist Episcopal Zion Church, October 21, 1817* (York [England], 1818).
65 Paul Cuffee, "A Brief Account of the Settlement and Present Situation of the Colony of Sierra Leone, in Africa; As Communicated by Paul Cuffee (A Man of Colour) to His Friend in New York" (1812), in *Early Negro Writing*, 259.
66 Ibid., 258.
67 Williams, Jr., *A Discourse Delivered on the Death of Capt. Paul Cuffee, Before the New-York African Institution, in the African Methodist Episcopal Zion Church, October 21, 1817*, 7, 17, 10, 9, 16, 28, 22, 21, 8.
68 Ibid., 23.
69 Ibid., vi.
70 *Freedom's Journal*, March 16, 23, 30 and April 6, 13, 1827. Benjamin Fagan links the serialization of Cuffee's memoir to the newspapers middle class ambitions in *The Black Newspaper and the Chosen Nation* (Athens and London: University of Georgia Press, 2016), 27.
71 Taylor, "Reconsidering the 'Forced' Exodus of 1829: Free Black Emigration from Cincinnati, Ohio to Wilberforce, Canada."
72 "Constitution of the American Society of Free Persons of Colour, For Improving Their Condition in the United States; for Purchasing Lands; and for the Establishment of a Settlement in Upper Canada, Also the Proceedings of the Convention, with Their Address to the Free Persons of Colour in the United States," in *Early Negro Writing, 1760–1837* (Philadelphia: I. W. Allen, 1831), 178. See also http://coloredconventions.org/.

73 Peter Williams, Jr., "A Discourse Delivered in St. Philip's Church, for the Benefit of the Coloured Community in Wilberforce, in Upper Canada, on the Fourth of July, 1830" (1830), in *Early Negro Writing*, 295, 297, 302, 298, 301, 300.

74 Richard Allen, "Address to the Free People of Colour of These United States," in "Constitution of the American Society of Free Persons of Colour," (1831), in *Early Negro Writing*, 180.

75 Taylor, "Reconsidering the 'Forced' Exodus of 1829: Free Black Emigration from Cincinnati, Ohio to Wilberforce, Canada," 293–294.

76 Ibid., 297.

77 P. Gabrielle Foreman, "The Colored Conventions Project and the Changing Same" *Common-place* 16, no.1 (fall 2015), http://common-place.org/book/the-colored-conventions-project-and-the-changing-same/. See also http://coloredconventions.org/

78 Schoolman, *Abolitionist Geographies*; Kerr-Ritchie, *Rites of August First: Emancipation Day in the Black Atlantic World*; Sinha, *The Slave's Cause: A History of Abolition*; Robert S. Levine, *The Lives of Frederick Douglass* (Cambridge, MA: Harvard University Press, 2016).

79 Elisa Tamarkin, *Anglophilia: Deference, Devotion, and Antebellum America* (Chicago: University of Chicago Press, 2007), see especially chapter 3, "Freedom and Deference: Society, Antislavery, and Black Intellectualism."

80 Gilroy, *The Black Atlantic: Modernity and Double Consciousness*, 37.

81 Ibid., 16.

CHAPTER 5

Robert Roberts's The House Servant's Directory *and the Performance of Stability in African American Print, 1800–1830*

Britt Rusert

> There are years that ask questions and years that answer.
>
> Zora Neale Hurston, *Their Eyes Were Watching God* (1937)

> [T]his is not your time you spend, but your employer's, for all your time belongs to them.
>
> Robert Roberts, *The House Servant's Directory, or A Monitor for Private Families* (1827)

African American print published between 1800 and 1830 is rife with silences, subtleties, and forms of political rhetoric that would fall out of fashion with the rise of Garrisonian Abolition and abolitionist movement literature in the 1830s. Indeed, Black writing published after the Revolutionary period but before the rise of organizational Abolition in the 1830s and 1840s does not fit easily within scholarly frameworks of Black agency, freedom, and progress, but as such, it potentially unsettles African American literary history in productive and sometimes surprising ways. I argue that the peculiar focus on *non-movement* and even stasis (in the sense of both immobility, but also, at times, stagnation) in Black texts that were at the same time moving through intricate networks of distribution and circulation might suggest different ways of conceiving Black politics and aesthetics in this period. Indeed, we still have much to learn about the political comportments and aesthetic particularities of Black literature in the post-Revolutionary period on its own terms.

In what follows, I take up Robert Roberts's 1827 manual, *The House Servant's Directory*, a handbook that instructed potential and newly employed servants on various "tricks of the trade," including how to master the performance of "everything is perfectly fine" in front of one's employers, even when everything was not. Roberts conceptualizes "the art of waiting," a phrase signaled in the author's lengthy subtitle, but also taken up throughout the text as a strategy of survival, of waiting things out

MISCELLANY.

From the House Servant's Directory.

A WORD TO THE HEADS OF FAMILIES.

A few words might be said to masters and mistresses, in behalf of those who are dependent on them for their present, and often times for their eternal good. "The labourer is worthy of his hire," and should be treated, in health or in sickness with pity and feeling; if it is necessary to place servants under strict surveillance, let them at least be treated as fellow beings and candidates for a future world. It would be presumption in me, a servant, to urge aught on this subject to my superiors; I beg leave, therefore, respectfully to conclude with the following extract in behalf of the cook and other servants, taken from the Cook's Oracle:

"A good dinner is one of the greatest enjoyments of human life; and as the practice of cookery is attended with so many discouraging difficulties, so many disgusting and disagreeable circumstances, and even dangers, we ought to have some regard for those who encounter them, to procure us pleasure, and to reward their attention, by rendering their situation every way as comfortable and agreeable as we can. Mere money is a very inadequate compensation to a complete cook; he who has preached integrity to those in the kitchen may be permitted to recommend liberality to those in the parlour; they are indeed the sources of each other.

Depend upon it, 'true self-love and social, are the same;' 'do as you would be done by;' give those you are obliged to trust, every inducement to be honest, and no temptation to play tricks.

When you consider that a good servant eats no more than a bad one, how much more waste is occasioned by provisions being dressed in a slovenly and unskilful manner, and how much a good cook (to whom the conduct of the kitchen is confined,) can save you by careful management, no housekeeper will hardly deem it an unwise speculation, it is certainly an amiable experiment, to invite the honesty and industry of domestics, by setting them an example of liberality; at least, show them, that 'according to their pains, will be their gains.' But trust not your servants with the secret of their own strength; importance of any kind, being what human frailty is least able to bear.

Avoid all approaches towards familiarity, which to a proverb is accompanied by contempt, and soon breaks the neck of obedience.

Servants are more likely to be praised into good conduct, than scolded out of bad; always commend them when they do right; to cherish the desire of pleasing in them, you must show them that you are pleased:

'Be to their faults a little blind,
And to their virtues very kind.'

By such conduct, ordinary servants will often be converted into good ones; few are so hardened as not to feel gratified when they are kindly and liberally treated.

Figure 5.1 Excerpt from Robert Roberts's *The House Servant's Directory* in the August 10, 1829 issue of *The Lynchburg Virginian*.

until other conditions of possibility emerge.[1] *Stasis* indicates equilibrium, and this was exactly what texts like *The House Servant's Directory* performed, even in the midst of, and perhaps because of, broader forces of social destabilization and dispossession within and beyond Boston, where Roberts lived and worked in the 1820s. But I also use stasis here in the sense of its etymological link to the Greek *στάσις*, meaning "party faction" or "civil strife."[2] Here, stasis emerges as a term of war, in which equilibrium is more like a tense stalemate between opposing parties in war. This definition helps to capture the precious but also precarious nature of stability for free African Americans in the early nineteenth century, who were treated with open hostility and often violently targeted in a post-war society that must have still felt like open warfare for both Black and Native people in the young nation. Moreover, Black writers like Roberts sought to counter the ephemeral and unstable nature of the US print sphere – an instability that was exacerbated for Black writers seeking publication in a racist public sphere – by performing stability in their texts. This rhetorical performance of stability was not an avoidance of the realities of the world, but a technique oriented toward self-protection and even community defense for nominally free Black communities in and beyond Roberts's Boston.

The circulation of early African American texts was fraught by irony and paradox. For example, *The House Servant's Directory* ultimately traveled more widely, and more easily, than many of the readers it addressed. It was reviewed in both northern and southern periodicals and was popular enough to warrant two subsequent editions, one in 1828 and another in 1837. It continued to be a standard reference text throughout the nineteenth century.[3] Roberts's racial identity and name were absent from the reviews and advertisements of the book that appeared in antebellum periodicals, but such erasure through print actually enabled his writing to infiltrate the print culture of the slaveholding South. In the last years of the 1820s and into the 1830s, Roberts's text circulated in the South, and in one spectacular instance, it ended up infiltrating and subverting the literature of slave management. The surprising story of *The House Servant's Directory*'s reprinting, circulation, and readership in the slaveholding South points to instances in which "out of bounds" early Black texts could move and do things in the world that other genres, especially the slave narrative, could not. In the contexts of works such as David Walker's *Appeal to the Coloured Citizens of the World* (1829–1830), the story of Roberts's *House Servant's Directory* suggests that seemingly non-political texts could take on newly politicized meanings through circulation and reproduction, as they reached new readerships and appeared in alternative formats or editions. Nuancing narratives about the Black Atlantic that privilege mobility and fugitivity, I conclude by theorizing a group I call "shore intellectuals," those activists and writers like Roberts who used their proximity to water to make connections and move ideas despite restrictions on their own movement.

The availability of an abolitionist printing press was crucial for Black voices in the 1830s; the lack of availability to the means of publication clearly limited the possibilities for publication in the earlier post-Revolutionary, pre-Abolition moment that is the focus of this volume. However, these inroads were largely eclipsed by the 1840s, when the abolitionist movement increasingly determined what stories could and could not be told about Black resistance as well as about cross-racial alliances between Blacks and non-whites that excluded white participation.[4] This chapter approaches 1800–1830 as a crucial period of *immobility* within Black life and politics, one that shaped the literature of the period in profound ways. Unlike the narratives of the Atlantic movement, revolt, and resistance privileged in accounts of the late eighteenth- and mid-nineteenth century, Black narratives in the first three decades of the nineteenth century were much more likely to emphasize conditions of stasis, imposed immobility, and sometimes even a debilitating "paralysis," often figured through an embodied language of disability. Before the golden age of antislavery literature in the later decades of the antebellum period, Black writers were more likely to bemoan their personal immobility and the frustratingly halted and stalled efforts to end slavery, rather than the optimism, activity, and activism highlighted in both the Age of the American Revolution and the Age of Abolition. Even Walker's *Appeal*, a kinetic text attempting to will a massive slave revolt into existence, includes scenes of immobilizing dread and exasperated despair. In this way, Black print of this period was structured by a crucial dialectic of movement and stasis, in which materially circulating Black texts rhetorically performed immobility, a canny reflection of the paradoxes of freedom and surveillance of movement for nominally free African Americans navigating a viciously anti-Black society.

Transition and Waiting

Waiting might be understood as one strategy for weathering a period of transition, particularly under the conditions of oppression. The first decades of the nineteenth century were ones of change and transformation for enslaved and nominally free populations across a geographically expanding nation, authorized by ideologies of racial destiny, commercial growth, and frontier individualism. Published in 1837, Hosea Easton's *Treatise on the Intellectual Character, and Civil and Political Condition of the Colored People of the United States* lays out the racist violence, intimidation, and rollbacks of political power that beset northern Black communities in the previous three decades. The difficulties discussed therein describe transitions in northern life for free Blacks like Robert Roberts, who was Easton's brother-in-law. It conveys the difficulties of free Black life in the post-Revolutionary period through Easton's own, largely traumatic, family history traced back to the Revolution itself. Writing from Hartford, Easton had recently experienced the premature death of his father, James Easton, as well as riots in Hartford, Connecticut, that had targeted the Black community, including its churches.[5] He figures Northern prejudice toward the "colored people" as an act of profound "injury," a term that is meant to capture both physical acts of violence as well as a juridical notion of injury, an act worthy of legal prosecution and redress.[6] The text is largely descriptive, interested more in illuminating the current condition of his "afflicted brethren" than in charting a way forward. An opening account of the fall and desolation of Africa suggests that Africa shall rise again, but Easton's account follows contemporaneous theories of history that understood the rise and fall of civilizations as cyclical, natural, and largely outside human agency.[7] Instead of offering a word of consolation, a plan for change, or a rally cry for political action or revolt, Easton closes with an image of African Americans waiting for a systemic change in American society, one that must be initiated and carried out by those in power. Since the "downtrodden colored Americans" are "half dead," they presumably need to wait for what Easton calls the "true emancipation," a complete overthrow of the system that would allow both the enslaved and the nominally free to "arise as from the dead."[8] Easton's image of patient anticipatory waiting and resurrection fits with Second Great Awakening-style, millenarian views of the Judgment, visible also in Walker's *Appeal* (Easton travelled in the same intellectual and religious circles as Walker), but it is also one of chilling immobility: of half-dead, frozen, even machinic bodies waiting for animation under a completely transformed social order.

Slavery is the most impactful social issue that shapes Easton's dark and pessimistic tone. It aligns with that of Maria Stewart and David Walker, reiterating a sentiment that characterized much Black writing, and the sermonic cultures to which it was deeply connected, before 1830.[9] His is a macabre text – grotesque, gothic, and often melancholic – that lays out how both structural and everyday forms of prejudice inhibit Black intellectual, political, and even physical development. In Easton's account, the traumas of whipping and sexual violence are passed down generationally: the pregnant mother's observation of "whipped slaves," around her are reproduced in the twisted, distended visage of her baby (a formulation that nonetheless evades acts of violence and harm committed against pregnant enslaved women themselves).[10] Slavery casts a long, painful shadow across the free states, and is figured, throughout Easton's account as an agent of gruesome maiming and collective deformation.[11] The constant surveillance of Black subjects is also figured as a crushing, immobilizing weight, one unlikely to be moved by any individual action or form of resistance. Complete, structural change is the only salve for this collective, festering wound.

Down South, the wide-scale transition to cotton production entailed a new phase of destabilizing upheavals for enslaved people.[12] Among other changes, the intensification of the domestic slave trade to feed the growing "Cotton Kingdom" in the Lower South instigated a new round of sales, dislocations and separations from biological and chosen kin. In other words, the re-organization of plantation labor and production was surely felt by enslaved people amid the transition to cotton production. The abolition of the (legal) British slave trade through the 1807 Slave Trade Act simultaneously created a labor supply problem within the United States, a demand that was met through an intensification of the domestic slave trade. Up north, the rise of the Cotton Kingdom and the growth of the domestic slave trade were felt through the threat of kidnapping and re-capture, which constantly loomed over fugitive and nominally free people.

But in other ways, the period must have felt not like one of change, but of the changing same ("nothing new under the sun"). Enslaved people continued to endure the endless brutalities and excruciating repetitions of their labor and nominally free people saw little change in their lives as slavery was outlawed and slowly withered away across the states of the North via gradual emancipation. Indeed, the transition to wage labor often registered little difference in the forms and conditions of Black labor, and into the mid-nineteenth century, domestic service in white households remained the most common occupation for free African Americans. Black women's labor was especially constricted to activities that mirrored an earlier history of domestic slavery in colonial New England: they continued to work as maids, domestic servants, cooks, and washerwomen, often laboring in the homes of white families while caring for their own families and children. Slavery remained powerfully imprinted on northern memory, even if white northerners sought to disavow and disconnect from the recent history and legacies of slavery in the North.[13] In the decades that preceded the rise of antislavery activism in the 1830s, African Americans waited through a period of economic deterioration and the rollback of voting and other rights that had been granted to African Americans after the Revolutionary War. While Black organization and politics in the post-Revolutionary period largely hinged on recourse to the nation's democratic principles as well as the importance of veteran war status for claiming freedom, such claims became more tenuous as the years passed.

African Americans continued to remind those in power about the promises of freedom made to them during the American Revolution, while they organized through literary societies, mutual aid societies, churches, and fraternal aid societies throughout the 1810s and 1820s. In their foundational study of Black Boston in the antebellum period, James and Lois Horton note that it is much more difficult to track the lives of Black activists who worked in the Black community than those who were tied to white abolitionists, their organizations, and, I would add, their printing presses.[14] At the same time, the records of Black organization that do exist in the first few decades of the nineteenth century often record a sense of dreadful waiting and frustration at social conditions that *were* actually changing while the racial system and hierarchy undergirding them remained solidly in place.[15]

Such conditions of dreadful waiting in the North were similarly connected to a set of legal, practical, and economic conditions that determined and surveilled the movement of Black people, from vagrancy and poor laws that disproportionately targeted African Americans, to threats of violence and kidnapping that served as more diffuse impediments to unfettered and unanxious movement. While vagrancy and poor laws, the looming threat of kidnapping, and the violence and intimidation directed at urban Black communities all worked to circumscribe the travels and movement of nominally free African Americans, Black life *within* particular cities was often marked by the conditions of periodic uprooting and movement. James Oliver Horton and Louise E. Horton highlight the transience of Black workers in Boston, who often followed jobs and moved between different types of temporary living arrangements. African Americans in the city often lived in multi-family homes, and single workers routinely moved between boarding houses and the homes of relations and friends.[16]

Rampant housing and employment discrimination worked to keep people on the move within and sometimes beyond the city's borders.

When employment opportunities didn't pan out in the city, Black workers, especially men, often took to the sea, where they worked in a variety of capacities. In fact, movement via the sea/ship was often easier than interstate travel, creating the seemingly paradoxical situation in which Black mobility was deemed acceptable beyond the boundaries of the United States but "out of bounds" within the nation itself. In his study of African American seamen, W. Jeffrey Bolster notes that "free and enslaved Black sailors established a visible presence in every North Atlantic seaport and plantation roadstead between 1740 and 1865."[17] His study illuminates the importance of seafaring for free Black men who were struggling to "create a footprint for freedom" in the decades following the American Revolution, noting that "seafaring became one of the most common male occupations," alongside domestic service.[18] Thus Black workers often found themselves working in conditions of either hyper-mobility (at sea) or hyper-confinement (in white homes).

Finally, the 1820s were an important transitional moment within the long history of Native dispossession and violence at the hands of the US government and, earlier, colonial settlers and imperial adventurers. It was a decade marking the changing tenor of "Indian relations" as models of cultural assimilation began to give way to theories of Indian "difference" and animosity.[19] Native Americans were increasingly figured as inassimilable threats in need of removal and containment, just as the American Colonization Society sought to remove troublesome free Blacks from the Republic and transport them to Liberia. Robert Roberts's *The House Servant's Directory*, which I discuss below, was published just two years before Andrew Jackson was elected into the US presidency and just a few years before Jackson's Indian Removal Policies would authorize a new wave of Native dispersal and dispossession.

The criss-crossing networks of Black and Native itinerancy across New England were shaped by interlocking and autonomous conditions of dispossession and expropriation, the theft of land and labor, and the attraction for both Black Americans and Native Americans of Methodism, a denomination that required its preachers to travel and, more broadly, promoted an itinerant ethic of evangelist preaching and conversion. With Narragansett, Wampanoag, and African ancestry, Easton also represents the forms of Afro-Native identity and alliance that marked this moment in 1820s and 1830s New England. Afro-Native intellectuals and sailors like Paul Cuffee and Robert Benjamin

Lewis further illuminate the movements of Black, Native, and Afro-Native peoples across New England, as well as the intersections between the Black Atlantic and the "Red Atlantic."[20] Recent scholarship by Ron Welburn has illuminated that the so-called "colored" sections of northern cities also included Native American inhabitants, many of whom arrived in cities like Hartford, founded in an important Native crossroads, as a result of resigned or coerced departure from their lands. Welburn's research on the poet Ann Plato further suggests that Plato was likely not a Black American, as has been assumed because of her membership in James Pennington's Colored Congregational Church, but a Native American originally from the Long Island Sound in New York. It is likely that she, like others, was an Indian congregant of a mostly Black church.[21]

These elements create an obstinate immobility at the heart of Easton's *Treatise* as a *strategy* and perhaps even as an *aesthetic* in its own regard. Black writing and preaching of this period both reflected and forged an aesthetic out of conditions of disappointment and betrayal, an aesthetic shaded by melancholy, dispossession and death (as well as death as transition), and that produced a distinct affect and political orientation, one of waiting rather than *movement* or even *resistance*.[22] Easton, and his interlocutors insisted that this was a time during which Black people in the United States would need to wait and see. In the meantime, they would need strategies for surviving the wait.

The Art of Waiting

Strategies of survival by serviceable, patient, and political waiting were precisely what Hosea Easton's brother-in-law, Robert Roberts, subtly interleaved into the text of his 1827 *The House Servant's Directory, or A Monitor for Private Families*, exactly ten years before Easton published his *Treatise*. The first American handbook to be published by a servant for other servants, Roberts's text is also the first book by a Black American author to be published by a commercial press. As Kyla Wazana Tompkins has noted, Roberts's text is routinely cited in histories of housework and domesticity, but it has been largely ignored by literary scholars and cultural critics, "no doubt because of the avowedly apolitical and non-subversive tone of the book."[23] Like Easton's *Treatise*, the politics of *The House Servant's Directory* must be understood and excavated within the particularities of Black life in the opening decades of the nineteenth century, before the mainstream abolitionist movement re-wrote and rendered invisible the vibrant history of Black resistance that existed before the founding of the American Anti-Slavery Society in 1833.[24]

The House Servant's Directory differs from the *Treatise* in tone, genre, theme, and intended audience. Roberts's was a commercially published how-to manual for "footmen," cooks, and their employers, while Easton's was printed by the abolitionist Boston publisher Isaac Knapp and circulated with the explicit intention of raising funds for Easton's church community through its sale. While Easton was identified as a "colored man" on the title page of his *Treatise*, readers of *The House Servant's Directory* could read Roberts's text without realizing he was Black.[25] *The House Servant's Directory* was popular enough to warrant two subsequent editions; Easton's *Treatise* was "stranded" in the ways that Joanna Brooks talks about early Black books, which usually needed social movements to survive in and through circulation.[26] But for all these differences, both Easton's and Roberts's texts were undergirded by a similar orientation to the future: the sense that waiting could be a practical and political tool. For Roberts, the "art of waiting" signifies in multiple ways: as domestic service, as a virtuous patience, as waiting around, as biding one's time until another opportunity arises.

While ostensibly a simple and straightforward handbook for domestics, offering instruction on the "art of waiting," Roberts's handbook might also be read as a guide for surviving and weathering conditions of precariousness, unemployment, and dispossession that plagued "free" Black workers in the period. And while Roberts's text clearly targeted a broad audience, including employers and servants – Blacks, whites, and immigrants on their way to the privileges of whiteness – there is a personal and urgent tenor to his text that hails Black readers, especially young Black men, within the concreteness and specificities of their circumstances.[27] Of course, the figuration of the domestic house as a (relatively) safe space is highly gendered, and it seems quite clear that this was a fantasy largely unavailable to Black women working in white homes. Texts like Harriet Wilson's *Our Nig* (1859) exposed the white home as a space of torture and terror for Black women while Harriet Jacobs' *Incidents in the Life of a Slave Girl* (1861) focused on the regime of sexual terror enabled and promoted by the specificities of servitude within the house. Jacobs's and Wilson's narratives thus serve as reminders of the violations and perversities of "service" for Black women, along with the structures of (gendered/racialized/sexed) terror that don't make their way into Roberts's representation of service as a protection from a racist world.

Deploying the popular rhetorical strategy of friendly, paternal advice that could be found in a wide range of pedagogical texts in the period, Roberts addresses his advice to two "young friends," Joseph and David, who are about to enter into "gentleman's service."[28] Roberts's paternalistic tone lends him authority as a dispenser of advice in print , but it is also a tone that seeks to protect its young male readers from the conditions of vagrancy and homelessness that might result from being fired. In his introduction, he specifically signals the conditions of vagrancy that domestic employment might help to counter: "How many have we seen going about a city, like vagabonds, diseased in mind and body, and mere outcasts from all respectable society, and a burthen to themselves, therefor I sincerely wish that my young friends may fulfill their several duties with honesty, integrity, and due respect to their employers and fellow servants in general."[29] In this way, *The House Servant's Directory* reads like something like *The Negro Motorist Green Book* (1936–1966), or, in the era of Black Lives Matter and driving-while-Black, the various flyers and fact sheets circulating on how Black motorists and pedestrians can try to protect themselves during encounters with the anti-Black police. Roberts's *Directory* is a roadmap and guide to surviving public life in a racist regime, and, in this case, of maintaining employment and housing in the contexts of rampant racial prejudice, violence, and discrimination. If the Boston streets, as Easton so harrowingly describes them in his *Treatise*, were nothing but spaces of racist intimidation, insults, and threats, the white home, while filled with its own terrors, in Roberts's estimation, was preferable to being on the streets.

In keeping with the genre of nineteenth-century advice literature, Roberts's handbook is heavy-handed and moralistic. Throughout, he promotes a Puritanical work ethic as well as a series of Benjamin Franklin-inspired virtues, especially moderation, thrift, neatness, industry and near-silence (don't speak unless spoken to). Franklin's "rags to riches" story clearly resonated with Roberts's own sense of himself as a self-made man, from a humble young boy in Charleston, South Carolina to a cosmopolitan footman working for an elite Federalist in Boston. Roberts even named one of his sons Benjamin Franklin (the son would go on to become a shoemaker, activist, and radical printer who published his uncle Hosea's *Treatise* in 1837). In his book, Roberts counsels neatness and thrift in everything, and plenty of sections in the text carry a distinct tone of shaming: servants must not waste nor destroy their employers' property; they "should be submissive and polite" at all times; and they must "never make more noise in the parlour than [they] can possibly help."[30] But even so, those who take their time with the narrative (and literate servants surely would have spent more time reading the book than their employers would have) can find an entirely different ethic at play: of protecting young servants from the humiliations and dangers of service. Male servants must not dress foppishly since it doesn't make sense to go into debt for clothes (our "circumstances do not allow it"), but also because extravagant dress may make a servant visible to his employer in a way that could put his physical person or job in jeopardy.[31] Roberts's words on servant dress are thus ultimately concerned with how the servant might protect his employment, cover his ass (quite literally), and thus, survive "the wait" in service.

Such advice is also geared toward helping servants stay off the radar of their employers in order to evade constant surveillance and to adhere to the expectations that servants remain "invisible" within the home. In the North, this structure of invisibility allowed northern elites, even liberal ones, to partition off their use of live-in Black "help" from slaveholding practices in the South. As Harriet Wilson's *Our Nig* powerfully expresses, the *experience* of both indentured and "free" service for African Americans regularly mirrored enslavement, irrespective of differences in legal standing among slaves, indentured servants, and nominally free workers – lest we forget that employers of servants in the antebellum North were still called "masters" and "mistresses."

Early on in his introductory comments, Roberts says that he wants to share wisdom on the many things that servants must do so that their work might, simply, end at the end of the day. He offers a chapter on the benefits of rising early that might be read as a Puritanical lesson on the importance of hard work and subservience, but its real lesson is contained in the fact that "masters and mistresses" are demanding, unreasonable people who won't let a servant get anything done once they are awake. Another section on "Trimming and Cleaning Lamps" advises that "when you first hire with a family, let it be your first object to examine all your lamps and see that they are in order; and if not, let your employers know immediately.[32] This is the servant's equivalent of taking pictures of a new apartment so that a tenant has the proof of evidence when the landlord inevitably steals the security deposit.

Throughout, Roberts gives hints and advice on how servants might protect themselves and their employment from the charges and accusations of their employers. In another section addressed to "my respected employers" and titled, "A Word to Heads of Families," Roberts at first allies himself with his employers by denigrating his fellow servants. Striking a tone of familiarity appropriate only for the head servant in a home, he explains that his manual uses simple language since it is intended not for masters and mistresses but for the servant class, "whose ignorance is sometimes very troublesome."[33] But Roberts's deferral here is likely strategic, knowing that an employer who picked up the volume for his or her servants may have flipped to this section, and this section only, before handing it to the footman or cook. One also gets the sense that this statement about the "ignorance" of the "servant class" may simply be a projection of the employer's prejudices. The necessity of a volume filled with a servant's knowledge and expertise suggests that it was actually employers who were ignorant of how to run and manage a household.

Roberts also uses this paragraph to "my respected employers" to ingratiate himself to these readers before introducing several paragraphs that forcefully remind employers that their servants must be treated kindly, humanely, and with "liberality."[34] Like the other sections of the text, Roberts thus aims to protect his fellow servants from the destabilizing and violent whims of the master class. And when we remember that this is a Black writer not known to be Black by all of his readers, his advice to "masters" and "mistresses" is revealed as nothing less than a supremely subversive piece of rhetoric.

Perhaps most subversively, Roberts figures service as a form of study.[35] And importantly, Roberts presumes the literacy of servants. As a young man, he himself had arrived in Boston literate. Born in Charleston, South Carolina, possibly free but maybe enslaved, he may have first traveled to Boston with an earlier employer, the Boston financier Nathan Appleton, after he visited Charleston from 1802 to 1804.[36] Before the lockdown on Black literacy in the South that occurred in the wake of the circulation of David Walker's *Appeal* and Nat Turner's 1831 uprising, southern cities like Charleston valued the literacy of Black workers as a boon to trade and business.[37] Roberts's text thus registers a critical moment, a historical blip in the nineteenth century, really, during which Black literacy in the United States was not criminalized in ways that it would be beginning in the 1830s. After laying down the stark and brutal reality that "once you hire yourself to a lady or gentleman [. . .] all your time belongs to them," Roberts suggests that new servants "study" service, in order to "give general satisfaction to your employers" but also "to gain credit to yourself" in the eyes of your employers.[38] The collective nature of this form of study is emphasized when Roberts notes that one's fellow servants are "comrade servants," who might provide comfort and a sense of "being-with" often denied within the isolating structures of the private homes of private (white) families.[39] Here, we might think of "study" in terms of the traditional sense of book-learning, of availing oneself of the books and other reading materials that might be covertly apprehended in a white home. Additionally, though, study also speaks to the more revolutionary dimensions of how David Walker conceives of the important role of study for the oncoming/inevitable revolution: of studying white people so that one might take them down in the end. Indeed, Roberts was clearly interested in the forms of study that might help to make the "art of waiting" more bearable, but there is also a sense throughout the text that service might be turned into an opportunity for knowledge acquisition, of knowledge to be stored for future use. In this way, the (perceived) immobility of study could be a powerful tool of and for organization under cover.

While Roberts's advice regarding "comrade" study seems specifically directed at his male readers, the text encodes other circuits of study connected to women's labor in the house. As Tompkins argues, the hearth has long been associated with orality, reading, and writing, and Roberts's text posits the (female) cook's mouth as a source of both vulnerability (the pitfalls of gossip) and power: the "cooks power lies [. . .] in exercising orality: in eating and speaking."[40] Tompkins further links the mouth of the cook to the erotic, a function of activity not explicitly available to the footmen addressed in *The House Servant's Directory*. Tompkins' notion of "kitchen insurrections" illuminates the forms of revolt and protest that always threatened to emerge from the space of the kitchen, from women and their work. That threat could emerge from the position of immobility itself, such as the performance of mundane housework, and from the performance of patience. Here, the metaphorical resonances of Harriet Jacobs' garret, not just with the shackles of enslavement, but also with the restricted, confining spaces of domestic service found in both the "free" North and the slave South, serve as a reminder that Black women's subversion and resistance within service had to come from spaces and experiences of even greater confinement and surveillance than Black male servants. Given the gendering of cooking as "women's work," we might further think about the "shadow texts" of *The House Servant's Directory* in the way that Kevin Young talks about the "shadow book," or those Black texts that have been lost, remained unfinished, or were conceived but never begun because of various historical contingencies.[41] In this case, the "shadow texts" of *The House Servant's Directory* might include Black women's knowledge and writing, including recipes and other kitchen "formulas" that Roberts could have used or adapted for his own purposes in his manual.

The Stable House/Unstable Frontier

The House Servant's Directory is a text borne out of the conditions of historical and economic transition, including the broad reorganization of labor across an expanding, imperial nation. Roberts's text occupies a historical moment that was witnessing the national "innovation" in slavery that Edward Baptist and Walter Johnson have discussed, the expansion and intensification of slave labor through the transformation of the US South into an economy defined by monocultures of cotton production on plantations across the region.[42] As a text that clearly wants to disconnect the noble duties of the servant from the degraded condition of the slave (even though, and perhaps because, the form of their labor often *looked* so similar), *The House Servant's Directory* ignores plantation slavery – and the slave – altogether. Roberts's text is, in this way, more backward- than forward-looking; it resonates more with the isolating, lonely forms of slavery in colonial New England that Wendy Warren has discussed than with the soul breaking but thoroughly "collective" forms of slavery in the cotton fields that would begin to define the representation of slavery itself in the 1830s.[43] The invisibility of Roberts's race in the text, his packaging as just a "servant" rather than as a Black servant, might be further linked to Joanne Melish's argument about New England's amnesiac, willful forgetting of its own very recent slave past.[44] In such a scenario, the actual presence of Black people in New England could serve as a kind of "return of the repressed" in human form for a region intent on forgetting its slaveholding roots. Practically, the erasure of Roberts's status as a (politically active) freeman in Boston likely garnered him a larger readership, including many white and immigrant readers in and beyond the northeast.

While the figure and the history of the slave is kept at bay throughout the text, *The House Servant's Directory* does register the changing racialization and gendering of domestic labor already underway in Roberts's New England in the 1820s. As Graham Russell Hodges writes in his 1998 introduction to Roberts's handbook, "The world of domestics was rapidly changing in this decade [the 1820s], when the final demise of slavery in the North, its replacement by free wage labor, the rise of middle-income families, and the entrance of women, many of them Irish, into competition for jobs in such homes were rapidly making traditional [male] servants like Roberts obsolete."[45] In this way, rather than positing *The House Servant's Directory* as a path-forging text, I want to hinge upon it as an almost anachronistic one: it is a text that reflects a weakening, withering early Republic along with its founding structures and sociopolitical organizations rather than an emergent order. At a time when Black men were decreasingly finding positions as footmen because of the whitening and feminization of domestic labor in the North, Roberts counsels those readers on how to clutch onto a form of employment – and a form of life – that was becoming increasingly scarce.

Roberts's text thus performs a kind of stasis and a stability in the face of conditions of dispossession and oppression. He speaks to the reserve army as if they are already employed, or surely on the cusp of employment, rather than what they were: structurally under-employed and only intermittently employed. But despite Roberts's performance of stability, repeatedly noting his long tenure "as a house servant in some of the first families in England, France, and America," the book itself is enmeshed in the racial politics of un/under-employment and dispossession.[46] Published just two weeks after the death of his employer and "master," former Massachusetts governor and senator, Christopher Gore, Roberts may have viewed the publication of his handbook as a pathway to securing his own future and finances after his employment for Gore ended. He clearly wanted to use the opportunity presented by Gore's long illness and eventual death: he began selling his book, complete with a prefatory endorsement from Gore himself, right when news of his death was circulating in and beyond newspaper obituaries. And given the fact that Gore was already ill when Roberts began working for him at his lavish country estate in Waltham, outside of Boston, Roberts may have been planning his *Directory* for a long time. James Miller notes that after the 1827 publication of his book, and after Gore's death, Roberts never again worked as a domestic servant.[47] Roberts's rhetorical performance of his own secure status as a long-standing servant was thus published right at the moment when he was no longer working as a servant. He preaches subservience and contentment to servants in order to escape the yoke of service. He promotes the art of waiting so he no longer has to wait.

But the performance of stability was not just the province of the oppressed. Anglo-elites like Gore were also clutching onto a way of life while the world changed around them. In Hodges' terms, the orchestration of gentility, formality, and manners within Federalist homes in the period was performed in opposition to the disorder of emerging "Democratic" mores and politics. Hodges notes that servants were critical in maintaining the gentility of Federalist dining and manners in an age of perceived "barbarism" that culminated in the 1829 election of Andrew Jackson: "Roberts's instructions reveal how carefully servants had to partake in these ceremonies of decorum intended to set elite families, such as the

Gores, *apart from the roguery of Jacksonian America*."[48] At the same time as servants were hailed into the labor of erecting symbolic and physical barricades against the wild vagaries of Jacksonian "roguery," the "civilized" home was also imagined as a kind of domestic garrison that, in Roberts's text, protects employers and servants alike against the dangers of the colonial frontier. *The House Servant's Directory* thus spectrally references ongoing anxieties about Native revolt and frontier violence, even as Native peoples were being "domesticated" and further dispossessed in the period. In this way, the text registers the uneasy alliances also found in Lucy Terry Prince's, "Bars Fight" (1746; 1855), the orally-transmitted ballad that recounts the deaths of whitesettlers in Deerfield, Massachusetts in 1746 at the hands of Natives seemingly moved to violence without provocation, a poem that reinforces negative stereotypes about Indians, while placing Black "settlers" on the side of the settler colonials rather than the Native peoples.[49]

The peppering of commodities from Asia throughout Roberts's recipes and instructions, including silk, tea, and even soy sauce, offers further glimpses of forms of subjugated labor in Pacific locales like tea plantations in India and coffee plantations in Java. The spectral presence of East Asian plantation workers in the *Directory* in mundane instructions on how to "Clean Japanned Tea and Coffee Urns," for example, enmesh Roberts and this world of New England service within a broader, multi-racial world of subjugation and coerced labor across global networks of European empire and imperialism. At the same time, the presence of Pacific commodities in the New England household looks forward to the forms of East Asian contract labor that replaced enslaved labor after the legal end of slavery in the mid-nineteenth century.[50] Closer to home, the spectral "savage" in Roberts's text brings into view networks of Native itinerancy and forced migration that overlapped, but also differed from the experiences of Black New Englanders of the period in key ways. Despite the protections afforded by the white home, then, Roberts's text registers the cultural instabilities and movements that defined a broader world of commodity exchange and movement, which disproportionately affected racialized populations in and beyond New England.

Southern Movements

In this period before the flowering of African American literature under the authorizing aegis of the Abolition movement, Black authorship was routinely obscured through the processes of editing, printing, circulation, and the unregulated yet completely normal practice of reprinting in American publishing.[51] But as Lara Langer Cohen and Jordan Alexander Stein have argued, depersonalization through print could afford certain possibilities for Black writers.[52] In the case of Roberts, the depersonalization of his text through circulation – a depersonalization that increased with distance from his hometown – brought him a wider audience (and presumably, more profit). Roberts's employer was a well-known, public figure in New England, and the *Directory's* prefatory advertisement carried an endorsement from Gore himself. Some readers in Boston may have known for certain that Gore's servant was Black. Roberts's Black readers in the city surely knew he was, though his "non-political" text was not reviewed in the *Freedom's Journal* or in the *Liberator* (which had a majority of African American subscribers). Roberts's family rented a house in the city's sixth ward, and he was involved with Black organizations and politics in the city, including the movement against the American Colonization Society. As the text circulated further from Boston, Roberts's text became "less Black": disconnected from local connections and coordinates, the text itself did not signal Roberts's race, nor explicitly address the situations of Black servants, or African diasporic people more generally.

The House Servant's Directory thus raises questions about the place of seemingly non-political texts in African American literary history.[53] When contextualized from the vantage of circulation, it becomes clear that the de-racialization of Roberts's book actually allowed it to become a subversive, even political text, working undetected in the least likely of places: the plantation South. In the South, the *House Servants' Directory* circulated detached from Robert's name, identity, and intentions. But re-contextualized within a slave system that was increasingly surveilling slave communication, Roberts's text became political by its very presence in the South. It was nothing less than a Black text circulating undercover. A brief advertisement for the *Directory* appeared in the *National Journal* in Washington, D.C., and another in the September 17, 1830, issue of the *Charleston Mercury* noted that the book would be "very valuable to heads of families," and was available at book-seller "S. Babcok & C.," alongside other titles on household management, including "'The Frugal Housewife,' by the author of Hobomok [Lydia Maria Child].'" Most spectacularly, the *Lynchburg Virginian* reprinted an entire section of *The House Servant's Directory* on the front page of its August 10, 1829 issue. As Lori Leavell argues, Black writers circulated in the antebellum South more than scholars have realized. Her research reveals that white southerners were aware of an emerging Black literature and they even read some of the texts.[54] But published without Roberts's name or a note about his identity, readers of the *Lynchburg Virginian*, including proslavery readers and slaveholders themselves, were unlikely to know or even think of the possibility that they were reading a Black text. They may have even thought they were reading advice from a fellow slaveholder. The editor of the paper may have thought the same thing.

Reflecting the prevalence of reprinting in American publishing in the early antebellum era, the *Lynchburg Virginian* reprints the section of *The House Servant's Directory* titled "A Word to Heads of Families," a section that itself relies on an excerpt from William Kitchiner's best-selling cookbook, *The Cook's Oracle*.[55] Roberts himself addresses his excerpting of Kitchiner (an attribution often not made in this age of rampant literary appropriation), noting "it would be presumption in me, a servant, to urge aught on this subject to my superiors."[56] Tellingly, the excerpt chosen by the *Lynchburg Virginian* begins with the writer-servant's statement of subservience and deferral to his superiors. The paper excises Roberts's actual opening in the section, which addresses his employers. Excising the language of "employer" in favor of the language of "master" found throughout the extract from Kitchiner, *The House Servant's Directory*, through excision and re-contextualization, is made to speak to and for a slave society. At the same time, the excerpt's re-signification of "master" within a master–slave context reveals the regimes of unfreedom and tyranny that also structured "free" domestic labor in the North. Similarly, the use of "servant" throughout the excerpt reveals the instability and slipperiness of that term on both sides of the Mason-Dixon line, as well as the long-standing practice of calling slaves servants in order to obscure their true status as property. Despite his opening deferral to Kitchiner's text, the "master" text from which Roberts cites, the erasure of Roberts's identity actually enables him to address white southern readers, including slave masters, and to do so as a peer rather than a servant. Arguably, the pedagogical tone of advice literature actually elevated his position over his readers. Like many of Phillis Wheatley's poems, didactic genres, while restricting and formulaic, allowed writers of color to "school" white readers from a position of cultural authority and knowledge. And as in northern contexts, Roberts uses Kitchiner's authority, and status as a white man, to insist that slaves/servants must be treated well by their "masters" and "mistresses." Meredith McGill has written about how reprinting often produced radical forms of decontextualization. In this case, such decontextualization allowed for a work of early African American literature to be (positively) featured on the front page of a southern newspaper, and for its free Black author to speak directly to a white southern readership, including slaveholders.

Despite the foundational role that Atlantic frameworks have played in the study of slave and post-slave cultures over the past two decades, they do not necessarily help to capture the forms of precariousness that plagued African Americans in urban environments in the period, including those forms of dispossession that could result in interminable confinements within northern, liberal institutions. Atlantic frameworks also often miss the rivers, creeks, and other coastal and inland bodies of water that have long been central to the lives and movements of indigenous people in the Native northeast. Indeed, from a Native perspective, the nineteenth-century northeast itself was not necessarily a land mass increasingly demarcated into the "city" and the "country," but still a complex network of waterways connecting Native homelands and crossroads.[57] Recent scholarship suggests that the framework of the Black Atlantic should not be discarded but instead put in closer conversation with additional archives, methods, and networks of movement and circulation, as well as with structures of immobility that operated in tandem with forms of coerced and chosen mobility.[58]

Despite their suggestiveness, tracking the subversions of Roberts's text-in-circulation might ultimately reflect the obliqueness of Black agency and evasiveness of mobility in the post-Revolutionary/pre-abolitionist phase of US history. The conditions of Roberts's world meant that his text had to be subversive rather than revolutionary. It is certainly possible to find in Robert Roberts's life an uplifting story about upward mobility and increasing stability across the decades of the antebellum period. The success of Roberts's book suggests that he never again had to work as a domestic servant (at least no records have been found suggesting he continued in this line of work). When he passed away in his eighties in 1860, on the cusp of a series of radical transitions and transformations produced by the Civil War, he was known as a community leader, a property-owner, and one of the wealthiest African Americans in the city at the time. But Hodges also notes that from 1828 to 1860, city directories listed Roberts's occupation as a "stevedore," a job that entailed unloading goods from ships in port.[59] The date range also indicates that Roberts began working Boston's port the year after the death of Gore and worked there right up through the year of his death. His last years were thus still marked by the conditions of his labor, not leisure and luxury.

No longer laboring within his Federalist employer's house and its structures of patient waiting, Robert's work as a stevedore enmeshed him within the tempos and geographies of Atlantic resistance, organization, and activity (though of course, sailors endured their own waits in between contracts/voyages at sea, as well as through the immobilities of impressment at sea). More specifically, Roberts's post-servant labor opens up a space to think about African Americans in the period who benefited from working *near* rather than *at* sea; a kind of port or shore intellectual positionality that allowed someone like David Walker to transmit his text to sailors and other maritime agents who could connect urban centers with plantations and plantation slaves. While surviving records document Roberts's involvement in the anti-colonization movement and the Black conventions movement, serving as a delegate to the National Convention of Free People of Color in the 1830s, we might also meditate on the furtive forms of communication and political organization that may have been enabled by his work unloading cargo from ships. In other words, we might also consider forms of politics – and engagement with a movement – that simply elude organizational records, newspaper notices, and other surviving documentation of Black activism and organizing in the period.[60]

In a fascinating way, Roberts's post-servant life illuminates that Black performances of stability on land were often forged in a dialectical relation with the realities of wandering/restlessness and riotous movement that defined life on the North Atlantic. As Bolster notes, in the decades following the Revolutionary War, the wages of Black sailors crucially "underwrote organizations such as churches and benevolent societies through which black America established an institutional presence and a voice."[61] In this way, the dangerous travels and relentless movement of sailors on the Black Atlantic actually helped to make possible the solid ground and stability that Black organization-building sought to establish in and for communities on land. "Maritime rhythms" also affected and accented many women's lives, as women took care of business at home while "waiting" for their husbands to return from stints at sea that could last weeks, months, or even years.[62] Some women waited, and others moved on.

Interestingly, the *Lynchburg Virginian* leaves out the final paragraph in "A Word to Heads of Families" from Roberts's book. Roberts's original text reads, "If the master and mistress of a family will sometimes condescend to make an amusement of this art, they will escape a number of disappointments, &c. which those who will not, must suffer, to the detriment of both their health and their fortune."[63] The excision of this final piece of advice could be chalked up, simply, to a lack of space: reprinted texts were often truncated for this reason within the fast-paced world of editing and cutting in nineteenth-century newspaper culture. But this seemingly mundane reminder that readers should heed the writer's advice regarding the proper treatment of servants would have carried a more sinister subtext in a southern context. In a South on constant watch for slave subversion, such language would have raised the specter of slave revolt and resistance. Kept in, Roberts's advice would have found kinship with the ideas of Nat Turner, David Walker, and other men and women who incited and planned slave revolts and organized actions in the South. It thus places Roberts closer to someone like Denmark Vesey, the former slave and "shore intellectual" who planned a revolt in Roberts's native Charleston, SC in 1822.

Robert Roberts's writing shows up in another publication in the period (his name also occasionally appeared in periodical publications in connection to his political involvements), this time enabled by the rise of white abolitionist organizations in Boston in the 1830s and their connections to the channels of publication. The first pamphlet in a series of publications entitled the "abolitionist's Library" and presented to the public by the Boston Young Men's Anti-Slavery Association for the Diffusion of Truth. The second, *Despotism of Freedom* (1834), prints a version of David Lee Child's speech at the first anniversary of the New England Anti-Slavery Society, and concludes with a set of affidavits from Black men in Boston giving first- and second-hand accounts of free men being kidnapping into slavery, including one from Roberts. Paralleling Hosea Easton's androcentric family history offered in his 1837 *Treatise* (violence and trauma tracked only through male family members), Roberts's contribution is an intergenerational and traumatic history in which he recounts the cases of three free men who were carried off and transported into slavery, two of whom were never heard from again. Laying out each case individually, and then dramatically revealing that all three of these men were the sons of his father-in-law, Jude Hall, Roberts's account shows that the systematic destruction of Black kinship did not only happen in the slave South. In so doing, his writing once again indicates the importance of "sheltering in place" for people of African descent in the early nineteenth century: the politics of stasis/immobility as a response to the conditions of emergency.

Notes

1 Robert Roberts, *The House Servant's Directory, or a Monitor for Private Families: Comprising Hints on the Arrangement and Performance of Servants' Work, with General Rules for Setting Out Tables and Sideboards in First Order;*

and the Art of Waiting in All Its Branches (Boston: Munroe and Francis, 1927). Subsequent citations come from the Dover edition of the text, which republishes the work as it appeared in 1827. See Robert Roberts, *The House Servant's Directory: An African American Butler's 1827 Guide* (Mineola, NY: Dover, 2006).

2 "Stasis," *Oxford English Dictionary*, www.oed.com.

3 Graham Russell Hodges, "Introduction," in *The House Servant's Directory* (Armonk, New York: M.E. Sharpe, 1998), xiii, xxxvi.

4 John Sekora, "Black Message/White Envelope: Genre, Authenticity, and Authority in the Antebellum Slave Narrative," *Callaloo* 32 (1987): 482–515.

5 For more on the Hartford riots and Easton, see David Swift, *Black Prophets of Justice: Activist Clergy before the Civil War* (Baton Rouge: Louisiana State Press, 1989). Easton served as a minister of the AME Zion Church in Hartford prior to his death in 1838; The AMEZ church originally shared space with the colored Congregationalist church in Hartford, the church to which Plato belonged and which Pennington led. See ibid., 176–177.

6 Easton, "Preface," *A Treatise on the Intellectual Character and Civil and Political Condition of the Colored People of the U. States* (Boston: Isaac Knapp, 1837), n.p.

7 On the rise and decline theory of civilization in universal/world history in the eighteenth and nineteenth centuries, see Stephen G. Hall, *A Faithful Account of the Race: African American Historical Writing in Nineteenth-Century America* (Chapel Hill: University of North Carolina Press, 2009).

8 Easton, *Treatise*, 52.

9 In *Fugitive Science: Empiricism and Freedom in Early African American Culture* (New York: NYU Press, 2017), I suggest that Black intellectuals in the 1820s and 1830s, including Maria Stewart, David Walker and Easton, often expressed ideas that today would be called Afro-pessimist. For an introduction to Afro-pessimism, see Frank Wilderson, *Red, White & Black: Cinema and the Structure of U. S. Antagonisms* (Durham, NC: Duke University Press, 2010).

10 Easton, *Treatise*, 24.

11 Throughout, Easton's *Treatise* traffics in the "monstrosities" of disability in order to emphasize the horrors of enslavement.

12 On the expansion of slavery to fuel the US's growing role in the global cotton economy, see Walter Johnson, *River of Dark Dreams: Slavery and Empire in the Cotton Kingdom* (Cambridge, MA: Harvard University Press, 2013); Edward E. Baptist, *The Half Has Never Been Told: Slavery and the Making of American Capitalism* (New York: Basic Books, 2014); Sven Beckert, *Empire of Cotton: A Global History* (New York: Alfred A. Knopf, 2015).

13 On the history (and forgetting) of slavery in New England, see Joanne Pope Melish, *Disowning Slavery: Gradual Emancipation and "Race" in New England, 1780–1860* (Ithaca, NY: Cornell University Press, 1998).

14 James Oliver Horton and Lois E. Horton, *Black Bostonians: Family Life and Community Struggle in the Antebellum North* (New York: Holmes & Meier Publishers, 1979), 53.

15 See, for example, David Walker's *Appeal to the Coloured Citizens of the World* (College Park: Penn State University Press, 2009), the *Freedom's Journal*, Hosea Easton's 1837 *Treatise* (which I address below), and the speeches and writing of Maria Stewart in *Maria W. Stewart, America's First Black Woman Political Writer: Essays and Speeches*, ed. Marilyn Richardson (Bloomington: Indiana University Press, 1987).

16 Horton and Horton, *Black Bostonians*, 15–26.

17 W. Jeffrey Bolster, *Black Jacks: African American Seamen in the Age of Sail* (Cambridge, MA: Harvard University Press, 1997), 4.

18 Ibid.

19 On the evolvement and entrenchment of theories of Indian difference in the nineteenth century, see Maureen Konkle, *Writing Indian Nations: Native Intellectuals and the Politics of Historiography, 1827–1863* (Chapel Hill: University of North Carolina, 2004), and Sean P. Harvey, *Native Tongues: Colonialism and Race from Encounter to the Reservation* (Cambridge, MA: Harvard University Press, 2015).

20 Jace Weaver, *The Red Atlantic: American Indigenes and the Making of the Modern World, 1000–1927* (Chapel Hill: University of North Carolina Press, 2015), 86–98.

21 Ron Welburn, *Hartford's Ann Plato and the Borders of Native Identity* (Albany, NY: SUNY Press, 2015).

22 My thinking on waiting in early African American literature of this period was first inspired by Amanda Waugh Lagji's dissertation, "Waiting for Now: Postcolonial Literature and Colonial Time" (University of Massachusetts Amherst, English, 2017).

23 Kyla Wazana Tompkins, *Racial Indigestion: Eating Bodies in the 19th Century* (New York: New York University Press, 2012), 46–47. Roberts has also showed up recently in emerging media coverage on Black American cooks and cookbooks. See, for example, Amanda Mouiz, "A Meal to Honor Early African-American Cookbook Authors," *NPR*, last modified 5 February 2014, www.npr.org.

24 While scholars have productively expanded the genres that "count" as African American literature, especially in the dynamic world of nineteenth-century print, texts like Easton's *Treatise* and Robert's *The House Servant's Directory* still seem marginal to narratives we tell about the politics, forms, and affects of Black literature. On the importance of expanding the genres and representational politics of African American literature, see Jordan Alexander Stein and Lara Langer Cohen, "Introduction," in *Early African American Print Culture* (Philadelphia: University of Pennsylvania Press, 2012), 1–18; Gene Andrew Jarrett, *Deans and Truants: Race and Realism in African American Literature* (Philadelphia: University of Pennsylvania Press, 2006); Gene Andrew Jarrett, ed., *African American Literature Beyond Race: An Alternative Reader* (New

York: New York University Press, 2006); Gene Andrew Jarrett, *Representing the Race: A New Political History of African American Literature* (New York: New York University Press, 2011).

25 Book reviews of the *Directory* highlight Roberts's many years of experience in service but do not mention that he is Black. See, for example, reviews in *Columbian Centinel* (Boston), May 23, 1827; *Poulson's American Daily Advertiser* (Philadelphia), March 31, 1827; *The Boston Statesman*, November 22, 1828; *The Critic: A Weekly Review of Literature, Fine Arts, and the Drama*, ed. William Leggett (New York), 1829: 157. *The House Servant's Directory* was not reviewed in the Black press.

26 Joanna Brooks, "The Unfortunates: What the Life Spans of Early Black Books Tell Us About Book History," in *Early African American Print Culture*, ed. Stein and Cohen, 51–52.

27 Such multivocality also characterizes Walker's *Appeal*, which shifts its addressees across the text, from free people to slaves, slave holders, and "liberal" white northerners.

28 Roberts, *The House Servant's Directory*, 11.

29 Ibid., ixi.

30 Ibid., 49.

31 Ibid., 61.

32 Ibid., 21.

33 Ibid., 122.

34 Ibid., 123.

35 On the revolutionary practice of study, see Fred Moten and Stefano Harney, *The Undercommons: Fugitive Planning and Black Study* (Brooklyn: Minor Compositions, 2013) and Jacques Ranciere, *The Ignorant Schoolmaster: Five Lessons in Intellectual Emancipation*, trans. Kristin Ross (Palo Alto: Stanford University Press, 1991).

36 James Miller, "Publisher's Note," in *The House Servant's Directory*, iii–iv; Hodges, "Editor's Introduction," in *The House Servant's Directory*, xv.

37 Grey Gundaker, "Give Me a Sign: African Americans, Print, and Practice," in *A History of the Book in America: An Extensive Republic: Print, Culture, and Society in the New Nation, 1790-1840*, vol. 2, ed. Robert A. Gross and Mary Kelley (Chapel Hill: University of North Carolina Press, 2010), 490.

38 Robert, *The House Servant's Directory*, 12–13.

39 Ibid., 56.

40 Tompkins, *Racial Indigestion*, 44, 50.

41 Kevin Young, *The Grey Album: On the Blackness of Blackness* (Minneapolis: Graywolf Press, 2012).

42 Baptist, *The Half Has Never Been Told*; Johnson, *River of Dark Dreams*.

43 Wendy Warren, *New England Bound: Slavery and Colonization in Early America* (New York: Liveright, 2016).

44 Melish, *Disowning Slavery*.

45 Hodges, "Editor's Introduction," in *The House Servant's Directory*, xix.

46 Roberts, *The House Servant's Directory*, xix.

47 Miller, "Publisher's Note," in *The House Servant's Directory*, iii.
48 Hodges, "Editor's Introduction," in *The House Servant's Directory*, xxxv; emphasis added.
49 Like Roberts's *Directory*, the transmission of Prince's ballad was heavily mediated by the interests and motivations of local white interlocutors. "Bars Fight" was transmitted orally for decades by white residents of Deerfield and did not appear in print until 1855 when it was published in Josiah Gilbert Holland, *History of Western Massachusetts*, vol. 2 (Springfield, MA: Samuel Bowles and Co., 1855), 359. For more on Lucy Terry Prince, see Gretchen Gerzina, *Mr. and Mrs. Prince: How an Extraordinary Eighteenth-Century Family Moved Out of Slavery and Into Legend* (New York: Amistad, 2008).
50 Lisa Lowe, *The Intimacies of Four Continents* (Durham, NC: Duke University Press, 2016).
51 See, for example, in an earlier moment, the different ways that John Marrant's authorship was packaged in editions of his *Narrative of the Lord's Wonderful Dealings with John Marrant* (1785). See *"Face Zion Forward: First Writers of the Black Atlantic, 1785–1798*, ed. Joanna Brooks and John Saillant (Boston: Northeastern University Press, 2002). On antebellum reprinting practices, see Meredith McGill, *American Literature and the Culture of Reprinting, 1834–1853* (Philadelphia: University of Pennsylvania, 2003).
52 Cohen and Stein, "Introduction," in *Early African American Print Culture*, 14–15.
53 See Jarrett, *Deans and Truants*; Jarrett, *Representing the Race*; Frances Smith Foster, "A Narrative of the Interesting Origins and (Somewhat) Surprising Developments of African-American Print Culture, *American Literary History* 17, no. 4 (Winter 2005): 714–740.
54 Lori Leavell, *Recirculating Radical: Black Authorship, Materiality, and Literary Impact in Antebellum America* (book manuscript in progress).
55 Kitchiner's *The Cook's Oracle* was first published in 1817 in England. It appeared in many American editions, including one printed by Roberts's own publisher in Boston in 1823. That edition may very well have served as the source-text for the excerpts found in *The House Servant's Directory*. See *The Cook's Oracle* (Boston: Monroe and Francis, 1823).
56 Roberts, *The House Servant's Directory*, 123; "From the House Servant's Directory. A Word to the Heads of Families," *The Lynchburg Virginian*, August 10, 1829.
57 Lisa Brooks, *Common Pot: The Recovery of Native Space in the Native Northeast* (Minneapolis: University of Minnesota Press, 2008).
58 Lowe, *The Intimacies of Four Continents*; Edlie Wong, *Racial Reconstruction: Black Inclusion, Chinese Exclusion, and the Fictions of Citizenship* (New York: New York University Press, 2015); Weaver, *The Red Atlantic*; Robbie Shilliam, *The Black Pacific: Anti-colonial Struggles and Oceanic Connections* (London: Bloomsbury, 2015); Samantha Pinto, *Difficult Diasporas: The Transnational Feminist Aesthetic of the Black Atlantic* (New York: NYU Press, 2013).

59 Hodges, "Editor's Introduction," in *The House Servant's Directory*, xx.
60 For the extensive records of the Black conventions movement, see *Colored Conventions*, http://coloredconventions.org.
61 Bolster, *Black Jacks*, 4.
62 Ibid., 5.
63 Roberts, *The House Servant's Directory*, 126.

CHAPTER 6

Dream Visions in Early Black Autobiography; Or, Why Frederick Douglass Doesn't Dream

Bryan Sinche

> For God speaketh once, yea twice, yet man perceiveth it not. In a dream, in a vision of the night, when deep sleep falleth upon men, in slumberings upon the bed; Then he openeth the ears of men, and sealeth their instruction . . .[1]
>
> Job 33:14–16

Over the past century of African American writing and political speech, there is no more potent idea than "the dream" invoked by Martin Luther King, Jr. during his 1963 speech on the National Mall. This still unrealized dream of a fundamentally just United States recalled the deferred dream of Langston Hughes's "Harlem" to which Lorraine Hansberry alluded in *A Raisin in the Sun*. And, looking forward, King's dream remained a potent force for Barack Obama, whose *Dreams From My Father* testifies to the enduring significance of the dream for Black Americans. For Hughes, Hansberry, King, and Obama, the dream obtains rhetorical significance insofar as it might be linked to hopefulness about the future; dreamers imagine a time to come when Black Americans will have access to the same possibilities as white Americans. These dreams, all of which gain their unifying power because they are publicly declared, speak to possibility and the eventual realization of community goals.

As a defining feature of African American speech and writing, the dream has a long history, and its earliest invocations remind us that – like any trope – dreams have served very different purposes depending on the rhetorical situation in which they were employed. Whereas leaders like King and Obama shared their dreams with others, early Black spiritual autobiographers used their dreams and visions to authorize themselves as religious and community leaders.[2] Such visions appear in a number of pre-1830 narratives and are characterized by the narrator's interactions with the incredible, the divine, or the phantasmagorical. It is important to remember that the presence of the dream in narrative is not evidence of an actual dream; rather, the dream is a rhetorical tool, a useful device for achieving particular narrative ends. Because dreams are idiosyncratic and unreal, describing those dreams allows narrators to communicate important ideas or goals that might be heterodox or forbidden. Moreover, since it is both personal and imaginary, the dream is entirely unverifiable. Or, perhaps it might be better to say that the reality of a dream is no different from its narration. This combination of imagination and narration is one reason early African American autobiographers made use of the dream vision as a rhetorical trope: the dream preserves a fictional space within a fact-based narrative. Within these fictional spaces, narrators could offer up visions of justice, morality, and faithfulness that deviated from white, European, and/or Christian norms. They could produce versions of self that were more capable, more powerful, or more insightful than the men who controlled the dominant institutions in the colonies and early United States. Ultimately, narrators could use dreams to make claims on their readers and – at the same time – to authorize their own actions in a world of prohibitions.

Inaugurating the Tradition

The rhetorical power of the dream vision finds its first evocation in one of the founding texts of African American autobiography: Olaudah Equiano's *Narrative* (1789). Equiano is a crucial figure for many reasons, and he stands out among early Black autobiographers for his ability to write and produce his text on his own terms.[3] Part of that ability stems from his intelligence, acumen, and networking, but another key component in helping Equiano achieve his commercial and narrative success is his use of the dream vision as a form of divine authorization for speech and status.

The first volume of Equiano's *Narrative* concludes with an image of a storm-tossed ship and a quotation from Job: "Thus God speaketh once, yea, twice, yet Man perceiveth it not. In a Dream in a Vision of the Night, when deep sleep falleth upon Men, on slumbrings upon the Bed: Then he openeth the Ears of Men & sealeth their instruction."[4] This quotation from Job is actually spoken by Elihu as he responds to Job's complaints about his own suffering. Elihu tries to explain to Job that God has been speaking to him through physical pains and other trials, and he indicates that God also communicates with man through dreams or night visions. Whether or not Equiano's readers were familiar with this particular quotation, they would have understood its significance to Equiano because of its place in his book: the image and quotation appear on the final pages and serve as both a preview of and advertisement for the second volume of the *Interesting Narrative*. While it is true that the image of a ship amidst a stormy sea offers readers a glimpse of the adventures that make up the second volume, Equiano's decision to append a biblical quotation to that image indicates that he wanted to highlight something more than the maritime settings of the second volume. Indeed, Equiano shows his readers that God has spoken to him and that his words carry a divine sanction.

In the second volume, readers realize why that divine sanction matters as Equiano relates his remarkable night vision: "I dreamt the ship was wrecked amidst the surfs and rocks, and that I was the means of saving every one on board; and on the night following I dreamed the very same dream."[5] After another night during which Equiano sees the same vision yet again, he awakens to find his ship amongst rocks and breakers and works tirelessly to save the crew from certain death. In the aftermath, the "dream now returned upon [his] mind with all its force; it was fulfilled in every part." Equiano the dreamer becomes Equiano the doer, and the divine warnings he receives through his dreams enable him to become the "principal instrument in effecting our deliverance."[6]

The scriptural citation that Equiano chooses to precede his tale gives a strong indication of how he and future narrators think about dreams; those who see visions are those whom God has chosen. And when Equiano compares his dream knowledge to his experience in the waking world, he finds that God has indeed selected him. Amidst the confusion of surging waves and threatening rocks, Equiano realizes that he serves an incompetent captain, but still he, "remembered the Lord" and "thought that as he had often delivered he might yet deliver."[7] That deliverance takes the form of inventiveness, and Equiano "began to think how we might be saved; and I believe no mind was ever like mine so replete with inventions and confused with schemes, though how to escape death I knew not."[8] It is through his own creativity, bravery, and savvy that Equiano manages to save the entire crew and cargo of twenty slaves, and he insists that "if any of these people had been lost, God would charge [him] with their lives."[9] Just as he had chosen Job, God also chose Equiano. Because he was chosen by God, Equiano was authorized to act despite his marginal position in both the command structure of the vessel and the prevailing racial hierarchy; by acting in response to God's choice and saving the ship from physical destruction, Equiano saves himself from spiritual ruin. This moment of empowerment is every bit as arresting and significant as those moments associated with the "trope of the talking book," and it provides an entirely different kind of warrant for speaking and writing: specifically, a divine warrant.

Equiano's use of the dream in his *Narrative* inaugurates a tradition in early autobiographies that was followed up by George White (1810), Boyrereau Brinch (1810), and Jarena Lee (1836). After Lee, the dream takes on very different forms in African American autobiographies. One reason for this shift is undoubtedly the dawning of the abolition movement in the 1830s; within the confines of that political movement, Black and white writers were constrained to tell a certain kind of story in a certain way, and the imaginative space offered by the dream vision may have seemed less useful and less attractive.[10] Indeed, as the slave narrative came to rely upon white authorities who could vouch for the character of former slaves and verify the accuracy of their accounts, the dreaming Black slave may have become a political liability. Absent the mechanisms of an abolition movement that might give shape and meaning to their life stories, White, Lee, and Brinch highlight their personal experiences and create entirely new forms in which they make sense of those experiences. Like Equiano, they highlight the power of divine authorization as both a personal force and a narrative device.[11]

George White and Jarena Lee: "My Mind was Led to Embrace the Divine Promises"

George White was born a slave in Accomack, Virginia, in 1764 and obtained his freedom in 1790 when his master died and emancipated White. In his autobiography, White skips over the period of his enslavement in just a few paragraphs; his story truly begins when he considers that "as God in his providence had delivered [White] from temporal bondage, it was [his] duty to look to [God] for deliverance from the slavery of sin."[12] From the beginning, then, White's concerns are not political but spiritual. Indeed, the slavery with which White contends for most of his narrative is that of sin, which presents torments greater than the physical and psychological pains White endured during the first twenty-six years of his life. Some thirteen years after he had left Maryland for New York and joined the Methodist church in his new home, White had his first "dream, or night vision," the effects of which would change his life:

> After the usual religious exercises in my family, I retired to rest at the late hour of about two in the morning; and falling to sleep, the place of the future torment of the wicked was presented to my view, with all its dreadful horrors. It was a pit, the depth and extent of which were too vast for my

discovery; but perfectly answering the description given of it in holy writ–a lake burning with fire and brimstone . . . one, which I particularly observed, and doubted from its smallness and singular appearance, whether it was a human being, had no sooner arrived at this place of misery, than it assumed the features and size of a man, and began, with all the other newcomers, to emit flames of fire, from the mouth and nostrils, like those I had seen there at first.

> I next beheld a coach, with horses richly furnitured, and full of gay, modish passengers, posting to this place of torment; but, when they approached the margin of the burning lake, struck with terror and dismay, their countenances changed, and awfully bespoke their surprise and fear.
>
> But having myself, while engaged with my conductor, stepped upon the top of the descent, and apparently burnt my feet, which he observing, said to me, "Go, and declare what you have seen." Upon which I awoke; but so overcome by the effect of what I had seen, that it was a considerable time before I was able to speak.[13]

I have quoted this at some length in order to convey the intensity of White's vision and to indicate the space that the vision occupies within the larger narrative. White spends little time questioning either the provenance or meaning of the vision but, instead, takes immediate steps to "declare" his vision far and wide. Though a friend from his church discourages White, he nonetheless follows God, who White believes had "called [him] to . . . obtain license as an exhorter."[14] White was unsuccessful in his first attempt "to" obtain such licensure, but he eventually succeeded and began his career on the lowest rung of the church hierarchy.

As an exhorter, White travels around New York, New Jersey, and Long Island and leads prayer meetings, primarily for African Americans.[15] After exhorting for two years, White experiences another vision, this one a counter to the dark dream that had launched him on his quest to become an exhorter. During a meeting at his home, White

> . . . fell prostrate upon the floor, like one dead. But while I lay in this condition, my mind was vigourous [*sic*] and active; and an increasing scene of glory, opened upon my ravished soul; with a spiritual view of the heavenly hosts surrounding the eternal throne, giving glory to God and the Lamb; with whom, all my ransomed powers seemed to unite, in symphonious strains of divine adoration; feeling nothing but perfect love, peace, joy, and good-will to man pervading all my soul, in a most happy union with God, my all and in all . . .[16]

Here White is overcome by God's love and believes himself "sanctifyed [*sic*];" soon thereafter, he "felt a greater desire than ever, to be able to read the scriptures."[17] With his daughter's help, he learns to read, but only by eschewing the "common spelling book" and focusing upon the word of God.[18] White's acquisition of literacy in this manner represents a reversal of the kinds of stories we have come to expect from formerly enslaved men and women. It is not literacy that frees him to read God's word but God's power that gives him the ability to read. And once he learns to read and write, White chiefly appreciates that he can record "the travels of [his] own soul in the way to the kingdom, and the dealings of God towards [him]."[19]

After his first dream vision, White secures a leadership role within the church; after his second vision, White learns to read; and, with that knowledge in hand, White seeks licensure as a preacher. As a preacher, White would be able to do more than lead prayer meetings and encourage others to come to Christ; he would also be able to stand in the pulpit and interpret the word of God. As he works to realize this goal,

> . . . I was lying in bed, about twelve o'clock at night, and ruminating upon the glories of heaven; all at once my room, which was before entirely dark, became exceeding light, and the appearance of three forms, like doves, presented themselves before my wakeful eyes, who, for some minutes looked me full in the face. A peculiar brightness, or light, surrounding each of them. Conceiving them to be angels, I was terrified with fear; but soon disappearing, and leaving the room dark as before, and me to reflect upon what I had seen, my mind was led to embrace the divine promises and I considered this vision as an omen of good, and that, in due time, I should reap if I fainted not . . .[20]

It is curious that a vision appears almost every time White wants to make progress within the church or otherwise change something about his life. The ministering angels who visit White do not speak or signal any particular promises, but White seems to believe that he will "reap" in the form of a license to preach. Even so, he was denied that license on six separate occasions in 1806 and 1807.

White's story is that of a talented, committed, and ambitious man who seeks both heavenly and mundane rewards, but he is careful to couch his pursuit of those mundane rewards within a spiritual frame. That frame, though, is not typical of the spiritual autobiography, a form that documents the religious journey of an individual as he or she moves away from sin and toward salvation. Perhaps the best-known example of such an autobiography in American literature is Jonathan Edwards "Personal Narrative," (1740) in which Edwards describes his hesitating and uncertain journey toward sanctification, a journey filled with setbacks, self-doubt, and frustration. Crucially, though, Edwards's struggles are all related to his personal salvation and a feeling of security in the same.

Among critics of African American literature, there is a sometimes a tendency to think about this payoff differently; that is, in less individualistic terms. Writing about White, Yolanda Pierce argues that "an individual's personal experience of a relationship with God is transformed into the possibility of liberating an entire community."[21] Though Pierce is right to note that White's account fits within the tradition of the spiritual autobiography, I believe that George White's spiritual journey does not direct us to believe in the possibility of divine liberation for all African Americans. As William L. Andrews notes, White was a man of surpassing "aspiration and will," and he very much wanted to realize his personal goals. This is not to diminish his faithfulness but merely to insist that White senses God's grace relatively early in his narrative and spends most of his book describing his efforts to employ his skills in a professional context. The dream visions White experiences do not guarantee salvation or hint at freedom; instead, they suggest divine authorization of his earthly efforts. In other words, what distinguishes White's spiritual narrative from Edwards's is not its relevance to a larger African American community but its relevance to White's career.[22]

As White's narrative leads readers to expect, his journey to the top rung of the church hierarchy requires another instance of divine authorization that can only manifest in the form of a vision:

> In my sleep, a man appeared to me, having under his care a flock of sheep; from which, separating a few, requested I would keep them. But I told him I was no shepherd. However, he went away and left them with me: as he was going, I called after him to know his name: he replied, that it was enough for me to know that he was a shepherd.
>
> This dream encouraged me to hope, that I should find some of the fruit of my labours, in the flock of the great Shepherd of the sheep, at the last day; and inspired me earnestly to pray to God that it might be so.[23]

Soon thereafter, White renews his quest to act as a shepherd for other Christians and is called upon to preach yet another trial sermon for the presiding elders of the church. For his text, he chooses a verse from Hebrews that very clearly applies to White and his professional quest: "Cast not away, therefore, your confidence; which hath great recompense of reward."[24] The reward that White has long sought is finally granted, and he remains a preacher in the AME church until 1829; he dies in New York in 1836.

According to his autobiography, White does not experience any more dream visions after he obtains a license to preach. Perhaps this reflects the actual state of affairs in White's life, or perhaps the dream vision has already fulfilled its narrative purpose and so he does not need to factor in a story of spiritual and professional ascent. Instead of dream visions, White appends the text of a funeral sermon he preaches for Mary Henery in 1809. This sermon, with its standard formulation (doctrine/interpretation/application) demonstrates White's mastery of both text and analysis; it also shows readers the same thing that White's several trials were meant to show church elders: White was indeed sanctioned by God to do the work of preaching. Though White does not press this point, it is clear by the end of the text that White – and not the elders – is the most skilled interpreter of divine "speech" in the form of the dream vision. The very skill that he needs to demonstrate in order to gain a license to preach is the skill that he mastered before he ever learned to read.

Like George White, Jarena Lee spent years trying to gain institutional sanction for her preaching. Whereas White had to convince Methodist church leaders that he was capable of reading and interpreting the Bible, Lee had to convince AME leaders that a woman could understand and proclaim God's word from the pulpit. As such, in the first edition of *The Life and Religious Experience of Jarena Lee* (1836) the preacher cum author plays the role of a religious entrepreneur seeking to spread both the good news and the idea that women could share that good news with a congregation. And, as she confronted institutional gender proscriptions, Lee, like White, used the dream vision as evidence of God's favor for her mission. In fact, near the conclusion of her 1836 *Life*, Lee seems to realize how important dreams have been to her religious growth and her narrative, and she offers readers an explanation for the outsize influence of these deeply personal religious experiences. Comparing herself to a blind or deaf person whose fully functional senses are more acute, Lee notes that since she "never had more than three months schooling," she "watched more closely the operations of the Spirit, and have in consequence been lead thereby."[25] Those "operations," manifest in a series of dream visions that shape and guide Lee as she grows in her faith; in fact, Lee describes no fewer than nine dreams and visions in her twenty-four-page *Life*.

As is typical of a spiritual autobiography, Lee's first vision is the one that leads her to conversion; appropriately enough, she experiences that vision in church as Richard Allen begins his sermon. Almost immediately after Allen speaks, Lee explains, "there appeared to *my* view, in the centre of the heart *one* sin ... at this discovery I said, *Lord* I forgive *every* creature. That instance, it appeared to me, as if a garment ... split at the crown of my head, and was stripped away from me ... when the Glory of God seemed to cover me in its stead."[26] The intensity of this vision accords with those of other narrators who commemorate their conversions, but what stands out as well is Lee's use of pronouns (my, me, I) that highlight the individual nature of religious experience. The vision and its meaning belong entirely to her, and she would continue to see and interpret visions in the years to come: a vision of the gulf of hell over which she stood balanced, a "form of fire," a shepherd and his sheep, and Jesus on the cross.[27] Of particular importance among these visions is the one she experiences after she asks the "Lord ... if he had called [her] to preach." Almost immediately, "there appeared to [her] view the form and figure of a pulpit, with a Bible lying thereon, the back of which was presented to me as plainly as if it had been a literal fact."[28] Her dreams leave her, as Frances Smith Foster insists, with a "strong conviction of her own authority."[29] As was true for George White, though, Lee uses dream visions to explain her personal ambitions and desires and justify those desires for readers and for church leaders.

The point of my analysis here is not to demonstrate that God did or did not speak to George White and Jarena Lee or to suggest that either person was a cynical opportunist who conjured visions in order to justify professional ambitions. Rather, I want to show how the dream vision functions within their narratives and those of other early Black preachers. Whereas many Black authors would present authenticating documents produced by white amanuenses or editors, White and Lee use their visions as justification for action and as evidence of divine favor. Those visions lead each person to seek and acquire the right to speak from a text, and that right, in turn, leads them to embrace the opportunity to speak within a published text. Moreover, since White and Lee published their books without the obvious interference of white gatekeepers, publication may have been less difficult for them to realize than licensure. Whether or not that is true, their assertion of a divine authorization to speak in public and their insistence upon that authorization within a self-published narrative allows these two authors to transcend the racial and gender hierarchies that made external authorization a necessity for many African American writers.

Boyrereau Brinch: The "Customs of my Forefathers"

During August of the same year George White published his autobiography, a "blind African slave" named Boyrereau Brinch and known locally as Jeffrey Brace published his life story at the press of Harry Whitney in St. Albans, Vermont.[30] Unlike White, Brace employed a white amanuensis (a young lawyer named Benjamin Franklin Prentiss) and therefore relied upon one form of authorization that was very much grounded in racial hierarchy.[31] Prentiss seems to have been sympathetic to Brinch's motives and concerns, and he probably negotiated the terms of publication with Whitney, the publisher of a short-lived local newspaper titled the *Franklin County Advertiser*.

According to his *Memoirs*, Broyreau Brinch was born in the Niger River region of Northwest Africa and was taken captive at the age of sixteen (around 1758). After being transported to Barbados, Brinch was purchased by a hotelier named Welch and then sold to a captain named Isaac Mills. Brinch served as a mariner on board Mills's ship and saw extensive action during the Seven Years War. After the war, he was taken to New Haven, Connecticut and – after being sold three times – was purchased by Mary Stiles, a widow who was "one of the finest women in the world" and taught him to read.[32] During the Revolutionary War, Brinch enlisted with the Stiles grandchildren and served in the Continental Army for the duration of the war. He eventually gained his freedom through that service and, after a brief stay in Massachusetts, moved to Vermont, and lived there until his death in 1827. Brinch's decision to dictate and publish his story seems to have been animated by his destitute condition. His wife had died in 1807, and by 1810 he was completely blind. Therefore, he may have hoped that book sales would "bring something to make [him] comfortable in [his] declining days."[33] Brinch's book sold through Prentiss and at the offices of the *Advertiser*, but it seems unlikely to have sold many copies. The book, which was the first one ever published in St. Albans, never achieved a wide circulation and remained in only a few libraries until it was re-published in 2004. Though Brinch relied upon the assistance of an amanuensis, in his *Memoirs* he uses dreams to highlight his unique perspective and the fundamental equality of Black Africans and white Americans. In other words, despite the fact that he courted or accepted Benjamin Prentiss's editorial control, and despite the fact Prentiss made the kinds of remarks and alterations we so often associate with what John Sekora calls the "white envelope" surrounding a "black message,"[34] Brinch's use of dreams helps him preserve a space outside either the editorial or experiential control of his amanuensis.

The first appearance of the dream vision comes when Brinch is thinking back on the celebrations and traditions practiced by his family. After explaining the origins of those traditions and their links to Christian practices, Brinch makes the leap to Christian scripture: "These things bring to my mind a chapter of sacred scripture which I often repeat, when memory brings me back to my native land; the visions of night cause me to read, while in the arms of Morpheus, the following scripture, which is verified by the ancient customs of my forefathers."[35] Brinch goes on to quote the entirety of Exodus 18, a chapter detailing the genealogy of Moses' family. Brinch's "visions of the night" seem intertwined with his memories, suggesting that the dream offers something other than – or, perhaps, in addition to – divine communication. Moreover, the night vision is a vision of reading that complements or verifies the oral tradition in Brinch's home. Ultimately, Brinch's dream reading confirms an equality between divine scripture and community practices among Brinch's African ancestors. By using scripture to certify the rightness of those community practices, Brinch seems to be gesturing toward an understanding of religion that is rooted in behavior and practice. The role of the dream vision, then, is to help Brinch explain the connection between those behaviors and the doctrine that his readers already know and, through that connection, to posit that "all mankind [are] naturally equal."[36]

As Brinch's narrative progresses, the division between his African home and his American home becomes more and more stark, and many of his dreams begin to take on a utopian, escapist quality that positions Africa as something akin to heaven on earth. His experience in the West instigates a violent dream, however, which he explains after narrating the experience of his torture and sale in Barbados:

> I met the most horrid nightly visions that the human mind can experience. Whether I slept or was awake, I am unable to say, at any rate, I thought, Maggots were devouring my inwards [*sic*] and whips were scourging my back; the furies of unprovoked vengeance were preying upon me to that degree that I was almost tempted to wish for annihilation . . . nothing but the arm of Almighty Jehovah saved my life.[37]

Interestingly, the only respite from the torture that leads to Brinch's nightmare is the act of a "humane African friend" who gives him food and water. Even with this kindness, the living hell of slavery and abuse is visited upon Brinch even as he sleeps, and that hellish reality continues in the waking world when Brinch is pressed into naval service and survives a sea battle against the Spanish before being sold to John Burrell, "a professed [*sic*] puritan."[38] Despite his religious professions, Burrell abuses Brinch numerous times and shows himself to be anything but Christlike; through Burrell, Brinch accentuates the division between religious profession and religious practice.

To insist upon the all-too-common problem of white religious hypocrisy, Brinch narrates a dream vision that contrasts African "felicity" with American terror.[39] First he goes to bed and dreams of "being in my native country, and conversing with one of my aunts, by the name of Zoah. In this vision, a region of imaginary happiness appeared before me. I was in a complete transport of earthly felicity; but alas! . . . When I awoke I found it was a dream."[40] And, then, at the moment of Brinch's waking,

> Something was said by my master. He spoke so quick that I did not understand him, then immediately jumped up, and the first salutation knocked me down with his fist. As I went to get up he took up a chair and struck me on the side of the head near where I had been wounded in the first battle I was engaged in, and pealed [*sic*] up a piece of my scalp about as big as my three fingers. I fell with the blow under a table, where he kicked and beat me until I became insensible.[41]

Brinch is rendered "insensible" and cannot dream; he wakes in the morning to find himself covered in blood and required to work anyway. Beyond undercutting claims about American civilization and religiosity, these contrasting experiences – one asleep and one awake – also highlight the value and significance of the family connections he has lost. In his dream, he can converse with his aunt; when he awakens, his family is nowhere to be found and communication is only possible through violence.

Still suffering from the brutal beating he has received from John Burrell and realizing that any hope for earthly salvation is becoming more and more remote, Brinch offers a final, detailed vision of lost happiness:

> At night I dreamed that the good spirit came to me, took me by the hand, asked me to accompany him, which I did without the least hesitation. He ascended with me high above the earth, and wafted me through vast space – at length we arrived at the African coast and came in sight of the Niger, following its course up the river, about one hundred yards above the earth. He shewed me the desolated town of Yellow Bonga. The shades of night seemed to break away, and all at once he gave me a fair view of Deauyah, my native town. The people were all asleep, and we hovered about the town until it was light. We then descended and sat upon the grass before the church.[42]

This vision closes chapter seven of the *Memoirs*, but the vision continues as the next chapter begins:

> I then thought I had died of my wounds, and that our great father, the Sun, was the good spirit, who conducted me back to my town. The spirit left me, and seemed to ascend into the air with dazzling light, which overpowered the strength of my eyes to behold. I started at the sight and awoke. The fire from the kitchen hearth had blazed up and shone bright in my face.[43]

Though Brinch remains, as he says, "a forlorn slave," this vision ends with the "dazzling light" of the kitchen fire and precedes Brinch's sale to Mary

Stiles, and his subsequent entrances into the Continental Army during the Revolutionary War.[44]

As a free man after the war, Brinch moves to Vermont, marries, and – eventually – embraces Christianity before publishing his memoir. These material changes do nothing to alter his vision of earthly felicity, a vision rooted in family ties, community religious traditions and practices, and West African geography. Indeed, nothing in the colonies or the United States seems to change Brinch's fundamental understanding of the world he inhabits or of his position in it. He closes *The Blind African Slave* with an antislavery plea and a quotation from Jeremiah: "Oh that my head were waters, and mine eyes a fountain of tears, that I might weep day and night for the slain of the daughter of my people."[45] Brinch, now a literate Christian, locates a scriptural parallel for the lamentations that occupy so much of his story and reiterates a connection with those he deems "my people." Whether Brinch uses that phrase to describe all kidnapped Africans, the family he left behind, or those who share religious traditions and practices, it seems clear enough that his people are reachable only in his dreams.

Brinch's autobiography is what Kari J. Winter calls a "hybrid, collaborative text" since it is episodic and therefore lacks that "graceful narrative shape" of some autobiographies.[46] Or, as Susan Willis puts it as she examines Brinch's narrative, "the narrator, not fully aware of an audience and the purpose to which his narrative might be put, is not constrained to supply meaning."[47] Though it is certainly true that Brinch does not supply the kind of meaning that readers would expect in later years, I am not so sure that he fails to "supply meaning" altogether. Given the shape of his life, it is no surprise that Brinch's narrative lacks a "graceful shape," and, given his treatment in the United States, it makes some sense that Brich's meaning would be more focused on religious and social equality than on the eradication of slavery. If we think about shape and meaning in these ways, Brinch's use of the dreams seems less random and more purposeful. As was true for White and Lee, Brinch's visions appear at key moments and lead Brinch to crucial realizations. Specifically, Brinch uses his visions to indicate the links between his native beliefs and the Christian knowledge he gains in the West (he was reputed to have memorized the entire Bible).[48] By drawing numerous parallels between life and scripture, Brinch shows readers that the religious arguments buttressing slavery are completely unfounded and claims "the biblical authority to rebuke Christians."[49] Moreover, as he locates God in both African experience and scriptural mastery, Brinch demands that we accept both forms of knowledge and – crucially – understand them as equivalent in terms of their purchase on his life. By positing a natural equality between African and Christian spiritual realms and verifying that equality through his use of dream visions, Brinch authorizes a powerful argument against white, Christian supremacy.

"Another Way of Knowing Things": The Rhetoric of Dreaming after 1836

Whereas the early spiritual autobiographies I have described are full of dreams and interpretations thereof, many of well-known texts written between 1830 and 1865 avoid dreams or use them in very different ways. For example: The only extended sequence on dreams in Douglass's corpus appears in reference to Sandy, the man who betrays Douglass and his compatriots when they planned to run away. Henry Bibb and William Wells Brown never even mention dreams. So, what is it about the early period that made the dream vision a crucial rhetorical device? One answer is fairly obvious and fits perfectly with long-standing critical paradigms that position the pre-1830 period as what Blyden Jackson calls the "Age of Apprenticeship" as opposed to the 1830–1895 "Age of Abolition."[50] Because early autobiographers were writing in a time before the abolition movement developed in the North, they were not attuned to the rhetorical strategies and political arguments that would define the slave narrative in the antebellum period. As such, earlier autobiographers were free to explore themes and situations that were more personal and less political whereas later autobiographers almost certainly felt constrained by the demands of their audience and their publishers. While it is certainly possible that Frederick Douglass slept so soundly that he never dreamed, it is more likely that Douglass and other post-1830 writers (many of whom were supported by abolitionist publishers) believed that it would be detrimental to even mention their dreams or the liberatory possibilities contained within them.

Though many antebellum authors rejected the dream as a rhetorical device, Sojourner Truth and Harriet Jacobs both used the rhetoric of the dream vision, though to very different effect. In her 1850 *Narrative* (which Truth published with the help of her amanuensis, Olive Gilbert), Truth recalls her "day-dreams" with her husband and admits that those dreams "turned to 'thin air'" because of her enslavement and that of her husband. Accepting these earthly disappointments, Truth also recalls her 1828 sanctification after Jesus "appeared to her delighted mental vision as so mild, so good, and so every way lovely, and he loved her so much."[51] As with Equiano, White, Lee, and Brinch, Truth communes with God through a vision and accepts the significance of that vision in shaping her life and commitments. In her biography of Truth, Nell Irvin Painter links this particular moment "the secret power that black women have tapped into over the generations to counter the negation they experience in the world."[52] As it was for her literary ancestors, Truth's dream vision is extraordinarily empowering, as it unites God's strength with that of the individual seeking to battle against "negation."

When Harriet Jacobs published *Incidents in the Life of a Slave Girl* eleven years after Truth's *Narrative*, she too employed the dream vision as a motivating force, though it would be most appropriate to place Jacobs on a continuum between the self-authorizing dreamers of the earlier period and the frustrated dreamers of the Civil Rights era and beyond. Indeed, Jacobs often writes of dreams ruined or deferred: the "love-dream" of her childhood is thwarted and, at the end of *Incidents*, she admits that "the dream of [her] life" was not realized because she could not occupy a common home with her children.[53] Moreover, just before she enters the garrett that will be her home for seven years, Jacobs experiences what "[s]ome will call . . . a dream, others a vision" that left her "certain something had happened" to her children.[54] This vision, though, proves to be false, for Jacobs's children had already been freed. Jacobs, then, positions the dream as a form of knowledge and insight, but it seems unreliable for her, and it does little to authorize action. Perhaps Jacobs's use of dreams signals her own uncertainties regarding both religion and the communities in which she lived as both an enslaved woman and a fugitive. For her, finally, the dream is a space of doubt and thwarted hopes. In this respect, Jacobs previews the future-oriented political dreams with which modern readers are most familiar.

These snapshots describing the evolution of the dream trope in the "age of abolition" are not definitive, but one thing does unite all of the of the autobiographies I have discussed above: their method of publication. White, Lee, Brinch, Truth, and Jacobs were all self-published, meaning that the authors themselves (or someone close to them) paid for the printing and distribution of their autobiography. Though such a strategy has obvious limitations in terms of circulation, in purely expressive terms, self-publication is enormously freeing; when self-published authors employ dreamscapes in their books, they highlight the imaginative space available to a self-financed author. While contemporary readers might imagine imaginative space as a positive feature in early Black writing, there is ample evidence that white sponsors and abolitionist organizations did not. The most effective antislavery speakers were Black subjects who could speak or write words that were both true and verifiable, verifications that might take the form of "public performances" in which audiences could "cross-examine [former slaves], and ... see scars from whippings or other traces of plantation violence."[55] Dreams, though, are entirely personal and idiosyncratic; the scars left by such visions are psychological and unverifiable. So, while dreams may have authorized individual actions (preaching, rebellion, writing), dreams were not – and could never be – proof.

The problem of form and verifiability almost certainly limited the usefulness of the dream as a rhetorical device during the abolitionist period, but one wonders why the early dreamers I have identified (White, Lee, Brinch) have not received more attention in our own era. One possibility has to do, again, with the inherently personal and subjective nature of the dream itself. When an individual narrator interprets dreams within the context of divine communication, that narrator marks himself as unique rather than representative, thereby setting himself apart from fellow slaves and the needs of the enslaved more generally. Even when African American writers stopped critiquing slavery or writing under the aegis of abolitionist organizations, such writers almost always remained committed to the racial communities of which they were a part.[56] And, the regnant pedagogical strategies in courses on African American literature privilege this communitarian ethos.

Ultimately, the very things that make books like those by White, Lee, and Brinch special – the formal innovation and imaginative freedom enabled by the authors' revision and expansion of the dream trope – sets them apart from much of what would follow in the antebellum period and beyond. But that does not mean that their version of the trope disappeared entirely, far from it. In the Harlem Renaissance era, writers like Nella Larsen and Richard Bruce Nugent conjured decidedly non-religious visions in which characters could imagine romantic or erotic possibilities that transcended racial and gender binaries.[57] And, across her corpus, Toni Morrison would link her herself to historical and literary ancestors by thematizing what "could be called superstition and magic" as "another way of knowing things."[58] Though it is probably fair to say that the dreams of King and Obama have the greatest purchase on our contemporary imagination, it is Morrison who comes closest to capturing the unique quality of the early dream visions and the "secret power" therein as she authorizes the supernatural as a source of knowledge about oneself and the world.

Unlike Morrison's bestselling novels, though, the earliest "dream autobiographies" were produced in small print runs, circulated across a limited temporal and geographic range, and limited in impact in a political context shaped by abolitionism. Such books can be classed with what Joanna Brooks calls "the unfortunates," since they enjoyed neither "movement nor movements" that would bring them to a wider readership in either the nineteenth century or today.[59] But as we conceive a more capacious history of African American literature and try to envision that literature in its fullness, we should preserve a place for the dreamers whose autobiographies provide us alternative ways to think about imagination and authorization.

Notes

1 Job 33:14–16 (KJV).

2 Though some narrators make a distinction between dreams (experienced by a sleeper) and visions (experienced while awake), in this chapter, I use the terms "dream" and "vision" interchangeably. Both terms speak to the idiosyncratic and unverifiable nature of personal imaginative experience.

3 On the history of Equiano as a bookseller and businessman, see Vincent Carretta, "'Property of Author:' Olaudah Equiano's Place in the History of the Book," in *Genius in Bondage: Literature of The Early Black Atlantic*, ed. Vincent Carretta and Philip Gould (Lexington: University of Kentucky Press, 2001), 130–151; John Bugg, "The Other Interesting Narrative: Olaudah Equiano's Public Book Tour," *PMLA* 121, no. 5 (Fall 2006): 1424–1442; and Ross Pudaloff, "No Change Without Purchase: Olaudah Equiano and the Economies of Self and Market," *Early American Literature* 40, no.3 (2005): 499–527.

4 Olaudah Equiano. 1789. *The Interesting Narrative of the Life of Olaudah Equiano, or Gustavus Vassa, the African. Written by Himself*, vol. I. Documenting the American South. University Library, The University of North Carolina at Chapel Hill. 2001. http://docsouth.unc.edu/neh/equiano1/equiano1.html, 278.

5 Olaudah Equiano. 1789. *The Interesting Narrative of the Life of Olaudah Equiano, or Gustavus Vassa, the African. Written by Himself, vol. II.* Documenting the American South. University Library, The University of North Carolina at Chapel Hill. 2001. https://docsouth.unc.edu/neh/equiano2/equiano2.html, 38.

6 Ibid., 47.

7 Ibid., 42.

8 Ibid., 43.

9 Ibid., 48.

10 On the ways that white editors and activists shaped slave narratives, see (among many others): William L. Andrews, *To Tell a Free Story: The First*

Century of Afro-American Autobiography, 1760–1865 (Urbana: University of Illionois Press, 1986); Houston A. Baker, *Blues, Ideology, and Afro-American Literature: A Vernacular Theory* (Chicago: University of Chicago Press, 1984); James Olney, "'I Was Born': Slave Narratives, Their Status as Autobiography and as Literature," in *The Slave's Narrative*, ed. Charles T. Davis and Henry Louis Gates Jr. (Oxford: Oxford University Press, 1985), 148–175; and John Sekora, "Black Message/White Envelope: Genre, Authenticity, and Authority in the Antebellum Slave Narrative," *Callaloo,* no. 32 (Summer, 1987): 482–515.

11 In some ways this accords with Katherine Clay Bassard's argument in "Gender and Genre: Black Women's Autobiography and the Ideology of Literacy," *African American Review* 26, no. 1 (Spring, 1992): 119–129. Bassard claims that "nineteenth-century Afro-American writers . . . 'bought into' the ideology of literacy, freedom, and economic advancement to varying degrees, and the extent to which they absorbed it into their system of values (and their texts) is directly related to a given writer's own social position" (119). For most of the writers Bassard examines, it was salvation rather than literacy that represented the ultimate goal.

12 George White, "A Brief Account of the Life, Experience, Travels, and Gospel Labours of George White, an African; Written by Himself, and Revised by a Friend," in *Black Itinerant Ministers of the Gospel: The Narratives George White and John Jea*, ed. Graham Russell Hodges (Madison, WI: Madison House, 1993), 53.

13 Ibid., 53–56.

14 Ibid., 56.

15 On White's work in the church, the best source is Graham Russell Hodges, "Introduction," in *Black Itinerant Ministers of the Gospel,* 1–49.

16 White, 58.

17 Ibid.

18 Same phenomenon as above – this is also page 59.

19 Ibid., 59.

20 Ibid., 62–63.

21 Yolanda Pierce, *Hell without Fires: Slavery, Christianity, and the Antebellum Spiritual Narrative* (Gainesville, FL: University of Florida Press, 2005), 25. One might point to numerous examples of religiously authorized community action amongst Black activists of the nineteenth century. In addition to the figures named by Pierce in *Hell without Fires* (John Jea, David Smith, Zilpha Elaw) David Walker, Harriet Tubman, and Henry Highland Garnet also fit within this paradigm.

22 Andrews, *To Tell a Free Story,* 55.

23 White, 66.

24 Ibid.

25 Jarena Lee, The Life and Religious Experience of Jarena Lee in *Sisters of the Spirit: Three Black Women's Autobiographies of the Nineteenth Century*, ed. William L. Andrews (Bloomington: University of Indiana Press, 1986), 48.

26 Ibid., 29.
27 Ibid., 30, 37, 39, 44.
28 Ibid., 35.
29 Frances Smith Foster, *Written By Herself: Literary Production by African American Women, 1746–1892* (Bloomington: Indiana University Press, 1993), 74.
30 Boyrereau Brinch, *The Blind African Slave, Or Memoirs of Boyrereau Brinch, Nicknamed Jeffrey Brace*, ed. Kari J. Winter (Madison: University of Wisconsin Press, 2004).
31 On Prentiss, see Kari J. Winter, "The Strange Career of Benjamin Franklin Prentiss, Antislavery Lawyer," *Vermont History* 79, no. 2 (Summer/Fall 2011): 121–140 as well as Winter's Introduction to *The Blind African Slave.*
32 Brinch, 157.
33 Ibid., 182.
34 Sekora, "Black Message/White Envelope."
35 Ibid., 115.
36 Ibid., In this respect, Brinch is continuing a technique also visible in Equiano's *Narrative* and Venture Smith's *Life*. In both books, African practices are described in relation to Christian morality or the lack thereof in the United States and England. See Venture Smith, *A Narrative of the Life and Adventures of Venture Smith, a Native of Africa, but Resident above Sixty Years in the United States of America. Related by Himself* (New London: Charles Holt, 1798).
37 Ibid., 146.
38 Ibid., 152.
39 Ibid., 153.
40 Ibid.
41 Ibid.
42 Ibid., 155.
43 Ibid., 156.
44 Ibid.
45 Ibid., 182.
46 Winter, "Introduction," 72.
47 Susan Willis, "Crushed Geraniums: Juan Francisco Manzano and the Language of Slavery," in *The Slave's Narrative*, ed. Charles T. Davis and Henry Louis Gates Jr. (Oxford: Oxford University Press, 1985), 202.
48 See Winter, "Introduction," 69.
49 Rhondda Robinson Thomas, *Claiming Exodus: A Cultural History of Afro-Atlantic Identity, 1774–1903* (Waco, TX: Baylor University Press, 2013), 37.
50 Blyden Jackson, *A History of Afro-American Literature, vol. 1* (Baton Rouge: Louisiana State University Press, 1989), 25. Jackson's focus is literary; the history of the change in abolitionist politics is ably given by Richard S. Newman, *The Transformation of American Abolitionism: Fighting Slavery in the Early Republic* (Chapel Hill: University of North Carolina Press, 2002).

51 Sojourner Truth, *Narrative of Sojourner Truth, a Northern Slave, Emancipated from Bodily Servitude by the State of New York, in 1828.* Documenting the American South. University Library, The University of North Carolina at Chapel Hill. 2000. https://docsouth.unc.edu/neh/truth50/truth50.html, 67.

52 Painter, 30.

53 Harriet Ann Jacobs, *Incidents in the Life of a Slave Girl.* Documenting the American South. University Library, The University of North Carolina at Chapel Hill. 2003. https://docsouth.unc.edu/fpn/jacobs/jacobs.html, 60, 302.

54 Ibid., 164.

55 Lara Langer Cohen, *The Fabrication of American Literature* (Philadelphia: University of Pennsylvania Press, 2013), 116. On the demands for veracity in the slave narrative, see also Andrews, *To Tell a Free Story;* Ann Fabian, *The Unvarnished Truth: Personal Narratives in Nineteenth-Century America* (Berkeley: University of California Press, 1999); and, Dwight McBride, *Impossible Witnesses: Truth, Abolitionism, and Slave Testimony* (New York: New York University Press, 2001).

56 On the idea of African American literature as a communal and community-building endeavor, see (among others) John Ernest, *A Nation within a Nation: Organizing African American Communities before the Civil War* (Chicago: Ivan R. Dee, 2011).

57 Here I am thinking specifically of Larsen's *Passing* and Nugent's "Smoke, Lilies, and Jade."

58 Toni Morrison, "Rootedness: The Ancestor as Foundation," in *What Moves the Margin*: *Selected Nonfiction* (Oxford: University Press of Mississippi), 61.

59 See Joanna Brooks, "The Unfortunates: What the Life Spans of Early Black Books Tell Us about Book History," in *Early African American Print Culture*, ed. Lara Langer Cohen and Jordan Alexander Stein (Philadelphia: University of Pennsylvania Press, 2013), 40–52.

PART III

Print Culture in Circulation

Essays in part three, "Print Culture in Circulation," consider the means by which African Americans distributed ideas to mass audiences, including the structures that supported these efforts and the rhetorical tropes that enabled a broad readership. In the earliest decades of the nineteenth century, countless networks organized around African American writing, thinking and speaking fostered literary engagement. Elizabeth McHenry explains that such societies reveal the value of education to free and enslaved African Americans who relied on these associations "for collective reading, writing, and discussion to combat charges of racial inferiority, validate their call for social justice, and alert their audience to the disparity between American ideals and racial inequality."[1] Educational associations provided opportunities to "develop leadership abilities, practice framing constitutions and bylaws," according to Julie Winch.[2] In Chapter 7, Teresa Zackodnik argues that a prototypical Black feminist politics emerged from such a network of Black women's literary societies and the early Black press. These organizations produced a lasting impact that continued into the nineteenth century, indicated in the transition from educational organizations to institutions of higher education such as Cheyney University in Pennsylvania. For example, The Female Literary Society founded in 1831 by Black women of Philadelphia had its grumblings begin in other meeting opportunities, and was one of three such organizations in the city – the others include the Female Minervian Association and the Edgeworth Literary Association. Beginning with Black women's news writing in the 1820s, Zackodnik reveals the political inclinations that inform how scholars should think about circulation in this period.

The interracial coalition of Black and white abolitionists also fueled publication vehicles with newspapers becoming the most prominent in this period. Although Black abolitionists provided funds and white editors were frequently the public-facing figures of such venues, antislavery papers faced their own tribulations for the promotion of incendiary ideas more than three decades before the Civil War. In 1821, Benjamin Lundy began printing his *Genius of Universal Emancipation* in Ohio (after writing for *The Philanthropist* in Mount Pleasant, Ohio); he moved the paper to Tennessee, Maryland, Washington, and finally Philadelphia in search of a safe and lucrative place from which to work. Likewise, readers of this periodical would have been familiar with the tribulations experienced by young William Lloyd Garrison who was imprisoned in Maryland for charges of libel after publishing his "black list." In the aftermath of this scandal, Garrison moved north to Boston to continue his work, and eventually set up his *Liberator* for publication with the help of funding from free Black elites.[3] Despite these significant contributions, the emergence of the Black press remains an essential turning point in thinking about the period. In New York, editor John Russwurm begins weekly printing of the *Freedom's Journal* on 16 March 1827 through its last issue on 28 March 1829, for a total of 103 issues. As it concludes, former co-editor Samuel Cornish releases *Rights of All* newspaper with sporadic publication in New York on 29 May 1829, printing five issues up through October 1829, with the tagline: "Righteousness Exalteth a Nation; Sin Is a Reproach to Any People." These items "recorded the disagreements within and among Black communities that accompanied attempts to define and enforce particular versions" of Blackness and Black exceptionalism according to Benjamin Fagan.[4] Thus the dynamics discussed by Brigitte Fielder revealing a gendered dimension to the concept of African American literature in *Freedom's Journal* tell us more about how those engaged with early Black newspapers were making meaning about national identity. Her chapter shows that author, venue, and subject matter were all pertinent with an examination of "Theresa – A Haitian Tale," published in the weekly. For Chapter 8, Fielder critiques this story of women's wartime heroism, which also addressed transatlantic transitions in race and nationhood, to reveal that the mixed-race figure undergoes a transition in terms of Black nationalism and racial identification.

While Black women propelled print venues and were discussed in newsprint, the life stories of Black men predominated the book format in this period. There are eight known autobiographies and three biographies written about formerly enslaved people between 1800 and 1830. While the biographies were all published in New York, the autobiographies were published in various northern locations, including London. In addition to publishing houses, Reverend Allen printed John Joyce's *Confession of John Joyce* in Philadelphia for 1808. Across sections, scholars in this volume write about all of the known autobiographies with the exception of Ottobah Cugoano's "Narrative of the Enslavement of Ottobah Cugoano, a Native of Africa; Published by Himself on the Year 1787" in *The Negro's Memorial; or, Abolitionist's Catechism; by an Abolitionist.* For this section on print circulation, Stefan Wheelock explores writing by formerly enslaved men of African descent at the turn of the nineteenth century. Critiquing autobiographies by Venture Smith, George White, and John Jea, the ninth chapter urges readers to think about Black autobiography in the context of early book circulation and to think of redemption as a rhetorical trope – one that no doubt facilitated the dissemination of these early narratives in a period still marked by the suppression of Black literacy.

Notes

1 Elizabeth McHenry, Forgotten Readers: Recovering the Lost History of African American Literary Societies (Durham, NC: Duke University Press, 2002), 41.

2 Julie Winch "'You Have Talents–Only Cultivate Them': Philadelphia's Black Female Literary Societies and the Abolitionist Crusade," *The Abolitionist Sisterhood: Women's Political Culture in Antebellum America*, eds. Jean Fagan Yellin and John C. Van Horne (Ithaca, NY: Cornell University Press, 1994): 103.

3 Henry Mayer, *All on Fire: William Lloyd Garrison and the Abolition of Slavery* (New York: W.W. Norton & Company, 2008).

4 Benjamin Fagan, *The Black Newspaper and the Chosen Nation* (Athens: University of Georgia Press, 2016), 8.

CHAPTER 7

Reading, Black Feminism, and the Press around 1827

Teresa Zackodnik

For the past decade, African American literary and print culture studies have been influenced by Frances Smith Foster's assertion that "early African-American print culture ... is virtually synonymous with the Afro-Protestant press."[1] Foster roots that print production in the benevolent and mutual aid societies African Americans established "much earlier than the late eighteenth century" when scholarship tends to date their emergence,[2] and in the "multicolony networks of friends and acquaintances" and the "organized literary circle[s]" that shared original literary "productions" amongst members.[3] Yet the focus of Foster's intervention has tended to be taken up as a reorientation of African American literary studies from a previously established centering of the slave narrative to the periodical press as the location of a diverse literary production. Doing so skirts the question of what it may mean that periodical literature emerged from the literary societies that were central to the development of a Black public sphere. Through inextricable links to both communal reading practices and orality, such societies were key to sharing and developing African American literature, in its broad sense, before its print publication. Literary societies also played a central role in the fledgling Black press and African American women's politics through this nexus of orality, reading, and print publication that mobilized a practice of recirculation. This chapter argues that African American women, as readers and writers, played a foundational role in the developing circulation of African American literature in the periodical press, that they did so in ways directly connected to their political use of the press, and that understanding women's centrality to the development of both the Black press and African American literature at this time is long overdue.

Histories of the Black press in the United States have long cited the Black convention movement as its birthplace, those eleven national conventions held in the northeast between 1830 and 1861 frequently led by male editors of the early Black press at which "an organized political response to American racism" in the form of a Black nationalist politics was formulated.[4] However, recent scholarship on African American readers enables us to understand that the Black press did not spring fully formed from the male-led convention movement but was, rather, fostered by literary societies that were central to its viability.[5] As Elizabeth McHenry contends, "it is no coincidence that the rise of the African American press paralleled the development of literary societies and literary culture in northern antebellum Black communities."[6] Literary societies, most predominant in the American northeast but documented in the Midwest, South,[7] and West,[8] as well as in Black communities in Upper Canada,[9] were staging grounds for early nineteenth-century Black political activism through what McHenry calls "the pursuit of a literary character" as a distinctive political strategy for African Americans.[10] Michelle Garfield contends that by the 1830s such literary societies were forming so frequently that the phenomenon "could best be characterized as a movement."[11] The politics of this "literary character" or "reading disposition" not only fueled the growth of literary societies and the Black press, but also sustained a distinctive site for women's literary production and political participation. African American women's literary societies were organized nearly as early as men's, and from 1830 through the 1850s they doubled in number those reserved for male membership in some locales,[12] meaning that the political activism and strategies that literary societies made possible were mobilized by women in particular. Through literary societies, these women in turn became anonymous and pseudonymous contributors to the radical abolitionist and early Black press.[13] In other words, the Black press and African American literary societies were far more than parallel developments. Rather, African American women and the literary societies they founded were crucial in establishing and sustaining a periodical press that they recognized as an important tool in their developing politics and central to their local, national, and transnational communities.[14] This chapter will argue that African American women used the recirculation enabled by a feedback loop established between literary societies and the abolitionist and Black press to pursue not only that broad politics of "literary character," but their particular politics of women's education, colonization, and a broader Black nationalism.

For Black feminist politics, the communal "literary character" promoted by literary societies was key, as was their value of shared or communal reading that meant "the power of formal or individualized literacy" was not prioritized "over communal knowledge."[15] Widely conceived to include both reading and listening to texts read aloud, literary societies did not require members to be textually literate as Foster, McHenry, and Shirley Logan have stressed. In fact, the oral presentation of texts was central to the program of any literary society, linking the twinned rhetorical forces of nineteenth-century American civic life – oratory and print – together in the development of Black politics, generally, and of Black feminism particularly. This imbrication of oratory and print also highlights the importance of what I call recirculation for the development of Black women's political culture in the early decades of the nineteenth century.[16] More than a site of democratic access to civic life not limited by textual literacy or gendered proscriptions regarding the "public," African American women's literary societies actively fostered the recirculation of writings, lectures, and addresses outward from their organizations to newspapers, which then circulated back into other literary societies where those published "productions" were, in turn, read to new audiences. That feedback loop of recirculation created not only an extended awareness of a developing Black feminist politics, but also constituted what Dilip Parmeshwar Gaonkar and Elizabeth Povinelli call a "circulatory matrix . . . through which new discursive forms, practices, and artifacts carry out their routine ideological labor of constituting subjects who can be summoned in the name of a public or a people."[17] Through the circulatory matrix formed by literary societies and the newspapers they sustained, Black feminist texts were effectively naturalized, and their recirculation, in turn, actively created a public for whom such texts were recognizable within a political culture that called women to listen to and/or read literary productions, including Black women's "original creations,"[18] whether oratorical, written, published, or unpublished.

The early Black press and the abolitionist press together testify to the importance of women's literary societies to Black communities and to their development out of the female mutual benevolent or mutual aid associations established at least as early as the late eighteenth century.[19] *Freedom's Journal* (1827–1829), the first paper owned, operated, and edited by African Americans, published the proceedings of female benevolent association meetings, which were an early form of Black women's political culture and often the training ground for women who would enter public politics through reform work. Such societies enjoyed community approval and support from the late 1820s into the 1840s.[20] As James Oliver Horton and Lois E. Horton argue, "Black women not only contributed to the welfare of their community," but also "participated in the political discourse of the day" through benevolent societies and associations, "a role unfamiliar to most American women of the time."[21] Philadelphia emerges as a center of note for African American organizing. Dorothy Porter argued that the city "took the lead in the establishment of literary societies" with the Reading Room Society for young men in 1828 and the Female Minervian Literary Association in 1833.[22] The founding of these literary societies was clearly fostered by a strong culture of mutual aid and benevolent association work amongst women; Erica Armstrong Dunbar documents that by 1830, of the eighty such associations Philadelphia could claim, sixty had been established by African American women and were for women only.[23] Scholarship on Black women's literary societies tends to focus on the Philadelphia Female Literary Association (PFLA), a twenty-member literary society founded in 1831 whose membership included Grace Bustill Douglass, Sarah Douglass, Harriett Forten Purvis, and Sarah Forten, largely because of the content its members contributed to the "Ladies' Department" in William Lloyd Garrison's *The Liberator* (1831–1865).[24] Through Boston's Afric-American Female Intelligence Society (1832), Maria Stewart delivered her first public address in the spring of 1832. That society's founding was reported in both *The Liberator* and Benjamin Lundy's *Genius of Universal Emancipation* (1821–1839).[25] Reading newspapers as records of women's literary societies, we find the late summer of 1827 announcement in *Freedom's Journal* of "A Society of Young Ladies . . . at Lynn, Mass. To meet once a week, to read in turn to the society, works adapted to virtuous and literary improvements."[26] We are only beginning to appreciate the roles of women who founded literary societies, to fully appreciate the geographical reach of the work they undertook through them, and to understand the transformations that they made possible in African American literature as a result of sustaining these societies, creating original literature through them, and publishing that literature in the pages of the newspapers they fostered and sustained.

One way to further that work would be to consider the ways in which women's benevolent societies fostered, and at times also operated as, literary societies. The African Dorcas Associations and the Female Dorcas Societies in the northeast were not only benevolent organizations, supplying children attending the African Free Schools with clothing or destitute and sick members with financial aid, but they were also strong monetary supporters of the Black press and seedbeds for female literary societies.[27] The *Colored American* (1837–1842) reported in April of 1837 on the Troy Female Benevolent Society, founded on February 13, 1833, which was also a literary society that read "compositions . . . written by the younger members of the Society." These societies flourished and maintained significant savings for mutual aid and benevolence drawn from membership fees.[28] In fact, Charles Ray, co-editor of the *Colored American* along with Philip Bell and Samuel Cornish, wrote in November 1837 of the Female Dorcas Society of Buffalo's donation of ten dollars "toward the Editor's Salary ... [and] incidental expense of the paper."[29] Like women's literary societies, the Dorcas Societies remained active through the nineteenth century. Reports of their activities indicate that the "mental feasts" women's literary societies offered were also central to Dorcas Societies.[30] At times, these benevolent associations also operated *as* literary societies. Benevolent societies, then, were venues for Black women to continue their active support for their communities and sources of sustained mutual support amongst women, and worked in ways related to African American female literary societies as outlets for Black women's creative and political writing, as acceptable venues to discuss concerns affecting the community and women within it, and as spaces which fostered an important sense of women's collectivity. Both enabled women "to practice and perform literacy ... to experiment with voice and self-representation in ways that approximated the ideals of civic participation,"[31] and to try on leadership roles. Women like Henrietta Green Regulas Ray, who was secretary of New York City's African Dorcas Society in 1828, would go on to participate in literary societies or lead them, as she did the Ladies' Literary Society of that city in 1834.[32]

The *Colored American* and *Freedom's Journal* actively supported literary societies as central to a politics of racial uplift, with the *Colored American* leaving us the most extensive records we may have of the formation and operation of benevolent associations and literary societies in the early decades of the nineteenth century.[33] By 1837 the *Colored American* was pronouncing literary societies "of more importance than any others in the present age of Societies and Associations,"[34] urging "African Americans to 'cultivate a reading disposition' as the foundational step toward a long process of elevation and communal self-determination."[35]

Freedom's Journal had published similar enjoinders a decade earlier that lauded literary associations as a well-known method to "remove the evil ... [and] create a spirit of emulation, and, of course, a disposition for reading which would tend to mature the judgment, and expand the mind."[36] As McHenry has established, African American literary societies were the "intellectual centers for an increasingly unified and politically conscious" Black public, through which "African Americans took the lead in calling for a substantive democracy."[37] Women's literary societies offered varied self-presentation possibilities for their members, who could present as "meek and vocal, submissive and assertive" through anonymous submission and pseudonymous publication, just as they could express themselves through multiple genres ranging from "lyric poetry" to the "radical political convictions" of "fiery rhetoric."[38] Logan argues that these organizations sanctioned women's "increased community activism" along a spectrum ranging from the rationale that "rhetorical skills would help women have a greater moral influence" in their families, to using female literary societies as "training grounds for, if not sites of," political activism such as antislavery work.[39] Indeed, some of the most recognizable Black female activists of the nineteenth century were members of, or addressed, literary societies. Sarah Mapps Douglass, Sarah Forten, Maria Stewart, and Elizabeth Jennings were all active in northeast literary associations in the 1830s.[40] Ida B. Wells participated in a Memphis literary society in the late 1880s.[41] Charlotte Forten Grimké welcomed Anna Julia Cooper to her "at home" literary society in Washington, DC in the late 1880s.[42] Mary Ann Shadd Cary and Mary Church Terrell were members of the Bethel Historical and Literary Society, and Terrell became its first female president in 1892.[43] Maritcha Lyons and Frances Harper crossed paths at the Brooklyn Literary Union (1866) in the late 1890s.[44] And Harper addressed the Boston Literary and Historical Association (1901) in the fall of 1902, which counted Pauline Hopkins as a founding member.[45]

The earliest African American women's literary societies also provided the abolitionist and Black press with content. Thus, these women quickly came to apprehend the press as an important political tool and to use its "reflexivity in the circulation of texts among strangers." The readers of their "original contributions" became what Michael Warner calls "a social entity," a public that comes to "exist *by virtue of being addressed*."[46] Notably for African American women, the distinctly African American communal reading practice of sharing printed texts orally, together with the circulatory matrix between women's literary societies and the press, meant they could capitalize upon its "punctual rhythm of circulation," which produced "the sense that ongoing discussion [was] unfold[ing] in a sphere of activity."[47] Black women harnessed that recirculation not only to transmit their politics, but to actively shape "new forms of subjectivity and identity"[48] for women in their communities.

Women's Education

Education was a central communal issue that drew women to literary societies and was also one of the earliest public goods for which they advocated within a circulatory matrix that linked their societies and the

Black press. In the late summer of 1827, Amy Matilda Cassey,[49] a founding member of the PFLA and Philadelphia's Gilbert Lyceum, signed herself "Matilda" in a letter to *Freedom's Journal* that argued for women's education. Published in the August 10 edition, "Matilda's" letter opens by indicting the paper for not having "said sufficient upon the education of females," a daring move given that *Freedom's Journal* was publishing pieces chastising women who did not hold their tongues at this time.[50] "Matilda" continued, "I hope you are not to be classed with those who think that our mathematical knowledge should be limited to 'fathoming the dish-kettle,' and that we have acquired enough of history, if we know that our grandfather's father lived and died." In what would become a refrain in women's contributions to the press and to their literary societies, "Matilda" argued that a woman's influence over children and spouse "demands that our minds should be instructed and improved with the principles of education and religion ... There is a great responsibility resting somewhere, and it is time for us to be up and doing."[51] Women like "Beatrice" would similarly argue before their literary societies in the early 1830s that "woman has a high destiny to fulfill" in "the domestic circle ... requir[ing] extensive exertions ... call[ing] for strict attention, on her part to the benefits of a good education."[52] Signing herself "A.," Sarah Forten would likewise see one of her contributions to the PFLA published in *The Liberator* couching the value of a "well educated female" in an "influence" and "power" she characterized as "absolute."[53] By the fall of 1837, Elizabeth Jennings was raising a very similar call to Black women through her address "On the Improvement of the Mind" at the third anniversary of the Ladies Literary Society of New York:

> [N]ow is a momentous time, a time that calls us to exert all our powers, and among the many of them, *the mind is the greatest* ... Awake and slumber no more – arise, put on your armor, ye daughters of America, and stand forth in the field of improvement ... The mind is powerful, and by its efforts your influence may be as near perfection.[54]

Hailed as the first American woman orator, Maria Stewart was a "published writer before she was a public speaker."[55] She emerged from this repeated contention for women's education recirculating in Black women's literary societies and the press, and entered print expressing herself as a reader (just as Amy Matilda Cassey did) by writing *Freedom's Journal* in 1827 to caution against the exclusion of Black women in a politics of racial uplift, as Joycelyn Moody has noted.[56] Moreover, what is frequently taken up in scholarship as Stewart's first published essay, "Cause for

Encouragement," was, in fact, a reader's press genre – "a letter to the editor." Marilyn Richardson has documented that Stewart wrote it in response to "William Lloyd Garrison's ... account of the 'Second Annual Convention of the People of Color,' held in Philadelphia June 4-15, 1832," in *The Liberator*.[57] "Cause" appeared in the July 14, 1832 edition of Garrison's paper. This gathering was, of course, part of the larger Black convention movement long credited with midwiving the Black press. Stewart's letter critiques a political event open only to Black men at the time,[58] and an event that sought to establish the Black press as an arm of Black public politics. If we re-center African American literary societies in their foundational and sustaining role in African American periodical culture and keep in sight that these societies were predominantly female spaces and political training grounds, the importance of understanding someone like Maria Stewart as influenced by this milieu or coming directly out of these sites becomes clear. Stewart's public career, in other words, began when literary societies were very quickly establishing the interrelatedness of reading, oral address, and writing for Black women's politics. She emerged in a context in which Black women's education was consistently being advocated in those spaces and in print. And given that she joined a literary society in New York after she left Boston in 1833,[59] she may well have belonged to one during the late 1820s and early 1830s when she was highly visible politically.

Women like Cassey and Stewart used the letter to the editor to argue for women's education by positioning their political intervention as the result of their readerly "disposition," and by amplifying their individual signatures or voices as collective. Benedict Anderson's contention that periodicals facilitated a "mass ceremony" of "imagined community"[60] has been so formative in studies of print culture that it has become standard to note that through the ritual of reading the newspaper, readers imagine themselves as part of a larger community partaking of the same solitary activity. Letters to the editor are that community made visible and tangible on the page, and they facilitate what Warner maintains as "the achievement of this cultural form," the press "allow[ing] participants in its discourse to understand themselves as directly and actively belonging to a social entity that exists historically in secular time and has consciousness of itself."[61] By sharing readers' views in a form that offers opportunity for debate, if not also actively courting or staging such debate, letters are a press form that intensifies that sense of direct and active belonging. They also lend a degree of authority to the individual writing them because the form signals a public voice, or a voice issuing from a recognizable collective. This genre enables us to see "cultures of circulation" performatively "shap[ing] new forms of subjectivity and identity that are grounded in the everyday ... through their inscription in specific social practices such as rational calculation, reading, and democratic voting,"[62] as well as the democratic or "rational" debate that Habermas argues is the hallmark of the public sphere.[63] Understanding the formative effects of literary societies upon Black women's writing and politics acknowledges women's letters to the editor as evidence of a civic identity and collective voice. Such letters may have been composed in the collaborative environment of literary societies in the late 1820s and early 1830s, or influenced by discussions and debates they hosted, including Stewart's writing to *Freedom's Journal* on women's respectability in early April 1828, "A Colored Lady in Medford" writing Garrison on slavery in *The Liberator* in April 1831, and May's letter on emancipation published in late October 1832 in *The Liberator*.[64] Letters to the editor effectively stage civic debate by presenting a position on an issue alive in "secular time," and this form might be said to assume, and thereby performatively create through its address, a public likewise engaged as Warner theorizes. Women's letters to the editor created, as they claimed an authority for, African American's women's voices and civic identity within the larger collective.

Stewart's "Cause" advocated for women's education through her social gospel as she centered religion in the work of racial uplift: "It is that holy religion ... whose precepts will raise and elevate us above our present condition, and cause our aspirations to ascend up in unison with theirs [antislavery societies], and become the final means of bursting the bands of oppression."[65] As Marilyn Richardson puts it, "resistance to oppression was, for Stewart, the highest form of obedience to God."[66] Social gospel was a hallmark of Stewart's public career, in which she repeatedly sought to "convert" African Americans through her oratory and writing to the necessity of uniting in order to better their collective condition, as she did in "Cause" when she wrote: "It is high time for us to promote ourselves by some meritorious acts." Here we can hear the refrain repeatedly offered in newspapers like *Colored American* and *Freedom's Journal* that advocated literary societies as routes not only to self-improvement, but also as representational correctives seen to be essential to both "race" advancement and abolition. An anonymous "Short Address; Read at a 'Mental Feast,' by a young lady of color," published in the May 11, 1833 edition of *The Liberator*, would also argue that "to elevate our condition, and alleviate our brethren in bondage from the bitter and galling yoke," all African Americans, including women called to "arise ... and resolve," must be educated or "enlighten[ed] in literature and knowledge."[67] At roughly the same time, Stewart also pressed African Americans to regard the Black woman and her education as integral to racial uplift: "Many bright and intelligent ones are in the midst of us; but because they are not calculated to display a classical education, they hide their talents behind a napkin." By stressing women's intelligence despite their lack of access to formal education, Stewart implicitly raised the question of just where they might be developing that intelligence. "One of the most significant ways literary societies were instrumental in establishing the place of African American women was by exposing them to education generally," documents McHenry. "Before formal education opportunities became available for Black women, literary societies served as 'school[s] for the encouragement and promotion of polite literature.' They were invaluable means of educating Black women beyond what was considered their 'proper sphere.'"[68] Female literary societies were, in effect, another way to consider Stewart's "napkin"; they provided the cover behind which African American women both acquired and argued more broadly for education when organizations such as the Black convention movement focused on formal education for Black men.[69]

Through recirculation, calls for women's education like Stewart's, Sarah Forten's ("A."), "Beatrice's," and Cassey's developed in women's literary societies and then were raised at the very heart of Black public politics – the pages of a newspaper. They joined women's letters on emancipation and slavery that were part of a larger discourse on freedom and the rights of "the race" pursued in women's literary societies that we see published as addresses and poetry in the early 1830s.[70] In the case of *Freedom's Journal*, women's writing could reach a national and transnational readership as far afield as the Caribbean, Canada West, and England.[71] Such calls for women's education reached a predominantly African American readership of *The Liberator*, since 80 percent of its initial 450 subscribers were free African Americans and Black "organizations, churches, societies, and prosperous Negro businessmen either donated funds or bought blocks of subscriptions" to the paper.[72] The organizations and societies Armistead Pride and Clint Wilson note as part of *The Liberator*'s subscription base would undoubtedly have included the African American mutual benevolent and literary societies predominant in the northeast in the 1830s. In Boston, as in Philadelphia, New York, and further south in Washington, DC, Black men's mutual aid societies "functioned as units of solidarity" by "identif[ying] and promot[ing] Black leaders ... [and] sponsor[ing] petitions and letters to the public addressing concerns of the African

American community."[73] Garrison envisioned *The Liberator* as a forum for Black activists and an interracial political coalition, and he represented the free northern African American community as politically active and organized by reporting on their meetings.

But these calls for Black women's education also reached readers in the South. Garrison made a deliberate use of the American "culture of reprinting" to heighten the sense of his paper's impact,[74] as Henry Mayer documents: "Southern editors not only saw the paper but reprinted material from it – accompanied by bitter condemnation – which was then picked up by other papers and eventually worked over again by Garrison in a lively cycle that . . . enabled *The Liberator* to make a noise out of proportion to its size or subscription base."[75] By the time Stewart approached Garrison in the fall of 1831, the effects of that "lively cycle" were evident: Georgetown, DC had passed a law prohibiting free African Americans from picking up copies of the paper at the post office and imposing a twenty-five dollar fine and thirty days imprisonment for those who did so; if they were unable to pay the fine, they would be "sold into slavery for four months."[76] Other southern cities offered rewards for whites found circulating the paper, posted rewards for Garrison's arrest, and raised calls for Boston's mayor to suppress the paper. Garrison received death threats both from the South and from within New England.[77]

Stewart wrote Garrison in "Cause for Encouragement" only a month after he had published Black women's contributions to the PFLA in *The Liberator*'s "Ladies' Department" and sought more such contributions for his newspaper with a report in the June 30, 1832 edition:

> Nearly all of [the members of this 'society of colored ladies'] write . . . original pieces, which are put anonymously into a box, and afterwards criticized by a committee. Having been permitted to bring with him several of these pieces, he ventures to commence their publication, not only for their merit, but in order to induce the colored ladies of other places to go and do likewise.[78]

The Liberator expanded the presence of women in its pages by its second volume; arguably Garrison gave "increasing prominence to women's voices, both Black and white" *because* he had content to fill that additional space from the PFLA and, later, news from female antislavery societies. African American women from the PFLA published anonymously and under multiple pseudonyms in Garrison's paper: Sarah Mapps Douglass published as "Zillah" and "Sophanisba," Sarah Forten as "Ada," "A.", and "Magawisca," along with other unidentified women signing themselves "Bera," "Anna Elizabeth," "Ella," "Beatrice," "Zoe," and "Woodby."[79]

Garrison's paper, *The Colored American,* and *Freedom's Journal* were an early part of what Logan documents as a system of "direct link[s] between these societies and various publication venues" by the late nineteenth century, meaning that "a paper presented at a literary society meeting might be published in a newspaper or by the society itself or ... be developed into a book for even wider distribution."[80] In other words, the imbrication of oratory and print, literary society and newspaper, that was commonplace by the century's close was being established by Black women in the late 1820s and through the 1830s. These links between literary society and newspaper were as fragile as Black newspapers themselves, many of which were in operation for less than a year, but they were also fundamental to the establishment of a Black press in the United States.

Colonization and Black Nationalism

Debates over colonization and assertions of Black nationalism were central to African American conceptualizations of and claims to home and national belonging. These notions were necessarily future-oriented in their imagining otherwise. As other contributors to this series make clear, such freedom dreams have fueled African American literature and its transformations since the earliest texts and it continues to be a preoccupation. Colonization debates and Black nationalist politics are often misunderstood as the purview of male political leaders and writers, yet Black nationalist politics were far from unusual in women's literary societies. Sarah Mapps Douglass published "Moonlight" under her pseudonym "Zillah" in the Ladies' Department just two weeks before Stewart's address appeared. What some may see now as a subtle Black nationalist argument against emigration and colonization was one of those "original piece[s]" that members of the PFLA "put anonymously into a box, and afterwards [were] criticised by a committee," and which in turn might make their way into print in *The Liberator.*[81] Born free in Philadelphia on September 9, 1806, Sarah Douglass was a co-founder of the PFLA and a member of the interracial Philadelphia Female Anti-Slavery Society, which her mother, Grace Bustill Douglass, had helped found in 1833. Sarah Mapps Douglass was a teacher, opened a school for African American children in Philadelphia in the 1820s, was active in abolition at a time when attending abolition meetings was "a life-threatening activity,"[82] and, like Stewart, entered masculinist political debates over emigration and colonization. "Moonlight" appears to be Douglass's first foray into Black nationalist politics in *The Liberator*'s pages. Contemplating the death of friends, Douglass recalled her "happy schooldays, – my school companions . . . O, my heart! where are they now? Two or three have left their native city for a foreign land; others have passed away." Likening emigration to death, she closed with her understated "hope" that African Americans would yet become citizens of the nation, rather than be forced to establish colonies in "foreign" lands: "Hope whispers, – 'The time is not far distant, when the wronged and enslaved children of America shall cease to be a "by-word and a reproach" among their brethren.'"[83]

Within the communal spaces of literary societies, women explored a range of sites for reimagined and realized Black freedom and belonging beyond the US as nation state. Douglass contributed regularly to the *Liberator*'s Ladies' Department throughout 1832, signing her contributions "Zillah" and "Sophanisba," and contributed as "Zillah" to *The Emancipator* in 1833.[84] On January 28, 1832, Garrison published a PFLA member's contribution to "the box" signed "A Colored Female of Philadelphia" that advocated emigration to Mexico or Upper Canada over Africa, framed as in keeping with "the sentiments of some of my Trenton brethren." This anonymous member cited "attach[ing] ourselves to a nation already established . . . in this hemisphere," lauding emigration as the exercise of "republicanism" and "that spirit of independence" made "manifest." She particularly advocated for emigration to Mexico, noting its climate and soil as "contribut[ing] to our wealth" and in turn enabling African Americans to "become a people of worth and respectability." Mexico, too, promised "the rapid growth of amalgamation amongst" its "eight millions of colored, and one million of whites," which the anonymous PFLA member argued had "every probability" of "becom[ing] one entire colored nation."[85] Come late July 1832, an extract from a letter Sarah Douglass wrote a friend in February of that year debating emigration to Upper Canada appeared in *The Liberator*: "You do not agree with me in regard to emigration. Would that I had eloquence enough to convince you that I am right!" wrote Douglass. "If we should bend our steps to Hayti, there is no security for life and property . . . If we go to Mexico, it is the same there. Why throw ourselves upon the protection of Great Britain, when thousands of her own children are starving? Do you suppose she can feel more love for us than she does for her own?"[86]

As James and Lois Horton document, Haiti had actively sought to attract African American immigration since 1804, and as contributors such as Ben Fagan and Marlene Daut explore in volume three of this series, Haiti fueled a Black literary imagination at mid-century. By 1818, Haiti was more than an imagined otherwise with the Haitian government offering African Americans land and paid passage. In the 1820s Jonathan Granville, a charismatic Haitian military officer, traveled through the American northeast and the upper South lecturing on the advantages of Haitian emigration to "large and enthusiastic" African American audiences.[87] The Haitian Emigration Society was formed in Philadelphia in 1824, and by the 1830s some 8,000 to 13,000 African Americans had emigrated to Haiti, only to face illness and hardship. In order to keep African American immigrants in the rural areas they were expected to settle, the Haitian government instituted the Rural Code of 1826, which African Americans experienced as enforcing "slave-like plantation labor."[88]

By the early 1830s when Sarah Mapps Douglass was writing on emigration for *The Liberator*, the disappointments of Haitian emigration and opposition to the ACS had rendered debates over emigration and colonization highly charged. Some African Americans were participating in Liberian colonization yet reports raised fears of their endangered health. Canada emerged as a viable alternative, said to have a healthier climate, and was seriously discussed at the national Black conventions in the early to mid-1830s. However, Black leaders were also ambivalent about Canada as a site for Black settlements, fearing that it would create the perception that African Americans had relinquished their fight for rights in the United States. Canada would re-emerge in the 1850s when Mary Ann Shadd Cary, Henry and Mary Bibb, Samuel Delany, and Frederick Douglass would all emigrate or temporarily relocate there, and a revolutionary Black imagination would be realized in John Brown's recruiting of Black resistance fighters from Chatham to the raid on Harper's Ferry. From the 1830s through the 1860s, 40,000 African Americans emigrated to Canada, more than emigrated to either Haiti or Africa, while the vast majority of African Americans remained in the United States.[89] These debates and emigrations, whether to Haiti, Liberia, or Canada, were part of both a transnational political Black imaginary and the transnationalism of African American literature.

Women's literary society members, including Douglass, were well-informed voices within evolving emigration and colonization debates in the 1820s and early 1830s. By August 1832, Douglass (as "Zillah") was on record in *The Liberator* as finding Haiti and Canada unsuitable colonies for African Americans and rejecting emigration altogether. She stood firm in a response to "Woodby," published in that same August 18, 1832 edition, correcting Woodby's mistaken impression that her letter extract published in the July 21, 1832 edition was a response to "A Colored Female of

Philadelphia," yet in that response Douglass also indicates she had "placed" that extract "in the box last week." In other words, Douglass seems to have used the double distancing of her "Zillah" pseudonym and what appears to be the pretense of a letter to someone outside the literary society in order to engage in that society's debates. Much as Maria Stewart fused her social gospel with her Black nationalist arguments, Douglass invoked God as ordaining that African Americans remain in their "own, native land": "I firmly believe it is his will that we remain. I would not give up this belief for a thousand worlds ... Cease, then, to think of any other city of refuge. Listen to the voice of our dear Redeemer! ... 'Fear not, little flock; it is your Father's good pleasure to give you the kingdom.'"[90] Douglass engaged with Woodby's position only through a social gospel rhetoric, invoking God, "the approval of Heaven," "the Rock of Ages," "our dear Redeemer" and the Father in her short four-paragraph response.

Maria Stewart's Black nationalist politics were not unusual in women's literary societies as we can see; rather, her ideas took shape through their growth and influence, thus rendering Boston's African American Female Intelligence Society (AAFIS) more than a venue for her work. Little has been made of the AAFIS as the site for her first public address in the spring of 1832, "Address Delivered Before the Afric-American Female Intelligence Society of America," beyond the fact that she spoke before a predominately Black female audience. Yet, it is far from accidental that Stewart first addressed a Black women's literary society, and the significance of this venue extends well beyond our expectation that she would have been as welcome to address them as any woman from their own membership. In fact, as scholarship on Stewart stresses, her message was not welcome. McHenry surmises that, like other societies of its kind in the 1830s and 1840s, the AAFIS counted roughly thirty members. Established in September 1831 and similar to the PFLA, Boston's AAFIS collected both monthly and yearly dues, using them to purchase books and hire the room in which they met.[91] Marilyn Richardson quotes its preamble to its constitution, which was published in *The Liberator* on January 7, 1832:

> Whereas the subscribers, women of color of the Commonwealth of Massachusetts, actuated by a natural feeling for the welfare of our friends, have thought fit to associate for the diffusion of knowledge, the suppression of vice and immorality, and for cherishing such virtues as will render us happy and useful to society, sensible of the gross ignorances under which we have too long labored, but trusting, by the blessing of God, we shall be able to accomplish the object of our union – we have therefore associated ourselves under the name of the Afric-American Female Intelligence Society. . .[92]

The group's constitution marks, through its listing of acceptable activities and interests, the links between women's literary and benevolent societies: community welfare, both economic and moral, and community service rendered in the name of womanly virtue. Rather than claiming the acquisition of knowledge for women, the association gathers for the "diffusion" of knowledge. To these ends, the society "rented halls and sponsored lectures by William Lloyd Garrison" and others, promoted "abolitionist debates, dramatic readings, fund-raising" and the establishment of "reading rooms, and other community welfare projects," but it "did not itself participate in public debates or lectures."[93] However supportive the AAFIS was of abolitionist politics, the fact that its members did not "participate in public debates or lectures" beyond presentations to their own small circle tells us something of their response to Stewart's address.

Maria Stewart took to Boston platforms from the fall of 1832 to her farewell address in late September of 1833 having already positioned herself as a selfless, lone voice, a martyr willing to be censured for the cause. She had closed *Religion and the Pure Principles of Morality, The Sure Foundation on Which We Must Build* (1831), published by Garrison a year before her first Boston lecture before the AAFIS, rather dramatically:

> I have never taken one step, my friends, with a design to raise myself in your esteem, or to gain applause. But what I have done, has been done with an eye single to the glory of God, and to promote the good of souls. I have neither kindred nor friends. I stand alone in your midst, exposed to the fiery darts of the devil, and to the assaults of wicked men. But though all the powers of earth and hell were to combine against me, though all nature should sink into decay, still I would trust in the Lord, and joy in the God of my salvation.[94]

In her first address to the AAIS in the spring of 1832, Stewart again presented herself as a martyr: "I have enlisted in the holy warfare, and Jesus is my captain; and the Lord's battle I mean to fight, until my voice expire in death. I expect to be hated of all men, and persecuted even unto death, for righteousness and the truth's sake."[95] In fact, she repeated these invocations so often that they became a hallmark of her lectures and writing as she cultivated a holy warrior persona serving the divine will of God and Black liberationist politics. Stewart worked deliberately, in other words, to protect her Black female peers in the AAFIS from community censure by association – she was a lone figure, not part of the female collective she first addressed – yet she also worked to direct that negative attention toward her political ends. I read this as Stewart's awareness of the rhetorical force of recirculation, not a "fatal rhetorical miscalculation."[96]

Stewart's deliberate courting of notoriety for its use in heightening recirculation is rooted in her appropriation of masculine political address in her religious rhetoric. Eddie Glaude notes that religion was central to Black politics and Black nationalism, in particular, in the early nineteenth century when "the nation [was] imagined not alongside religion but precisely *through* the precepts of Black Christianity ... [O]ut of Black religious life emerged a conception of Black national identity."[97] For antebellum northern African Americans, political discourse and "political languages were tied to a Black Christian imagination."[98] Stewart's social gospel, then, was firmly in step with male-dominated political debate, and her militancy was conventionally masculine. Her spirituality and evangelism were more than a matter of rhetorical style, but instead were part of that larger masculine Black nationalist political discourse that saw Black national identity emerge from Black Christianity.

Stewart opened her lecture before the AAFIS in step with its constitutional focus on virtue, morality and humility: "religion is held in low repute among some of us; and purely to promote the cause of Christ, and the good of souls, in the hope that others more experienced, more able and talented than myself might go forward and do likewise."[99] But in just two sentences she moved to a fiery jeremiad that ran for paragraphs, indicting the African American clergy for failing to "faithfully discharge their duty" to keep the truth and the Black community for working against its own interests.[100] "Our own color are our greatest opposers," claimed Stewart.[101] She then quickly moved to the Black nationalist call for community solidarity and collective uplift that was also ringing out in the Black convention movement:

> [U]nless the rising generation manifest a different temper and disposition towards each other from what we have manifested, the generation following will never be an enlightened people. We this day are considered as one of the most degraded races upon the face of the earth. It is useless for us any longer to sit with our hands folded, reproaching the whites; for that will never elevate us.[102]

Patrick Rael has noted that in the antebellum North "theodicy and jeremiads" were "meld[ed] ... with important principles of nationalism" in the rhetoric of Black leaders that "told African American northerners they were part of a special community with a divine mission."[103] Stewart's movement in this address, from a focus on religion, to an indictment of the clergy, and on to a call for Black collectivity, indicates her appropriation of a Black nationalist politics, making her closing even more outrageous than her claim to be "fired ... with a holy zeal" to call her community to account for their "envious and malicious disposition." Stewart's address ends with her exhorting the women of this literary society to form the backbone of a renewed Black nationalism: "O woman, woman! Upon you I call, for upon your exertions almost entirely depends whether the rising generation shall be any thing more than we have been or not. O woman, woman! Your example is powerful, your influence great; it extends over your husbands and your children, and throughout the circle of your acquaintance."[104] While Stewart closed with a nod to woman's influence, in keeping with gendered notions at the time, she was also resting her Black nationalist call for collectivity and racial uplift upon it. This is a move that scholars have characterized as beyond the comfort zone of her audience.

Yet, Stewart was deliberate in all she did. She knew she would cause a stir in Boston and presented herself as the world-weary martyr to the Black nationalist cause whose "soul has been so discouraged within me, that I have almost been induced to exclaim, 'Would to God that my tongue hereafter might cleave to the roof of my mouth and become silent forever!'"[105] In this closing she effectively invited her female listeners at the AAFIS to indict and martyr her, and then she took the text of her address to Garrison's *Liberator* offices. He published it in the April 28, 1832 edition with the header, "It is proper to state that the Address of Mrs. Stewart, in our Ladies' Department to-day, is published *at her own request*, and *not by desire of the Society* before whom it was delivered."[106] Stewart recirculated her lecture as the anomalous and independent act of a marginal figure to the Boston Black community in a paper she already knew would reach most Black Bostonians, Black communities in the northeast, and part of an anxious southern reprinting circuit. She made Black women's role in Black nationalism newsworthy beyond Boston by understanding that she could use recirculation and the force of Garrison's incendiary paper and personal reputation in ways that not only benefited her political work but were beneficial to Garrison's cause and *The Liberator*'s viability. Marilyn Richardson notes that advertising the lectures of a Black woman and printing them along with her essays gave Garrison items of "news in and of themselves," as well as "strong statements in support of his publication's stands."[107] Stewart very clearly set in motion a program that saw her follow the *Liberator* print shop's printing and the paper's advertising of her tract *Religion and the Pure Principles of Morality* in 1831, with its publication of her AAFIS lecture in April 1832. Her letter to the editor, "Cause for Encouragement," was then published in July 1832, followed by advertisements for reprintings of three further public lectures she gave in Boston. These reprintings ran "By Request"[108] from the fall of 1832 through the fall of 1833. It is worth underscoring here that the AAFIS constitution was printed in the *Liberator* in the midst of Stewart's political program and four months before her address before the society was recirculated.

Even appearing to have been run out of Boston seems to have worked well for Maria Stewart if we understand recirculation as foundational to her Black feminist politics. Stewart left Boston in 1833 for New York City, where she remained active in reform and Black feminist politics by joining the Ladies' Literary Society of New York and attending the Woman's Anti-Slavery Convention of 1837.[109] Alexander Crummel recalls "listening, on more than a few occasions, to some of her compositions and declamations" produced for that society.[110] She continued to be visible in the press and to lecture after she left Boston, becoming a "regular contributor" to the AME *Repository of Religion and Literature, and of Science and Art* in the late 1850s to mid-1860s.[111] Stewart evidently continued to work through that feedback loop between the Black press and literary societies, for

> many of the features that were included in the *Repository* were lectures that had been given before or were prepared in the context of men's and women's literary societies, and the editors appealed regularly to members of the literary societies that sponsored the magazine to employ "their rich thought and polished pen" toward the productions of "contributions of great value."[112]

One of the *Repository*'s regular columns was the "Young Ladies' Lecture Room," and the paper's 1858 genesis was in its publication by "select 'Literary Societies of the African Methodist Episcopal Church.'"[113]

Maria Stewart crafted a public persona in Boston at the beginning of her career that, in many ways, scholarship has adopted with little question. Yet we should pay attention to the afterlife of her work in that city because it signals the likelihood that her Boston orations developed in the collective sites of women's literary societies, sites that continued to be a value to her in New York. Rather than an isolated individual pursuing an unusual politics, Stewart was a participant among many, and her work was possible not only because it was shared by other women who had been making related arguments through literary societies that we can document since 1827, but also because women's societies – benevolent and literary – had been training grounds for their communally-oriented political work as early as the eighteenth century, as Foster reminds us. Stewart's career as a reader, writer and orator may be one of the best known in Black women's historiography of the early nineteenth century, but its development in women's literary societies is far from unique. In fact, these societies supported the growth of Black women's politics and literature, broadly conceived, of which Stewart was a part, not a rejected renegade. That growth was fostered by and included women such as Amy Matilda Cassey, Elizabeth Jennings, Sarah Mapps Douglass, Sarah Forten, and their fellow members of the PFLA. The writing that emerged from and was influenced by women's literary societies, such as Stewart's, Forten's, and Douglass's, employed techniques that Richardson notes became characteristic of African American women's writing by the late nineteenth century, such as the work of "Frances Harper, Emma Kelley, Alice Dunbar-Nelson, and Pauline Hopkins," including hybrid historical and autobiographical writing, shifts in narrative point of view, and "sentimental ... cliff-hanging moments of uncertainty, cruel misunderstandings which compromise the heroine's reputation, ... scene[s] of bleak despair ... and, of course, prayers answered in the fullness of time."[114]

Women's literary societies not only fostered and shaped the development of both Black women's politics and writing, but they also continued to sustain the Black press – the central site of Black literary circulation at this time – as it established its critical mass across the nation. Sarah Mapps Douglass helped found the all-Black Women's Association of Philadelphia in 1848 to support "Frederick Douglass's call for Black nationalism."[115] Its constitution's preamble, written by Black nationalist Martin Delany, stressed "self-elevation" and "self-exertion," and a program of fundraising through fairs and bazaars that would "support ... the Press and Public Lecturers devoted to the Elevation of the Colored People."[116] The Association clearly articulated its intention to participate in Black nationalist efforts and its sense that the press was central to such a politics: "Whereas, believing Self-Elevation to be the only true issue upon which to base our efforts as an oppressed portion of the American people; and believing ... that the Press and Public Lecturer are the most powerful means by which an end so desirable can be attained."[117] Sarah Mapps Douglass went on to found in Philadelphia the Sarah M. Douglass Literary Circle in September 1859.[118] She did so when Black newspapers such as *The Weekly Anglo-African* were "inspir[ing] the formation of both informal literary coalitions and a formal reading room," publishing readers' calls for "literary gatherings or circles," and printing letters that characterized reading rooms as "productive of good, especially if the ladies patronize [them] and enter into discussions upon the merits of different periodicals." The Weekly Anglo-African Reading Room on Prince Street in New York City held lectures and meetings "often sponsored by independent literary societies," including women's societies.[119] In the west, come the late

1860s, African American women were financially sustaining Black newspapers through benevolent organizations, such as San Francisco's Ladies' Pacific Accumulating Society, which had formed the "Elevator Aid Association" to financially support Phillip Bell's *Elevator* (1865–1898). As F.H Grice wrote the paper in October 1868, "our ladies show far more interest in sustaining the press, and they intend to continue their benevolent undertaking in aid of a journal which fearlessly vindicates our rights, not as a distinct race, but as American citizens. If the gentlemen would only rally and support the ladies, we would gain a complete victory."[120]

Literary societies remained important well into the nineteenth century. They continued to promote the "understanding of reading, writing, and print as technologies of power and political agency" at mid-century, and McHenry documents that "in the aftermath of the failure of Reconstruction, literary societies were reorganized in the North" as "the staging ground for Black communities' increased activism."[121] Black feminists like Mary Church Terrell were shaped by this reconfigured landscape of literary societies that by the 1880s included racially integrated clubs like "the Aelioian Literary Society which 'provided women with a forum for debate and oration' and was founded in 1852 as a more progressive branch of the Oberlin College Ladies Literary Society." Terrell, "quite possibly [its] first Black member ... credit[ed] the society with exposing her to some of the best speakers in the country and with enabling her to argue extempore, preside over meetings and hold her own in formal debates."[122] Though the "link between newspapers, literary clubs, and subsequently published works" is an "often overlooked" one, at least as early as 1827 we see it registered, with women swiftly coming to dominate literary societies as the primary site in which that link was forged and sustained through African American communal reading practices that made the oral inextricable from Black print culture.

Notes

1 Frances Smith Foster, "A Narrative of the Interesting Origins and (Somewhat) Surprising Developments of African American Print Culture," *American Literary History* 17, no. 4 (2005): 715.

2 Foster cites "a confederation of African Union Societies in Rhode Island, Massachusetts, and Pennsylvania" formed "as early as 1780." Ibid., 726. Sharing Foster's reiteration of Dorothy Porter's original documentation of the African Union Societies, Shirley Wilson Logan also dates formally organized literary societies from the Rhode Island African Union Society (1780). Shirley Wilson Logan, *Liberating Language: Sites of Rhetorical Education in*

Nineteenth-Century Black America (Carbondale: Southern Illinois University Press, 2008), 58. See Dorothy Porter, ed., *Early Negro Writing 1760–1837* (Boston: Beacon Press, 1971), 5.

3 Foster, "A Narrative," 721. Foster, Shirley Wilson Logan, and David Proper all speculate that literary circles or societies fostered the emergence of early African American poetry such as Lucy Terry Prince's ballad "Bar's Fight" (1746). Proper cites Prince's home as a site for "recitations, music and poetry on the order of an adult literary circle." David R. Proper, "Lucy Terry Prince: 'Singer of History,'" *Contributions in Black Studies* 9 (1990–1992): 192. Foster also sees Phillis 'Wheatley's *Poems on Various Subjects* (1778) as emerging from such a context of communal literary production and recitation. Foster, "A Narrative," 721. See also Logan, *Liberating Language*, 60.

4 Martin E. Dann, ed., *The Black Press, 1827–1890: The Quest for National Identity* (New York: G.P. Putnam's Sons, 1971), 17.

5 Book-length studies that have dramatically altered scholarly understanding of early African American readers are Elizabeth McHenry, *Forgotten Readers: Recovering the Lost History of African American Literary Societies* (Durham: Duke University Press, 2002) and Shirley Wilson Logan's *Liberating Language*, as well as selected essays in Kristin Waters and Carol B. Conaway, eds., *Black Women's Intellectual Traditions: Speaking Their Minds* (Burlington: University of Vermont Press, 2007). One marker of literary societies' role in the developing Black press would be *Freedom's Journal* and its campaign to promote these societies, begun in 1827, co-incident with the space it devoted to African American writers such as Phillis Wheatley and George Moses Horton and reviews of their work. Another related marker is the way in which the *Colored American* operated as what McHenry calls a "coworker of these societies, operating in conjunction with them to further their shared mission." *Freedom's Journal* is widely acknowledged as the first African American paper, in publication from 1827 to 1829, while the *Colored American* began publication in 1837. McHenry, *Forgotten Readers*, 97–99, 104. I go on to note some of the literary societies that interacted with the *Colored American*.

6 McHenry, *Forgotten Readers*, 85.

7 Dorothy Porter documents African American literary societies in Cincinnati and Columbus, Detroit, Baltimore, and Washington, DC. Dorothy Porter, "The Organized Activities of Negro Literary Societies, 1828–1846," *Journal of Negro Education* 5 (1936): 558.

8 Logan notes the 1853 founding of the San Francisco Athenaeum as "the first Black literary society in California," which "established a library and reading room and launched the city's first Black newspaper, *Mirror of the Times*," and an 1855 report in *Frederick Douglass's Paper* of the Sacramento Musical and Literary Society. Logan, *Liberating Language*, 64.

9 Logan documents the "first mixed-sex literary society in Ontario," the African Canadian Wilberforce Lyceum Education Society (1850) and Mary Bibb's organization of the Windsor Ladies Club or Windsor Mutual Improvement

Society in 1854. Ibid., 66 and 64. See also Heather Murray, *Come Bright Improvement! The Literary Societies of Nineteenth-Century Ontario* (Toronto: University of Toronto Press, 2002).

10 McHenry, *Forgotten Readers*, 86.

11 Michelle N. Garfield, "Literary Societies: The Work of Self-Improvement and Racial Uplift," in *Black Women's Intellectual Traditions: Speaking Their Minds*, eds. Kristin Waters and Carol B. Conaway (Burlington: University of Vermont Press, 2007), 126.

12 Porter documents the first women's literary society as the 1831 Philadelphia Female Literary Society and the first men's society as that city's 1828 Reading Room Society. Porter, "Organized," 557. McHenry documents the greater growth of women's over men's societies as the century progressed and notes that women's benevolent societies in cities like Philadelphia nearly doubled their male counterparts as early as 1831. McHenry, *Forgotten Readers*, 57.

13 Foster has argued that "by 1827, when public education for men was scant and for women almost nonexistent, enough African-American women could and did read newspapers that their interests affected the papers' content. (In fact, from the first issues, some women writers appeared as subjects and as contributors.)" Frances Smith Foster, "Genealogies of Our Concern, Early (African) American Print Culture, and Transcending Tough Times," *Early American Literature* 22, no. 2 (2010): 355.

14 When I mention transnational communities, I have in mind not only the literary societies that worked in connection with the Black press in Canada, but also papers such as *Freedom's Journal* which publicized their transnational circulation via agents in the Caribbean, England, and Canada. See Jacqueline Bacon, *Freedom's Journal: The First African-American Newspaper* (Lanham: Lexington Books, 2007), 53.

15 McHenry, *Forgotten Readers*, 13.

16 I use recirculation to distinguish the deliberate and self-reflexive circulation of texts from women's literary societies through the Black press and back into the literary societies as distinctive and different from the journalistic practice of reprinting. I stress that distinction because I see Black feminist recirculation as having a political intent and effect that I would argue exceeded reprinting as a practice in the American press in the absence of copyright law. On reprinting, see Meredith McGill, *American Literature and the Culture of Reprinting, 1834–1853* (Philadelphia: University of Pennsylvania Press, 2003). I also choose recirculation and not remediation to name this practice because I seek both to highlight the movement of Black women's texts and their circulation as subtending a fledgling Black press and to avoid positioning their print publication as either altering their meaning or as achieving a more developed media form.

17 Dilip Parameshwar Gaonkar and Elizabeth A. Povinelli, "Technologies of Public Forms: Circulation, Transfiguration, Recognition," *Public Culture* 15, no. 3 (2003): 386.

18 Elizabeth McHenry, "'An Association of Kindred Spirits': Black Readers and Their Reading Rooms," *Institutions of Reading: The Social Life of Libraries in the United States*, eds. Thomas Augst and Kenneth E, Carpenter (Amherst: University of Massachusetts Press, 2007), 102.

19 Foundational scholarship on literary societies includes Sandra Moon and Jean Libby, "A Successful 19th Century Literary Society," *Negro History Bulletin* 41 (1978): 850; Porter, "The Organized Activities of Negro Literary Societies, 555–576; Dorothy Porter (ed.), *Early Negro Writing 1760–1837* (Boston: Beacon Press, 1971); Dorothy Sterling, *We Are Your Sisters: Black Women in the Nineteenth Century* (New York: Norton, 1984).

20 See "Notice . . . The African Dorcas Association," *Freedom's Journal* February 1, 1828.

21 James Oliver Horton and Lois E. Horton, *In Hope of Liberty: Culture, Community and Protest among Northern Free Blacks, 1700–1860* (New York: Oxford University Press, 1997), 128.

22 Porter, "The Organized Activities of Negro Literary Societies, 558–559. An undated letter written by a white man to *The Liberator* published in its 30 August 1832 edition dates the Philadelphian Minerva Society as being in operation "about 9 months," with Henrietta Matthews then its president. The writer notes she "frequently visited them on their meeting nights . . . to see and hear my oppressed sisters. read and recite pieces, some of which were original, and which would have done credit to the fairest female in America – the republican land of liberty." McHenry refers to such touristic attendance as forming "a steady stream of observers." J.C.B., "Literary Societies," *The Liberator,* August 30, 1834. McHenry, *Forgotten Readers*, 79.

23 Erica Armstrong Dunbar, *A Fragile Freedom: African American Women and Emancipation in the Antebellum City* (New Haven: Yale University Press, 2008), 60.

24 Philadelphia was home to at least "nine different literary societies" between 1828 and 1841, including "the Reading Room Society, formed in 1828," the PFLA (1831), "the Library Company of Colored Persons, formed in 1833; the Philadelphia Association for Moral and Mental Improvement of the People of Color, formed in 1835; the Rush Library and Debating Society, both began in 1836; the Demosthenian Institute and the Edgeworth Society, formed in 1837; and the Gilbert Lyceum, formed in 1841." Phyllis M. Belt-Beyan, *The Emergence of African American Literacy Traditions: Family and Community Efforts in the Nineteenth Century* (Westport: Greenwood, 2004), 115–116.

25 *The Liberator*, May 5, 1832; *Genius of Universal Emancipation,* March 1832. See Belt-Beyan for the other African American literary society and the two reading rooms founded in Boston in 1835 and 1836, respectively. She also documents the formation of literary and debating societies during the late 1830s through the mid-1840s in Detroit, Washington, DC, Baltimore, New Bedford, and cities in Rhode Island. Belt-Beyan, *The Emergence*, 116.

26 "Summary," *Freedom's Journal*, August 24, 1827, 3.

27 For reports on the Female Dorcas Association of New York City, see *Freedom's Journal,* February 1, 1828, February 15, 1828, March 7, 1828, September 26, 1828, October 3, 1828, November 21, 1828, January 9, 1829, February 7, 1829, March 14, 1829; for reports on the Female Dorcas Society of Buffalo, NY, see the *Weekly Advocate,* February 11, 1837, and the *Colored American,* November 4, 1837. Women did not always see literary societies as succeeding benevolent associations in a trajectory of civic participation. For example, Boston's Afric-American Female Intelligence Society of Boston was led by Elizabeth Riley, who went on to lead the Colored Female Union benevolent society. See Martha Jones, *All Bound Up Together: The Woman Question in African American Public Culture, 1830–1900*, (Chapel Hill: University of North Carolina Press, 2007), 221 n. 69.

28 In four years, the Troy Female Benevolent Society had grown from ten to sixty-one members and held in savings $236.10. Troy also supported a United Sons and Daughters of Zion's Benevolent Society, in operation since 1833 with forty-eight members and an account worth $112. J. J. Miter, "Colored People of Troy," *Colored American,* April 1, 1837, 1.

29 C.B.R, "For the Colored American," *Colored American,* November 4, 1837. On this trip, $100 was raised "from the Colored Citizens of Buffalo," though the Dorcas society is the only organization named.

30 On mental feasts, see McHenry, *Forgotten Readers,* 78. For example, *The Christian Recorder* was reporting on the Philadelphia Dorcas Society in the early 1860s. See, *The Christian Recorder,* November 23, 1861, November 22, 1862, and November 29, 1862.

31 McHenry, *Forgotten Readers,* 56. Here I am extending McHenry's insight into how literary societies functioned for women to benevolent societies that at times operated *as* literary societies.

32 Jones, *All Bound,* 39.

33 The *Colored American* reported on the Phoenixonian Society (1833–1841), sister literary society to the male Phoenix Society (1833–1839), and The Ladies' Literary Society of New York (founded 1834). See Amicus, "Our Literary Societies," *Colored American,* March 11, 1837. The paper also linked literary and benevolent societies in its reporting, such as in its September 1839 report on Poughkeepsie's "2 or 3 female benevolent associations" and the Phoenixonian Library, a "well attended" literary society connected with a debating society in the city. See "For the Colored American, Poughkeepsie, Sept 19th 1839," *Colored American,* September 28, 1839. A month later the paper described the Philomathean and Phoenixonian Societies, the Eclectic Fraternity, The Franklin Form, and the Tyro Association" as "praiseworthy literary institutions" of New York City. See "Literary Societies," *Colored American,* October 5, 1839.

34 Amicus, "Our Literary Societies."

35 Quoted in John Earnest, *Liberation Historiography: African American Writers and the Challenge of History, 1794–1861* (Chapel Hill: University of North Carolina Press, 2004), 295. McHenry refers to the *Colored American* as "a

great supporter of African American literary societies" and, so, a primary historical record of their formation and work. McHenry, *Forgotten Readers*, 327 n. 63. Indeed, its editors were active in the organization and management of such societies. Dorothy Porter documents that Charles Ray was on the Board of Directors of New York City's Phoenix Society; Samuel Cornish, who had left his co-editorship of *Freedom's Journal* over differences with John Russwurm regarding African colonization, was "at one time" its librarian; and Phillip Bell acted as "Chairman of the Board of Associates of the Philomathean Society." Porter, "Organized Activities," 566 and 568.

36 Muta, "Messrs. Editors," *Freedom's Journal*, July 27, 1827.

37 McHenry, *Forgotten Readers*, 41. African Americans continued to see literary societies as central politically and to see the literary as part of a respectability politics that centered the moral and religious as late as the 1880s, when we see the AME Church calling for the increase of its "Bethel Literaries . . . accumulating all over the country," so that the Church itself would come to be seen as a literary center and "not only a moral and religious" one. "Bethel Literaries," *The Christian Recorder*, January 31, 1884.

38 McHenry, *Forgotten Readers*, 63.

39 Logan, *Liberating Language*, 65.

40 Mapps Douglass and Forten were members of the PFLA; Stewart was a member of the Ladies Literary Society of New York after she left Boston in 1833; Elizabeth Jennings addressed that society in the fall of 1837 and in 1854 successfully sued against racial segregation on public transport in the city. On Jennings see Logan, *Liberating Language*, 74; on Stewart see Marilyn Richardson, ed., *Maria W. Stewart, America's First Black Woman Political Writer: Essays and Speeches* (Bloomington, Indiana University Press, 1987), 81.

41 Logan, *Liberating Language*, 44.

42 On Forten Grimké and Cooper see ibid., 56 and 87.

43 On Shadd Cary in the BHLS in the late 1880s and Terrell see McHenry, *Forgotten Readers*, 184–185 and 361 n. 94. Logan also notes that Terrell was "possibly the first Black member" of Oberlin's Aelioian Literary Society (1852) in the early 1880s. Logan, *Liberating Language*, 86.

44 Maritcha Lyons would also co-organize a Lyric Hall (New York) fundraiser in 1892 that launched Wells's transatlantic anti-lynching campaign.

45 McHenry, *Forgotten Readers*, 361 n. 89.

46 Michael Warner, *Publics and Counterpublics* (New York: Zone Books, 2002), 11–12, 67, original emphasis.

47 Ibid., 96.

48 Benjamin Lee and Edward LiPuma, "Cultures of Circulation: The Imaginations of Modernity," *Public Culture* 14, no. 1 (2002): 194.

49 Amy Matilda (Williams) married Joseph Cassey in 1827; Cassey was a sales agent for *The Liberator* and Erica Dunbar documents him as "already entrenched in early antislavery activity, Black improvement societies, and the creation of the first African American newspaper, *Freedom's Journal*" by

the time of their marriage. Erica R. Armstrong (Dunbar), "A Mental and Moral Fest: Reading, Writing, and Sentimentality in Black Philadelphia," *Journal of Women's History* 16, no. 1 (2004): 83. On Amy Matilda Cassey as "Matilda" see Mary Kelley, "'Talents Committed to Your Care': Reading and Writing Radical Abolitionism in Antebellum America," *The New England Quarterly* 88, no. 1 (2015), 69. Kelley does not note how she has arrived at this attribution of that signature.

50 The paper printed such sage cautions as: "A babbling tongue is the 'object of my implacable disgust.'" "Observer No. V," *Freedom's Journal*, October 5, 1827. See also, for example, "A Sketch of Comfort," *Freedom's Journal*, June 22, 1827.

51 "Matilda," "Messrs. Editors," *Freedom's Journal*, August 10, 1827, 2.

52 "Beatrice," "By a young lady of color. For the Liberator. Female Education," *The Liberator*, July 7, 1832.

53 "A.", "By a member of the Female Literary Association," *The Liberator*, November 22, 1834.

54 "Third Anniversary of the Ladies' Literary Society of the City of New York," *The Colored American*, September 23, 1837.

55 Richardson, "Introduction," in *Maria W. Stewart, America's First Black Woman Political Writer: Essays and Speeches* (Bloomington: Indiana University Press, 1987), 26.

56 Joycelyn Moody, *Sentimental Confessions: Spiritual Narratives of Nineteenth-Century African American Women* (Athens: University of Georgia Press, 2001), 26. Moody does not document this letter she attributes to Stewart beyond what I note here.

57 Richardson, *Maria W. Stewart*, 126 n. 68.

58 Martha Jones documents that by 1836 women "were seated as delegates and [were] signing petitions" at the Colored Conventions. Jones, *All Bound*, 45.

59 Richardson, *Maria W. Stewart*, 81. Dorothy Porter documents two Black women's literary societies in New York City in the 1830s, "The Ladies Literary Society of the City of New York" and "The New York Female Literary Society." Porter, "Organized," 557.

60 Benedict Anderson, *Imagined Communities* (London: Verso, 1983), 35.

61 Warner, *Publics and Counterpublics*, 105.

62 Lee and LiPuma, "Cultures of Circulation," 194.

63 See Jürgen Habermas, *The Structural Transformation of the Public Sphere: An Inquiry into a Category of Bourgeois Society*, trans. Thomas Burger (Cambridge: MIT Press, 1989).

64 Maria, *Freedom's Journal*, April 4, 1828; "A Colored Lady in Medford," *The Liberator*, April 9, 1831; May, *The Liberator*, October 27, 1832. See also "Phila," on women's respectability in antislavery in *The Liberator*, March 17, 1834 and "S.," praising the paper in the March 22, 1831 edition of *The Liberator*. These join two letters to the editor by Sarah Mapps Douglass. See "Zillah" (Sarah Mapps Douglass), "To a Friend," *The Liberator*, June 30, 1832; Sarah Mapps Douglass, "Dear Brother," *The Liberator*, September 30,

1837. These letters were part of a larger discourse on freedom and the rights of "the race" pursued in women's literary societies that included addresses and poetry in the early 1830s.

65 Maria Stewart, "Cause for Encouragement," *The Liberator*, July 14, 1832.

66 Richardson, "Introduction," 9.

67 Anon., "A Short Address," *The Liberator*, May 11, 1833.

68 McHenry, *Forgotten Readers*, 68.

69 In 1833, the Black Convention movement proposed a "mechanical arts" high school and a college for men in New Haven, Connecticut. This was the same year that Prudence Crandall founded her academy for Black women in Canterbury, Connecticut when her school for girls, first established in 1831, drew censure because she had admitted an African American pupil. Whatever the social stigma against educating Black male youth, the education of Black girls and women was regarded as much more controversial in the 1830s.

70 See: Anon., "Address to the Female Literary Association of Philadelphia, On their First Anniversary: By a Member," *The Liberator*, October 13, 1832.

71 McHenry, *Forgotten Readers*, 89.

72 Armistead S. Pride and Clint C. Wilson, II, *A History of the Black Press* (Washington, DC: Howard University Press, 1997), 26. Benjamin Quarles notes that by the spring of 1843, African Americans formed three-quarters of *The Liberator*'s 2,300 subscribers. Benjamin Quarles, *Black Abolitionists* (Oxford and New York: Oxford University Press, 1969), 20.

73 McHenry, *Forgotten Readers*, 44–45.

74 Meredith McGill argues that in the absence of copyright, a "culture of reprinting" sustained newspapers in the US and gave local happenings and marginalized voices the appearance of much greater influence and reach. See her *American Literature and the Culture of Reprinting*.

75 Henry Mayer, *All on Fire: William Lloyd Garrison and the Abolition of Slavery* (New York: St. Martin's Press, 1998), 117.

76 Ibid., 122.

77 The Washington, DC, *National Intelligencer* called for the paper's suppression; a Raleigh, North Carolina jury indicted Garrison and his partner Isaac Knapp for distribution of incendiary material; a vigilance association in Columbia, South Carolina posted a $1,500 reward for whites found circulating the paper; and the Georgia legislature offered a $5,000 reward for Garrison's arrest. Ibid., 121–123.

78 William Lloyd Garrison, "Female Literary Association," *The Liberator*, June 30, 1832.

79 Julie Winch has speculated that Ella was either Sarah or Grace Douglass, but Marie Lindhorst notes she has "uncovered nothing to make that identification with any certainty." Marie Lindhorst, "Politics in a Box: Sarah Mapps Douglass and the Female Literary Association, 1831–1833," *Pennsylvania History* 65 (1998): 278 n. 29. Dorothy Sterling identified Sarah Douglass as "Sophanisba" and "Zillah" a decade earlier, which has been widely followed in

scholarship on African American women's contributions to *The Liberator*. Sterling, *We Are Your Sisters*, 110–111. However, Mary Kelley cites Winch as she attributes the pseudonyms "Ella" and "Sophanisba" to Sarah Douglass, while leaving "Zillah" as an unattributable pseudonym. Kelley, "Talents Committed," 43. And Gay Gibson Cima takes "Ella." to be both a sufficiently common pseudonym that it may have been used by a variety of women, yet she also argues that Douglass used it in *The Liberator*. Gay Gibson Cima, *Performing Anti-Slavery: Activist Women on Antebellum Stages* (Cambridge: Cambridge University Press, 2014), 112–114, 133–134, n. 60.

80 Logan, *Liberating Language*, 69.

81 Garrison, "Female Literary Association, *The Liberator*, June 30, 1832.

82 Shirley Yee, *Black Women Abolitionists: A Study in Activism, 1828–1860* (Knoxville: University of Tennessee Press, 1992), 21.

83 Sarah Mapps Douglass ("Zillah"), "Moonlight," *The Liberator*, April 7, 1832.

84 In 1849 and 1850 Douglass reported on the activities of the Women's Association of Philadelphia, as its corresponding secretary, to Frederick Douglass's paper *The North Star*, and in the spring of 1859 wrote under her own signature for the new monthly *Anglo-African Magazine*. *The Emancipator*, edited by Joshua Leavitt in New York City, was a weekly publication of the American Anti-Slavery Association. Frederick Douglass's *North Star* was published in Rochester, NY, from 1847 to 1851. *The Anglo-African Magazine*, edited by Thomas Hamilton in New York City, was established in January 1859 and "appeared only sporadically for the next six years. Thomas Hamilton died in 1861, but his brother, Robert, saw the publication through the Civil War and into the first stages of freedom for the slaves." Pride and Wilson, *A History*, 46.

85 "A Colored Female of Philadelphia. Philadelphia, January 2, 1832," "Emigration to Mexico. Mr. Editor," *The Liberator*, January 28, 1832. Lindhorst notes that *The Liberator* then published a series of responses to this member from the PFLA "box" in its August 1832 edition. Mapps Douglass's response as "Zillah" was one of these, as was "Woodby"'s, both of which I go on to discuss.

86 Sarah Mapps Douglass, "Extract from a letter written to a friend, February 23, 1832," *The Liberator*, July 21, 1832.

87 Horton and Horton, *In Hope*, 193.

88 Ibid., 196.

89 Ibid., 197–199, 211.

90 Sarah Mapps Douglass ("Zillah"), "Reply to Woodby," *The Liberator*, August 18, 1832.

91 McHenry, *Forgotten Readers*, 69.

92 "Constitution of the Afric-American Female Intelligence Society of Boston," *The Liberator*, January 7, 1832.

93 Harry Reed, *Platform for Change: The Foundations of the Northern Free Black Community, 1775–1865* (East Lansing: Michigan State University Press, 1994), 77–78.

94 Maria W. Stewart, *Religion and the Pure Principles of Morality, The Sure Foundation on Which We Must Build. Productions from the Pen of MRS. MARIA W. STEWARD [sic], Widow of the Late James W. Steward, of Boston*, 1831, reprinted in *Maria W. Stewart, America's First Black Woman Political Writer: Essays and Speeches*, ed. Marilyn W. Richardson (Bloomington: Indiana University Press, 1987), 41.

95 "For the Liberator. AN ADDRESS, Delivered Before the Afric-American Female Intelligence Society of Boston. By Mrs. Maria W. Stewart.," *The Liberator*, April 28, 1832, 2.

96 Carla L. Peterson, *"Doers of the Word": African-American Women Speakers and Writers in the North (1830–1880)*, (Oxford: Oxford University Press, 1995), 68 and Richardson, "Introduction," 24.

97 Eddie S. Glaude, Jr. *Exodus! Religion, Race, and Nation in Early Nineteenth-Century Black America* (Chicago: University of Chicago Press, 2000), 6, emphasis added.

98 Ibid., 111.

99 Stewart, "An Address," 2.

100 Stewart's most frequently used rhetorical appeal was the Black jeremiad, explaining why she is so often understood as heavily influenced by David Walker's *Appeal*, which indicted American racism and encouraged Southern slaves to rise up and overthrow their white masters. Stewart followed the Black jeremiad's focus on warning "whites ... [of] the judgement that was to come for the sin of slavery." Wilson Moses describes the Black jeremiad as a "mainly pre-Civil War phenomenon ... often directed at a white audience ... Sometimes its warnings were militant and direct ... At other times ... the tone was that of a friendly warning, couched in the rhetoric of Christian conciliation." Wilson Jeremiah Moses, *Black Messiahs and Uncle Toms: Social and Literary Manipulations of a Religious Myth* (University Park: Penn State University Press, 1982), 30–31, 37.

101 Stewart, "An Address," 2.

102 Ibid.

103 Patrick Rael, *Black Identity and Black Protest in the Antebellum North* (Chapel Hill: University of North Carolina Press, 2002), 266–267.

104 Stewart, "An Address," 2.

105 Ibid.

106 Ibid., emphasis added.

107 Richardson, "What If I am a Woman?" in *Maria W. Stewart, America's First Black Woman Political Writer: Essays and Speeches* (Bloomington: Indiana University Press, 1987), 193.

108 Stewart's publications of her speeches in the paper and these advertisements ran with headers that made clear Garrison did not instigate or solicit them, but that they were published at Stewart's "request" or instigation. These are clear indications that Stewart made *The Liberator* part of a multi-faceted political program.

109 Richardson, "Introduction," 27.

110 Quoted in Sterling, *We Are Your Sisters*, 158–159.
111 Richardson, "What If I am a Woman?," 205 n. 1. The *Repository* was published monthly from 1858 to 1864 and sold for one dollar per yearly subscription and twenty-five cents per copy.
112 McHenry, *Forgotten Readers*, 133.
113 Ibid., 132.
114 Ibid., 82–83.
115 Dunbar, *A Fragile Freedom*, 95.
116 Jones, *All Bound*, 83.
117 Quoted in Sterling, *We Are Your Sisters*, 17. Shirley Yee notes the association's inaugural meeting was held in Rachel Lloyd's home and that Sarah Douglass and Hetty Burr "held leadership positions" in it. Delany addressed its members at this meeting. Yee, *Black Women Abolitionists*, 108.
118 Quarles, *Black Abolitionists*, 105.
119 McHenry, *Forgotten Readers*, 133, 136.
120 F.H. Grice, "Elevator Aid Association," *Elevator*, October 16, 1868, 2. See also Mary, "A Response," *Elevator*, February 14, 1868, 2. Mary wrote in response to Mrs. D.D. Carter's proposition that women "contribute a dollar each to sustain *The Elevator*: 'women have always felt an interest in your paper. The ladies do not neglect you as contributors, and I know they will not neglect you as financial contributors.'"
121 Ibid., 19–20.
122 Logan, *Liberating Language*, 86.

CHAPTER 8

"Theresa" and the Early Transatlantic Mixed-Race Heroine

Black Solidarity in Freedom's Journal

Brigitte Fielder

In the 1828 anonymously authored story "Theresa – A Haytien Tale," three women escape the French army while also aiding the Black revolutionary effort. Madame Paulina saves her daughters, Theresa and Amanda, from being captured by the French – inadvertently allowing Theresa to gain the military intelligence she later provides to Toussaint L'Ouverture's army – by posing as a French officer and pretending her daughters are her prisoners. Paulina does this, in part, by assuming an officer's uniform and affect, but in order to perform this disguise believably, she must also be able to pass as white. These are mixed-race heroines, and this story of Black heroism and women's political action is also one of mixed-race alliance with the revolutionary Haitian cause.

Questions of self-identification and political engagement drive the actions of "Theresa's" women. "Theresa's" appearance in *Freedom's Journal* inserts this story of women's wartime heroism into the broader literary history of the Haitian Revolution, painting an image of mixed-race womanhood that was not insignificant for both this American venue and for a larger transatlantic context. Like the anonymously authored British epistolary novel *The Woman of Colour, A Tale* (1808), "Theresa" depicts mixed-race women aligned with Black racial uplift rather than white assimilation.[1] Both of these texts present mixed-race heroines who differ significantly from the most popular literary tropes of the mixed-race woman: the treacherous seductress of eighteenth-century depictions of the West Indies and the "tragic mulatta" genre that would gain popularity during the antebellum period. Working in opposition to texts in which mixed-race women are measured by ideals of white womanhood, "Theresa" frames its mixed-race heroines as models of Black solidarity and radical abolitionist action. In this, "Theresa" anticipates postbellum mixed-race heroines like Frances Ellen Watkins Harper's Iola Leroy, although it foregoes depicting mixed-race women's heterosexual union with Black men over their political action alongside them.

In this chapter I discuss the significance of "Theresa's" mixed-race heroines within the context of US abolitionist and antislavery literature that would later mark mixed-race womanhood as a site for white abolitionist failings rather than Black solidarity. Reading Black-authored texts with regard to their relation to white-authored ones is by no means the only – or the best – context in which to understand literature of the African diaspora during the early nineteenth century, and "Theresa's" unknown authorship further complicates such a comparison. However, reading this story alongside other transatlantic depictions of Black and mixed-race heroines helps to illustrate how "Theresa" departs from predominant tropes of mixed-race womanhood. "Theresa's" protagonists play with and against familiar tropes around mixed-race literary heroines and are therefore worth exploring further.

Paulina's disguise illustrates possible generic scripts for mixed-race heroines within the story's early nineteenth-century context. The story thereby allows us to read its characters with relation to the possibilities it might otherwise be understood to avoid. "Theresa" hints at the configurations of racial relations in which mixed-race characters would most often be depicted in nineteenth-century literatures – in relations to white men, to white women, and to Black men and women, all of which ultimately work to frame these characters as Black women. This chapter works through these relations in order to show how the performances of race in "Theresa" consciously push against dominant orientations for reading mixed-race characters already in operation by the time of its publication.

I situate "Theresa's" publication in *Freedom's Journal*, among other historical fiction of the Haitian Revolution, and within a broader context of mixed-race heroines in early antebellum fiction. Reading "Theresa" alongside texts including the anonymous novel *Marly; or, a Planter's Life in Jamaica* (1828), excerpted in *Freedom's Journal* in August 1828; *Zelica the Creole* (1820); and the anonymous epistolary novel, *The Woman of Colour* (1808), I show how "Theresa's" performances and allegiances of race and gender position it within a broader transatlantic genre. "Theresa's" representation of mixed-race womanhood in the West Indies depends both on what is said and unsaid and which relationships are present and which are absent. It calls for a comparative reading within the context of African American literature about mixed-race women and transatlantic writing about gender and slavery in the West Indies. We have debated the status of "Theresa" based on ideas about the identity of its author – questioning if he or she was white or Black – but the way the story itself interrogates identity and affinity requires us to move outward.

"Theresa" asks us to put it in relation to other works that make choices it forgoes or that its readers would find familiar within *Freedom's Journal*'s world of Black print. My work here situates a reading of mixed-race womanhood in "Theresa" that extends beyond the usual assumptions surrounding this trope in antebellum literature and argues that the story shows mixed-race heroines as oriented toward solidarity with Black people, rather than as conservative mediators of white racism, within this broad horizon.

"A Haytien Tale" in *Freedom's Journal*

"Theresa – A Haytien Tale" was published serially in *Freedom's Journal* between January 18 and February 15, 1828. Founded by Samuel E. Cornish and John B. Russwurm in 1827, the New York publication was the first African American owned and operated newspaper. Elizabeth McHenry shows how, by the 1820s, northern Black communities "understood text, identity, and public access to be linked."[2] *Freedom's Journal* endeavored to give voice to and unite a diasporic Black community, reflecting editorial interests in Haiti among its broader investments in Black identity, rights, nationalism, history, literature, and uplift. The publication of "Theresa" followed a wave of African American immigration to Haiti, peaking in 1824 (though declining by 1826).[3] As editor Russwurm continued to support Haitian immigration as a form of Black self-determination in opposition to the American Colonization Society's white-centered interests, *Freedom's Journal* serialized a five-part history, "Hayti," in spring 1827. "Theresa" appeared alongside the paper's array of short fiction and poetry, domestic and foreign news, historical vignettes, marriage and death announcements, advertisements for youth and adult schools, and reports of women's activist organizations. These issues featured antislavery sentiment via news stories, poetry, and meeting minutes alongside news of infringements upon free African American rights.

Writing under the simple pen name, "S," "Theresa's" author has not yet been identified and their unknown race and gender makes the text difficult to classify among identity-based literatures. Acknowledging the many difficulties of dealing with a "problem" text such as "Theresa," scholars have speculated as to this authorial "S." Frances Smith Foster suspects Prince Saunders, who worked as a teacher and missionary in Haiti.[4] Dickson Bruce suggests the young James McCune Smith as another alternative.[5] Marlene Daut argues that we ought to consider the possibility that "Theresa" was written by a radical African American woman, given its alignment with other writing by radical Black women writers such as Maria Stewart and Sarah Forten.[6] "Theresa's" unknown authorship raises the question of how scholars ought to treat texts published in African American contexts when we do not know the racial or gender identity of their authors. In addition to Black-authored texts, even African American-owned and edited periodicals with predominantly Black readerships, such as *Freedom's Journal* and the *Christian Recorder*, often republished pieces written by white writers.[7] However, the story's description as an "Original Communication" for *Freedom's Journal* suggests that it was written explicitly for this venue. Scholars including Foster, Daut, and Jean Lee Cole concur that this designation, along with the newspaper's commitment to publishing material written by African American writers, makes it probable that "Theresa's" author was a writer of color.[8] This possibility is intriguing when thinking through the story's implications for Atlantic circulations of print and the Black diaspora.

I hold, however, that the text's appearance in *Freedom's Journal* alone is sufficient for the story to be considered as part of a larger African American literary culture. As Meredith McGill has shown, the nineteenth century's "culture of reprinting" ensured a wide circulation of texts. More recently, scholars such as Daniel Hack and Britt Rusert have indicated the various ways African American writers have engaged, rather than ignored, a broad range of literary and other intellectual work, whether Black-authored or not.[9] While some scholars have relied upon a narrow frame for African American literature, others have developed nontraditional methodologies for demarking what the category "African American literature" might include and with which texts it might be in conversation.[10] Dickson Bruce, for example, organizes his study of African American literature "in a historical context that includes, among other things, African and American oral traditions, European conventions, American race relations, and political activism."[11] In this spirit, "Theresa" can and should be read within the wide context of shared transatlantic histories and literary tropes. I therefore approach this story within the larger frame of print production that includes the transatlantic and African American print contexts of *Freedom's Journal.* Elsewhere I have argued that an African American readership is sometimes reason enough to consider texts among what we call "African American literature," for example, in the case of the reader-oriented genre of children's literature.[12] Regardless of the author's racial identity, and given these wider contexts, we should construe the category "African American literature" broadly enough to include "Theresa."

The story's opening pages describe the social position of Paulina and her family. In the midst of the uprising of enslaved people, "provoked to madness, and armed . . . against French barbarity; Madame Paulina was left a widow, unhappy–unprotected, and exposed to all the horrors of the revolution."[13] Though not apparently enslaved herself, Paulina is not French but West Indian, presumably belonging to the colony's large population of *gens de couleur libres*. While later African American abolitionist and racial uplift literature would align mixed-race characters with their Black counterparts by virtue of their mutual enslavability, this racial alignment is not guaranteed within the context of the Haitian Revolution. Distinctions between Black people with and without known white ancestry were important in the context of Saint Domingue's colonial order, where divisions of class and free status aligned with those of color for people who had inherited some of the privilege of their white relatives. Although various historians of Haiti have acknowledged the familial affiliations and socio-political oppression that caused even some free mixed-race people to identify with the Black enslaved population, this alignment was not inevitable. In *The Black Jacobins*, C.L.R. James discusses the intricate relations of power between Saint Domingue's variously racialized populations, noting how white supremacy and colorism, property relations, and French law combined to complicate free mixed-race people's potential to align themselves with enslaved Black people.[14] The possibility of racial solidarity among people of African descent nevertheless alarmed French colonial power.

Men and masculinity figure into "Theresa's" treatment of revolution, but the story centers on women and women's relationships. We later read that Paulina's brother has joined "his patriot brethren, who, like him, distained slavery, and were determined to live free men, or expire in the attempts for liberty and independence."[15] Although her father and uncle are absent from this story, Theresa aligns herself with Black revolutionary men like these relatives. Edlie Wong writes that "Theresa's" women protagonists "emphasize the forms of black social reproduction engendered–not destroyed–by the Haitian Revolution, building upon the very promises that Boyer extended to all black American emigrants."[16] Wong compares this to texts like Leonora Sansay's 1808 *Secret History; or, the Horrors of St. Domingo* and Victor Séjour's 1837 "Le Mulâtre," which frame the revolution as familial drama, while "Teresa" positions L'Ouverture as Black patriarch and ends with familial reunion.

In this representation, we also see an early instance of mixed-race heroines who align themselves with antislavery and antiracist causes. In

"Theresa," those with class privilege or free status must participate in revolutionary action in order to secure "liberty and independence, and to obtain the rights of which they have been unjustly deprived."[17] "Theresa" foregrounds a woman of color who knows that the French government will not protect her family from violence or displacement and who looks to the Black-led revolution for assistance. The question of whether the mixed-race population would accept the second-class citizenship offered to them by the French government or take part in the revolution for a free, Black-led nation did not always have a clear answer. *Freedom's Journal* printed "Theresa – A Haytien Tale" within its ongoing conversation about the importance of Haiti for African Americans and other people of the Black diaspora. The history of the Haitian Revolution figured amid antislavery and antiracism strategizing and emigration debates in the Black press. This piece of historical fiction offers a fictionalized past as it imagines unknown women's experiences of and participation in the revolution. It also presents mixed-race characters as ideals of racial solidarity and radical action.

Theresa's Mixed-Race Women

As the story begins, the revolution is already underway. Paulina has been widowed and her daughters have been left fatherless by the "French barbarity" perpetrated against "the oppressed natives of St. Nicholas."[18] They have also been displaced by the violence. Paulina and her daughters leave the village, evading the French military through disguise. As a result, Paulina's daughter Theresa overhears French military plans against the revolutionaries. Out of a proto-nationalistic sense of duty to Haiti, Theresa leaves a note to her family and departs to convey the information to Touissant L'Ouverture and his army. Theresa is successful, and her assistance helps the revolutionaries to ultimately defeat the French. While Theresa at first believes her mother and sister to have been killed, at the story's close we learn that they are alive and the small family is reunited.

My reading of "Theresa"'s heroines as mixed-race depends upon the following scene, quoted here at length, in which we see Paulina's ability to successfully pass as white:

> The party of horsemen being now very near, she gave necessary instructions to her daughters, and conducted them onward with no little confidence in her success. The lieutenant, by whom the French were commanded, observing her attired in the uniform of a French officer, took her for what she was so well affected to be – (a captain of the French army) he made to

> her the order of the day, and enquired the time she left St. Nicholas, and whether conducting the two prisoners, (for Paulina had the presence of mind to disguise her daughters as such) she replied, and taking forth her letter, she handed it to the lieutenant. Succeeding thus far admirably, our adventuress was led to make some enquiries relative to the welfare of the French troops, stationed west of St. Nicholas, and having collected much valuable information, they parted, and Madame Paulina favoured by a ready address, and with much fortitude, escaped death – conducting the dear objects of her tender solicitude far, from the ill-fated village of their infancy.[19]

In this scene, Paulina's ability to pass – as white, male, and French – is due, in part, to her ability to perform. She "so well affected to be" a French officer that we understand as effective her combined performance of race, class, and gender, as well as some knowledge of the French military's operations. While we observe Paulina's performance of an officer's concerns and affect, as well as her donning of the (male) uniform, to take on this guise, we read no accompanying description of what her racial performance must entail. The fact that this part of her performance seems to require nothing at all suggests this character's probable racial appearance. Given the nature and success of Paulina's disguise, these characters must be mixed-race Black people. Daut argues that these characters' mixed race is not ancillary to the story's plot, but that "the differential skin color of its heroes and heroines alike . . . has much more to tell us about the sweeping essentialism to be found in cultures of slavery, whereby all people of color may not have been slaves, but all people of color were certainly subject to color prejudice."[20] In discussing these characters as mixed-race protagonists, I read their racialization as not merely incidental to the story, but as a detail both apparent enough in the story's plot and mundane enough that it does not become its driving force.

However, if we think carefully about this story as a reframing of mixed-race heroines, we can read "Theresa" as also pushing against familiar genres and themes in which such characters appeared in antebellum literature. Paulina's disguise speaks to assumptions about the visuality of race (i.e., that race is "visible" on/in the body) and the confusion produced by mixed-race bodies (i.e., that race is discernable) in nineteenth-century literature. It also speaks to notions of racial identification and allegiance. I discuss Paulina's disguise at length in order to better understand how the story hints at the very racial relations that it pushes against. These hints lay bare the relations of race that the story otherwise refuses, making this refusal even more pronounced.

In addition to creating the plot-driving opportunity for Theresa's military knowledge, Paulina's disguise suggests the familial relations to whiteness upon which other literature of mixed-race heroines would dwell, particularly their relation to white men. Theresa's closest encounter with white men is this scene in which her mother poses as a French officer. While we learn nothing of the genealogical relations that produce Paulina as a woman who is light enough to pass but who identifies with Saint Domingue's people of color, nineteenth-century readers, especially, might have imagined the possibilities. The absence of racial family drama in the story's plot decenters white people's importance – an unusual decentering, even in African American literature featuring mixed-race characters. Most often, white family members ironically serve to illustrate the workings of hypodescent for mixed-race Black people. If readers imagined a racial backstory for "Theresa's" characters, they would have known that white ancestry was secondary to African descent. Even if we were to imagine Paulina as the daughter of a Frenchman, it is not unfeasible that she would still align herself with Black people or even the revolutionary cause. In this same spirit, we see later mixed-race heroines who willingly identify with enslaved mothers rather than enslaver fathers, as in anti-passing novels like Frances Harper's *Minnie's Sacrifice* and *Iola Leroy*.

In this scene of Paulina's disguise, readers are given a glimpse of how Theresa might otherwise have been oriented – as the child of not only a mixed-race mother, but also of a white, French father. Although the story does not explicitly give Theresa this particular genealogy, the scene of Paulina's passing shows readers – however briefly – this possibility. The complex race relations of the French colony make the political alignment of mixed-race people a matter of foremost discussion in literature about the revolution. In her discussion of Victor Séjour's 1837 short story, "Le Mulâtre," Daut notes a common trope of this brand of historical fiction. Following Doris Garraway's discussion of white men as both "real and symbolic fathers" to enslaved Black people, Daut writes "the idea that miscegenation might make 'black' sons want to kill their 'white' fathers constitutes one of the primary metaphors of the Haitian Revolution in the nineteenth century."[21] Paulina's passing scene simultaneously hints at this context for mixed-race descent and reveals its protagonists' white ancestry as insufficient to garner white protection.

Antebellum-era mixed-race heroine literature would not only feature white men as adversaries to women of color, but in this role, as fathers. These fathers of mixed-race children were less likely to be killed in acts of parricide but were overwhelmingly subject to premature death. Moreover, they died in the manner of "kind" enslavers of abolitionist literature – unexpectedly, in debt, and without having properly manumitted their enslaved wives and children. Like the "tragic mulatta," what we might aptly call the "ineffectual white father" was a prominent literary type in fiction by writers like Lydia Maria Child, William Wells Brown, and Frances Harper. Not simply an adversary, these men were often well-intentioned, though negligent; their paperwork was never quite in order. Upon their deaths their proslavery relatives or creditors would descend to claim their beloved family members as property. In the United States' matrilineally-inherited system of slavery, such stories pointed to the structural nature of the problem. No matter what well-meaning relatives or "kind" enslavers did, slavery's worst dangers loomed. In a twist of the parricide plot, we find white fathers who lack the powers of white patriarchal protection. When it comes to protecting nonwhite family members, such men are effectively useless; they cannot save their Black wives or children from slavery.

"Theresa" frames this paternal relation as neither a reality nor a metaphor of its plot, but as a masquerade. The figure of the "white father" is absent from "Theresa" in any literal sense but is present here in the image of Madame Paulina done up in drag for the purpose of protecting herself and her daughters. Paulina's disguise is a necessity for her family's survival. Their deception flies in the face of white authority, undermining colonialist military operations and the project of maintaining racial hierarchies: The result of Paulina's disguise of white masculinity is the betrayal of military information to the revolutionaries. In effect, Theresa's masquerading as a white Frenchman suggests this relation of mixed-race people to white fathers as masquerade, itself. In this system of racialization and racial oppression, white fathers cannot – or will not – protect people of color from anti-Black racism. The Haitian Revolution's goals of Black self-determination are here embodied by a mixed-race Black woman who displaces the white male emblem of colonialism and slavery. This centering of Black characters in literature about Haiti is unsurprising among *Freedom's Journal's* broader focus on Black voices and reliance on Black community.

Paulina's disguise might remind readers of later nineteenth-century antislavery literature of the escape of Ellen and William Craft, told in their 1860 self-emancipation narrative, *Running A Thousand Miles to Freedom.* In 1848 Ellen Craft disguised herself as a white gentleman with her husband, William, posing as her enslaved valet to escape their Georgia enslavers. Like Ellen Craft, Paulina does not pass into but, as P. Gabrielle

Foreman puts it, "through" whiteness.[22] Just as Ellen Craft posed as a white man alongside her husband disguised as her own property, Paulina positions her daughters as captives of war. These disguises hide people who cannot pass for white in plain sight, boldly acknowledging the dangers posed to Black bodies by staging a preemptive masquerade of that threat. By pretending captivity, they find the means to escape it.

In the story's final paragraphs, when Theresa believes her mother and sister to be dead (her other family members having been killed before the story's opening) she considers where she might turn for support. We read that

> friendless and disconsolate, she was now left exposed to many evils, and at a time when the assiduous care of a mother was most essential in the preservation of her well being. Theresa was on her way back to the camp of the kind Touissant L'Ouverture to claim his fatherly protection, and seek a home in the bosom of those, to whom she had rendered herself dear by her wisdom and virtue.[23]

L'Ouverture has become a father figure to Theresa and a father, in the historic sense, of Black nationality. L'Ouverture was described as "one of the most extraordinary men of his age" and an exemplar of "negro character" in a three-part biography *Freedom's Journal* reprinted from the British *Quarterly Review* in May 1827.[24] This framing of L'Ouverture fit with the newspapers' conception of a unifying Black history and with its associations of freedom and masculinity.[25] While we might see L'Ouverture here as the antithesis of the white enslaver father, the true antithesis lies in the story's turn away from patriarchal care altogether. Theresa's mother and sister emerge from a baggage cart, abandoned by the French in their retreat. Inasmuch as this story is about a young woman's heroic support of Black male revolutionaries, it is also about women's familial relationships with and care for one another in the midst of wartime trauma. Paulina has successfully protected her daughters. Theresa has not sacrificed mother or sister for the sake of saving her country and has maintained her own safety while conveying her information. For the story's protagonists, the protection that mixed-race women can provide to one another and for themselves is enough.

Paulina's encounter with the French soldiers and her posturing as one of them drive home the fact that this story decenters male figures in favor of mixed-race African American women. Hortense Spillers notes the ways in which "the African-American woman, the mother, the daughter, becomes historically the powerful and shadowy evocation of a cultural synthesis long evaporated."[26] By giving only a glimpse of a mixed-race woman affecting the guise of a white man, Paulina reveals this synthesis and not only decenters the white male figure of mixed-race heroine genres, but displaces him, putting herself – a woman of color – in his place. Not white men, but woman of color have the power and will to protect other women of color. While neither "Black sons" nor "white fathers" are at the center of "Theresa," Black and mixed-race women are at the center of the popular cultural narrative of "Black sons" and "white fathers" in Haiti; as such sons are understood to side with their matrilineally inherited race, these mothers are implied. This implication of matrilineage, though racializing along lines of relative power, is not simply disempowering, but reveals the safest alignment for mixed-race people in a white supremacist society.

As in "Theresa," mixed-race motherhood is most often depicted under threat in nineteenth-century fiction. Harriet Beecher Stowe's Eliza Harris crossing the ice of the Ohio River with her child in her arms would come to be the century's most visible image of mixed-race motherhood.[27] Dead, dying, or otherwise absent mixed-race mothers would haunt texts like Lydia Maria Child's 1842 "The Quadroons" and 1867 *Romance of the Republic*, William Wells Brown's 1853 *Clotel*, Julia C. Collins' 1865 *The Curse of Caste*, Frances Ellen Watkins Harper's 1869 *Minnie's Sacrifice* and 1892 *Iola Leroy*, and Charles Chesnutt's 1901 *The Marrow of Tradition.*[28] In these texts, we see mixed-race characters who have most often been discussed in relation to their white genealogies.[29] Early twentieth-century African American fiction with mixed-race protagonists – such as Chesnutt's 1900 *The House behind the Cedars*, James Weldon Johnson's 1912 *The Autobiography of an Ex-Colored Man*, and Nella Larsen's 1929 *Passing* – would shift depictions of mixed-race identification even further toward whiteness, even as these writers critiqued "passing."

"Theresa" marks a moment for mixed-race protagonists who have not yet taken on the norms of antebellum-era "tragic" mixed-race heroine fiction. In the next section I turn to earlier mixed-race protagonists. Just as "Theresa" imagines its "Haytien Tale" in the mixed-race historical context of Saint Domingue and for an African American audience familiar with the particularities of racialization in the United States, it did so in a larger literary landscape. By disguising her daughters as the prisoners of a white French officer, Paulina recognizes a potential point of mixed-race women's vulnerability. If this disguise is necessary because these particular young women cannot pass for white, it also speaks to the foreclosure of stable whiteness for mixed-race literary characters – or perhaps more accurately, to their refusal of whiteness. In this respect, we might distinguish "Theresa" as an early version of what P. Gabrielle Foreman calls "anti-passing narratives."[30] In order to more closely examine "Theresa's" position within this larger genre, I turn first to another representation of mixed-race heroines in *Freedom's Journal.*

The Transatlantic Mixed-Race Heroine

On August 1, 1828, *Freedom's Journal* published an "Affecting Incident," excerpted from *Marly; or, a Planter's Life in Jamaica*, an anonymous British novel published the same year, recounting the life and experiences of a Scottish enslaver. This excerpt describes the circumstances of three mixed-race young women of "the caste denominated Mustees their mother having been a Quadroon, and their father a white man."[31] Much in the fashion of later "tragic mulatta" fiction, these women are revealed to be legally enslaved when their father dies without having successfully manumitted their mother. In what would become a familiar story by the late antebellum period, "these girls were brought to the hammer to pay their father's debts, being held to be part of his moveable property."[32] Similarly to other antebellum mixed-race heroine fiction, *Marly* recounts these women's apparent markers of whiteness, in both physical appearance and adherence to white middle-class standards of education and culture. We read of "the handsome forms, apparently cultivated manners, the soft and pleasing faces wholly European, even more fair than numbers of our country women, and the neatness, nay elegance of their dress ... Their genteel manners, liberal education and pleasing appearance."[33] Antislavery texts relayed such characteristics of mixed-race women in order to challenge notions of racial essentialism and argue that a system of slavery that would enslave such "near-white" people must be flawed. This fiction often employed these characters' tragic deaths to evoke feelings of enhanced injustice in a white readership that might care more about white-seeming enslaved characters than dark-skinned ones. This excerpt from *Marly* departs from the dominant narrative of later antislavery fiction, however. Rather than being sold and dying an untimely death as a result of their abrupt exposure to slavery's horrors, these women turn out not to be saleable at all. "No offers appeared ... and it was the very same reason that prevented any one in Jamaica from making a purchase of them because the neighborhood would have cried shame, had they been put to any laborious or even servile employment."[34] Rather than enhance their value on the market (as is the case for many antebellum mixed-race heroines), these women's "white" characteristics render them unenslavable.

While the original novel is by no means abolitionist in its orientation, for readers of *Freedom's Journal*, the excerpt from *Marly* may have signaled antislavery sentiments in the context of northern print culture.[35] This excerpt is reframed as an abolitionist story within *Freedom's Journal*. The scene of white, British refusal to purchase these women might therefore have been read in contrast to a US enslaver culture in which mixed-race women were often sold at high prices in the sex market of slavery known as the "fancy trade." At the end of the excerpt, we read that these women "were allowed to roam at large, in the same manner as if they were free."[36] The "Affecting Incident" of these mixed-race women's ultimate freedom frames readerly affect in sympathy with these characters, even while acknowledging their position of privilege relative to other stories of slavery, which did not always include (de jure or de facto) freedom for mixed-race characters.

As Daniel Hack shows, "African American writers and editors [were] immersed in the transatlantic literary culture of the day . . . working with and against prevailing generic norms and conventions."[37] The editors of *Freedom's Journal* chose to reprint this excerpt from *Marly*, in part, because the plot of these characters had resonance beyond its original context. Such a depiction of mixed-race women could have been of interest to readers of *Freedom's Journal* because they, like the editors presumably did, knew the original text, or because they were familiar with various genres of writing about slavery. The women in this incident appear in circumstances that are not only familiar to antebellum fiction, but also for mixed-race people in the West Indies, as various colonial systems of racialization and enslavement were similar in the precarious position they created for free people of color. While this story's possibility of inherited enslavement looks much like antebellum American representations of slavery, it is not entirely unlike the precarious state in which we find "Theresa's" heroines.

Marly's mixed-race women presumably benefit from their white privilege. We are to assume that "no offers appeared" and "the neighborhood would have cried shame" at their sale because they are visibly white. Abolitionist arguments were reinforced by the fact that "even" white-looking women were sold, relying on white supremacist notions about enslavability. These women find no buyers because of the qualities "that would have entitled them to comfortable marriages in Britain."[38] But if we read this story in the context of *Freedom's Journal*, we might look beyond these women's whiteness to the fact of their neighbors' refusal to purchase them. The community's refusal to participate in these women's enslavement might be compared to *Freedom's Journal*'s other calls for free people of color to resist any compulsion to help return fugitives to slavery (a point to which I will return in my final section). Recognizing free Black people's positions of privilege, the newspaper urges its readers not to betray their self-emancipated neighbors, even if it would serve their own self-interest.

Apart from this message, *Marly* presents the common abolitionist argument that mixed-race genealogy (or economic or educational opportunities) will not necessarily save someone from slavery. These women remain free in practice, but not in law: "they were allowed to roam at large, *in the same manner as if* they were free."[39] They remain legally enslavable and therefore precarious in their roaming, as though someone of means may at any time disregard the local sentiment about enslaving white-looking women and seize them. The "affecting incident" has no unqualifiedly happy ending. *Marly*'s mixed-race women might be compared to the most prominent – and the most prominently discussed – version of the mixed-race heroine, the "tragic mulatta" trope. Teresa Zackodnik argues that this figure is double-voiced in its simultaneous performance of whiteness and Blackness.[40] Similarly, Eve Allegra Raimon reads the "tragic mulatta" figure of US antislavery fiction as a character "who could successfully mediate between militancy and gentility," in the case of Cassy in Richard Hildreth's 1836 *The Slave, or, Memoirs of Archy Moore.*[41]

The antebellum period, and abolitionist literature in particular, would produce a wide range of literature around mixed-race figures, their racial identification, and their enslavability, by both white and Black writers. This excerpt from *Marly* might have interested readers of *Freedom's Journal* for some of the various reasons mixed-race characters would become widely popular in antebellum literature. A litany of scholars has written at length on mixed-race figures in eighteenth- and nineteenth-century literature. Lisa Ze Winters argues that the figure of the "free mulatta concubine" becomes central to understanding Black diasporic intersectional identity as early as the eighteenth century.[42] Jennifer DeVere Brody shows that the mixed-race figure of nineteenth-century English literature varied over the course of the century and was not always a sympathetic character, as evidenced by William Makepeace Thackeray's racist-comic depiction of Rhoda Swartz in *Vanity Fair* (1848).[43] Radiclani Clytus notes the transatlantic nature of these depictions of people of African descent, referring to "that shared socio-aesthetic vision, acknowledging the cultural fluidity whereby depictions of African-American and African-Caribbean subjects reside both within and outside conceptual abstractions of 'antebellum' and 'Victorian' culture."[44] Kimberly Snyder Manganelli traces the transatlantic movement of the "tragic mulatta" trope in American, British, and French fiction of the eighteenth and nineteenth centuries, arguing that the trope more complexly represented various, contradictory stereotypes of mixed-race womanhood.[45] Zackodnik describes the different work done by mixed-race heroines in Black-authored texts over time, "to invoke and manage both American and British abolitionist empathy and identification; to contest racialized notions of womanhood in the postbellum United States; to critique the politics and proclivities of the 'New Negro Renaissance'; to play on the taxonomic fever of early-twentieth-century American culture; and to question postwar optimism at midcentury."[46] Elsewhere, I have argued that both pre- and post-antebellum mixed-race heroine fiction reveals more radical racial solidarity than the "tragic mulatta" trope when we turn our focus away from these characters' relationships to white family and white love interests and toward their relationships with Black characters and Black community.[47]

While "libidinous" or "sexually imperiled" versions of this trope have dominated discussions of mixed-race women in eighteenth- and nineteenth-century fiction, these were not the only versions of mixed-race characters available. Perhaps "Theresa's" most drastic departure from mainstream mixed-race heroines is the absence of any heteronormative love plot in this text. Theresa is uncoupled at the story's close. Whether "libidinous" or "imperiled," mixed-race women characters' sexuality is central to most fictional depictions. Such heroines are overwhelmingly paired with white male suitors of varying quality and, as the "tragic" moniker suggests, these love stories seldom end well. Later nineteenth-century African American fiction would reject the trope of the ineffectual white lover and instead pair mixed-race women with African American men, as in Harper's late-century anti-passing novels, *Minnie's Sacrifice* and *Iola Leroy*. The absence of any such love plot in "Theresa," however, marks it apart from most other depictions of mixed-race women. This absence of coupling is one reason "Theresa" might not be legible as belonging to either earlier or later bodies of mixed-race heroine fiction. However, I count the story here in part to recognize the wider range of work mixed-race women characters do in nineteenth-century fiction.

While the de-sexualized mixed-race woman is a rare literary phenomenon, these characters' relationships to other women are often just as important as their relationships to white fathers or lovers. In the anonymous 1808 *The Woman of Colour* and Leonora Sansay's 1820 *Zelica the Creole*, the titular characters forego heterosexual romantic relationships out of necessity for the larger part of their plots.[48] Relationships to women, rather, frame their racial performance and identification. This emphasis on mixed-race women characters' relationships with other women shows the non-genealogical and non-heteronormative workings of their racialization.

The term "creole" marks Zelica's race as ambiguous. Although she is phenotypically white and "passing" as such, readers learn that Zelica has African ancestry. Manganelli describes Clara, the white woman to whom Zelica is devoted, as a mirror of Zelica, whose racial ambiguity amounts to her approaching white womanhood, writing "there is no difference between them; they are both imperiled by patriarchy and empire."[49] This is not true of mixed-race heroines falling within the "tragic mulatta" trope, of course, as the rules of hypodescent and legal enslavement bar them from even the limited privileges afforded to white women. Later characters of African American literature – Harper's Minnie Carpenter and Iola Leroy – would choose African American identity in allegiance with both dead and living Black family members. Zelica, however, rejects identification or allegiance with Black people on familial grounds. Her white father has promised her in marriage to Henry Christophe, a Black revolutionary general. Zelica shows no love for Christophe, however; she loves Lastour, a white, French soldier to whom she remains faithful.

Her proximity to and influence among the revolutionaries allows Zelica to assist her white friends throughout the novel. Unlike Zuline in Sansay's *Secret History*, who uses her sexual prowess to save the lives of white men threatened by the revolutionaries, Zelica works primarily in the interests of the American Clara, also saving the life of Clara's French creole husband, Louis.[50] While Zelica cannot claim white womanhood herself, she participates in its idealization via this uneven, self-sacrificial friendship. Taking on a task traditionally ascribed to white male characters, Zelica the protector takes the generic role that might be ascribed to Clara's lover. Louis is unfaithful, (he is involved with a white creole woman), and lacks both the local power and knowledge that Zelica wields. Zelica's devotion to Clara is unmatched. In the novel's third volume, she tells Clara "I have devoted my life to your safety – a life that has no other object – that is enlivened by no hope of happiness."[51] Ironically, like the ineffectual father or lover of mixed-race women in antebellum antislavery fiction, Zelica is ultimately unable to protect Clara. Clara is accidentally stabbed by Zelica's father in an attempt to rescue Clara from a kidnapping. Zelica outlives her, spending the novel's final pages in mourning. By framing Zelica as Clara's devoted protector, the novel removes her from the realm of treacherous mixed-race people found in other literature about the revolution, such as Victor Hugo's 1826 *Bug-Jargal*. As protector, Zelica also avoids sexual competition with Clara. Far from de-sexualized, Zelica and Clara are both objects of various men's unrequited love and must negotiate this while simultaneously negotiating their safety. Zelica remains faithful to her own lover and uses whatever sexual power she has for the cause of Clara's safety.

Zelica's role is not exactly that of a masculinized lover-protector, but of a devoted subordinate. The only person who approaches her devotion to Clara is Madelaine, a "faithful slave" who refuses to leave her mistress even in death and who we learn in the novel's final lines "passed the remainder of her days in watching over the grave of the fair and unfortunate Clara."[52] Zelica's devotion, too, seems to stem from ingrained notions of racial hierarchy. Despite her father's attempts to educate her against color prejudice, racism prevents Zelica from aligning herself with other people of color. Comparing her imposed marriage to slavery, Zelica rejects Christophe not only because her love lies elsewhere, but also because her aversion stems from a pronounced colorism. She explains, "my long residence in France had entirely effaced from my mind all idea of the people of colour; nor can I, even now, accustom myself to them. Conceive, then, the horror with which I recoiled from the presence of Christophe."[53] Having been raised in France, Zelica finds people of color foreign; she cannot identify with Saint Domingue or the revolutionary cause. At the novel's end, she is en route to the United States along with Lastour and St. Louis, who are escaping from the island. While Daut reads in Zelica a figure of "powerful … 'black' female identity" this identity does not translate into revolutionary solidarity.[54] Manganelli wonders if Zelica will pass into whiteness upon her arrival abroad, as would be necessary for her to legally marry her lover in several states.[55] One must wonder if Zelica's devotion to Clara is based in her own aspirations to whiteness and what her racial status will be when she reaches the United States. Zelica's ability to pass renders her among the potentially treacherous mixed-race characters of earlier fiction, rather than the "tragic" heroines of later antislavery literature. The novel leaves us with the racial "danger" of failing to define a mixed-race character by her experiences of anti-Black racism: legal Blackness and its accompanying enslavability.

In contrast, *The Woman of Colour* forecloses whiteness for its protagonist. Rather than aspiring to whiteness, Olivia Fairfield embraces her identity as a woman of color. Olivia travels to England from Jamaica in order to marry her white cousin, Augustus Merton, following the condition of her father's will. After a surprising turn of events in which she discovers that Augustus is already married, Olivia receives a proposal of marriage from another Englishman, Charles Honeywood. Even though readers understand her to hold real affection for Charles (and he seems to be otherwise unobjectionable), Olivia decides to return to Jamaica with her Black servant, Dido. Olivia's goal is to "zealously engage myself in ameliorating the situation, in instructing the minds–in mending the morals of our poor blacks."[56] This potentially condescending approach to racial uplift is countered in part by Olivia's continual claims of kinship and identification with her Black "*brothers and sisters.*"[57]

Olivia is among the mixed-race heroines who Jenifer DeVere Brody distinguishes from those who are light enough to "pass" as white.[58] Perhaps because Olivia cannot deny her Blackness, she chooses to embrace kinship with people of African descent, articulating this as part of (though not separate from) her Englishness. Rejecting Honeywood's marriage proposal also amounts to a rejection of white society. Literary critics have characterized this move as one ranging from a radical rejection of domesticity to a conservative refusal to promote further amalgamation in the plot. Both of these readings, however, prioritize the (potentially reproductive) heteronormative relationships of the text. Olivia cannot and does not pass into white womanhood. Lyndon Dominique regards Olivia's refusal to participate in white, reproductive futurity as working against the paternalism in which she is caught.[59] This move is not simply a turn away from her father's paternalism, but a turn toward her ultimate alignment with Black Jamaicans, and Black women, in particular. As I argue elsewhere, *The Woman of Colour* might be best addressed by attending to how it represents women of color's relationships with one another. While both Olivia and Zelica are driven by their relationships with women, Olivia's racialization and political alignments are framed vis-à-vis her relationship with her Black servant, the one person with whom Olivia has a sustained relationship throughout the novel.[60] So, too, would "Theresa's" mixed-race heroines provide one another the necessary support and protection that would see them through the Revolution.

Solidarity and Self-Interest

As with mixed-race Black characters in later nineteenth-century literatures, who (like Harper's Iola Leroy) would respond to the question of whether they would attempt or be able to "pass" as white, racial solidarity involves a complex nexus of racial genealogies, visual markers, interpersonal relationships, and intersections with other modes of identity. As we de-emphasize mixed-race figures' white ancestry, as Foreman and I suggest we do, other relationships to whiteness become visible. In the scene in which Paulina passes as a white man, she twists the common tropes of mixed-race heroines who are either mistaken for or believe themselves to be white women. While Paulina is light enough to pass, it is this (temporary) resemblance to white men, rather than her biological relation to white people, that racializes her in the story. If she is the daughter of a Frenchman, the story does not give us this information. Her connection to white defenders of slavery is not here imagined as familial, or even romantic, (as with the overwhelming majority of mixed-race heroines), but as resemblance.

This resemblance, we see, does not amount to identification. Paulina and her daughters clearly identify with the Black revolutionary cause, despite the fact that their own racial and class position might afford them some limited privileges in the French colony's hierarchy. In the scene in which Paulina poses as a French officer, she escapes with her daughters as prisoners. Here we also see evidence of her careful planning. Paulina "had the presence of mind to disguise her daughters," suggesting that this disguise is necessary for their escape (641). It is unclear, though, what disguise her two daughters require. We may surmise that their dress somehow signals their imprisonment. But are we also to understand them as less able to pass as white than their mother and therefore needing to assume the role of prisoners? Paulina's plan is not impromptu or haphazard, but careful, taking into consideration the possibilities for disguising her family and what might be necessary given their individual embodiments. If Paulina might pass as a French officer, perhaps her daughters cannot. Theresa and Amanda are presented as they are: young women of color, who might be taken captive by the French army. This non-disguise illustrates the daughters' vulnerability and a possible alternative to their escape.

These women's vulnerability is a point with which readers of *Freedom's Journal* might have identified. In the United States, free African American people were similarly vulnerable as people who were, themselves, in danger of being enslaved. Along with other antislavery items, the paper habitually printed articles about kidnappings. Jacqueline Bacon writes that these "conveyed a general sense of the precariousness of freedom for African Americans and the oppression that threatened them continually."[61] No person of African descent was entirely safe. Because free Black people did not hold full rights of citizenship, they were even more fully aware of the conditionality of their freedom.

It is unsurprising that antislavery newspapers called for their readers – both white and Black – to identify with the enslaved. Perhaps surprisingly, though, *Freedom's Journal* also acknowledged the privileged position of free African Americans in the possibility of their complicity in slavery. In late 1828 the newspaper ran a series of articles documenting the arrest of several self-emancipated people in New York. The series, titled "Self-Interest," reports that "most of those who have been carried back into bondage, have generally been betrayed by coloured persons – brethren of the same flesh and kindred, for the sake of paltry lucre." The editors go on to call these betrayers "traitors to liberty – to their kindred."[62] Continuing to chastise its readers even in subsequent issues, the editors argue that "any man of colour who will betray one who is a runaway, would not hesitate one moment toward assisting to kidnap those who are free."[63] They even go so far as to print the names of alleged informants.

This indictment of African American people who turn fugitives from slavery over to enslavers is not only a condemnation of slavery; it is also a call for Black solidarity. In one case, we learn that "the villain who testified against the young woman, was her own cousin!"[64] Whether this cousin was white or Black, the writer does not say, but the series implies that this kind of betrayal is even more treacherous when it is also a betrayal of race. The paper's continual emphasis of (both literal and figurative) kinship between free and enslaved Black people marks these cases as even more egregious, perhaps, than white participation in slavery. The assumption is, of course, that Black people ought to act in solidarity with one another to work against slavery. Reading "Theresa" alongside this conversation, we see the story as reflecting a model of Black participation in the antislavery movement that demands radical antiracist action, regardless of one's potential kinship to white people. In this context, Theresa's devotion to the revolutionary cause is not only a model of heroism, but a call to radical action for racial justice.

In "Theresa," the readers of *Freedom's Journal* may well have perceived a call toward radical action, or at the very least, a testament against complacency. Undoubtedly, the story offered readers a heroic protagonist who displays ideals of self-sacrifice and filial duty. However, there is something universalizing in the story's focus away from the wartime heroes of the historical record. As a work of historical fiction, the story paints the margins of the Revolution, rather than its iconic leaders. Shifting its focus away from a figure like Toussaint L'Ouverture, "Theresa" imagines the work of others who might have assisted the revolutionary effort, never to be remembered in the official history. Jean Lee Cole describes the story's characters as "simple, ordinary women" who are "meant to represent a *kind* of person rather than a specific individual."[65] Theresa's heroism is born of opportunity and necessity and stems from a sense of personal obligation to "raise up some few of those, who have been long degraded–give to them dominion, and enable them to govern a state of their own."[66] Theresa feels a duty to help the revolutionary effort in whatever way she can, even if this means putting herself at risk, and even if she must leave her immediate family in order to do so. What might the alleged "ordinariness" of Theresa and her family mean for readers? For the Black diasporic readers who were the intended audience of *Freedom's Journal*, "Theresa's obligations of racial solidarity" may well have seemed ordinary for Black-identifying women.

To imagine Theresa as a mixed-race heroine whose plot does not depend upon her sexuality is, in some way, also to think of her as ordinary – as having other interests and needs beyond her hypersexualization. This is also to imagine these characters outside the realm of plots that would prioritize mixed-race women's sexuality. Manganelli describes the emergence of the "tragic mulatta" as a shift from eighteenth-century literary depictions of mixed-race women, from the "libidinous, avaricious mistress" to a "virtuous but sexually imperiled figure" in British and American literatures. The turning point for this shift, she argues, is the Haitian Revolution, as "The Tragic Mulatta grew out of this history of interracial violence in Saint-Domingue."[67] The heroines of "Theresa" might best be understood to illustrate this trajectory by refusing to fall neatly into either of these extremes. They are both avaricious and imperiled, neither libidinous nor tragic. Paulina is successful in ferrying her daughters past the French troops and out of harm's way; Theresa is successful in conveying military intelligence to L'Ouverture's camp; the revolutionary effort is successful. There is no love plot; Theresa need not marry; the family of women is reunited at the story's end.

The affinities between "Theresa"'s women and other mixed-race characters of the nineteenth century allow us to see the various ways racialization works there. Just as these characters are racially ambiguous, neither can the authors of texts like "Theresa," *The Woman of Color*, *Zelica,* or *Marly* be definitively identified. This leaves us without some of the standard tools for analyzing the political leanings or representations of literatures dealing with race. What we can learn about these texts might therefore be best worked out through relations and similarities of genres and tropes. The texts I discuss here have an affinity with one another that becomes legible in much the same way that these mixed-race characters are racialized through their affinities of relations to other people. Reading "Theresa" within the tradition of other mixed-race heroines shows us how this story frames mixed-race women's racialization and identification against the backdrop of other available possibilities.

Notes

1 On how racial mixture and racial solidarity work in this novel, see Brigitte Fielder, "*The Woman of Colour* and Black Atlantic Movement," in *Women's Narratives of the Early Americas and the Formation of Empire*, ed. Mary Balkun and Susan Imbarrato (New York and London: Palgrave, 2016), 171–185.

2 Elizabeth McHenry, *Forgotten Readers: Recovering the Lost History of African-American Literary Societies* (Durham, North Carolina: Duke University Press, 2002), 24.

3 On the history of African American emigration to Haiti, see Sara Fanning, *Caribbean Crossing: African Americans and the Haitian Emigration Movement* (New York: New York University Press, 2015).

4 See Frances Smith Foster, "How Do You Solve a Problem Like 'Theresa?'" *African American Review* 40, no.4 (Winter 2006): 636.

5 See Dickson D. Bruce, Jr., *The Origins of African American Literature, 1680–1865* (Charlottesville: University of Virginia Press, 2001), 172.

6 See Marlene Daut, *Tropics of Haiti: Race and the Literary History of the Haitian Revolution in the Atlantic World, 1789–1865* (Liverpool: Liverpool University Press, 2015), 291–293.

7 See Jacqueline Bacon, *Freedom's Journal: The First African American Newspaper* (Lanham, MD: Lexington Books, 2007) and Eric Gardner, *Black Print Unbound: The Christian Recorder, African American Literature, and Periodical Culture* (New York: Oxford University Press, 2015).

8 See Foster, "How do you Solve," 636; Jean Lee Cole, "Theresa and Blake: Mobility and Resistance in Antebellum African American Serialized Fiction" *Callaloo* 34, no. 1 (2011): 160; and Daut, *Tropics of Haiti*, 289.

9 See Meredith McGill, *American Literature and the Culture of Reprinting, 1834–53* (Philadelphia: University of Pennsylvania Press, 2003);Daniel Hack, *Reaping Something New: African American Transformations of Victorian Literature* (Princeton: Princeton University Press, 2016); and Britt Rusert, *Fugitive Science: Empiricism and Freedom in Early African American Culture* (New York: New York University Press, 2016).

10 See, for example, Kenneth Warren's definition in *What Was African American Literature?* (Cambridge: Harvard University Press, 2011), which is so alarmingly narrow that it excludes most writing by African American women and, alternately, the expansionist approach to the slave narrative genre in *The Oxford Handbook of the African American Slave Narrative*, ed. John Ernest (New York: Oxford University Press, 2014).

11 Bruce, *The Origins of African American Literature*, ix.

12 See Brigitte Fielder, "'No Rights that Any Body Is Bound to Respect': Pets, Race, and African American Child Readers," in *Who Writes for Black Children?: African American Children's Literature before 1900*, eds. Katharine Capshaw and Anna Mae Duane (Minneapolis: University of Minnesota Press, 2017), 164–181.

13 "S." "Theresa–A Haytien Tale" *Freedom's Journal*, January 18–February 15, 1828 reprinted in Frances Smith Foster, "How Do You Solve," 639.
14 See, especially, C.L.R. James, *The Black Jacobins: Toussaint L'Ouverture and the San Domingo Revolution* (New York: Random House, 1963), 27–61.
15 "Theresa," 639.
16 Edlie Wong, "In the Shadow of Haiti: The Negro Seamen Act, Counter-Revolutionary St. Domingue, and Black Emigration," in *The Haitian Revolution and the Early United States: Histories, Textualities, Geographies*, eds. Elizabeth Maddock Dillon and Michael J. Drexler (Philadelphia: University of Pennsylvania Press, 2016), 182.
17 "Theresa," 645.
18 Ibid., 639.
19 Ibid., 641.
20 Daut, *Tropics of Haiti*, 305.
21 Dorris Garraway, "Race, Reproduction and Family Romance in Moreau de Saint-Méry's *Description ... de la partie française de l'isle Saint Domingue*," *Eighteenth-Century Studies* 38 (2005): 230. Marlene L. Daut, "'Sons of White Fathers': Mulatto Vengeance and the Haitian Revolution in Victor Séjour's 'The Mulatto'" *Nineteenth-Century Literature* 65, no. 1 (June 2010): 5.
22 P. Gabrielle Foreman, "Who's Your Mama? 'White' Mulatta Genealogies, Early Photography, and Anti-Passing Narratives of Slavery and Freedom," *American Literary History* 14, no. 3 (2002): 508.
23 "Theresa," 645.
24 "Toussaint L'Ouverture," *Freedom's Journal* 1.8, (May 4, 1827): 30. See also Bacon, *Freedom's Journal*, 167–168.
25 On the newspaper's gender politics and conception of the Black diaspora community, see Bacon, *Freedom's Journal*, 121–146 and 147–175, respectively.
26 Hortense J. Spillers, "Mama's Baby, Papa's Maybe: An American Grammar Book," *Diacritics* 17, no. 2 (Summer 1987): 80.
27 Similarly fraught depictions of enslaved motherhood appear in a wide variety of texts and genres, from slave narratives like Harriet Jacobs' 1861 *Incidents in the Life of a Slave Girl* to plantation nostalgia fiction such as Mark Twain's 1894 *Pudd'nhead Wilson*.
28 I discuss further implications for mixed-race women's orientation toward Black communities in "Radical Respectability and African American Women's Reconstruction Fiction," in *African American Literature in Transition: 1865–1880s*, ed. Eric Gardner (Cambridge: Cambridge University Press, 2021).
29 Foreman discusses the problem of overemphasizing mixed-race figures' white ancestry. See "Who's Your Mama?," 506–507.
30 Foreman, "Who's Your Mama?," 507.
31 "Affecting Incident," *Freedom's Journal* 2, no. 1 , August 1, 1828: 147.
32 Ibid.
33 Ibid.

34 Ibid.
35 On *Marly's* politics regarding slavery and free people of color, see Sara Salih, *Representing Mixed Race in Jamaica and England from the Abolition Era to the Present* (New York: Routledge, 2010), 56–74.
36 "Affecting Incident," 147.
37 Hack, *Reaping Something New*, 2.
38 "Affecting Incident," 147.
39 Ibid., emphasis added.
40 Teresa C. Zackodnik, *The Mulatta and the Politics of Race*, (Jackson: University of Mississippi Press, 2004), xvii–xxviii.
41 Eve Allegra Raimon, *The "Tragic Mulatta" Revisited: Race and Nationalism in Nineteenth-Century Antislavery Fiction* (New Brunswick, NJ: Rutgers University Press, 2004), 21.
42 See Lisa Ze Winters, *The Mulatta Concubine: Terror, Intimacy, Freedom, and Desire in the Black Transatlantic* (Athens, Georgia: University of Georgia Press, 2016).
43 See Jennifer DeVere Brody, *Impossible Purities: Blackness, Femininity, and Victorian Culture*, (Durham, NC: Duke University Press, 1998), 17–19.
44 Radiclani Clytus, "At Home in England: Black Imagery across the Atlantic," in *Black Victorians: Black People in British Art, 1800–1900*, ed. Jan Marsh (Burlington, VT: Lund Humphries, 2005), 24–25.
45 Kimberly Snyder Manganelli, *Transatlantic Spectacles of Race: The Tragic Mulatta and the Tragic Muse* (New Brunswick: Rutgers University Press, 2012), 8.
46 Zackodnik, *The Mulatta and the Politics of Race*, xi.
47 See Fielder, "*The Woman of Colour* and Black Atlantic Movement" and "Radical Respectability and African American Women's Reconstruction Fiction."
48 While this novel was published anonymously and some debate still remains about its author, I follow scholars such as Philip Lapsansky and Monique Allewaert, who argue for Sansay's authorship and refer to the author of *Zelica* as Sansay. My reading, however, is more interested in the text's use of popular tropes of mixed-race women characters than its authorship. See Philip S. Lapsansky, "Afro-Americana: Rediscovering Leonora Sansay," in *The Annual Report of the Library Company of Philadelphia for the Year 1992* (Philadelphia, PA: Library Company of Philadelphia, 1993), 29–46 and Monique Allewaert, *Ariel's Ecology: Plantations, Personhood, and Colonialism in the American Tropics* (Minneapolis: University of Minnesota Press, 2013), 152.
49 Manganelli, *Transatlantic Spectacles of Race*, 35.
50 Daut discusses connections between Zuline and Zelica. See *Tropics of Haiti*, 259–265. *Secret History* also depicts mixed-race women in sexual competition with white women, similarly to the "tragic mulatta" genre that contrasts white women's legal marriages with legally enslaved women's extra-legal attachments or their rape. See Melissa Adams-Campbell, "Romantic Revolutions: Love and Violence in Leonora Sansay's *Secret History, or The Horrors of St. Domingo*," *Studies in American Fiction*, 39, no. 2 (Fall 2012): 138.

51 [Leonora Sansay?] *Zelica, the Creole. A Novel, By an American*, vol. 3 (London: William Fearman, 1820), 122.
52 Ibid., 308.
53 Ibid., 130.
54 Daut, *Tropics of Haiti*, 267.
55 Manganelli, *Transatlantic Spectacles of Race*, 35–36.
56 *The Woman of Colour, A Tale*, ed. Lyndon J. Dominique (Peterborough, Ontario: Broadview, 2008), 189.
57 Ibid., 77.
58 Brody, *Impossible Purities*, 16.
59 See Lyndon J. Dominique, *Imoinda's Shade: Marriage and the African Woman in Eighteenth-Century British Literature, 1759–1808* (Columbus: Ohio State University Press, 2012), 228.
60 I discuss the circumstances and stakes of Dido's enslavement and freedom more thoroughly in "*The Woman of Colour* and Black Atlantic Movement."
61 Bacon, *Freedom's Journal*, 239.
62 "Self-Interest," *Freedom's Journal*, November 7, 1828.
63 "Self-Interest," *Freedom's Journal*, November 14, 1828.
64 Ibid.
65 Cole, "Theresa and Blake," 162, 161.
66 "Theresa," 642.
67 Manganelli, *Transatlantic Spectacles of Race*, 28.

CHAPTER 9

Redemption, the Historical Imagination, and Early Black Biographical Writing

Stefan M. Wheelock

The Black biographical production which appeared at the dawning of the nineteenth century marked a turning point in the evolution of a literary genre. This era in literary expression was not as direct or explicit in its condemnation of slavery when compared with the later antebellum narratives which appeared in the 1840s and after. But the Black life writing of the period spanning from the late 1790s up through the 1820s, nevertheless, transformed Black biography into a far most robust commentary on slavery and its social ills. Works such as Jeffrey Brace's *The Blind African Slave, Or Memoirs of Boyrereau Brinch, Nicknamed Jeffrey Brace* (1810) and William Grimes's *The Life of William Grimes, the Runaway Slave, Written by Himself* (1825 and republished in 1855) are fairly representative, as neither text advocates outright for abolition. But both Brace and Grimes express their contempt for an unjust institution and chronicle a host of abuses they suffered at the hands of brutal masters (for Brace, in the Caribbean and New England, and for Grimes, in Virginia and Georgia).

This chapter investigates the function of a biblically-derived rhetoric of redemption in writings by turn-of-the century Black narrators who discussed slavery in the United States of America. Operating as a principal and a vocabulary, the rhetoric of redemption enlarged possibilities for Black narratives to critique both the early practices of racial slavery and the historical character of freedom in the North American context. Rather than offer an exhaustive survey of the biographical writings produced during the era, I focus on three key texts: Venture Smith's *A Narrative of the Life and Adventures of Venture, A Native of Africa, But resident above seventy years in the United States of America* (1798); George White's *A Brief Account of the Life, Experiences, Travels, and Gospel Labours of George White, An African* (1810); and John Jea's *Life, History, and Unparalleled Sufferings of John Jea, The African Preacher.* White and Jea infuse the account of their freedom from the bondage of sin and their subsequent regeneration in God with a riveting chronicle of their experiences both as slaves and as roving Atlantic freedmen, while Smith incorporates his experiences as a slave and a freedman within a Franklinesque account of personal fiscal successes and exploits.

The word "redemption" carries theological and economic meanings that bore directly upon the historical character of (and possibilities for) Black liberation in the late-eighteenth and nineteenth centuries. There is the grander sense of the term, denoting what was believed to be the eventful and providentially ordained salvation of individuals, oppressed communities, and, more broadly, the nation from sin, from slavery, inequality, and from the imperfections of Old World social orders. Redemption signaled national revival and renewal, and for Blacks, increasingly reflected a heightened call for the nationalizing of Black consciousness, identity, and resistance. Black narrators during this early period would most likely have known about (or been directly influenced by) the Second Great Awakening, a spiritual and cultural movement which swept across the early United States, affecting virtually all quarters of American society from the late 1790s into the 1840s. With its stress on redemption, revival, and spiritual regeneration, the Second Great Awakening significantly diminished the threat which deism posed to orthodox Protestant Christianity during the early national period. The movement helped democratize religious experience and presented opportunities for Blacks and women to voice their concerns over emergent practices of racial and gender oppression in the North American context.[1]

On the other hand, there was the juridical and economic practice that allowed slaves or sympathetic whites to buy back, or "redeem" Blacks' freedom from slaveholders through paying slaveholders for their apparent loss in property and labor power. Antislavery proponents were increasingly disturbed by the economic practice of redemption as the nineteenth century wore on, believing that the ransoming of slaves, by implication, sanctioned the legality of slavery. The guiding principle of abolition was that slaves belonged to no one but themselves. But moral outrage did not completely quash antislavery ambivalence over redemption as an effective (and legal) practice of emancipating slaves. By 1857, the Massachusetts antislavery leader William Lloyd Garrison wholly denounced the practice of redeeming slaves; but when the Black abolitionist Frederick Douglass was ransomed by British antislavery sympathizers ten years earlier, Garrison, at the time, conceded that "To save a fellow-being, it is no crime sometimes to comply with even unjust demands."[2] In these instances, the potential to reconstitute families torn apart by slavery, and the opportunity for antislavery proponents to promote the civility of

Blacks who were industrious and thrifty enough to purchase themselves and others out of slavery was compelling.

I argue that Black narrators during this early period deployed the rhetoric of redemption as a way of highlighting the ideological and legal failings of an early republic mired in a culture of race oppression. Early Black autobiography, at the turn of the century, artfully exploited the ironic contrasts in the meaning of redemption, and, in so doing, portrayed how an early culture of slavery enabled and warped possibilities for a more substantial Black liberation and agency. The Black narrators of this period depicted how redemption set them on a path to spiritual and/or legal emancipation from slavery. But as they chronicled their redemption from legal and spiritual bondage, they also described how slavery precluded the full reclamation of selfhood and autonomy in a market-driven circumstance of racial subjugation. Offering an important point of departure in the line of enquiry pursued here, critic Yolanda Pierce observes that much like their white literary predecessors, Black narrators marshaled the rhetoric of redemption as a way of allaying anxieties regarding their own racial alienation and enslavement in New World settings.[3] The rise of white nationalist conceptions of citizenship after 1790 and the flourishing of southern slavery after the closing of the slave trade in 1808 brought Blacks face to face with a new set of pressing concerns. For those precious few Blacks who procured their freedom, they lived "free" with limited mobility and autonomy in a world governed largely by slavery and race discrimination.[4] The acquisition then of freedom could not fully reclaim dignity and equality for the emancipated. The Black biographical writings of this era recounted personal redemption (and the redemption of other Blacks) in ways that provided unsettling and thoughtful responses to the concerns of their historical moment.

This chapter focuses on a brief, albeit significant, period (*c.*1800–1830) in early Black literary expression, when men's published narratives constituted the bulk of the Black life writing which appeared in print. Discernable traditions in Black women's conversion narratives and ex-slave autobiography, however, would appear on the scene with the publication of Maria W. Stewart's record of her conversion to the Christian faith in her political sermon "Religion and the Pure Principles of Morality, The Sure Foundation on Which We Must Build" (1831). Stewart's speeches formed some of the earliest efforts by Black women to interrogate post-revolutionary American political self-understanding. There was also Mary Prince's dictated narrative, *The History of Mary Prince, a West Indian Slave* (1831) which was published with the imprimatur of London's

Antislavery Society, and later, Jarena Lee's recounting of her call to ministry in *The Life and Religious Experience of Jarena Lee, A Coloured Lady, Giving an Account of Her Call to Preach the Gospel* (1836). The reasons Black women's published narratives appeared later than their male counterparts are suggested, in part, by the women writers themselves: early Black women's biographical accounts chronicled their efforts to assert their voices while creating spaces for other women within public spheres dominated by men's perspectives. For the Black women writers of the period, redemption entailed a mode of reclamation which not only involved their liberation from racial domination and spiritual bondage but also involved the reclaiming of their bodies, identity, and sexual agency from male domination and, not infrequently, from sexual violence.[5]

An investigation, then, into redemption's semantic contrasts offers a window into how Blacks first imagined their agency and strategized resistance in a world governed by slavery. The writers examined below anticipate a rich intellectual tradition unfolding in nineteenth-century African American literature. Black autobiographers in the early nineteenth century advanced their indictments of slavery, in part, by recalling for reading audiences how difficult it was for them to reclaim some semblance of self-worth in a world where slavery touched virtually all facets of American life. Smith, White, and Jea impugned the character of slavery before the public eye by revealing the ironic consequences of their redemption.

Venture Smith and the Paradoxes of Redemption

Venture Smith's narrative offers an autobiographical glimpse into early Atlantic economies. Smith, early on, came to see wealth as intrinsic to personal freedom and nobility of stature long before being brought to North America. Born Broteer Furro, the scion of a wealthy African (probably Fulani) king, the young Smith was taken as a slave, eventually to be sold from the port city of Anomabo (in what is present-day Ghana). The young Broteer stood by helplessly as his father was captured and then killed by a rival village of people. During the raid, young Smith was forced to witness Saungm Furro (Smith's father) die to protect his wealth, an event that thrusts Smith headlong into a violent trade in African bodies that had grown substantially in volume since 1700. At the time of Smith's birth in 1729, the volume of the slave trade had grown to between fifty to sixty thousand captive souls per annum. This figure climbed to somewhere between seventy and eighty thousand captives per annum in the 1780s.

After being captured, Smith was taken to Barbados and then New England where he labored as a slave in Rhode Island, Fishers Island (New York), and Connecticut.

What seems to have been seared in Smith's memory is his father's final noble act of defiance. Saungm chose to hide his wealth from his captors, and would never betray the location of his money, even at the expense of his life. For the young Smith, Saungm's courage to protect personal wealth only enhanced the virtue of his father. This market-informed sense of nobility translated into Smith's sense of his own potential standing with his captors. The acquisition of money came to signify virtuous achievement for the young slave. If this traumatic moment first sowed the seeds of manly virtue in a boy no more than twelve years old, Smith's contractualist-oriented outlook on interpersonal relations – his belief in just business dealings and promise-keeping as a virtuous path to emancipation – came of age in a mid-eighteenth-century New England culture of slavery.

Smith's first masters, the Mumfords, were a prominent New England family that could trace their proud roots as far back as the 1630s. Over the course of the eighteenth century, the Mumford clan acted as itinerant agents, brokers, and managers for others who needed ships, slaves, and other provisions for the triangular trade. His subsequent owners, the Stantons were a family of Revolutionary War heroes, and Smith's final owner, Oliver Smith (whose last name Venture took) knew General George Washington personally. In his narrative, Smith recounts his journey to legal emancipation, which proved to be anything but simple. Smith knew that the autonomy he craved involved redeeming his wife, Meg, his daughter Hannah, and his sons Solomon and Cuff from their status as property. Smith eventually purchased his freedom in 1765 from Oliver Smith as relationships between the American colonials and the British government became increasingly strained. Venture Smith is silent on what was surely a politically tumultuous circumstance that bore directly on his status as a slave in colonial and rebellious New England. He could not claim his "natural rights" as his white rebellious contemporaries did (many of whom were slave owners) during the war years of the American Revolution.[6]

Smith's *Narrative* is an example that connects to a number of other early Black Atlantic autobiographical accounts of enslavement and freedom. The work is anticipated by *The Interesting Narrative of the Life of Olaudah Equiano, or Gustavas Vassa, the African, Written by Himself* (1789). Smith's work, like Equiano's, emphasized the racial particularities in modernity's logic of capitalism: racism and emergent ethnic nationalisms coincided with the logic of a free market to severely limit the entry of free Africans into a competitive market place.[7] The seminal claim Houston Baker makes about the ex-slave Olaudah Equiano – that Equiano "realizes, in effect, that only the acquisition of property will enable him to alter his designated status as property"[8] – also applies to Smith. Generally speaking, late-eighteenth-century Anglo elite sensibilities ground the Enlightenment's emphasis on rational freedom in the very potentialities of the market to foster individual agency. The individual's capacities for freedom and agency are expanded through the acquisition of property, so the logic goes, and market logic, in turn, further humanizes and civilizes modern subjects through "mannered" encounters between participants of roughly equal standing operating under the banner of commercial exchange. African Americans were arguing for freedom from slavery, but the fact of their second-class racial status in this market-driven world contradicted any idealism they may have had. One might question the extent to which Smith's emancipation, shaped by the logic of the market, was satisfying to him. Smith's endeavors to redeem his family and other Blacks coincide with his emphasis on the various opportunities presented to him for investment. But, the practice of redemption would shield neither Smith nor his family from the vagaries of Atlantic market logic.

Smith highlights his commercial successes, recalling how he economically redeems (purchases) himself and others from slavery. Generally speaking, scholars have been troubled by Smith's economic outlook on the purchase of both things and people, as it reveals the cold and calculating predisposition of a narrator who prizes wealth and real assets over human life. Philip Gould, for instance, has pointedly observed that in "[s]uccumbing to the epistemological trap endemic to slave capitalism, Smith commodifies even the most intimate of familial relations."[9] After Smith purchases his son Solomon's freedom, for example, Solomon is enticed by the promise of wages and a "pair of silver buckles" to sail on a whaling voyage financed by the Massachusetts merchant, Charles Church.[10] By the time Smith discovers his son's intentions and attempts to stop him, Solomon is out to sea. Smith later learns that Solomon dies of scurvy while on this voyage, and Church, a white man, does not remunerate Smith for the loss of his son. Smith laments the loss of his son but also the fact that he loses "equal to seventy-five pounds,"[11] the rough equivalent of money he originally spent to manumit Solomon. Still, Elijah Niles, the amanuensis who wrote down what Smith related concerning his life, found Smith's accomplishments truly remarkable, rivaling the genius and industry of Benjamin Franklin. And by the end of his memoir, Smith touts his freedom as a "privilege which nothing else can equal."[12] The word "privilege" is suggestive of the way he views the liberation of his family and other Blacks as we shall see. Scholars have imagined these remarks as a cresting moment in the life of a former slave who, with remarkable business savvy, promulgates the logic of an Atlantic market.

Smith literally works his way into emancipation, and, by sheer force of will, is able to redeem himself, his wife and children "besides three negro men."[13] Striking a deal with his master, Oliver Smith, to purchase his freedom, Smith agrees to pay the extravagant sum of seventy pounds, two shillings "towards redeeming my time,"[14] enough to buy hundreds of acres of land in 1765.[15] Additionally, he accrues the requisite amount to pay for his manumission while handing his master a quarter of his earnings for the "privilege" of working for himself. Smith's experience suggests that the practice of redemption performs as the economic (and salvific) antidote to bondage – a restorative measure aimed at reclaiming family while fostering new investment opportunities for the narrator in the face of all that race slavery has wrought. The redemption of his family from various masters presents the best opportunity for emancipating his family. The language of redemption, then, serves a double duty, first, by touting the entrepreneurial savvy of the narrator, and second, by demonstrating how the narrator forges a dignified existence initially brought low by the violence of the slave trade. Still, Smith's efforts are tested by the volatility of his economic situation. An accidental fire consumes Smith's chest containing clothing and a considerable amount of money – thirty-eight pounds in fact – while his wife and children are in bondage. Through thrift and industry he would more than make up what he lost in the fire: he had enough money to purchase his sons, Solomon and Cuff for two hundred dollars each with one hundred pounds to spare, and he went on to purchase his wife and his daughter. While redeeming his family, he purchases three Black men for sixty pounds, four hundred dollars, and twenty-five pounds, respectively.[16] But if he redeems these men from slavery, it is not clear whether Smith intends to fully emancipate these men, make them indentured servants, or perhaps slaves.

Smith's economic rhetoric of redemption is murky and it raises somewhat thorny questions about his views on the freedom of his family and other Blacks. Does Smith "enslave" the Black men he redeems? Does Smith "own" his family in the way masters own slaves? Has he (in eighteenth-century parlance) "bound out" (or placed in the status of temporary servitude) his son Solomon? The word "hire" lends itself to a few possibilities when it comes to Solomon. Perhaps, Smith saw an opportunity to increase his family's wealth through his son's work. Or perhaps, Solomon's hiring out was the way the son paid his father back. After he redeems Solomon from slavery, Smith "hires" out his son to the aforementioned Church so that Solomon may earn "twelve pounds and an opportunity of acquiring some learning."[17] (It isn't clear whether he or his son would be the recipient of the earnings.) On the other hand, Smith redeems his wife Meg "for love"[18] and by extension, his daughter Hannah and his sons as a way of repairing his family. The history of Blacks owning other Blacks only complicates matters. In speaking about the practices of the early nineteenth century, one historian observes that "many of the colored slaveowners inherited slaves from Black relatives as well as white kinsfolk." Sometimes marriages between free Blacks and slaves resulted in the free Black owning the spouse and children. In other instances, Black owners purchased other Blacks for humanitarian reasons or as outright slave labor to procure profits.[19] Smith could have been engaged in any of a number of these practices. In any case, by this point in the third chapter of the narrative, he deploys the rhetoric of redemption with increased momentum, and, ironically, the rhetoric of redemption figures as part of a tangled and condensed account wherein his efforts are encumbered by a culture based on slaveholding. I wish to suggest that Smith's muddled chronicle of purchasing the Black men, in particular, points to the rather pesky issue of whether Smith's practices of redemption are liberating at all for Blacks in the *Narrative*. (I return to this point below.)

The slave's redemption was a practice of negotiation, which Smith rightly intuited might be agreeable to masters. Smith, in one instance, attempts to strike a bargain with Hempsted Miner to purchase his freedom from his previous master, Thomas Stanton.[20] Smith's first North American master, Robinson Mumford could not have possibly known that the mocking name he gave his slave would come to signify the slave's smart participation in market activity –the slave turned venture capitalist whose exploits result in the substantial acquisition of land, houses, and money. What seems clearer is that Smith views Black emancipation as operating under market-informed constraints, and that this view is influenced by his experiences as a slave. Especially intriguing is how Smith's views on emancipation and indebtedness, at times, mimic the honorific dynamics behind slave's negotiations with masters in acquiring freedom. It seems that his understanding of liberation is influenced by the experiences he has with the masters of his youth. All along in the narrative, Smith repeatedly proves his worth as a valuable commodity to his various masters, through his virtue, industry, and integrity. And Smith, indeed, proves to be a dependable and sturdy worker, despite occasional moments of defiance. In the narrative, Smith's path to emancipation hinges upon preserving his status as a virtuous laboring subject. The narrative chronicles how his fortunes are tethered to his status as a manageable or unmanageable form of capital, and in this sense, Smith is the living embodiment of the master's risk in financial investment. Smith recalls protecting Mumford's valuables from Mumford's father; he cites Mumford's proclamation, that "his young Venture was so faithful" including this instance in the narrative as proof of his fidelity as a virtuous slave.[21]

But Smith would later have to reckon with the fact that his business encounters with his masters are hardly equitable, based on an asymmetry in power relations that grants the master the absolute prerogative to keep (or not keep) his word. In an act of personal defiance, Smith aims to flee from Mumford with an Irish indentured servant, Joseph Heday to Mississippi. But after Heday absconds with clothes and provisions, Smith partners with local authorities to help catch Heday.[22] Soon thereafter, Smith is sold to Thomas Stanton. While a slave under Stanton, Smith physically subdues Thomas and his brother Robert when they attempt to beat Smith after an altercation he had with Thomas's wife, Elizabeth.[23] Robert Stanton cheats Smith out of some money Smith entrusts to him.[24] Hempsted Miner attempts to purchase Smith from Thomas Stanton, and for a time it seemed that Smith belongs to Miner, although Miner never pays Stanton for the purchase of his slave. Miner, however, attempts to sell Smith to William Hooker and Daniel Edwards for sale. Edwards asks Smith why Miner would want to part with such an "honest negro." Smith speculates that Miner wants to "convert me into cash, and speculate with me as with other commodities."[25] Despite these transactions, Thomas Stanton ultimately sells Smith to his final master, Oliver Smith.[26] Although Smith has some say in who he works for, promoting the value of his labor to prospective masters, and working assiduously to obtain the requisite capital to free himself, it is the master's choice to free him. Smith's path to freedom, then, is dependent upon a somewhat fragile circumstance where the master's regard for Smith's honor, integrity, and capacities for generating money is the deciding factor in the decision to manumit the slave.

Smith mimics these honorific, obligatory, and contractual dynamics in his redeeming of the Black men, some of whom he endeavors to employ as laborers. Smith redeems three Black men. For the first man, Smith expects work as a form of repayment, though the man ultimately flees. The second man also leaves Smith, deciding to return to "his old master;"[27] Smith gives no reasons for why he parts with the third man he purchases. On another occasion, Smith hires two other Black men, both of whom decide to run away. Mingo, a Black man who Smith hires, flees in debt to Smith, but Smith stops him and hauls him to court. Mingo, appealing to Smith's sense of decency and humanity, asks Smith whether treating him this way for unpaid debts is not "a hard way of treating our fellow creatures." Smith sardonically responds that it would be "hard thus to treat our honest fellow creatures,"[28] thus highlighting Smith's belief that Blacks too were accountable to forms of contractual and moral obligation to those for whom they labor. Jacklin, another man working for Smith, intends to use his wages to enter the comb trade, but also runs away with the combs that Smith could rightly claim as his investment.[29] All in all, Smith's dealings with the men he redeems and hires capture a key irony. In Smith's mind, the freedom that these Black men possess is a privilege based in fidelity to an agreed-upon contract between persons. And this mindset is suggested in Smith's lament over the "perfidy"[30] of his countrymen. But for these Black men, Smith's terms for work are intolerable. Their attempts to free themselves from obligation assume a form that upsets the expectations of the narrator. For these men, freedom may very well have meant flight from indebtedness to yet another master. It is tempting to think that Smith himself had become something of an enterprising slaveholder. But if this conclusion sounds too extreme, he may have regarded himself as a guiding and directing hand in the fortunes of the lives he saved from slavery and destitution.

There is, however, another, more robust, way of reading Smith's murky chronicle of legally redeeming other Blacks. Smith's recounting of his efforts to redeem others frustrates readers because it does not offer a straightforward idea of how he views freedom. But the murky sense around freedom in the narrative is, nonetheless, valuable. The *Narrative* offers subtle clues for why redemption is, at best, a weak practice of Black liberation, suggesting that in a culture based on contracts, obligation, and duty, a person's redemption of a slave oftentimes requires a return on his or her investment (perhaps in the form of labor) from the person manumitted. In such cases, the redeemer might conceivably invoke the rhetoric of obligation, duty, and virtue as a way of reinforcing (and reinscribing) both power and presumption over the recently manumitted subject.[31] Smith, at the very least, seems to adhere to this general principle in his perspective on the Black men he redeems. In Smith's mind, the men he ransoms break faith with him by running away, suggesting to Smith that these Blacks' flight and contentiousness is ingratitude, dishonesty, or worse, beneath virtuous behavior. Smith's views on their behavior hint at how late-eighteenth-century principles of civility, operating in the shadow of the slave trade, reinforce an asymmetry in power relations, even among Blacks themselves. That early Black freedom comes with a price is stark in moments such as the ones just described and allows the *Narrative* to unveil an important truth: that economic and legal redemption for Blacks in a culture of slavery is not, in the fullest sense, liberatory.

Smith reinforces this sense of disappointment with the sobering recognition of the social constraints placed on him as a Black person with considerable financial means. Smith sails to New London with an "Indian" who had been placed in charge of "two hogsheads of molasses" which belonged to a white man, Elijah Hart. And upon arrival at New London, one of the hogsheads is lost overboard. The Indian doesn't have the money to pay for Hart's financial loss, and Hart, eager to recuperate his money, threatens to sue Smith. Smith, who claims to have had nothing to do with the loss of Hart's property, is forced to pay "ten pounds lawful" to Hart or face court proceedings. Outraged, Smith characterizes this incident as having no foundation "in reason and justice, whatever it may be called in a christian land [*sic*]."[32] Smith concludes that this maltreatment is because Hart is white with America's laws and customs on his side; Smith believes himself to be a man reduced to the low status of a "poor African," and a "black dog," berated and defenseless in the face of unfortunate circumstances like this one.[33] Critic David Kazanjian observes that Hart is able to cheat Smith by participating in the early American "ritual" of excluding Smith as a racial outsider.[34] Smith, I would add, suggests that American ideals of reason, justice, and religion are hollowed out in the face of these rituals of racial exclusion. Smith's efforts, then, to redeem Black personhood from physical and spiritual bondage achieved only so much in a historical circumstance where race prejudice renders reason, religiosity, and justice a mockery. Smith's remarks offer a tacit admission that his herculean efforts as a Black entrepreneur have been, to a degree, pointless – vain – where racism undercuts the equity market-logic promises for those who participate in it.

Smith's rhetoric of redemption offers clues into the vexed role the concept plays in early Black historical perspectives generally. Smith employs the economic rhetoric of redemption as a counterbalance to the cultural and economic ravages of slavery, which, in turn, helps to anchor the narrator's own sense of identity and agency. But Smith's chronicle of his redemption (and the redemption of his family) also focuses attention on the extent to which race slavery has circumscribed possibilities for Black liberation. The fact that Smith's account is unusual (and that it is spare in its commentary on Black oppression) may, however, explain why the narrative had limited influence during the early antebellum period. Charles Holt published the *Narrative* and the four-page newspaper in which it appeared, *The Bee*, in New London, Connecticut, each selling for one shilling. By the time he died in Haddam Connecticut in 1805, he had become a legendary figure, regarded as the "Black Paul Bunyan."[35] Still, Smith's legendary status happens against a backdrop where Atlantic commercialism has mixed consequences for the narrator's emancipation. Smith's efforts to redeem his family and other Blacks from chains express the salient ways in which Atlantic slavery warps early Black freedom and its prospects.

Black Redemption, Regeneration, and the Word

Despite the uncertainties of economic redemption, Black narrators imagined that they could reclaim their identity and agency in other ways. Spiritual redemption under Christ is a persistent rhetorical trope in this period, even as these writers found that spiritual redemption could not fully ward off the negative effects of slavery. George White and John Jea emphasized spiritual redemption as central to narratives regarding the plight of Atlantic Africans in a world of slavery. White and Jea embraced their respective callings as ministers of the Gospel during a pivotal moment after Black homiletics and the Black Church solidified into more formal institutions in the 1770s. As itinerant preachers who could not fully look to denominational affiliation as a viable source of economic support, both men sought to sustain their ministries through the limited means of income available to free Blacks at the turn of the century. White sold fruit and oysters in rural areas up and down the east coast, opened his home in New York to boarders, and made shoes as a way of making a living. Jea made his money primarily as a sailor, and particularly as a ship's cook, which was commonplace for Black men who were often denied opportunities for advancement at sea in the early 1800s. The emphasis on spiritual redemption in both their personal lives and their ministries enabled them to bear the indignities they endured as emancipated Blacks. They both understood that the Bible's emphasis on spiritual liberation was a powerful tool for self-realization and equality through Christ. As we shall see, Jea chronicles in the *Life* his espousal of a theology which transcends early American slaveholding perspectives, while White looks to overcome institutional (read racial) barriers in Methodism to preach the Word of God.

In a period of religious exodus from segregated churches, the Methodists treated Blacks better than other religious denominations of the early national period. Methodism offered Black preachers opportunities to spread the Gospel under a regimented itinerancy, it appealed across racial lines because of the egalitarianism implied in the Methodist doctrine of salvation freely available to all, and, finally, it emphasized the immediate and dynamic spiritual regeneration of the individual which also connected to African practices of spirituality. Accordingly, White and Jea both affiliated with Methodist doctrine, with White procuring a license to preach from the Methodist clergy in 1807 after several appeals, and Jea expanding his ministry beyond the dogmatic constraints of Methodism and Dutch Reformed religious circles.

White's *Brief Account* is distinct for being the first Black American to compose his autobiography with no amanuensis. White's autobiography was preceded by a number of biographies which chronicle Black American preachers' attempts to establish Baptist religious congregations in the American South, Jamaica, and Sierra Leone. Two notable examples are George Liele's *An Account of Several Baptist Churches, Consisting Chiefly of Negro Slaves* (1793), and David George's *An Account of the Life of Mr. David George, from Sierra Leone, Africa* (1793). And White's biographical account contained his "Sermon Preached on the Funeral Occasion of Mary Henery" (1809), which trended with the more formal homiletic structuring one finds in Lemuel Haynes's "Universal Salvation" (1805). Meanwhile, Black preaching was developing into an explicit mode of social commentary, as evidenced in Prince Hall's "Pray God Give Us the Strength to Bear Up Under All Our Troubles" (1797), Absalom Jones's oration on the abolition of the slave trade, "A Thanksgiving Sermon" (1808), and Richard Allen's "Eulogy for Washington" (1799). Jones and Allen went on to found the African Methodist Episcopal Church that White eventually joined and helped expand over the northeast United States.

White's and Jea's narratives reflect the cultural challenges that circumscribed the rise of Black evangelicalism at the dawning of the nineteenth century. Both authors' narratives signify a forward step in the emergence of early Black biographical writing as social commentary. White and Jea deploy redemption in ways that turn the Black conversion narrative into a salient critique of slaveholding and its theological presumptions. The narrators recast Christian redemption as one way to diminish the significance slavery has over the personal destinies of Black peoples, even as the institution of slavery maintains a material hold over Black bodies and labor. White and Jea each aim to imagine slavery and the racist forms of paternalism that accompany the institution as false and temporal enterprises which God's redemption nullifies. In so doing, they are able to focus attention on spiritual redemption and to place limitations on a tragic historical circumstance in which Blacks find themselves.

White stands in the gap between Olaudah Equiano's conversion narrative and a generation of nineteenth-century Black autobiography for the way it imagines the role of Christian redemption in the psychological, social, and spiritual regeneration of early Black peoples. White was inspired by the antislavery activism of New York's Black community and would be involved in a number of noteworthy projects in community reform. He joined the John Street Methodist church in New York City in the early 1790s but would leave the white-controlled Methodist congregation in 1796 in protest against white denunciations of the Saint Domingue Revolution. He joined the first separatist "African Society" which petitioned New York's Common Council in 1795 to purchase land to build a church and burial ground. As Graham Russell Hodges notes, he was among the "trustees of dissident Black Methodists who built the African Methodist Episcopal Zion Church on a lot at Church and Leonard streets after gaining a charter from the New York legislature."[36] After settling down in New York's Black community, White and his family tried their hand at an oyster business during this period and may have even gone into the printing business. But White mainly helped to more firmly establish the presence of the AME Church's congregation in New York State. Richard Allen eventually made White a deacon over the White Plains circuit in upstate New York. His 1810 narrative was published by the New York City Methodist printer, John C. Totten.[37]

White's theology is reflected in the recounting of his own life. Born on a plantation in Accomack, Virginia, in 1764 and separated from his mother soon after birth, White was sold three times when his last master (who White does not name) decided to free him on his death bed. It would be, as White phrases things, "the infinitely wise disposer of events" that "delivered him" from the "temporal bondage" of slavery. It is slavery, White contends, which divests the individual of "almost every privilege and enjoyment," and thus undermines the happiness and joy to be found in God. Hence, slavery is contrary to the "well-being of society, and repugnant to the will of God."[38] In White's case, God's plans for redemption charted a new course for the former slave in terms of spirituality and led White to look to God for deliverance from the "slavery of sin."[39] Offering a counter-narrative to slavery and its corruptions, God's redemption performs a double duty for White: if the institution enslaves both soul and body, God reclaims physical freedom for White and is in the process of reclaiming the narrator's soul.

White experiences God's soul-regenerating ability through a powerful encounter with Methodist preaching. After years of searching for his mother, he decides to leave the "brutal barbarity"[40] of the South and in 1787, at the age of twenty-five, makes his way north. Here, White finds the complicated landscape of gradual emancipation, which Graham Russell Hodges notes, did not completely end servitude in New York until 1827 and New Jersey's slaves were not entirely free until the passage of the Thirteenth Amendment in 1865.[41] White was arrested and detained for a month in New Jersey on the suspicion that he was a fugitive slave. White's manumission papers from his ex-master proved to be genuine; and some years after he arrived in New York City, he heard the transformative preaching of a Methodist minister named Stebbens. The first step toward White's spiritual redemption is coupled with a terrifying dream of Hell, as White experiences souls that are dragged headlong into a burning pit by devils to their final doom. The scene is so terrifying to carefree travelers in White's dream that they are also gripped by fear. White's "conductor" instructs him, in Dante-esque fashion, to tell others what he witnessed while in Hell.[42] This moment contrasts with another soul-regenerating moment in New York in the spring of 1806 where White has an ecstatic conversion experience, encountering the glory of God which steeps his soul in "perfect love, peace, joy, and good-will toward man."[43]

White's visions, dreams, and conversion set him on the path toward claiming his calling from God to preach. He felt duty-bound to call all sinners, and especially his fellow Blacks, to repentance through ministry. But he also longed for institutional acceptance from a largely-white controlled Methodist leadership. He would be denied five times before given a license to preach, one Methodist official regarding him as "delusional" in his aims.[44] Still, White was persistent, convinced of his calling. White experienced yet another level of spiritual regeneration through the literacy he obtains while learning how to read the Bible under the direction of his daughter. It was this regenerative form of literacy – taking the form of God's redemptive Word – that emboldened White to persist in procuring his preaching license. White, with God's promises in view, believed that he "was too much circumscribed in his privileges"[45] to be kept from preaching. White preached to various denominations and sects without a license, and was so convinced of his role in the spiritual regeneration and democratization of religious communities that he united a Long-Island camp meeting in prayers against detractors who viewed the "displays of divine power" as "unnecessary and prejudicial to society."[46]

White aligns with Methodist doctrine when he imagines the spiritual regeneration of the sinner as a process that involves "self-denial, mortification, self-renunciation, conviction and contrition for sin," given that these practices counter the "corrupt nature" and buoy the soul under divine Grace.[47] In general, his remarks set the stage for how he views the life of the regenerated believer under the providence of God. The Christian "rejoices in the wisdom of God, as ordering all events, and as being engaged for his direction, in whatever station or condition of life, Divine Providence have placed him" and the believer is "contented and happy" in the face of adversity and suffering, knowing these things "shall no less turn to his advantage, under the direction of infinite wisdom and goodness, than prosperity, ease, health, and wealth."[48] These remarks are troubling when considered with regard to the commercial enslavement of Africans. African slaves (including White) desired actual freedom and equality, and if God's wise purposes in the salvation of the believer surpass the limited sense that individuals have concerning their historical circumstances, then White's remarks seem to imply that slaves trust God's wisdom as they bear up under the master's yoke. Still, White's theological pronouncements are interlaced with subversive notions where White urges his largely African congregations to stand and to reach for new sources of strength in the face of race subjugation, reminding them that the power and omnipresence of God not only purifies the believer's heart from sin, but gives "him victory over all his temporal and spiritual enemies, and afford support under every trial and burden."[49] For White, God's redemption of sinners is victory, and like Jea, White's emphasis on God's redemptive victory over "temporal enemies" hints at a spiritual victory he believes Africans can rightly claim over the white oppressors who have racially subjugated them. White suggests that God's providence fortifies the believer's identity and supplies a sense of individual destiny which cannot be diminished by the temporalities of slavery-induced suffering.

White's comments prefigure what would become a general trend in slave autobiography. Repeatedly, White crafts sermons to highlight the soul-liberating consequences of a repentant turn toward God. After recounting for readers the sermon he preaches at the passing of Sister Mary Henery, a slave and White's now deceased wife, White takes a moment to explain that Mary dies "happy and triumphant" as opposed to other Blacks who he believes died in a state of "mad despair."[50] This idea of spiritual freedom is repeated in other period texts, for example, *The*

Life, Experience and Gospel Labors of the Rt. Richard Allen (1833). White believes that through God, the souls of his African brethren are set free, if their bodies, in fact, are not. He believes that if his African brothers and sisters are forced to bear the yoke of slavery, they can experience a regenerating form of psychological and spiritual freedom that the temporal bondage of racism and slavery cannot fully vanquish. Most notably, Frederick Douglass, in his 1845 autobiography, *Narrative of the Life of Frederick Douglass, An American Slave, Written by Himself* argued for the psycho-spiritual liberation of slaves. Douglass spends a significant portion of his narrative describing how a slave's being ultimately languishes under plantation life. After having bested his master, Edward Covey, in a fight, Douglass experiences a "glorious resurrection, from the tomb of slavery, to the heaven of freedom" which leads him to conclude that "however long I might remain a slave in form, the day had passed forever when I could be a slave in fact."[51] Douglass's acquisition of literacy had already liberated his mind to critique slavery and ignited his desire to gain freedom. But here we have a cresting moment: Douglass's exhortation is suffused with religious language that leads him to characterize his freedom as, first, an internal spiritual redemption from enslavement.

Jea, by contrast, sought to surpass the somewhat narrow ideological constraints placed on him by American and Western religious orthodoxies and would preach a redemptive Gospel across the world. Written sometime between 1800 and 1815 with the assistance of an unidentified amanuensis, the *Life* is the harrowing story of a man whose road to spiritual redemption was paved by violence, suffering, and neglect. Born in Old Callabar, southern Nigeria, in 1773, Jea and his family were stolen from their homeland, made to cross the Atlantic Ocean, and sold as slaves in New York to violent masters, Oliver and Angelika Triehuen. The Triehuens worked their slaves mercilessly, and the abusive treatment Jea endured under the Triehuens prefigured what were generally his experiences with several masters until his manumission. The Triehuens were congregants in the conservative Dutch Reformed Church, a religious organization that eventually acknowledged the equality of Blacks and whites under God, yet opposed the conversion of slaves to Christianity. When Jea has a life-transforming encounter with Christianity at fifteen years old, the Triehuens do all they can to nullify his soul-regenerating experience, including beating him. Emboldened, nevertheless, by his conversion experience and beginning to entertain an amateur career in preaching and exhortation, Jea desires to learn how to read (particularly, the scriptures), prays earnestly to God to become literate, and is miraculously granted his request. The news of this miracle spreads rapidly, eventually leading to Jea's manumission under the authority of local magistrates, and these new capacities for biblical literacy qualify him to enter society as a freedman. Driven by his calling, Jea eventually leaves his final unnamed master, roving up and down the Atlantic seaboard and sailing across the Atlantic as a ship's cook on several voyages, travelling as far as Boston, Rotterdam, Amsterdam, Liverpool, Sunderland, and Brest, sharing the Gospel with anyone who listens.

Jea's rhetoric of redemption lays the groundwork for a theory of slavery, religion, and Black destiny in the making of a post-Revolutionary American Atlantic identity. Jea's liberation ethic has been criticized by scholars as rather self-absorbed, informed by the individualism of free-will evangelical Arminianism rather than by a Calvinist world view which emphasized community and election in early Black theological understandings of freedom and destiny in the latter eighteenth century.[52] There is truth to this assertion. But I would also argue that this kind of sensibility misses some of the nuanced ways Jea's historical outlook frames Christian redemption in early Black liberation praxis. Refusing to subscribe to any particular religious orthodoxy, Jea grounds his theology, first and foremost, in the redemptive and liberating power of the Word. It is Jea's theological anchoring in the Word that allows him to refuse an identity circumscribed by narrow Western nationalisms or imperial rivalry. As scholars generally note, religious conversion and literacy fostered possibilities for the slaves to claim psychological and spiritual freedom for themselves, as White's and Jea's narratives make clear. Generally speaking, Jea imagines his biographical account as a Lazarus narrative – as a life-story paralleling that of Jesus' resurrection of Lazarus from the dead. Jesus raises Lazarus from the dead after having been in a tomb for days, and Jea believes his conversion experiences raise him from the death of slavery into a life of spiritual and material freedom through the soul-regenerating capacities of the Word. Facing opposition to his preaching while traveling in Sunderland, England, Jea is derided by a Mr. Chittle as a "poor Lazarus." Jea quotes from the gospel of John, chapter 11 to both remind his audience of the power Christ demonstrated in reviving Lazarus and to suggest to his listeners the applicability of these scriptures to Jea's own life.[53]

Jea's literacy begins with his miraculous capacity to read the first chapter of St. John, which characterizes God as the transcending and eternal Logos. The author of the Gospel writes that "In the beginning was the Word, and the Word was with God, and the Word was God," and that "the Word was made flesh, and dwelt among us" in the divinity of Jesus.[54] Jea recalls that "From that hour, in which the Lord taught me to read, until the present, I have not been able to read in any book, nor any reading whatever, but such as contain the word of God."[55] The redemptive power of the Word radicalizes Jea's understanding of his personal destiny as God's own. As we shall see, from his reformed views about God and salvation emerge a radically life-altering awareness of his historical circumstances. After his spiritual conversion, Jea, in what appears to parallel the story of the Apostle St. Paul's life, preaches Christian redemption but lives a life beset by suffering, much of which is brought on by the precarious status of being Black and free in a slaveholding Atlantic driven by imperial rivalry. It is his newfound literacy in the Word which spiritually emboldens him to pursue his calling, almost to what some readers have described as a somewhat naïve sense about the precariousness of his circumstances and the tragedy of his life. Nevertheless, he felt "enabled, by the assistance of the Holy Spirit" to go everywhere, preaching and teaching sinners, even as people "mocked and scoffed" at him, saying there goes "*the preacher.*"[56]

For Jea, God's word is eternal and larger than justifications for slavery. Forming the basis for his new-found vision from the moment he is converted onward, Jea's profound encounter with the Word made Flesh (and with the Word of God generally) produces in him an outsized view of God's relationship to the whole of creation, forever altering his understanding of the place he occupies in America's enslaving culture. He now views "the smallest insect … as none but the Almighty could make them."[57] His master and family thought he was insane. Being directed by the Spirit of God, Jea informs his master (and his family) that he will be delivered "from their tyrannical power" and that "whatsoever grace had begun, glory would end."[58] Recognizing the transcendence of God's saving Word, Jea now understands his personal redemption as that which overcomes the temporal hold slavery has over his Black body. Also importantly, the saving power of God's Word reveals to Jea the temporal limitations in theologies beholden to Atlantic slavery, capitalism, and imperialism, which might explain his hesitance to espouse any particular Christian doctrine. The master's catechism of racial subordination to which he was brutally exposed as a child – and to which he is continually subjected throughout his life – is revealed in the light of God's salvation as limited and to a great degree, false. God's redemption is, then, a liberating act. But even more, it forms the basis for a latent social critique which runs through the text.

Jea recounts his early life as an eventual awakening from the nightmarish experience of both the slaveholders' violence and perverse views concerning the slave's place in the world. Reflecting on his early experiences as a child, Jea remembers how the Triehuens indoctrinated slaves, lamenting that "[w]e [the slaves] were often led away with the idea that our masters were our gods," while at other times, the slaves "placed ideas" in the sun, moon, and stars.[59] The racial subjugation of slaves seems then to fracture the slaves' theologically-informed sense of being, forcing them to vacillate between two competing cosmologies, one African and the other American and proslavery in character. One way of justifying slaveholding violence and domination would be to imagine it as a local expression of God's absolute control over nature (and over the slave's destiny), which is exactly what Jea's masters do: Jea and other slaves were urged to believe that their masters were gods and that the slaves were not unlike "the beasts that perish."[60] Jea counters this outlook through a hermeneutic engagement that brings down masters from their godlike status and thus imagines them as fragile and limited. In Jea's theological view, the master cannot sustain what God in His wisdom removes or destroys. Jea recalls how his master lamented when his crops were eaten by worms, "God thus showing him his own inability to preserve the fruits of the earth." Jea recalls, in another instance, how his masters' crops were devoured by locusts.[61] In listing these instances, Jea stresses that while they were tyrants, his masters were hardly lords over nature. The slaves, Jea suggests, were being led away by a deception – one which imagined slaveholding brutality as the transcendent language of divine authority and proscription. Jea's aim is to show how his masters were, in fact, not gods, but subject to God's wise judgment and activity through time and space. Recalling his master's economic misfortunes with losing crops, Jea, in retrospect, confidently asserts that the master's godlike authority is temporary in the face of God's sovereignty: turning the psalmist's words into a riposte, Jea asks rhetorically whether God should be feared "seeing that he can build up and he can cast down, he can create and he can destroy."[62]

This post-conversion historical sensibility fans out as an outright commentary on the fleeting quality of history (and by implication, Jea's present). Jea's conversion is such that he no longer fears death. God's redemption has given Jea power over the last enemy, death, which "hath no more respect for the crowns of kings, the pope's mitre, and the cardinal's cap, than for the shepherd's crook, or the poor slave's chains,"[63] leading Jea to sermonize, for pages, over the various ways death "reduces to nothing" all historical possibilities. Life is, then, "vanity" for those who do not sufficiently recognize God's ability to redeem sinners from spiritual death. Jea likens fearful persons to "so many wretched slaves, that tremble under the inhuman power of a merciless tyrant";[64] and it is God's redemption that supplants the fear of death which has subjected so many to a life of bondage. This new sense enables him to endure a host of trials. During one of his preaching stays in Liverpool, he is beaten while on a ship.[65] On another preaching tour, he travels to Virginia only to be threatened with re-enslavement.[66] As if things could not be any worse, none of his children (one of whom was killed by his first wife Elizabeth) survive him.[67]

Jea nevertheless persists in his preaching of redemption. This redemption-driven historical sense enables Jea to engage in a mode of social displacement that, in turn, has significant consequences for his self-understanding as a global citizen. By the end of the narrative, Jea portrays himself as a post-national subject. He both eschews narrow Atlantic nationalisms and also an affinity with imperial aggression and is rendered stateless, in part, by finally grounding his identity in God's salvation. Jea affirms this identity as his fortunes turn for the worse during the War of 1812. The United States won its independence from Britain, but struggled to stave off British imperial aggression either in the form of the Royal Naval impressments of American sailors or in Britain's efforts to impede American expansion into northwestern territories on the North American continent. Even more, the United States would have to contend with British economic and maritime hegemony by forming temporary alliances with France, if the nation was going to establish itself as a viable trading partner in Atlantic markets. Jea had been en route to England on the *Iscet of Liverpool* when the brig was captured by a French privateer. This capture resulted in his eventually being brought to Brest and given into American hands.

Jea refuses to fight on the side of the Americans against the English, even as they threaten him while being held prisoner by the American consulate. Jea rather faces starvation and vagabondage than be made to choose sides, remarking that "for far be it from *me* ever to fight against Old England, unless it be with the sword of the gospel, under the captain of our salvation, Jesus Christ."[68] To be sure, Jea's pacifism was less about embracing England than about rejecting narrowly national agendas and the narrowly mercantilist and imperial agenda of the Americans. As the *Life* suggests, Jea's objection to the war would most likely have been overlaid by his unwillingness to fight for the land that made him a slave in the first place. I will conclude by proposing that his post-nationalism was anticipated by a resolute theological view. Jea's conversion experience and his subsequent interrogation of the Old Testament scriptures –and of antiquity – enabled him to see empires in terms of their transience rather than permanence. Jea concludes,

> Man, created in the image of God, at his first appearance seems to be very glorious, for a while, and become terrible, but as soon as death strikes at the earthly part, and begins to break his flesh and bones, all the glory, pomp, power, and magnificence of the richest, the most terrible, and victorious monarchs, are changed into loathsome smells, into contemptible dust, and reduced to nothing. "*Vanity of vanities, all is vanity.*"[69]

These are not the ruminations of a pessimist but of a man convinced that only God's plan of salvation is permanent and transcends limited modes of cultural self-understanding. It is not unreasonable to assume that he would have extended this biblically-based view to his understanding of his identity as post-American. The legacies of his theological views are found in the rather elastic form his identity takes as an Atlantic African and itinerant preacher. While in Brest, Mr. Dyeott and Mr. Veal, the directors of the American consulate, not only attempt to force Jea into service through imprisonment and starvation, they also revert to the all-too-familiar tyrannical language of the white master to do so. The consulate threatens Jea, stating that "[w]e will cool your Negro temper, and will not suffer any of your insolence in our office." The consulate expects Jea to cower under racial threats, but instead, Jea, asserts that he is not an American, but a "poor African, *a preacher of the gospel*."[70] The remaining pages of Jea's narrative are spent recounting how Jea and Dyeott, in particular, contend over this key question concerning Jea's identity until the French mayor provides Jea with a passport to England. Jea credits God with delivering him out of their hands, imagining himself as a Black subject redeemed from America's cultural shackles. But if Jea advances a post-national identity, he doesn't care to advance a post-racial one. David Kazanjian astutely observes that by making labor a means to evangelistic ends, Jea attempts to pry his Black subjectivity from the Atlantic currencies of racial capitalism.[71] Indeed, Jea would much rather see himself as a Black vagabond preaching the liberating Gospel than be made subject to America's slaveholding and imperialist excesses; and in this way, he authors a bold and innovative alternative for early Black agency and identity.

* * *

Venture Smith, George White, and John Jea, employed biographical writing to address tragedies surrounding Black liberation. Each anticipated the contradictions in Anglo-informed notions of liberty, and like others writing during this period, they understood that Black redemption was paradoxical. Theological redemption and economic redemption functioned thematically as contrasting modes of emancipation in Black biography and ironically, this double-sided form of hope was circumscribed by the ideological pervasiveness of slavery.

Redemption enabled a richly textured portrayal of freedom in early Black biography. Smith, for instance, largely avoided religious talk, perhaps because, early on, he recognized that America's national culture (ostensibly based on Christian ideals) prized the economic value of Blacks above all else. White and Jea, on the other hand, were raising explicitly theological considerations in their narratives. Both autobiographers wanted to make readers aware of the great extent to which their spiritual redemption bolstered their sense of personal freedom. And while both hoped in the spiritual "deliverance" of their African brethren from bonds, their narratives subtly commented on a tragic historical circumstance: they were living out their faith and its liberating potential in a world where Christianity largely functioned as a tool for slavery and empire. White saw that slavery "menaced society," and would spend his life preaching spiritual deliverance to his "coloured brethren" in chains, and Jea, recalling his childhood, imagined that masters were subjugating him and other Blacks through religious trickery, making themselves out to be lords over their slaves. Jea, in particular, saw in his spiritual redemption and acquired literacy the possibilities for revolutionary biblical hermeneutics. Together, Smith, White, and Jea were commenting (if subtly) on slavery's deleterious effects, a discursive foundation upon which the narrators of the late antebellum period built.

These historical writings of the early national period might be considered as intellectual foundations that transitioned African American literature toward the bold claims made by Frederick Douglass. By 1845, Black biographical writing exhibited an astonishing capacity to critique American civilization as Douglass came to view white American Protestantism as renegade in its religiosity, indulging in falsehoods, practicing a "false" spirituality and promoting retrograde and savage national sensibilities.[72] In the appendix to his 1845 autobiography, Douglass hoped that his "little book may do something toward throwing light on the American slave system, and hastening the glad day of deliverance to the millions of my brethren in bonds."[73] And yet, Douglass's recounting of his life and times forced readers to consider the historical potential of Black redemption in modern historical contexts based so thoroughly on the savagery of slavery.

What was redemption in a society where theological understandings of salvation were shaped by racist practices of subjugation? Although abolitionists were offering an alternative vision for redemption, Douglass surmised that efforts to redeem the slave's soul had become a thin excuse for violence. Douglass described this contradiction, lamenting that "[w]e have men-stealers for ministers, women-whippers for missionaries, and cradle-plunderers for church members," noting the hypocrisy in "the man who wields the blood-clotted cowskin during the week fills the pulpit on Sunday, and claims to be a minister of the meek and lowly Jesus."[74] These contradictions only intensified a growing paradox in the consciousness of a young nation and complicated what redemption could mean for Blacks in America.

Notes

1 See the section entitled "The Second Great Awakening and African American Religion," in *The Second Great Awakening and the Transcendentalists*, ed. Barry Hankins (Westport, CT: Greenwood Press, 2004), 68–77.

2 Margaret M. R. Kellow, "Conflicting Imperatives: Black and White American Abolitionists Debate Slave Redemption," in *Buying Freedom: The Ethics and Economics of Slave Redemption,* eds. Kwame Anthony Appiah and Martin Bunzl. Fwd. Kevin Bales (Princeton: Princeton University Press, 2007), 205–206. See William Lloyd Garrison, "The Ransom of Douglass" in *The Liberator* 17, no. 10 (1847): 38.

3 Yolanda Pierce, "Redeeming Bondage: The Captivity Narrative and Spiritual Autobiography in the African-American Slave Narrative Tradition," in *The Cambridge Companion to the African American Slave Narrative,* ed. and Intro. Audrey A. Fisch (Cambridge: Cambridge University Press, 2007), 84–85. Yolanda Pierce, *Hell without Fires: Slavery, Christianity and the Antebellum Spiritual Narrative* (Gainesville: University of Florida Press, 2005).

4 See Erica Armstrong Dunbar's important thesis on the fragility of freedom in the North in Erica Armstrong Dunbar, *A Fragile Freedom: African American Women and Emancipation in the Antebellum City* (New Haven, CT: Yale University Press, 2008).

5 Joycelyn Moody argues that there were, however, precursors to women's conversion narratives in Belinda's 1783 "Petition of an African Slave, to the Legislature of Massachusetts" and in Phillis Wheatley's "On Being Brought from Africa to America," published in 1773. For excellent discussions of Black women's contributions to nineteenth-century religious investigation, please consult Joycelyn K. Moody, *Sentimental Confessions: Spiritual Narratives of Nineteenth-Century African American Women* (Athens: University of Georgia Press, 2001), Rosetta A. Haynes, *Radical Spiritual Motherhood: Autobiography*

and Empowerment in Nineteenth-Century African American Women (Baton Rouge: Louisiana State University Press, 2011), and J. Kameron Carter, *Race: A Theological Account* (Oxford: Oxford University Press, 2008).

6 Chandler B. Saint and George A. Krimsky, *Making Freedom: The Extraordinary Life of Venture Smith* (Middletown, CT: Wesleyan University Press, 2009), 41–76.

7 David Kazanjian, "Mercantile Exchanges, Mercantilist Enclosures: Racial Capitalism in the Black Mariner Narratives of Venture Smith and John Jea," in *New Centennial Review* 3, no. 1 (2003): 147–152.

8 Houston *Baker, Blues, Ideology, Afro-American Literature: A Vernacular Theory*. (Chicago: University of Chicago Press, 1984), 35.

9 Philip Gould, "Free Carpenter, Venture Capitalist: Reading the Lives of the Early Black Atlantic" in *American Literary History* 12, no. 4 (2000): 676.

10 Saint and Krimsky provide a facsimile reprint of Smith's narrative in their volume with the original page numbers. All subsequent citations of Smith's narrative are taken from this reprint. Venture Smith, *A Narrative of the Life and Adventures of Venture, A Native of Africa, But resident above sixty years in the United States of America* ([New London]: 1798), 26.

11 Smith, *A Narrative*, 26

12 Ibid., 31.

13 Ibid., 27.

14 Ibid., 22.

15 Saint et al., *Making Freedom*, 66.

16 Smith, *A Narrative*, 25–27.

17 Ibid., 26.

18 Ibid., 31.

19 Larry Koger, *Black Slaveowners: Free Black Slave Masters in South Carolina, 1790–1860* (Jefferson NC: McFarland and Co., publishers, 1985), 2.

20 Smith, A Narrative, 22–23.

21 Ibid., 24–25.

22 Ibid., 17–18.

23 Ibid., 18–19.

24 Ibid., 21.

25 Ibid., 21–22.

26 Ibid., 22.

27 Ibid., 27.

28 Ibid., 28–29.

29 Ibid., 29.

30 Ibid., 31.

31 George Boulukos makes a related point in his discussion of the sense of gratitude Equiano felt toward his final master, Robert King, for allowing Equiano to purchase his freedom. Boulukos argues that King is able to exploit Equiano's labor for another year after Equiano is freed by having Equiano view his manumission as an "enforceable debt" he owes his master. See George Boulukos, *The Grateful Slave: The Emergence of Race in Eighteenth-*

Century British and American Culture (Cambridge: Cambridge University Press, 2008), 191–192.

32 Smith, *A Narrative*, 30.

33 Ibid., 30.

34 David Kazanjian, "Mercantile Exchanges," 160–161.

35 Vincent Carretta, "Venture Smith, One of a Kind" in *Venture Smith and the Business of Slavery and Freedom,* ed. and Intro. James Brewer Stewart (Amherst, MA: The University of Massachusetts Press, 2010), 165.

36 Graham Russell Hodges, *Black Itinerants of the Gospel: The Narratives of John Jea and George White* (Madison WI: Madison House, 1993), 12.

37 Ibid., 12–16.

38 All citations from White's and Jea's narratives are taken from Graham Russell Hodges's edited volume. George White, *A Brief Account of the Life, Experience, Travels, and Gospel Labours, of George White, an African, Written by Himself, and Revised by a Friend,* in *Black Itinerants of the Gospel*, 53.

39 Ibid.

40 Ibid.

41 Hodges, *Black Itinerants*, 2–3.

42 White, *Brief Account*, 56.

43 Ibid., 58.

44 Ibid., 65.

45 Ibid., 63.

46 Ibid., 60.

47 Ibid., 79.

48 Ibid., 83.

49 Ibid.

50 Ibid., 75, 82.

51 Frederick Douglass, *Narrative of the Life of Frederick Douglass, an American Slave, Written by Himself.* Ed. and Intro. Houston A. Baker, Jr. (New York: Penguin, 1986), 113.

52 William Andrews views White as an early racial accomodationist, anticipating writers such as Booker T. Washington, and John Saillant argues rather provocatively that Jea's perspectives on freedom are naïve, self-absorbed, and, therefore, not radical. I challenge both claims by examining how the early rhetoric of black intellectual resistance is suggested in their theological views about redemption and freedom. See William L. Andrews, *To Tell a Free Story: The First Century of Afro-American Autobiography, 1760–1865* (Urbana: University of Illinois Press, 1986), 52–56. John Saillant, "Traveling in Old and New Worlds with John Jea, the African Preacher, 1773–1816," in *Journal of American Studies* 33, no.3 (1999): 483–486. See also Pierce, *Hell without Fires*, 17.

53 John Jea, *The Life, History, and Unparalleled Sufferings of John Jea, the African Preacher, Compiled and Written by Himself* in *Black Itinerants of the Gospel*, 130–131.

54 St. John 1:1, 1:14 New King James Version.

55 Jea, *The Life*, 115.
56 Ibid.
57 Ibid., 103.
58 Ibid., 106.
59 Ibid., 90.
60 Ibid.
61 Ibid., 91.
62 Ibid., 92.
63 Ibid., 106–107.
64 Ibid., 109.
65 Ibid., 128.
66 Ibid., 147.
67 Ibid., 122.
68 Ibid., 155.
69 Ibid., 108.
70 Ibid., 155.
71 Kazanjian, "Mercantile Exchanges," 162.
72 Frederick Douglass, "The Meaning of July Fourth for the Negro," in *Frederick Douglass: Selected Speeches and Writings*, ed. Philip S. Foner. Abridged and Adapted, Yuval Taylor (Chicago: Lawrence Hill Books, 1999), 195.
73 Douglass, *Narrative*, 159.
74 Ibid., 154.

PART IV

Illustration and the Narrative Form

Chapters in the fourth and final section, "Illustration and the Narrative Form," explore transitions in visual culture of the early nineteenth century. By 1830, there was a growing diversity of Black portrayals in visual culture, ranging from the well-meaning but often misguided antislavery imagery to the purposefully hostile proliferation of anti-Black caricature. In materials that circulated privately, such as the friendship albums passed among free Black women, illustrations appeared alongside writing as hand-painted flowers denoted sentimental notes and poems.[1] Similarly, southern newspapers printing runaway advertisements for fugitive free Blacks hailed readers with the iconic stereotype of a runaway man or woman, on the move with stolen property. In addition to images, social activity also wielded an impact on visual culture. For instance, the 1808 ban on new importations of slaves from Africa was clear and present in the minds of African Americans. Not only did they mark these occasions with sermons and pamphlets produced to discuss these events, but also their freedom celebrations – public ceremonies and parades in Boston's free Black community, for example – were meant to take up space in public with visual demonstrations about abolition's significations.[2]

A number of transitions in visual technologies took shape in this period as well. Although lithography – that chemical process of printing on smooth surfaces – first emerged in 1796, its growing availability is seen throughout print materials of the early nineteenth century. Inventors continued to tinker with the lithographic process, making it easy to print pictures and "influence the pictorial representation of the news" well into the 1870s, and after the establishment of photography.[3] Similarly, although Louis-Jacques-Mandé Daguerre's photographic invention – the silver-plated glass prints known as daguerreotype – entered popular culture in 1839, the earlier photographic process of heliography enabled artists to fix images, making them permanent, as early as 1822. Each of these chemical processes with origins in France had immediate and lasting impact in the US and on African Americans of means who began documenting themselves with photographic processes as soon as they were available.

However, African American artistry would not wait for photography. Chapters in this section consider Black engagements with portraiture before the photograph. In Chapter 10, Sarah Blackwood takes a close look at sources not typically regarded in canonical treatments of African American literature or visual culture of the nineteenth century. In her explorations of Boyrereau Brinch's *The Blind African Slave*, and paintings by Baltimore portraitist Joshua Johnson, Blackwood presents new fodder for thinking about vision and race in the minds of early Black cultural producers. She examines key elements of perspective and visual philosophy that reveal "the white image in the black mind"[4] through concepts of vision and aesthetics. Born in slavery and working in the first decades of the nineteenth century, Johnson may still be situated among artists who came after him, such as daguerreotypists Augustus Washington, Black men who used their skills specifically for creating portraits of both whites and Blacks.

Following this discussion, Aston Gonzalez examines portraits of African American preachers, including Reverend Allen and Reverend Absolom Jones in Chapter 11. He situates these images as part of a conscious political self-fashioning and unpacks the extent to which these powerful men were thoughtful about visual representation, specifically. Gonzalez's focus on portraits of Black men is in keeping with the thirty years explored in this volume. Although the first image has yet to be identified, evidence suggests that audiences would wait until the 1840s to see portraits of Black women in public circulation when the AME Church published an image of Juliann Jane Tillman in 1844 and later, the frontispiece for Jarena Lee's *Religious Experience and Journal of Mrs. Jarena Lee, Giving an Account of Her Call to Preach the Gospel, Revised and Corrected from the Original Manuscript Written by Herself.* Still, portraits of free Black people were of immense importance in this first thirty years of the new century. While slavery proliferated, imaging practices supported the objectification of African descendants as women were forced to pose as "nurse" in family portraits with slave owners and zoologist Louis Agassiz employed the camera of Joseph T. Zealy to create portraits of Renty and Delia, naked.[5]

The multifaceted use of imaging technology, including the employment of photographic portraits for the pursuit of runaways,[6] likely compelled the earnestness of Frederick Douglass. The value Douglass placed on portraiture in particular, and not simply pictures or photography, is indicated by his choice to offer three different frontispieces for his life writing. Moving across the nineteenth century, his *Narrative of the Life of Frederick Douglass, an American Slave. Written by Himself* (1845) and *My Bondage and My Freedom. Part I, Life as a Slave. Part II. Life as a Freeman* (1855) feature portraits of a younger Douglass, and still differ from the image in his *Life and Times of Frederick Douglass: His Early Life as a Slave, His Escape from Bondage, and His Complete History to the Present Time* (1881). The final chapter of this section and the volume, Chapter 12, Martha J. Cutter takes on the abject illustrations of the enslaved in antislavery materials as well as frontispieces and illustrated antislavery books of Moses Roper and Henry Bibb. Cutter traces a visual inheritance that informs the posture of Douglass for example, whereby free Blacks made decisive choices about how to "cut a figure" in such a manner that refused the hostile portrayals of Blackness in other venues.[7]

Notes

1 Jasmine Nichole Cobb, 'Forget Me Not': Free Black Women and Sentimentality. *MELUS: Multi-Ethnic Literature of the United States* 40:3 (fall 2015): 28–46.

2 Mitch Kachun, *Festivals of Freedom: Meaning and Memory in African American Emancipation Celebrations, 1808–1915* (Amherst: University of Massachusetts Press, 2006).

3 Joshua Brown, *Beyond the Lines: Pictorial Reporting, Everyday Life, and the Crisis of Gilded Age America* (Berkeley: University of California Press, 2002), 67.

4 Mia Bay, *The White Image in the Black Mind: African-American Ideas about White People, 1830–1925* (New York: Oxford University Press, 2000).

5 Deborah Willis and Barbara Krauthamer, *Envisioning Emancipation: Black Americans and the End of Slavery* (Philadelphia: Temple University Press, 2013).

6 Rachel Hall, "Missing Dolly, Mourning Slavery: The Slave Notice as Keepsake," *Camera Obscura* 61: 21 (Number 1): 70–103.

7 Richard Powell, *Cutting A Figure: Fashioning Black Portraiture* (Chicago: University of Chicago Press).

CHAPTER 10

Theorizing Vision and Selfhood in Early Black Writing and Art

Sarah Blackwood

This chapter aims to snap into focus two examples of fascinating but understudied early nineteenth-century Black writing and art: the 1810 composite autobiography by Boyrereau Brinch, *The Blind African Slave*, and work by Baltimore portraitist Joshua Johnson. Highlighting Brinch's and Johnson's aesthetic techniques, I argue that their work provides new insight into how race and selfhood were visualized in the early nineteenth century. I attend here specifically to the formal details of Brinch's and Johnson's work, including point of view, horizontality, pigment, ornamentation, texture, and scale. The complexity of their aesthetic experiments reflects the complexity of their transitional historical moment, which nurtured a form of experimentation with ideas about selfhood, race, and beauty. Brinch's text was composed after the eighteenth-century Black "travel narratives" but before the "slave narratives." And while Johnson's portraiture sits squarely inside the long, conventional history of family portraiture, it also stands apart for how his aesthetic techniques comment on portraiture's role in reproducing racialized family structures. Both Brinch's and Johnson's aesthetic experiments are signal contributions to the archive of Black life and art-making before the Civil War, both under and out-from-under enslavement.

Brinch's narrative is an as-told-to autobiography recorded by a white amanuensis, Benjamin Prentiss. Stylistically, it falls in the gap between what would become the well-established tropes and conventions of the nineteenth-century US slave narrative, and what scholar Vincent Carretta calls the "varied picture" of Black life and the institution of slavery offered by writers of African birth or descent in the eighteenth century.[1] Though it contains first-person accounts of the Middle Passage, the Seven Years War, the Revolutionary War, and slavery in New England, the narrative is challengingly hybrid in genre and point of view and has remained relatively absent from scholarly conversations about nineteenth-century Black writing.[2] *The Blind African Slave's* reliance on an amanuensis perhaps challenges our ideas of "authorship" too much, and its sketchy narrative style feels almost experimental in comparison with the first-person realism achieved in post-1830s slave narratives.

Similarly, though a substantial number of Joshua Johnson's paintings have been identified and preserved, his work has not emerged into a larger cultural conversation about Black art as fully as it could. Johnson could be a towering figure in discussions of early Black art: after all, the formerly enslaved man made his living painting portraits of white merchant-class families in Baltimore. His work provides a window into not only how these families presented and perceived themselves, but also how Johnson himself perceived them, their familial wealth, relations, and racialized selfhood. It expands our understanding of a world in which slavery was still institutionalized, but white families readily invited a Black artist into their home (or visited him in his studio) to scrutinize their appearance and comportment. Apparently self-taught, Johnson's portraiture is accomplished and stylistically unique; art historians usually describe it as vernacular or "folk." To the best of our contemporary knowledge Joshua Johnson was one of only a very few Black portraitists working in the years before photographic technology was introduced in the United States and perhaps the only free Black artist who regularly painted white people.[3]

The Blind African Slave and Joshua Johnson's portraiture both manifest the productive instability of art produced by Black writers and artists in the period between 1800 and 1830. The antebellum slave narrative had not yet solidified into the form it would take in the late 1830s and 1840s, and the texts that free and formerly enslaved Black writers produced in this period are often provocative and unusual in their generic instability. Likewise, visual art produced by free and formerly enslaved Black artists before the Civil War is challenging to study, because early Black visual artists often worked in vernacular forms that are less likely to have been preserved and/or taken seriously, and because we are still in the midst of the active art historical and scholarly recovery projects related to early Black visual artists.[4]

In particular, I am interested in how the aesthetic techniques used by both Brinch and Johnson speak to their specific historical moment and how close attention paid to these aesthetic techniques helps scholars better understand the ideas about – and institutions of – race and enslavement that shift between the late-eighteenth and early-nineteenth centuries. For example, one of the nineteenth-century slave narrative's major innovations was its individualist, first-person, Black "I." The as-told-to structure of Brinch's autobiography lacks this "I," a feature which is often interpreted as merely a regrettable by-product of the cultural realities surrounding Black authorship in the early nineteenth century: limited literacy meant that Black people were not always able to write their own life stories. But a close aesthetic read of *The Blind African Slave* reveals that its vexed "I" (and, indeed, as I will go on to discuss, its visual "eye") presents the self as relational rather than singular, which is a significant idea worth engaging with on its own terms. Likewise, though we have no access to documents (letters, diaries) that might tell us directly what insights Johnson, the historical person, may have had into ideas about racialized selfhood, the aesthetic and formal characteristics of his art communicate much. The fascinatingly skewed scales and linear compositions of Johnson's portraits of his white sitters depict (quite modern) relationships between figure and ground, person and representation, subject and object, self and other.

As many historians and scholars have noted, the archives of slavery are compromised. The voices of the enslaved are absent or muted, their visual representation often perverted through the eyes of the racist whites who composed them.[5] The archive induces many frustrations, at times eclipsing aesthetic engagement with the texts produced by writers and artists of African descent. For example, the turn-of-the-nineteenth-century, white, itinerant portrait painter Ammi Philips – whose "naive," folk style is similar to Johnson's – is regularly put into aesthetic conversation with "high art" figures like Mark Rothko. Meanwhile, Johnson's work seems stuck in the frustrations of the archive as scholars keep hoping to find more biographical or historical information about this fascinating figure who is repeatedly described as "mysterious."[6] To be sure, knowing more about Johnson would be a radical addition to our understanding of him as an artist and the period in which he lived, as well as our own cultural and artistic genealogies. But still, something feels amiss in the attempt to wring blood from the silent stone of Johnson's biographical archive when we have the aesthetic techniques and surfaces of some eighty paintings of his that are full of insights into and innovations in the representation of race, beauty, and the (il)logic of slavery.

I do not conceive of an interest in the aesthetic as divergent from an interest in the archives of slavery. To the contrary, in this chapter I assert that, together, *The Blind African Slave* and Joshua Johnson's portraiture are major contributions not only to the archives of slavery but also to the archives of nineteenth-century visual theory, especially as these theories intersected with developing ideas about selfhood. Nineteenth-century Black writers and artists were often keen visual theorists, and their general absence from historical accounts of nineteenth-century visual culture, as well as from the critical genealogies deployed to explain our own contemporary visual culture, have left us with a dull sense of what vision is, how it works, what it might entail, and how its field of reference has been contracted by its unrelenting theoretical whiteness. For example, one of the most significant scholarly works of visual theory in the late twentieth century – Jonathan Crary's *Techniques of the Observer* – examines how "subjective vision" (the idea that vision is individual, physiological, and subjective rather than objective) developed in the first half of the nineteenth century, but it does so without a single reference to writing, thinking, or aesthetic work by any people of color.[7] This is a scandal not only because it passively fails to expand a canon, but because it actively misses the contributions of some of the most insightful visual theorists of the era – the very texts and works of art most committed to thinking through the complicated relationship between sight, embodiment, subjectivity, surveillance, and social control.

Brinch and Johnson both use a spectacular arsenal of aesthetic techniques and visual theory to explore these questions related to selfhood and subjectivity, questions which are manifested in their work's interest in surfaces. Specifically, Brinch's narrative obsesses over beauty and ornamentation as it offers its own unique theory of vision as embodied and material. And Johnson's portraiture of middle-class white sitters – with its focused interest in horizontality and scale – explores the relationship between subject and object. Their work poses a series of provocative aesthetic questions: Where is the place of beauty under enslavement? How are subjective individuals and objects drawn into grotesque relation with one another through slavery? What is the relationship between the physiological "eye" and the "I"? These aesthetic questions, in turn, help us understand more fully a particular transitional moment in Black art. How do the surfaces produced by an early Black visual artist speak to and against developing cultural notions about inner life in the 1830s? How does the text of one early Black writer contribute to, push against, and/or evade the ascendance of the self as "first person" in mid-nineteenth-century narratives about slavery?

The Blind African Slave's *Embodied Vision*

Though Boyrereau Brinch's 1810 narrative is titled *The Blind African Slave, or Memoirs of Boyrereau Brinch, Nicknamed Jeffrey Brace*, most critics and scholars agree that, as the editor of the modern edition of the narrative

Kari J. Winter notes, his "lack of sight does not appear in the text to loom large in his consciousness."[8] This is true to the extent that blindness, understood narrowly as an individual physiological reality, is not a topic or theme in this narrative. Indeed, the narrative doesn't once mention Brinch's blindness. Yet the narrative relies on metaphors of sight and vision to significant effect. The importance of the visual in *The Blind African Slave* has gone ironically unnoticed, which in turn has also left unnoticed how early Black writers were fascinated by theories of vision. In the case of Brinch's tale, the narration's interest in observation, ornament, and reflection brings together the visual and the embodied, the pictured and the remembered, in a vision of selfhood that demands a reader consider sight as a relational exchange, rather than a unidirectional and surveilling force.

This innovative perspective on sight itself is highlighted by the narrative's formal techniques. The first two chapters of this composite text, which combines elements of multiple different genres (travel literature, exotica, autobiography, slave narrative, religious conversion narrative, and more), are told from a third-person plural perspective: a "we" who surveys and describes the flora, fauna, "luxuries" and customs of the "kingdom of Bow-woo, which is situated between the 10th and 20th degrees of north latitude, and between the 6th and 10th of west longitude."[9] This third person is, as Kari J. Winter notes, a blended voice: both the white lawyer Prentiss (the "author") and the Black formerly enslaved farmer Brace/Brinch (the "narrator").[10]

An attentive reader can pinpoint the moment when Brinch claims the first person "I" from his white interlocutor Benjamin Prentiss at the beginning of chapter 3. Here, the perspective winnows: it is 1758 (rather than some unspecified general time), and there is suddenly a possessive individual telling us the story:

> While my Father and Mother had some gentle dispute about the quality of the silk (for here the writer takes the language of the narrator) I was busy snapping and observing the beauties of the pistol. As soon as an opportunity offered I asked my father where the pistols came from, and where he had obtained them, he said, they came from the white people, who lived on the waters and came to our shores and landed at Morocco, where he purchased them. White people! said I, what kind of beings are they?[11]

What is this "I" doing? "Snapping and observing," handling a weapon with his hands while also taking in its appearance through his eyes, joining the understanding gained through visual perception and bodily touch, all while building toward what would become one of the key questions of the antebellum abolitionist slave narrative: "White people! What kind of beings are they?"

Like Whitman breaking into free verse for the first time in his notebook as he ponders the relationship between the I, the slave, and the master, the break into a new perspective in *The Blind African Slave* is a significant moment of formal meaning.[12] The "I/eye" of this slave narrative comes into focus as someone who observes through contact, who gathers information about the world through touch and sight. This knowledge and way of inhabiting the world is figured as powerful, artful, and dangerous. It is attuned to beauty and death and to the inhumanity that lurks in the exact thing ("White people!") that figures itself as the horizon of humanity. Slave narratives often depict the experience of being surveilled (Olaudah Equiano's depiction of a portrait hanging on the wall "watching" him; Frederick Douglass's representation of the "slave breaker" Covey's snake-like technique of making the enslaved feel always already watched); but many slave narratives also include the suggestion that the enslaved were always looking back at and watching those who enslaved them (Harriet Jacobs in her attic, the fictional Hannah Crafts looking back at the portraits of whites hanging in the plantation's gallery). Brinch's frankness (and it's important to remember he is still free here) – White people! what *are* they? –is an early example of the power of such an act.

Brinch's sort of free-wheeling frankness in depicting a Black person *looking* is not the only place where his autobiography flips conventional slave narrative tropes of subjugation. Where many slave narratives necessarily tried to push back on racist visual regimes that asserted racial inferiority to be visible and observable, Brinch in multiple places, in fact, highlights the significance of visual appearance, but in order to condemn and critique whiteness. Take, for example, the extended satiric description of the commander who boards the ship on which Brinch has been transported to Morocco prior to its Middle Passage journey to Barbados. The bravura description starts with "his eyes resembled a bowl of cream in a smoky house" and ends a good twenty lines later with "his mind agreed with his appearance, and his dress was emblematical of his feelings, which were bedaubed with iniquity and grown very stale."[13] Lynn R. Johnson has argued that Brinch "combines the lexicon of caricature with eighteenth- and nineteenth-century philosophies of physiognomy" to "develop a commentary on cannibalism through his comic yet uncanny image of the captain's body."[14] Here, Johnson points out, Brinch uses sophisticated rhetorical tools to adhere a reader to a perspective that sees the body of white authority as animalistic and savage, doubling down on physiognomy's often problematic fusing of surface appearance with interior truth. Brinch employs physiognomy's familiar Western language (understood as a science in the era) of appearance against the very figures who have long wielded it to assert Black inhumanity.

Brinch's consideration of white appearance as "emblematical … of iniquity" is intriguingly contrasted by the narrative's interest in Black bodily ornamentation, which it figures as beauty, memory, and value given material form. In chapter 5, at the start of a particularly affecting tale of the brutality that the recently enslaved experienced when they arrived in Barbados, Brinch notes that "All of us had been stripped of our ornaments; in fact, everything of value was taken from us, and instead of gold rings, bracelets of gold beads, chains and jewels, we had an old piece of sail cloth tied round our waists."[15] The enslavers were covetous of the economic value not only of the slave's bodies and labor but also the ornaments that testified to their positions in the complex social and cultural systems from which they'd been stolen.

Brinch emphasizes the connection between memory and material when he tells the story, in this chapter, of a young girl who is whipped to death in front of her 6-year-old brother. "'I should not feel so bad" she begins, prior to being whipped for trying to comfort her crying brother:

> if the white people had not taken from me the bracelet of gold, which was on my right arm, as my grandfather, when my grandmother died, took it from her arm and gave it to me (on account of my bearing her name) as a token of remembrance and affection, which was always expressed; and now I have nothing in this foreign land to remember her by.[16]

This particular theft recalls Orlando Patterson's classic formulation of slavery's "social death": it participates in a systematic stripping of an individual from the rich familial and social systems that ballast one's experience of life. But the repeated eruption of ornamentation into this narrative exceeds those ornaments' role as social/familial utility. The specificity with which the ornaments are described – rings, bracelets, beads, chains, jewels here, but elsewhere "purple silk dress," "twelve plumes"[17] – suggest the presence of beauty, and the ineffable: memory and affection as filtered through aesthetic enjoyment.

Marcus Wood has noted that "The place of beauty in the description of slave experience, and particularly slave trauma, is not an easy place to be."[18] The experience of enslavement, we know, was brutal and violent on an almost unimaginable scale. And yet, Wood's analysis, coupled with other provocative recent work, like Tara Bynum's thoughtful consideration of pleasure and friendship under slavery, suggests we consider carefully how and why formerly enslaved authors valued beauty.[19] To what end does Brinch weave these stories that have beauty – and beauty stolen and destroyed – at their center? Shortly after describing the above young girl's brutal murder, he returns to the figure of a "princess," whose presence he's tracked through the Middle Passage journey. Here again is a person who has been "stripped of her ornaments."[20] But here, also, is a person who tells a tale of white brutality through a song "in her native language" that places beauty at its center:

1. Ye happy maids beyond the ocean's wave,
Who live secure from all these dread alarms,
Take heed from me, now dire affliction's slave,
Despise the beauties of the white man's charms.

2. Among my friends I play'd with every grace,
My hopes my prospects and my heart was free,
Amid this scene I view'd the white man's face,
He lur'd me trembling o'er the foaming sea.

3. With voice of Siren cloath'd with subtle guile,
He told the beauties of his native shore;
All these he said should court my placid smile,
All that my taste could wish or heart implore.[21]

The song continues, but what emerges is a remarkable tale in which a young Black woman's "taste" and love of beauty are used against her. Brinch presents the reader with the complete inverse of the racist ideology developed by writers and thinkers like Thomas Jefferson who insisted that people of African descent had no aesthetic taste or talent, and thus were not as fully human as whites. This is a stunning and scathing indictment in which it is no longer Blacks who lack aesthetic talent, but rather enslavers who are revealed to be engaged in a systematic attempt to deliberately decrease both aesthetic appeal and economic wealth among Blacks.

Like the "I/eye" that erupts into the narrative in chapter 3, the place of ornamentation in this early slave narrative suggests Brinch's sensitivity to visual culture and the place of the visual in representing key aspects of selfhood and subjectivity under slavery. Further, the way that he employs the visual emphatically turns away from a Western understanding of the visual as disembodied and abstracted in favor of presenting the visual as material and embodied in observation and touch, ornament and memory. Where Ralph Waldo Emerson developed the theory of the "transparent eyeball" ("I see all; my head is bathed in the blithe air"), Boyrereau Brinch narrates a different perspective on sight, sensation, memory, and consciousness.[22]

He does so by narrating a "vision" that he has one night after being sold to "John Burrell, a professed puritan."[23] Burrell follows the all-too-familiar tenets of Christian cruelty under slavery:

> If he had charity, that crown of christian virtues, how could he pray for all mankind and then starve a poor negro boy, who could look to no other person for food. If he had a hope of grace and mercy from his Lord and Master, how could he freeze his slave, and then unmercifully beat him for attempting to make a fire to warm himself.[24]

Brinch extends his consideration of his master's hypocrisy into a larger and more general condemnation of the racist thinking – scientific, humanist, philosophical – that has enabled slavery to thrive. He focuses especially on feeling and intellect as the key qualities that testify to the common humanity across race and ethnicity: "If I have the same propensities and feelings, and am endowed with the same intellectual reason, then where is the distinction? . . . From what fountain does the Ethiopian, Turk, Indian, Chinese, Tartar or Englishman receive all their sensations?"[25]

Burrell starves and beats Brinch such that a neighbor is led to intervene: "Mr. Samuel Eals came and took me up, and very charitably led me into the house, told Burrell that such abuse was inhuman and unchristian."[26] Eals brings Brinch to his home and provides him with a bed. Brinch's vision comes over him that night, as he lies in the "first bed I had slept upon after . . . [being] taken into bondage."[27] The bed is a place, finally, for bodily rest, and Brinch describes how the simple humanity that it represents "opened my wounded feelings and brought my sorrows up afresh to my view." These sorrows take the form of a vision in which Brinch accompanies the "good spirit" and "ascend[s] high above the earth, and wafted me through vast space" to return to his "native town."[28] While Brinch's consciousness ascends in a way that recalls Emerson's "transparent eyeball," his representation of vision also departs from Emerson's philosophy. Brinch understands sight as a "sensation" that flows from a fountain, that is deeply connected to the body's rest and well-being, and that is engaged in the work of *feeling* and memory, rather than of self-forgetting. *The Blind African Slave* repeatedly describes vision in embodied, sense-based, and memorial terms.

Brinch's "vision" late in the story importantly also recalls an earlier passage from the narrative. There, in narrating his last moments before being stolen into slavery, Brinch leans on the language of sight to underscore his loss: "I, before I descended the hill which shut me from the sight of home forever cast behind me one last and longing look to see if I could catch one pleasing glance of a fond mother; but alas! I could discover no trace of home."[29] Here, Brinch's memory is of not-seeing, of being stripped from home by an inability to see it. His later vision by the fireplace works in multiple ways: reparatively, in restoring his consciousness to the thing it has so long been unable to see and take comfort in, but also, I would argue, proleptically, in asserting a form of "vision" specific to the enslaved and formerly enslaved. This unique form of vision exists in the face of past, present, and future objections that would discount such a unique way of seeing exists.

Why has it been so easy not to see the significance of vision and sight in an early slave narrative titled *The Blind African Slave*? The final line of the narrative quotes from the Book of Jeremiah: "Oh that my head were waters, and mine eyes a fountain of tears, that I might weep day and night for the slain of the daughter of my people."[30] There are a multitude of ways to think about these closing words. One might consider the passage in the context of a generic transition: a new genre (the slave narrative) is working within an established genre (the conversion narrative) to intensify its critique of slavery. Another way of reading might be to think of the ending as reworking the jeremiad form that has been so foundational for the American literary tradition, which is to say as a rhetorical technique that pushes back against proslavery rhetoric and practices that use the Bible to justify the evil of slavery. And still another way to interpret this ending might be as a fascinating aspect of *The Blind African Slave's* place in the African diaspora. Brinch's autobiography has not been central to our study of nineteenth-century Black American literature because it is so odd and so multiplicitous, so difficult to situate within a tradition. But perhaps that is precisely its value.

In the end, the autobiography's remarkably expansive conclusion should also be considered in relation to the text's philosophy of vision. Its specific biblical citation ends a story on an image of eyes that give, eyes that produce, a consciousness that flows, and sight that memorializes. Many of the most important moments in *The Blind African Slave* feature sight and vision to produce significant formal meaning. The narrative truly begins when it erupts into the "I/eye" of chapter 3 when it tells its stories of loss and claims Black humanity through vision, aesthetic beauty, and ornamentation; and, importantly, it ends with an assertion of eyes that turn sorrow, love, and memory into material form.

Portraiture and the Archives of Slavery

The portraiture painted by formerly enslaved Baltimore artist Joshua Johnson represents similar themes, ideas, and theories about vision to those featured in *The Blind African Slave.* His art features insightful visual depictions of selfhood by a man whose job it was to look directly at whiteness while practicing an art form – family portraiture – that was explicitly oriented around memorializing and reproducing whiteness as property. Early-nineteenth-century family portraiture depicted its sitters' class status and the patriarchal structures that organized them into a family unit, while also functioning as materially inheritable property that imagined into being the racialized family lines that such inheritance would follow. Joshua Johnson would have had special insight into the socially reproductive role of portraiture. Formerly inheritable racialized property himself, Johnson was now in the business of tracing the lines of whiteness that often sought to make themselves invisible.[31] Close aesthetic analysis of a series of Johnson's portraits reveals the multitude of ways that he made these lines visible and suggests that he did so by honing a particular set of artistic skills and preoccupations: for example, his unique interest in and skill at depicting and experimenting with linearity, lace, and scale in his canvases. These preoccupations ultimately made the logic of slavery – and its manifestations within the sentimental frame of the white family – sharply visible. In its formal self-awareness, Johnson's portraiture of white families has an interestingly inverse relationship with the strategic use of frontispiece portraits by early- and mid-nineteenth-century Black writers who were seeking to re-envision middle-class identity markers. Where Black writers often sought to use portraiture's conventions to affirm their humanity, Johnson's portraits use those same conventions to reveal the inhumanity inherent in white familial life as it existed under slavery.[32]

Johnson's position as a Black portraitist who painted white sitters is obviously unique and fascinating, and it is odd that his work is not considered more significant than it is. He is, to the best of contemporary scholarly knowledge, one of only a very few Black portraitists working at all before the Civil War, let alone working in a slave state regularly depicting white sitters.[33] I would argue that scholarly conversations about Johnson have stalled out in part because his subject position was so unique that scholars have mostly focused on discovering more about him as a historical person. I don't view this as a faulty approach; if and when archival sources come to light that give us access to more information about Johnson as a historical person and practicing artist, those sources will be invaluable. But what should we do with the resources we do have? Nearly eighty paintings have been identified as Johnson's, which is a substantial body of work out of which to glean meaning – and not just about the sitters depicted, but about the insights that the artist who painted them had into questions of selfhood, race, and thought.

Scholarship on Johnson seems to have followed a boom and bust pattern. The 1980s saw a number of important exhibitions in art museums that forefronted pre-twentieth-century African American artists. The Smithsonian American Art Museum's 1985 exhibition "Sharing Traditions: Five Black Artists in Nineteenth-Century America" highlighted work by Johnson, Robert Scott Duncanson, Edward Mitchell Bannister, Edmonia Lewis, and Henry Ossawa Tanner. This show was followed by the Maryland Historical Society's 1987–1988 "Joshua Johnson: Freeman and Early American Portrait Painter," an important solo show (and accompanying major catalog) dedicated to Johnson's work. Both of these exhibitions can be placed in the context of the recovery projects and canon expansion of the 1980s. Additionally, the record-breaking price garnered at auction by Johnson's painting *Emma Van Name* (*c.*1805) (which I will discuss on page 278) in 1988 inspired a flurry of mainstream attention for the painter, especially around questions related to the inflated art market of the era.[34]

The next major moment for Johnson came in the mid-1990s, in part spurred on by a significant archival discovery related to Johnson: the bill of sale and manumission records related to his enslavement, found in one of three volumes of Baltimore County court chattel records that were given to the Maryland Historical Society. An image of the manumission papers was used to illustrate the 1996 issue of the *Archives of American Art Journal*, which featured an essay by art historians Jennifer Bryan and Robert Torchia about the significance of the new documents. As they note:

> The discovery of the bill of sale and manumission record points the way toward a total revision of Johnson's career, and many of the speculative but widely accepted ideas about his origins and training can now be dismissed. It is now clear that he was not a refugee who fled Santo Domingo following the slave insurrection of 1793, that he was never a "slave artist" as he has often been described, and that he was not a slave or apprentice to any members of the Peale family.[35]

But what Bryan and Torchia call "the new and fascinating avenues of inquiry opened by the newly discovered documents" have ultimately not been especially heavily trafficked.

W.J.T. Mitchell has argued that "[r]ather than talk of what we 'know' about slavery . . . we must talk of what we are prevented from knowing, what we can never know, and how it is figured for us in the partial access we do have."[36] There are many things that we are prevented from knowing about Joshua Johnson: historical and biographical details that we are, for example, not prevented from knowing about many of his sitters, who were often from prominent Baltimore merchant families. But rather than focus my energy on these blank spaces, I want to think through Mitchell's provocative theory of "partial access," especially as it relates to the richly detailed surfaces of Johnson's portraits of his white sitters. Like *The Blind African Slave*'s exploration of beauty, ornamentation, and vision, Joshua Johnson's formal aesthetic techniques are meaningful not only within his own historical and biographical contexts, but also for our own contemporary struggles to understand the relationship between race, selfhood, and art-making in the nineteenth century having been given only "partial access" to the evidence that helps us theorize.

In the following, I want to trace a speculative route through the remarkable experiments with texture, linearity, and scale found in Johnson's portraits of white sitters. Attending to the rich aesthetic techniques embedded in these surfaces reveals the works' sophisticated commentary on and experimentation with evolving ideas about selfhood in the era. In particular, through close reading of Johnson's depiction of lace, horizontality, and his canvas's skewed expression of scale, we can see an artist thinking through family/lineage, the relationship between subjects and objects, and the perversity with which these lines and relations are wrought under slavery.

Joshua Johnson's Portraits of Whiteness

Let us begin with lace. Art historians agree that Johnson's painterly treatment of lace is unique. Analysis of it not only provides information about Johnson's individual aesthetic style, but also about the daily limitations and opportunities that a Black painter might have encountered in the early nineteenth-century while trying to make a living as an artist. Paint was expensive, and even as he depicted sitters wearing luxurious fabrics and accoutrements, he would have been mindful of the skewed relationship between their ability to adorn themselves expensively and his ability to translate that expense on the canvas while simultaneously conserving his own limited financial resources. Johnson's lace is a record, then, both of his distinctive aesthetic expression *and* his social and economic position.

Carolyn Weekley urges viewers and scholars of Johnson's work to pay particular attention to "hands, collars, and other dress details . . . to realize his particularly consistent style."[37] Johnson's lace is unique in itself, as well as within the context of his general use of paint on his canvases (see Figure 10.1).

Figure 10.1 Joshua Johnson, *Mary Ann Jewins Burnett*, oil on canvas, c.1812. Courtesy of Maryland Historical Society, 2002.1.2

Johnson consistently used a particularly thin application of oil paint, with areas of primer often showing through the figures and settings that populate the ground of his paintings. As conservator Sian Jones notes, Johnson "painted quite thinly with only the lightest colored areas have any *impasto* at all. Often his sitters' collars, ruffs, cravats, and lace can be seen to have small areas of low *impasto*. Johnson's darker colors are thinly painted and often allow the priming color to show through."[38] Scholars have speculated that the thinness of the paint could be a result of a thrifty approach to materials, conserving expensive resources where he could.

But his lace was one area where Johnson seemed to build up his paint. The low *impasto* seen in the lace is intriguing because its effect is not exactly one of likeness. That is, where other Baltimore portrait painters of the era (Charles Willson Peale, James Peale Polk, Cephas Thompson, Charles Bird King, Thomas Sully, among others, all of whom we know a lot about, given that they were white, well-established, and mostly academically trained) depicted the lace worn by their female sitters with volume and an apparent aim to likeness – attempting to show what the lace the women wore looked like to the everyday eye – Johnson seems to have approached lace as an opportunity to focus on the contrast between outline and transparency. His lace is always transparent against his sitter's skin and hair, with the exception of the characteristic scalloped and waving edges that often rise off the surface of the canvas in that low *impasto*.[39]

Art historians often use the word "crisp" to describe Johnson's figures, in part to highlight the bright lines he often uses to set off edges. Another way to look at his distinctive lace-work might be as a suggestive eruption of drawing techniques into the (thin) painterly brushwork applying pigment to the canvas. Here it is useful to think through art historian Margaretta Lovell's foundational work on the significance of what she calls "drawing in painting" in colonial America. Lovell shows how theories about drawing were of particular importance and interest to eighteenth-century colonial painters, and she traces the influence of British art theory on a number of well-known aristocratic and academic painters from the era. In these treatises, she notes, drawing is understood as "evidence of the mind thinking ... Drawing embodies the *intellectual* aspect of the painter's and the designer's craft."[40] If it seems odd to bring Lovell's generous thinking on influential colonial and early Republic academic and aristocratic painters such as John Smibert and John Singleton Copley to bear on the more vernacular techniques of Joshua Johnson, I'd argue that is only because we have traditionally brought too-conservative analysis to Johnson's formal and aesthetic techniques. This is because, at least in part, we lack the deep knowledge about his artistic training, influences, and intention that the archive has preserved for painters like Copley.

Lovell continues, in a dazzling passage on what she speculates is a moment of "drawing in paint" in the depiction of lace in John Singleton Copley's *c.*1770 portrait of Joshua Henshaw:

> Look, for instance, at the strokes of white pigment that Copley used to describe ("draw" in paint) the right wrist ruffle of Joshua Henshaw . . . [W]e cannot resist seeing in these impasto strokes *mind*–in Norman Bryson's terms, "intention and decision"–that elsewhere in the painting hides itself but here rises to a doubleness in which image as image and "image as trace of performance" coincide. These passages of drawn pigment are rare in eighteenth-century American work. They concern us here as evidence of a wedding of drawing and painting, not in the initial stages of plotting a complex narrative picture, but in the final touches that animated a portrait's surface in the hands of a few masters.[41]

My aim in highlighting this gorgeous passage is not to suggest that Joshua Johnson's work is heir to, or influenced by, or even informed by the same artistic theories, training, treatises, or self-conception as were Copley's. I highlight it, rather, because of the generosity of imagination it shows toward the artist it concerns, its willingness to imagine the artist at work and with intention, as someone engaged in a process of world- and self-making. And I highlight it because it identifies in a small gestural detail – what she calls the "drawn pigment" of fabric edging – the mark of a mind at work.

I propose we bring a similar sort of speculative openness to the aesthetic surfaces of Johnson's work, despite our lack of knowledge related to him as a historical person or working artist. Johnson's lace – one of the most consistently unique aspects of the eighty-plus canvases that have been identified as produced by him in the early nineteenth century – is applied to the canvas as if having been drawn on. The clear, crisp lines that make his lacework both pop and flow across his figures' bodies are precise and thoughtful, and, importantly, make a deep sort of sense when considered in relation to two other characteristics of his paintings: their horizontal linearity and skewed approach to scale.

Johnson regularly places his figures on a sofa featuring brass upholstery tacks, which the curatorial files for *The McCormick Family* describes as a part of Johnson's "penchant for meticulously accurate delineations of furniture."[42] Johnson's meticulousness is the exact inverse of the care taken in depicting Black people in domestic scenes around the same time. Many white painters included Black figures in the background or shadows of their paintings; for example, Edward Savage's *The Washington Family* (1789–1796) depicts a liveried Black servant standing next to a column off to the right side of the titular family. The Black man is depicted as, literally, faceless; his head is just a circle of undifferentiated brown pigment. Johnson's careful attention to the inanimate aspects of his paintings

Figure 10.2 Joshua Johnson, *James McCormick Family*, oil on canvas, c.1804–1824. Courtesy of Maryland Historical Society, 1920.6.1

takes on meaning within such a context: in an era in which Black figures were portrayed (when they were at all) so off-handedly – as if they were objects – Johnson brings an unusual level of care to his representation of the actual objects he depicts.

The sofa is not only evidence of Johnson's alertness to slavery's objectifying logic, but also enabled his compositions to be particularly linear. What does his repeated return to the *line* – lines of inheritance, straight compositional lines, lines in a sketchbook – tell us about the world in which he lived, and his position in this world? Scholars have noted that Johnson's compositions – especially the large family portraits such as *Mr. and Mrs. James McCormick and Their Children* (1804–1805) (Figure 10.2) and *Mrs. Thomas Everette and Her Children* (1818) (Figure 10.3) – use a "distinctive horizontal composition . . . to simplify [the] potentially complex multi-figure groupings."[43]

The horizontal linearity of these family portraits might have been the solution to a compositional problem (the sofa allows a large number of people of differing heights to be united in depiction), but the effect, especially when considered in conjunction with the eruption of drawing

Figure 10.3 Joshua Johnson, *Rebecca Myring Everette and Her Children*, oil on canvas, 1818.
Courtesy of Maryland Historical Society, 1976.96.4

techniques into his paintings, is suggestive. His horizontal compositions bring his sitters up to the picture plane; in effect, the compositions flatten the figures *and* the space that they occupy. Johnson did occasionally use traditional eighteenth-century portrait techniques for suggesting depth beyond a sitter – a window or other architectural element opening onto a vista beyond – but he never did so in family group portraits and seems to have employed these illusions of depth beyond the picture plane less and less as he developed.

Compositionally drawing his figures up toward the picture plane, Johnson then often indulges a different interest in line as a kind of luxurious and slow connective thread. His lines, for example, find expression in the beautifully rendered white dresses worn by the mother and daughters in *The McCormick Family*, which contrast with the flatly rendered sofa and father and son's clothing. The Maryland Historical Society catalog entry for this painting suggests that "The picture is thinly painted, as are most of Johnson's portraits, but the intricate folds and feathery quality of the thin fabrics are reduced to rather more linear forms. In this respect, the McCormick picture is more painterly in overall style."[44] The compositional horizontality of the painting unites with the linearity of his depiction of fabric to suggest familial connection or ties that bind. And yet, in an effect that is common in Johnson's paintings, a few slightly "off" details prick the viewer. For example, the child John's awkward placement in between his father's legs, the baby Sophia's direct and confrontational gaze while holding, and seemingly glutting, a large bowl of strawberries, and the oppositional energy manifested in John's and his father's simultaneously grasping a single piece of paper between them. Family portraits are almost always about lines of inheritance; here we have an artist who was once enslaved using a variety of aesthetic techniques (composition, fabric modeling, and more) to depict a family line that appears binding at first, but starts to disintegrate upon a closer look.

The linear forms of Johnson's lace and fabrics also find echo in the "highly unusual" inclusion of a pencil drawing in *Mrs. Thomas Everette and Her Children*. Each of the children in this painting holds his or her own attribute –from left to right: two roses, strawberries, pencil and open sketchbook, and book. The oldest son holds the pencil, sketchbook, and depicted sketch in a moment of meta-artistic representation that scholars like Lovell (and, indeed, Michel Foucault, in his famous analysis of Velasquez's *Las Meninas* in *The Order of Things*)[45] have found suggestive. The representation of art within a work of art provides a rich opportunity to speculate about an artist's self-understanding and aesthetic techniques.

Here, the oldest son holds in his hand both pencil and sketch. Johnson would not know the significance that the "sketch" would come to hold for formerly enslaved people writing their stories about life under slavery. But as Teresa Goddu and Janet Neary have written, the visual language of slave narratives often included what was termed a "sketch" of slavery: both a brief account and a visual shorthand meant to make slavery's injustices and brutality vivid and urgent to readers.[46] The power of the sketch is its provisionality: it is quickly rendered, and is meant to one day be properly replaced or turned into something more permanent. It is always attuned to its own process, as a form of artistic expression not ever meant to be understood as complete.

The difference between a sketch and an oil painting is important. As Lovell has argued of Smibert's inclusion of the provisional chalk drawing in his painting *The Bermuda Group*, "Smibert's 'chalk drawing' is different in subject, scale, and medium from the larger work in which it is presented, and in these differences it complicates and *marks as artificial* our experience of it and of the painting as a whole."[47] The inclusion of something like sketching or drawing inside an oil painting occasions a productive split perspective in the viewer; an oil painting aims to reproduce "reality" but the insistent two-dimensionality and schematic nature of a drawing inside an oil painting challenges the viewer to acknowledge that the "reality" depicted is an illusion.

But where the drawing in Smibert's painting pops because of its qualitative difference – in medium, scale, and subject – from the rest of the canvas's visual world, Joshua Johnson's *Mrs. Thomas Everette* weaves together the sketchbook and the world of the painting. The lines depicted as drawn in the sketchbook are echoed in the lines that delineate the lace and fabric details, and the two-dimensionality of the sketchbook underscores Johnson's unique and skewed insistence on the two-dimensionality of the plane in which his sitters (three-dimensional humans) are featured. Johnson's group family portraits call attention to the flatness of the picture plane and the lines that connect and traverse person and object.

Nowhere is Johnson's interest in the relationship between subject and object more pronounced than in his wonderfully odd portrait *Emma Van Name* (*c.*1805) (Figure 10.4), which features an anachronistically almost modernist sensibility in its playful and disordered sense of scale and likeness.[48]

The painting depicts a young girl standing on an oil cloth floor wearing a gorgeous pink dress and shoes, a frilly lace cap, and fine white embroidered overdress. A window opens onto dark sky and greenery to the side and slightly behind her, and she wears coral bar pins on her shoulders, a coral necklace, and a long cloth chain with coral-and-bells hanging from it.[49] The most engaging part of this portrait is the "almost surreal" stemmed glass goblet filled with strawberries standing next to her.[50] This piece of glassware is nearly half her height, its scale entirely off-kilter in relation to both the room and figure depicted. The child brings one strawberry to her mouth while simultaneously reaching for another in the nearly overflowing gigantic goblet.

The relationship between the goblet's scale, the child's jewelry, and the child's gestures are significant. This child, wearing emblems of protection and safety, stands in possessive relationship to the goblet and its contents. She simultaneously consumes and reaches for more. In a sense, this is a picture of bounty and well-being. But at the same time, the goblet's scale threatens to overwhelm the figure, producing an off-kilter energy that calls to my mind two other early-nineteenth-century painters, Raphaelle Peale and Martin Johnson Heade. Peale's still life paintings, such as *Still Life with Watermelon* (1825), often feature combinations of rind, moist innards, fecund seed, decay, and violently akimbo slices cut into foodstuff's

Figure 10.4 Joshua Johnson, *Emma Von Name*, oil on canvas, *c.*1805. Courtesy of Metropolitan Museum of Art, 2016.116

flesh. These elements come together into what critic Alexander Nemorov has called a form of "grostequeness."[51] Likewise, Heade's landscapes offer similarly skewed perceptions. As Maggie M. Cao has written of Heade's depictions of the "exotic," landscapes of Brazil, which he visited in 1863, and which seem at first to conform to nineteenth-century romanticized ideals about tropical lands, "when examined closer, Heade's paintings reveal strange and uncanny effects: the confrontation of life-size objects with miniaturized landscapes; the conflicting cues as to scale where they meet; and the lattice-like overlay of brilliant, fecund foregrounds encircled by dark decay."[52] The traditional genres within which Peale, Heade, and Johnson worked – still life, landscape, portraiture – provided the rules and conventions that each artist subtly distorted to fascinating and meaningful effect.

When considered in this light, Johnson's painting of a young white girl standing in the midst of a world of bounty is incredibly suggestive. It asks us to consider: What happens when people and objects are rendered in similar scale? Recall Lovell's claim that part of the philosophical function of the drawing included in Smibert's painting is to "mark as artificial" the viewer's experience of the painting – we are not and were not there (and, further, that in any case of depiction, there is no "there" there). But again, I would argue that in Johnson's paintings we see the reverse of this process happening. Johnson's use of skewed scale, this unbelievably huge piece of glassware, may not be working to mark the viewer's experience of the painting as artificial, but rather to mark as *all too believable* the possibility that a person might be viewed as of the same size, volume, and value as an object. In other words, *Emma Van Name*, a delightful and aesthetically provocative painting, embodies the logic of slavery under which Johnson lived.

The political and social dimensions of *Emma Van Name* are intertwined with the painting's formal and aesthetic techniques and features. Though we don't know much about Johnson's perspective on his enslavement, his manumission, or his experience as a free Black man in Baltimore around the turn of the century, we have the surfaces of his paintings, which provide significant insight into the aesthetics of subjectivity and objecthood that are central to questions about race and slavery in the era. The rare moments of low *impasto* seen so often in the crisply detailed fabrics in his canvases, his enduring interest in linearity and two-dimensionality, and his skewed experiment with scale in *Emma Van Name* come together to produce a vision of a world where ornamentation (such as lace) is both a delight and part of a larger system that draws people and objects into grotesque relation.

Early Black Aesthetics of Vision

The Blind African Slave was written and published during the period just prior to the consolidation of "the slave narrative" as a recognizable and marketable literary genre. Brinch's tale is part eighteenth-century Enlightenment philosophy (its interest in exotic flora and fauna and transatlantic routes of exchange and influence), part spiritual autobiography, and part slave narrative. While it shares some of the better-known, mid-nineteenth-century slave narrative's conventions – authenticating documents, a William Cowper reference, and accounts of enslavement featuring cruel slave masters, daily details, violence, and escape – these conventions take less recognizable shape in *The Blind African Slave*. The conventions that the mid-nineteenth-century US slave narrative teaches us to recognize appear jumbled and chaotic in Brinch's tale when compared to the tightly honed and focused point of view and structure featured in the later narratives. But the very thing that makes *The Blind African Slave* somewhat less legible to us today – its complex understanding of the "I/eye" that roves its pages – is exactly the element that might be most useful for scholars looking to deepen our understanding of the vast and idiosyncratic qualities of Black thought and philosophy before 1830.

For his part, Joshua Johnson's position is both legible within the history of portraiture and not. Johnson's paintings are simultaneously reminiscent of, yet more aesthetically accomplished than, much itinerant and vernacular portrait painting of the era. At the same time, however, they have none of the luxurious markers of the canvases produced by the academically-trained Baltimore portraitists I listed above. Johnson is a unique figure working within a hoary, established, and conventional art form. As Margaretta Lovell has written, the colonial and early Republican period in the United States was marked by an almost insatiable taste for – on the part of those who could afford them – portraits. Colonists and early Americans, she notes, "did not buy landscapes, still lifes, or genre scenes; they did not even branch out into portraits of horses or houses. They focused solely – but enthusiastically – on portraits of individuals, couples, and occasionally families ... Portraits, it seems ... actively fulfill[ed] a specific, chronic, social need."[53] Perhaps this overwhelming taste for portraits was part of what enabled Johnson's unusual career. This market for painted portraiture held relatively steady until 1839, when the introduction of photographic technology to the United States forever changed individuals' relationship to painted portraiture. And while the nineteenth century saw a handful of Black portraitists rise up and add their perspectives, skills, and interests to the long history of portraiture – early photographers J.P. Ball and Augustus Washington, engraver Patrick Reason, New Orleans portraitist Julien Hudson, Philadelphia painter and lithographer Robert Douglass, for example – Joshua Johnson's aesthetic accomplishment remains unique: he developed a specific and provocative style (even within the relatively staid conventions of family portraiture), and while we still do not know much about him as a historical person, we have a comparative wealth of his canvases to study and think alongside of.

Ultimately, the historical and artistic contexts of the period between 1800 and 1830 can tell us a lot about these two fascinating artists. But I would argue the aesthetic and formal techniques that Brinch and Johnson employ in their art help us imagine beyond context and history. And because they both worked in unexpected forms that lie somewhat outside of the most legible histories of Black writing and art, their work helps prod and invent new ways of thinking about selfhood, beauty, and the visual. *The Blind African Slave's* narrative perspective and its interest in aesthetic beauty offer a theory of vision insisting that sight is an embodied experience, that the self is produced in a sense-based exchange between individual and world, and that aesthetic beauty is a form of memory and memorialization, not a world apart. Ultimately, *The Blind African Slave* advocates for a way of seeing, creating, and memorializing beauty that is specific to the experience of those who have been enslaved.

Joshua Johnson did not depict the experience of enslavement in his work. That he does not paint or represent "the Black experience" has perhaps been a factor in the difficulty of situating his work within a particular canon. But he did depict the logic of slavery in his portraiture of white sitters. And, crucially, his depictions take beautiful and charming form: the logic of slavery in Johnson's work does not take overtly racist or evil shape. Rather, it delights and perverts through an endlessly fascinating set of formal choices and techniques on the part of the artist. It takes the form of skewed lines and lineage and goblets the size of a child. It takes shape in the ease with which an appealing vignette starts to feel askew when sat with and considered and thought over.

Together, the work produced by Brinch and Johnson that I've analyzed here helps scholars, too, with a more meta question: What to do with the limitations of the archive when it comes to art produced by people of color before 1830 (or 1900 or 1960 for that matter). Where the archive is silent, Brinch's and Johnsons's art reveals the cacophony of the aesthetic: composition, point of view, adornment, pigment, pose, and more. The archival silences that mark (and mar) our understanding of early Black writing and art will likely never be made fully to confess. But the aesthetic and formal techniques of these works of art do more than tell: they show and embody and provoke.

Notes

Thank you to Jasmine Cobb for sharp editorial feedback on early drafts of this chapter, to Charmaine Nelson for inviting me to share my work on Joshua Johnson at the generative *The Precariousness of Freedom* seminar at Harvard University in Spring 2018, and to Elizabeth Kornhauser, at the Metropolitan Museum of Art and Allison Tolman, Alexandra Deutsch, and Mark Letzer of the Maryland Historical Society, for generously allowing me to consult curatorial and research files on Johnson, as well as a substantial number of his paintings, many of them in storage or otherwise not on display.

1 For more on the differences between eighteenth- and nineteenth-century cultural, political, and economic ideas about race and how historical transitions of the period shaped the writing produced by people of African descent, see Vincent Carretta, "Introduction," in *Unchained Voices: An Anthology of Black Authors in the English-Speaking World of the Eighteenth Century* (Lexington: University Press of Kentucky, 2003), 1–16. For more on the well-established tropes of nineteenth-century US slave narratives, see James Olney, "'I Was Born': Slave Narratives, Their Status as Autobiography and as Literature," *Callaloo* 20 (Winter 1984): 46–73. For more on the complexities of the white amanuensis, see Joycelyn K. Moody, "Frances Whipple, Elleanor Eldridge, and the Politics of Interracial Collaboration," *American Literature* 83, no.4 (2011): 686–717.

2 Kari J. Winter's meticulously researched and edited edition of *The Blind African Slave* puts it this way: "In 1810 in St. Albans, Vermont, a small town near the Canadian border, an anomalous narrative of slavery was published by an obscure printer. Entitled *The Blind African Slave; Or, Memoirs of Boyrereau Brinch, Nicknamed Jeffrey Brace*, it was greeted with no fanfare, and it has remained for nearly two hundred years a faint specter in our cultural memory" (3). Kari J. Winter, "Introduction," in *The Blind African Slave, or Memoirs of Boyrereau Brinch, Nicknamed Jeffrey Brace* (Madison: University of Wisconsin Press, 2004), 3–84. While Brinch's narrative often shows up in the footnotes of scholarly work on late-eighteenth- and early-nineteenth-century Black writing, it has been mostly marginal to this work. For an important exception, see Lynn R. Johnson, "Narrating an Indigestible Trauma: The Alimentary Grammar of Boyrereau Brinch's Middle Passage" in *Journeys of the Slave Narrative in the Early Americas*, ed. Nicole N. Aljoe and Ian Finseth, (Charlottesville: University of Virginia Press, 2014), 127–142.

3 For more on the intersection of portraiture and racial identity in the nineteenth century, see Richard Powell, "Cinqué: Antislavery Portraiture and Patronage in Jacksonian America," *American Art* 11, no.3 (October 1997): 49–73; Richard Powell, *Cutting a Figure: Fashioning Black Portraiture* (Chicago: University of Chicago Press, 2008); Richard Powell and Gwendolyn DuBois Shaw, *Represent: 200 Years of African American Art* (New Haven, CT: Yale University Press, 2014); Gwendolyn DuBois Shaw, *Portraits of a People: Picturing African Americans in the Nineteenth Century*

(Seattle: University of Washington Press, 2006); Maurice O. Wallace and Shawn Michelle Smith, eds., *Pictures and Progress: Early Photography and the Making of African American Identity* (Durham, NC: Duke University Press, 2012); and Shawn Michelle Smith *American Archives: Gender, Race, and Class in Visual Culture* (Princeton: Princeton University Press, 1999).

4 See Metropolitan Museum of Art curator Amelia Peck's 2015 article on the enslaved colonial artist Prince Demah Barnes and the story of how the Met came to purchase one of his paintings is a part of this important current work. She notes that "Prince's story and canvases point to the likelihood of uncovering other significant contributions to the visual arts made by enslaved African Americans in the eighteenth century. While some are recorded as working as printmakers, silhouette cutters, and stone carvers, the only other recorded fine artist is Scipio Moorhead, the slave of a Boston minister who is thought to have drawn the portrait of Phyllis Wheatley that appeared as the frontispiece to a volume of her poems. Until the discovery of Prince's work, the earliest African-American portraitist in oils was thought to be Joshua Johnson, whose mother was enslaved and whose father, a white man, purchased and freed him while he was still a young man. Largely self-taught, Johnson lived in the Baltimore area, where he painted appealing portraits of the Maryland elite." Amelia Peck and Paula M. Bagger, "Prince Demah Barnes: Portraitist and Slave in Colonial Boston," *The Magazine Antiques*, January/February 2015: 154–159.

5 Stephen Best describes the problem of working with the archive of American slavery as a "pursuit of degraded fragments in an impoverished archive" (159). See "Neither Lost Nor Found: Slavery and the Visual Archive," *Representations* 113, no.1 (Winter 2011): 150–163. Saidiya Hartman calls the challenges of this archive an "impossibility": "a story predicated on impossibility–listening for the unsaid, translating misconstrued words, and refashioning disfigured lives–and intent on achieving an impossible goal: redressing the violence that produced numbers, ciphers, and fragments of discourse, which is as close as we come to a biography of the captive and the enslaved." See Saidiya Hartman "Venus in Two Acts," *Small Axe*, 12, no. 2 (June 2008): 1–14. Lauren Klein employs digital tools to shift perspective on slavery's impossible archive in her essay on Thomas Jefferson's enslaved chef James Hemings: Lauren Klein, "The Image of Absence: Archival Silence, Data Visualization, and James Hemings," *American Literature* 85, no. 1 (2013): 661–668.

6 Jennifer Bryan and Robert Torchia, "The Mysterious Portraitist Joshua Johnson," *Archives of American Art Journal* 36, no. 2 (1996): 2–7.

7 Jonathan Crary, *Techniques of the Observer: On Vision and Modernity in the Nineteenth Century* (Cambridge, MA: MIT Press, 1990).

8 Winter, "Introduction," 82. Winter uses "Jeffrey Brace" throughout her introduction, as this was the name used in historical records related to the historical person she has researched, and the name under which the volume is published. I have chosen to use Boyrereau Brinch in the body of the essay, not

because I think it is more accurate, but because the formal cues of the text indicate this to be the name of the authorial persona featured in the text.

9 Jeffrey Brace, *The Blind African Slave, or Memoirs of Boyrereau Brinch, Nicknamed Jeffrey Brace* (Madison: University of Wisconsin Press, 2004), 91.

10 Winter, "Introduction," 3–4.

11 Ibid., 109.

12 Ed Folsom and Kenneth Price, "Racial Politics and the Origins of *Leaves of Grass*," *Walt Whitman Archive*, www.whitmanarchive.org/biography/walt_whitman/index.html#racial

13 Brace, *The Blind African Slave*, 124.

14 Johnson, "Narrating an Indigestible Trauma," 133.

15 Brace, *The Blind African Slave*, 130.

16 Ibid., 131.

17 Ibid., 110.

18 Marcus Wood, *Black Milk: Imagining Slavery in the Visual Cultures of Brazil and America* (Oxford: Oxford University Press, 2013), 33.

19 See Tara Bynum, "Phyllis Wheatley on Friendship" *Legacy* 31, no. 1 (2014):42–51 and Tara Bynum, "Phyllis Wheatley's Pleasures," *Common-Place* 11, no. 1 (October 2010), www.common-place-archives.org/vol-11/no-01/bynum/

20 Brace, *The Blind African Slave*, 134.

21 Ibid.

22 Ralph Waldo Emerson, "Nature," in *Essays and Lectures*, ed. Joel Porte (New York: Library of America, 1983), 10.

23 Brace, *The Blind African Slave*, 152.

24 Ibid., 154.

25 Ibid., 155.

26 Ibid., 154.

27 Ibid., 155.

28 Ibid.

29 Ibid., 118.

30 Ibid., 182.

31 For more on whiteness as property and inheritance see Cheryl L. Harris, "Whiteness as Property," *Harvard Law Review* 106, no. 8 (June 1993): 1707–1791. For more on how normative White patriarchal family structures are in violent relationship to "illegitimate" Black family structures, see Hortense J. Spillers, "Mama's Baby, Papa's Maybe: An American Grammar Book," *Diacritics* 17, no. 2 (Summer 1987): 64–81.

32 Joycelyn K. Moody, "Tactical Lines in Three Black Women's Visual Portraits, 1773–1849," *a/b: Auto/Biography* 30, no. 1 (2015): 67–98 and Lynn Casmier-Paz, "Slave Narratives and the Rhetoric of Author Portraiture," *New Literary History* 34, no. 1 (Winter 2003): 91–116.

33 Enslaved by the well-known artist Charles Willson Peale, Moses Williams seems to have been active as a silhouette artist. See Gwendolyn DuBois Shaw, "Moses Williams, Cutter of Profiles: Silhouettes and African American

Identity in the Early Republic," *Proceedings of the American Philosophical Society* 149, no. 1 (March 2005): 22–39. Other Black artists working in portraiture before the Civil War include Scipio Moorhead and Prince Demah Barnes, both discussed in footnote 4.

34 See Rita Rief, "New Attention for Early Black Artist," *New York Times*, February 7, 1988. The catalogs accompanying the exhibitions noted are Lynne Roscoe Hartigan, ed., *Sharing Traditions: Five Black Artists in Nineteenth-Century America* (Washington, DC: Smithsonian Institution Press, 1985) and Carolyn Weekley and Stiles Tuttle Colwill, eds, *Joshua Johnson: Freeman and Early American Portrait Painter* (Colonial Williamsburg, VA: Abby Aldrich Rockefeller Folk Art Center and Maryland Historical Society, 1987).

35 Jennifer Bryan and Robert Torchia, "The Mysterious Portraitist Joshua Johnson," *Archives of American Art Journal* 36, no. 2 (1996): 5.

36 W.J.T. Mitchell, *Picture Theory: Essays on Verbal and Visual Representation* (Chicago: University of Chicago Press, 1995), 190.

37 Carolyn Weekley, "Who Was Joshua Johnson?," in *Joshua Johnson: Freeman and Early American Portrait Painter* (Colonial Williamsburg, VA: Abby Aldrich Rockefeller Folk Art Center and Maryland Historical Society, 1987), 63.

38 Sian Jones, "Johnson's Materials and His Techniques," in *Joshua Johnson: Freeman and Early American Portrait Painter* (Colonial Williamsburg, VA: Abby Aldrich Rockefeller Folk Art Center and Maryland Historical Society, 1987), 66.

39 Compare the transparency and weightlessness of Johnson's lace with the substantial rendering of lace in Charles Willson Peale's *Anne Catherine Hoof Green* (1769) or Charles Bird King's *Margaret Bayard Smith* (*c.*1829).

40 Margaretta Lovell, *Art in a Season of Revolution: Painters, Artisans, and Patrons in Early America* (Philadelphia: University of Pennsylvania Press, 2005), 189.

41 Ibid., 209–210.

42 Ibid., 4.

43 Maryland Historical Society, curatorial file for *The McCormick Family*, 3.

44 Weekley and Colwill, *Joshua Johnson,* 124.

45 Michel Foucault, *The Order of Things: An Archeology of the Human Sciences* (New York: Vintage, 1994), 3–16.

46 Teresa Goddu "Antislavery's Panoramic Perspective" and Janet Neary, "Representational Static: Visual Slave Narratives of Contemporary Art," both in *MELUS: Multiethnic Literature of the United States* 39, no. 2 (Summer 2014).

47 Lovell, *Art in a Season of Revolution,* 186.

48 This portrait was purchased by folk art collectors Edgar and Bernice Garbisch in the 1950s (no history of the painting before the twentieth century has been discovered), and then given to the Whitney Museum of American Art in 1969. The Whitney deaccessioned this early nineteenth-century work in 1987; the painting went on to garner a record-breaking purchase price at

auction to an art dealer in 1988, then onto the significant private Manoogian Collection, and then, most recently, in 2015, was acquired by the Metropolitan Museum of Art for its permanent collection.

49 As Marcia Pointon notes of eighteenth- and nineteenth-century children's jewelry, "Often, children's jewelry was prophylactic: coral (the origins of which lay, according to Ovid, with the beheading of the Medusa) was believed to ward off the evil eye of sickness and protect children from the plague" (12). Marcia Pointon, "Women and Their Jewels," in *Women and Material Culture 1660–1830*, ed. Jennie Batchelor and Cora Kaplan (New York: Palgrave Macmillan, 2007), 11–30.

50 Stiles T. Colwill, "Joshua Johnson's Portrait of Emma Van Name," *Sotheby's Catalogue*, January 1988: 1274.

51 Alexander Nemerov, *The Body of Raphaelle Peale: Still Life and Selfhood, 1812–1824* (Oakland: University of California Press), 124.

52 Maggie M. Cao, "Heade's Hummingbirds and the Ungrounding of Landscape," *American Art* 25, no. 3 (Fall 2011): 48.

53 Lovell, *Art in a Season of Revolution*, 9.

CHAPTER 11

Embodying Activism, Bearing Witness
The Portraits of Early African American Ministers in Philadelphia

Aston Gonzalez

Bishop Richard Allen, the founder of the African Methodist Episcopal Church, sat for several portraits between 1784 and 1823. After the completion of the last two, artists transformed these unique oil paintings into reproduced engravings for a larger viewing audience. As the first portraits of Black ministers appeared depicting Allen and several other early Black ministers in Philadelphia, the production of these images paralleled an increase in the publications authored by African Americans in the United States during the first three decades of the nineteenth century. The two phenomena are not unrelated. In Philadelphia and elsewhere, Black ministers advanced projects to build Black institutions and organizations such as schools, fraternal orders, factories, and churches as the nation's free Black population greatly increased from immigration and Pennsylvania's 1780 Act for the Gradual Abolition of Slavery.[1] The portraits speak to the social conditions created by the heightened Black presence in public spaces and the mounting demands for the end of racial oppression experienced by free and enslaved people of African descent, as well as to the activism of several early Black ministers in Philadelphia – the Revs. Absalom Jones, Richard Allen, John Gloucester, and Jeremiah Gloucester.[2]

By examining images of early African American male ministers in Philadelphia with their speeches, public writings, and private correspondence together, this chapter illustrates how visual and literary culture became intertwined as sites of activism and commemoration. This chapter analyzes the strategies of producing and circulating portraits of early African American ministers in Philadelphia that challenged denials of Black participation in the public sphere. These images countered powerful visual and print cultures of racism in simultaneous circulation. Religious portraits overlaid ideas about Black education, citizenship, and religiosity during the 1810s and 1820s in the face of racial prejudice against free Black northerners. While the portraits were often self-reflexive and highlighted each sitter's achievements, they also directly engaged in debates over the social and political positions of Black people in the United States at the time of their creation.

Scholars have increasingly examined the racial and political critiques represented in Black portraiture before the Civil War.[3] Joycelyn Moody has cogently argued that portraits of African American women during this era highlighted not just Black women's intellectual and economic productivity, but also their arguments for Black people's rights.[4] Similarly complex, religious portraits represented Black churches, institutions that intensified the growth of Christianity among people of African descent and propagated a liberation theology that subverted the institution of slavery. Embedded within sermons on moral living were stories about resisting slavery and promoting liberatory policies. In addition, the growing wealth, population, and strength of free Black institutions inspired ministers to advocate for increased political representation that previously did not exist in the early republic. Where the autonomy of African American churches came to symbolize a threat to the racial status quo, portraits of African American ministers commemorated the leaders of this movement.

The portraits of early African American ministers existed alongside derogatory images of African Americans and further revealed the climate of racial animus before the Civil War. Contrary to portraits of Black leaders, printers circulated "bobalition" prints, crude woodcut images of African Americans that ridiculed Black public culture. These items featured images and text that mocked the commemoration of the abolition of slavery in Massachusetts and the federal law that ended the legal importation of enslaved people to the United States at the beginning of 1808. For more than a decade, a series of "bobalition" prints attacked more than Black Americans' attire, physicality, and intelligence. These malicious imprints argued that Black people's participation in the body politic and their construction of benevolent and religious institutions undermined democratic republicanism with Black deviance.[5] They instructed viewers to discount Black men and women's political engagement as beyond the bounds of citizenship; they attacked Black claims to national belonging on the grounds of education, moral behavior, and respectability. Black Philadelphians modeled their claims when they gathered to celebrate the ban on the importation of enslaved people, deeming it "the Day of Our Political Jubilee," while community members read aloud congressional acts, the Declaration of Independence, and presidential addresses.[6] Portraits of Black ministers such as the Revs. Absalom Jones, Richard

Allen, John Gloucester, and Jeremiah Gloucester immortalize these figures who led the charge as separate Black churches of Methodist, Episcopalian, and Baptist denominations formed against race prejudice in white churches. These ministers and their churches hosted festive assemblies in celebration of abolition, while "bobalition" prints circulated to undermine their political activities.

This chapter examines images of Black leadership that shared a cultural landscape with the derisive "bobalition" prints to explore political, religious, and cultural debates that African Americans engaged in during the first decades of the nineteenth century. The production of images laden with religious and political referents illuminates the stakes of visual representations of race in the early republic and in the minds of religious leaders. Portraits were key sites for reshaping assumptions about Black leadership, Black cultural institutions, and Black political engagement. Projecting both the interior and exterior characteristics of those depicted, the images of early ministers supported religious education, antislavery commemoration, and fundraising efforts. Analyzing the circulation (when known), the intended viewership, and the medium of the portraits, this chapter enriches our understanding of African American ministers as cultural curators committed to the auspicious of blackness. The practice of producing postmortem portraits also enabled Black communities to honor the survival and celebration of a minister's life and work. These images became sites of struggle on which Black religious communities engaged in contemporary debates about Black authority and national belonging.

Richard Allen and The Making of Good Citizens

Reverend Richard Allen sat for his first portrait in 1784 or 1785, producing an image that revealed his commitment to Methodist ministry (see Figure 11.1). Born enslaved in 1760, Allen learned to read and write as an adolescent through biblical study.[7] After his conversion to Methodism in the 1770s and working for years to buy his freedom, he began attending St. George's Church in Philadelphia, which instituted the policy of removing Black people from the ground-level pews to the segregated balcony. Allen and others, including Reverend Absalom Jones, who would establish St. Thomas's African Episcopal Church, walked out in protest. Allen soon formed the Bethel African Methodist Episcopal Church, building his own congregation and church edifice. His portrait represents a man who taught himself to read, who secured his freedom, and who traveled throughout the Middle Atlantic states as an itinerant preacher.[8] His attire evidences his

Figure 11.1 Anonymous, [*Portrait of Richard Allen*], *c.*1784. Moorland-Spingarn Research Center at Howard University

religiosity and employment. The portrait's lack of background detail is in keeping with other portraits of Methodist ministers of this era and encourages the viewer to focus on Allen's face and religious calling.

By 1813, the portrait that Allen commissioned displays an accomplished Black leader heralding the promise of religious faith. The half-length

Figure 11.2 Anonymous, *Rev. Richard Allen, founder of the American Methodist Episcopal Church, in the United States of America, 1779*. 1813. Library Company of Philadelphia

portrait shows Allen in a dark coat and white cravat making eye contact with the viewer while he points down with his right index finger to a large, open Bible he grasps in his left hand. The book rests on a large, cushioned surface covered with a richly textured material that echoes the luxurious folds of fabric drawn back into a curtain behind Allen. The weight of the curtain, evident in the thick creases of the fabric, indicates a space filled with well-appointed materials. Such surroundings hint at the wealth that Allen had accumulated.[9] More importantly, however, Allen meets the viewer's gaze and directs their attention to a Bible passage with his pointed finger to emphasize religiosity as a priority over the worldly possessions around him. As evidenced by his personal real estate transactions and the eventual purchase of the land under Mother Bethel Church, Allen understood the importance of capital, especially for people of African descent.

One written reaction to the portrait of Allen reveals its positive reception (see Figure 11.2). Neat handwriting above one of the copies of Allen's engraved 1813 portrait signals its importance to one viewer:

> The curiosity of the portrait below is that it was made for the first Black Bishop in the UStates and perhaps the world! He is indeed a self created Bishop; nevertheless, as such he has now, in his 65 years, in 1824, probably

> created 100 ministers, by his ordination! He was born & bred in Philada. He was originally a slave of Benjn Chew's Esqre & learnd the trade of a Shoemaker; & like St. Paul, "labored with his own hands," while he ordained[10]

That the writer begins with the "curiosity of the portrait" underscores the rarity of a Black religious leader, and the perhaps unique existence of a Black bishop. The writer underscores Allen's work ethic and determination by describing him as a "self created Bishop" and conveys his excitement that Allen had ordained an estimated 100 ministers. Recounting his past as an enslaved man, the writer clearly seems taken with Allen, describing in biblical terms the manual labor he performed as an enslaved man while working to become ordained. The image was preserved in a large collection that recorded the early history of Philadelphia, and on its verso was placed a portrait of Benjamin Lay, the social justice advocate and fervent anti-slavery Quaker activist. In mentioning that the portrait "was made for" Allen, the writer communicated that Allen commissioned the stipple engraving which could be reproduced many dozens of times to create prints of excellent quality. After all, reproduction and circulation lay at the core of the technology of engraving. The high quality of Allen's engraving demonstrated the importance of the sitter; likely modeled on an oil portrait, the engraving required considerably more time, skill, and money to produce than standard woodcuts of the era. The precise reason for its publication is unknown; however, it is possible that such a printing was sold to raise funds for a cause important to Allen or his congregation. Those who purchased the print almost certainly would have known Allen and his labors and purchased the image as a pedagogical tool or commemorative object that documented and endorsed Allen's accomplishments as well as his stakes in the visibility of Black leadership and institutions.

The religious overtones in Allen's engraving coupled with the symbols of class and respectability create a didactic portrait stressing religious study and its benefits. Allen communicates the priority of religiosity over worldly possessions around him by meeting the viewer's gaze and directing their attention to a Bible passage with his pointed finger. His upright posture, fixed mouth, and especially his rigid index finger convey a serious gravity to his persona. The physical heft of the velvety curtain behind him further echoes this weighty atmosphere of importance. Salvation resulted from religious belief and practice, not the acquisition of material goods. While Allen's directive to read evokes his own personal history of teaching himself to read and write via Bible study, his pointing is also a pedagogical command to study more generally. Education, particularly religious instruction, was a means by which individuals would come to realize the national sin of slavery.

African Americans' acquisition of formal education, symbolized in Allen's portrait by his instructive finger pointing to the Bible, marked an essential characteristic to dismantle racial barriers and enjoy the fruits of citizenship. As Moody has written, the depiction of literacy and academic prowess in the portrait of Phillis Wheatley serves as both a qualifier for and productive component of citizenship.[11] Allen's directive to read was simultaneously self-reflexive and didactic because it draws attention to his self-education and acquisition of religious knowledge as an enslaved man. Allen instructs those who meet his gaze: study and know the sacred text. Learning to read the Bible enabled the faithful to read other materials and prove their intelligence, often denied by their white detractors. The portrait of Allen challenges these misconceptions because the specific way in which Allen holds and points to the book underscores his commanding grasp of its information. In other words, Reverend Allen embodies the educational and moral potential for all African Americans, and his portrait underscores what could be possible if citizens adopted Allen's abolitionist teachings, which were grounded in biblical instruction. The image of a self-educated, formerly enslaved man now in a prominent position as one of the few Black ministers in the United States powerfully displayed the possibilities and realities of abolition.

For Allen, education was a conduit to citizenship and respectability. Eulogizing the death of President George Washington in 1799, Allen proclaimed that religious education and service to one's nation held deep political importance for African Americans. Allen described Washington as a respected symbol of the nation who decided not just to call for the emancipation of his enslaved property, but also to grant these formerly enslaved people "lands and comfortable accommodations."[12] Like Allen's index finger directing viewers of his portrait to focus on biblical teaching, his eulogy of Washington guided his audience to tools with which to disassemble slavery: religion and morality. For Allen, the guidance of religious teaching and the liberatory promises of the Revolutionary Era buttressed the notion that "we [people of African descent] had a right to liberty."[13] By making external their internal faith, Allen wrote, Black Americans could prove that they could form themselves into citizens who would then be recognized as worthy members of the body politic. Allen instructed his audience:

> Let me intreat you always to bear in mind the affectionate farewell advice of the great Washington – 'to love your country – to obey its laws – to seek its peace – and to keep yourself from attachment to any foreign nation.' Your

> observance of these short and comprehensive expressions will make you good citizens – and greatly promote the cause of the oppressed and shew [*sic*] to the world that you hold dear the name of George Washington.[14]

Religious faith as well as the exercise of republican ideals, which Allen espoused, would clothe African Americans in the norms of respectable citizenship. They could enact their citizenship by observing the laws of the country in much the same way that, in his portrait, Allen entreats them to enact the lessons of the Bible in their lives. Long engaged in the struggle for abolition – first his own, and then that of other enslaved people – Allen fervently believed that biblical education provided guidelines for living a moral and upright life.[15]

The timing of another portrait of Allen just ten years later in 1823 hinted at a rift forming in Allen's church. Published on December 10, 1823, the portrait shows a noticeably older Reverend Allen with white hair and fatigued eyes.[16] No luxurious fabric hangs in the background, nor does any cushion rest beneath the Bible that he holds upright with his right hand drawn across his body. Respectably attired in a black coat and white cravat like his 1813 portrait, the image lacks the symbols of material wealth present in his previous portrait. This less extravagant image appeared after Jonathan Tudas, a dismissed member of Bethel AME issued a pamphlet in 1823 charging Allen with financial misconduct. Suspicion of Allen's financial dealings may have inspired the modest presentation in Allen's portrait from the same year. Additionally, however, less money may have flowed through his church as former AME congregants broke away from Allen's church in 1820 and formed the Wesley Church in Philadelphia, taking their tithes with them. Although a few members voted to reunite with Bethel, other congregants ultimately prevented Allen from entering the Wesley Church and later assaulted him. Wesley members then took Allen to court for allegedly assaulting them and attempting to take control over the Wesley Church. Allen again turned to the press to share his side of the story. His published response to Tudas's pamphlet denied any financial impropriety and presented Tudas as a miscreant.[17] The 1823 portrait of a wearied Allen entered circulation during the midst of the lawsuit and soon after the printed rebuttal appeared. While the pamphlet offered a written denial of these charges, the portrait depicted Allen as an aged Black leader, perhaps too senior to resort to physical assault, committed to religious worship for Black Philadelphians. The image served to counter defamations of Allen's character, much like the pamphlet (see Figure 11.3).

Portraiture helped Allen maintain his stature as a prominent man of the cloth. Despite controversy, Allen's portraits identified him as a man of social rank with a long career in the city of Philadelphia. The multiple

Figure 11.3 John Boyd, *The Rev. Richard Allen, Bishop of the First African Methodist Episcopal Church, in the U. States.* 1823. Library Company of Philadelphia

portraits of Allen completed during his lifetime both documented and endorsed his authority as a Black leader within a country that routinely rejected African Americans' claims to freedom and equality. They bore witness to Allen's accomplishments and made space for Allen within the public sphere.[18] The inclusion in the caption beneath his 1823 portrait that Allen was the "Bishop of the First African Methodist Episcopal Church" alludes to the numerous AME churches that had arisen since his portrait of 1813, thereby reaffirming his prominence and success in building a network of Black churches with robust Black congregations. His grip on the Bible signals his continued command of the religious text, and by extension the moral teachings that it advances, visually rebutting the claims made by Tudas. The persona projected in Allen's 1823 is one of a wise and weathered, but undeterred, leader who maintained his position as an essential architect to the Black institutions of Philadelphia.

Absalom Jones and Acts of Commemoration

The Rev. Absalom Jones also used portraiture to mark his position as a foremost leader among the African American community in Philadelphia.

Given his belief in three interrelated practices to engender the end of racial oppression in the United States – behaviors informed by religious beliefs, activism for racial equality, and African Americans' private and public conduct – portraiture became one vehicle of an overall philosophy on Black visibility. The 1823 lithograph, made after Jones sat for an oil portrait in 1810 by the renowned painter Raphaelle Peale, signaled the importance of making visible Black achievements and leadership. More than sixty years old at the time of the painting, Reverend Jones had lived most of his life in Philadelphia. Born enslaved in nearby Delaware, Jones acquired literacy at school after his owner sold away Jones's family members. After having been freed and purchasing the freedom of his wife, Jones jointly founded the Free African Society in 1787 with Reverend Allen several years before Jones won approval to begin the African Episcopal Church of St. Thomas in Philadelphia. Jones's engraved portrait recorded and projected his achievements as a person of African descent who dedicated himself to the social and racial revolutions from which he envisioned African Americans and all Americans would benefit.

The engraved portrait modeled from the painting contains numerous elements that communicate the respectability of Reverend Jones (see Figure 11.4). His flowing religious vestments evidence his respected social status as a minister and provide his person with additional mass that nearly covers the upholstered and ornamented chair on which he sits. The background of the portrait, like the 1813 portrait of Reverend Richard Allen, features hanging fabric that conveys wealth and luxury. Drawn across his body, his right hand rests on an upright Bible, which visually forms the foundation of a pyramid that reaches its apex in Reverend Jones's face. Here, Jones directly engages the viewer of the print with direct eye contact. The Bible was one of the many books that Jones owned, and its presence in the portrait, in addition to communicating his profession, was self-reflexive. The Bible is essential to the vision of the man we see in the portrait. The material elements featured in the print symbolize both the monetary success that Jones had acquired before the engraving as well as the visual forms of respectability he would have wanted to demonstrate to white Americans. His formidable presence as a Black religious leader resting literally and metaphorically on the sacred text further constructs his visual persona as one marked by morality and honor.

Jones's portrait also displays his enormous investment in religious and secular education for Philadelphia's Black youth and adults. While the Bible displayed in Jones's picture emphasizes his position as a minister, it also acts as a referent to the decades that Jones labored to establish schools

Figure 11.4 W.R. Jones and John Boyd, *The Revd. Absalom Jones, Rector of St. Thomas's African Episcopal Church in the City of Philad.* 1823. Mother Bethel AME Church

for Black Philadelphians who were largely excluded from the city's schools. In 1804, he served as the president of the Society of Free People of Colour, which opened the fourth school to admit Black children in the city. That it quickly enrolled approximately fifty students illustrated both the demand for formal education among Black Philadelphians but also the closed doors they encountered at other schools throughout the city.[19] To further illustrate the mission of the society over which Jones presided, "an open door [was] offered without distinction of sect or party" to interested Black pupils for the inclusive reason that they could "become useful members of Society."[20] Furthermore, Jones co-taught reading, writing, and arithmetic in a school within his church aimed at educating Black children regardless of sex. The school also welcomed apprentices and servants. If potential pupils could not attend classes by day, there was also a night school that opened in the church and Jones served on the committee to assess applicants.[21] Such inclusive policies expanded educational opportunities and served to train citizens who would benefit their communities and the country more broadly.

Reverend Absalom Jones's commitment to strengthening the Black community of Philadelphia and providing opportunities for Black Philadelphians extended well beyond his educational involvement and his leadership at St. Thomas. He, along with Reverend Richard Allen and Cezar Wetherington, built a nail factory and advertised that they wished to hire "a number of Africans, or their descendants, as Journeymen and Apprentices."[22] Doing so provided Black Philadelphians with an economic foothold in a city where finding such employment proved difficult. Fellow members of the Union Society appointed Jones to publish the group's constitution, which described the "difficulty there is in obtaining places for children of colour to learn useful trades ... thus depriving them of the means of becoming useful citizens."[23] Transforming African Americans into "useful citizens" who made public contributions to society provided an avenue to demonstrate that people of African descent deserved space within the body politic. Jones also served as administrator to settle estate payments and demands thereby assisting families in need after the death of loved ones.[24] Jones delivered sermons at St. Thomas's to raise money "for the relief of the poor and distressed" in Philadelphia, which further evidences his outreach to those at the margins of society, a core belief of his Episcopalian faith.[25] Although one of the schools that Jones helped establish did not teach denominational beliefs, religious study formed the underpinning of his worldview and activism.

The federal ban on the importation of enslaved people into the United States beginning in 1808 marked a transition in African American print culture because it prompted Black ministers like Jones to celebrate and commemorate the abolition of slavery publicly. In his 1808 sermon, published in pamphlet form, Jones celebrated the suppression of the slave trade in the United States.[26] Jones's oration opened with verses from Exodus that described the divine intervention that delivered the enslaved Jews from their Egyptian oppressors. More than recounting the grueling physical demands of enslavement, Jones spoke about the cruelties of slavery known well by his Black audience: the theft of children from mothers, the murder of enslaved people, and measures taken to protect the state from insurrection.[27] If the parallels between the enslaved Jews in Egypt and the enslaved people of African descent in the United States had not been clear, Reverend Jones refers to the enslaved as "our countrymen" and details their sufferings.[28] Jones thrice describes enslaved people as "our countrymen," elucidating the common nature shared between enslaved and free people who, by logical extension, shared an interwoven past, present, and future.

Jones taught that continued religious belief and practice were one way to end racial oppression. Frequently citing the influence of the divine, Jones calls on those gathered before him and those reading his pamphlet to "beseech [God] to extend to all the nations in Europe, the same humane and just spirit towards them, which he has imparted to the British and American nations."[29] Such a reference to the antislavery currents on both sides of the Atlantic highlights Jones's critique of the governments that had yoked people of African descent with inhumane and unjust laws. Jones repeatedly thanks "all our friends and benefactors, in Great Britain, as well as in the United States" and hints at the transatlantic antislavery campaigns which were deeply rooted in Christian morals opposing systems of slavery.[30] Such antislavery pursuits seemed logical and moral because, in beseeching God during his oration, Jones declares: "thou has made of one blood all nations of men."[31] Jones explains and justifies activism with religious tenets while simultaneously proffering the belief that all races belong to the human race and therefore should be treated equally under the law and through social practice. Such a radical claim reverberates in Jones's repeated address of enslaved Americans as "our countrymen" who deserve deliverance from their oppressed condition. Just as Reverend Richard Allen calls on his audiences to be "good citizens" who serve the "oppressed" among them, Reverend Jones beseeches his audiences to do the same while laying claim to African Americans' national belonging as "countrymen" in spite of their subjugated status. As powerful, published leaders calling for improved social conditions and as individuals with respectable portraits demonstrating their achievements to viewers, Revs. Jones and Allen offered themselves as examples that countered claims of African American inferiority. In their published portraits and orations, both minsters modeled the kind of social and racial change toward which they spent their lives laboring.

In his 1808 *Thanksgiving Sermon*, Jones identified the work of antislavery activists and organizations as a second strategy to free African Americans from racial oppression. Jones recognized the power of antislavery activism in various forms but identified "publications" as powerful tools not only to enlighten individuals but to provoke them to enact laws ending slavery. In particular, Jones believed print was a powerful engine of social change. He recorded that the activism of "our benefactors" became crucial to "enlightening the minds of the rulers of the earth, by means of their publications and remonstrances against the trade in our countrymen."[32] Furthermore, "[a]bolition societies and individuals have equal claims to our gratitude."[33] In describing his faith in the power of God and the persuasion of print, Jones published his pamphlet knowing that antislavery publications resulted in the evolution of legal culture and contributed to stopping one process by which slavery rooted itself in the United States. As a published author and speaker, Jones participated in a radical print culture that aimed to engender social and racial change.

Jones argued that the public actions of free African Americans themselves would be a third factor to end Black Americans' suffering. Jones tasked the members of his audience "to dispose the hearts of our legislatures to pass laws, to ameliorate the condition of our brethren who are still in bondage."[34] He proffered the idea that his African American audience "let our conduct be regulated by the precepts of the Gospel" as a means to demonstrate to other members of the public the deservedness of freedom of their enslaved brethren.[35] Jones enacted this philosophy before he delivered his 1808 sermon when he chaired a meeting that organized three concurrent religious services at different Philadelphia churches to celebrate the federal law banning the importation of enslaved people effective January 1, 1808.[36] Grounding African Americans' actions in biblical teachings, in theory, could leave no justification for the denial of Black rights enjoyed by other members of society. More pointedly, Jones urges his audience "to act as becomes a people who owe so much to thy goodness" in order to prove their worthiness, by private and public actions, of the rights of citizenship.[37]

The 1794 pamphlet that Jones jointly authored with Reverend Richard Allen provides a strident example of Jones's belief that Black respectability politics and public service were necessary to form public perceptions of Black people. It marks another example of early African American ministers shaping their public persona with images and text printed to broadcast the urgency for a radical social and racial future for people of African descent. Reverend Jones's pamphlet, like the printing of his later 1808 *Thanksgiving Sermon* oration and engraved portrait, became evidence circulated among public audiences of Black achievement and respectability that ran counter to dominant claims otherwise. After Mathew Carey published an account castigating Black nurses caring for those suffering from the 1793 yellow fever epidemic, which decimated Philadelphia's population, Jones and Allen published a rebuttal titled *A Narrative of the Proceedings of the Black People, During the Late Awful Calamity in Philadelphia*.[38] Together, they corrected the public record about African Americans' sacrifices during the crisis. In doing so, scholars have argued that this publication represents a new foray into Black claims of an American identity as well as new forms of Black leadership.[39] Revs. Jones and Allen advance in their circulated document evidence that public Black actions displayed the moral, upright, and respectable behavior of African Americans generally as well as their investment in American society.

Moral uprightness and respectability, as embodied and displayed in Jones's 1823 portrait engraving, were espoused as key components in securing the end of racial oppression. More specifically, Jones foresaw the end of slavery and improved conditions for all people of African descent when three forces worked together. The appearance of the engraved portrait of Reverend Absalom Jones points to its creation being an act of commemoration. It honors one of Philadelphia's greatest champions of Black social institutions during and after the Revolutionary Era. Published on December 12, 1823 by Joseph How in Philadelphia, the engraved portrait very closely resembles the 1810 oil painting completed by Raphaelle Peale after which it was modeled.[40] Reverend Jones, however, had passed away in 1818, five years before the publication and circulation of his engraved portrait. It is unclear precisely what factors prompted the production of the print, though 1823 also witnessed the publication of Reverend Allen's portrait. The delayed publication of the Jones print echoed the delayed 1813 publication of his 1808 *A Thanksgiving Sermon* in Lebanon, Ohio. The sermon sold for six and a quarter cents and spread considerably further than its initially anticipated audience given the description on the title page claiming the publication was "printed for the use of the congregation."[41] Given the sermon's theme of free and enslaved African Americans as persecuted members of society wishing to be recognized as equal before the law, the widespread circulation is precisely what Jones supported. Increased visibility of Black ministers' beliefs and activism reinforced ideas of Black achievement.

Individual and National Salvation in the Gloucester Portraits

In 1823, Reverend John Gloucester of Philadelphia's First African Presbyterian Church would have his portrait published to commemorate Black institutional leadership and the possibilities of emancipation (see Figure 11.5). Like Allen and Jones, Gloucester had been born enslaved and answered the call to religious life. Raised in Tennessee and freed by his slaveowner, he soon attracted a following on the streets of Philadelphia and, like Revs. Allen and Jones, became the first Black ordained minister of

Figure 11.5 W.R. Jones and B. Tanner, *Revd. John Gloucester, Late pastor of the First African Presbyterian Church in Philadelphia.* 1823. Library Company of Philadelphia

his denomination. Gloucester knew Reverend Allen and Reverend Jones well; all three claimed membership in the African Bible Society along with Black antislavery activist Russell Parrott. Each of these Black men published early nineteenth-century pamphlets on the US ban on the international slave trade.[42] The portrait of John Gloucester embodies his religious teachings and educational philosophies. The multiple layers of geometric borders that surrounded Gloucester's portrait create the illusion of a frame while it echoes the classical education that Gloucester championed. Gloucester's raised finger points to the open Bible above his portrait to direct viewers to the words of salvation inscribed therein: "Behold, the Lamb of God which taketh away the sin of the world John 1:29." The line embodies the religious teachings of Gloucester but it is also a choice selection for a postmortem portrait because it was the apostle John who uttered these words as Christ approached him according to biblical verse. While the "sin of the world" typically means original sin, the quotation also evokes the national sin of slavery.

A formerly enslaved man who was a strong antislavery advocate, John Gloucester worked to spread Christianity and end slavery using various strategies throughout his life. Gloucester's portrait conveys his belief that, education, particularly religious education, illuminated the possibilities of

African-descended people in the United States and abroad. Like Jones and Allen, Gloucester also participated in the 1818 commemorations of the abolition of the international slave trade. He delivered the annual address at Bethel church after celebratory participants wound through the streets of Philadelphia.[43] Later, after becoming pastor of his own church in Philadelphia, Gloucester traveled to Salem, Massachusetts to preach. The advertisement for his sermon specifically invited "AFRICANS of this town who are particularly invited to attend and hear a very respectable preacher of their own colour."[44] Unlike the practice of segregating African Americans to the church balcony, Reverend Gloucester made sure that "[t]he whole of the galleries, excepting the singing seats, will be assigned to them."[45] Gloucester preached that the "sin of the world" in the form of racial oppression would have no place in his place of worship.

Gloucester testified to his belief in the power of religious education when he notified the public of a successful, new seminary for young Black men in an 1816 newspaper circular. Augustine Hall provided a "classical and scientific education," and Gloucester made sure to include that the institution had been "long talked of," even discussed among members of the General Assembly of the Presbyterian Church, but that the seminary had been "commenced . . . among the Africans themselves."[46] Gloucester's circular details the process of organizing the school, raising funds, and hiring its principal no doubt to emphasize the capabilities of Black leadership.[47] To emphasize a burgeoning cadre of Black leaders, Gloucester names "five remarkably promising African youth" who studied at Augustine Hall. These included one of his sons, Jeremiah, as well as Richard Allen's son, Richard Jr. Appealing to the widespread contemporary calls for the Christianization of Africa during this era, the circular argues that youthful devotion to the ministry "[is] surely the true way to strengthen the African missions."[48] The promise of the new seminary, Gloucester documented, arose from the broad financial support from Philadelphia's "different denominations," charitable local African Americans, and the 500 African American students in twelve area schools that would "be leaders to Augustine Hall."[49] Reverend Gloucester's leadership continued a tradition of Black Philadelphian ministers building institutions to create avenues for the success of Black communities.

While Gloucester and others were committed to Black freedom as an ideal achieved through separate institutions, many remained ambivalent about a separate nation. A number of Black ministers supported the spread of Christianity in Africa, but a powerful group of Philadelphia's Black pastors made clear their disdain for Black emigration from the United

States. Absalom Jones, Richard Allen, and John Gloucester initially supported emigration in the face of domestic prejudice and foreign prospects, but ultimately they joined a committee that published a list of resolutions condemning emigration in 1817. "Feel[ing] ourselves entitled to participate in the blessings of [the United States]," those who drafted the resolutions make claims of national belonging and criticize emigration plans as "not only cruel, but in direct violation of those principles which have been the boast of the republic."[50] Furthermore, they directly align themselves with the enslaved population of the United States and vow "that we never will separate ourselves voluntarily from the slave population in this country, they are our brethren by the ties of consanguinity, of suffering, and of wrong."[51] Here, the drafters of the resolutions point to unfulfilled ideals of freedom that they experienced as Black people in the United States who shared experiences with the enslaved. While the writers argue that a plan to return to Africa "seems to us a circuitous route to return [us] to perpetual bondage," they write of "the strongest confidence in the justice of God, and the philanthropy of the free states" to deliver them from such schemes.[52] In other words, they trusted their "destinies" to the interworking of divine plan and political activities of the free states.[53] Black freedom, for Reverend Gloucester, began with religious observance, advanced in Black institution-building, and could be fulfilled in the United States. His portrait exhibits religious devotion and African American education, embodied in the figure of an accomplished Black minister, as one promise of Black freedom.

Reverend Jeremiah Gloucester inherited this commitment to institutionalizing Black freedom from his father John, and like his father, Jeremiah commemorated these values with a portrait. Trained at Augustine Hall, Jeremiah Gloucester, received more religious training in Parsippany, New Jersey, under the care of Reverend John Ford in 1817 after passing examinations and "coming well recommended from a number of gentlemen in Philadelphia."[54] He had not yet received his ordination when his father died in May 1822. A large minority of the congregants belonging to the First African Presbyterian Church supported the ascension of Jeremiah to the pulpit after John's death, but congregants expressed an urgent need for an ordained minister.[55] Seventy-five congregants signed a petition to form the Second African Presbyterian Church which was granted, and Reverend Jeremiah Gloucester became its pastor.

The 1828 engraved portrait completed after Jeremiah Gloucester's death bears a striking resemblance to the 1823 engraved portrait of his father (see Figure 11.6). The similarity of the portraits hints at the tumultuous history

Figure 11.6 Robert Tiller, *Revd. Jeremiah Gloucester, Late pastor of the Second African Presbyterian Church in Philadelphia*. 1828. Library Company of Philadelphia

of African Americans in Philadelphia's earliest Black Presbyterian Church. The image of Reverend Jeremiah Gloucester marks him with a visual lineage that many of his followers believed had been denied him in life. The open Bible and its verse, from which rays of light stream forth over Jeremiah's head, say as much. The Hebrews 4:16 verse instructs individuals to use their faith to find grace and mercy in times of need, a directive familiar to the congregation of the First African Presbyterian Church in Philadelphia before its bifurcation. More generally, however, the Bible verse evokes the political activities and oratory of Reverend Jeremiah Gloucester. His portrait contains a reassuring message of the religious and institutional guidance he provided for African Americans in Philadelphia, much like the 1823 portrait of Reverend Allen published during a trying period in his leadership. The portrait also constructs Gloucester as an exemplar of the social, religious, and racial revolutions from which he envisioned African Americans and all Americans would benefit.

The verse from Hebrews invokes Reverend Jeremiah Gloucester's condemnation of slavery and his support for the Revolutionary ideals of freedom and equality. In a speech delivered in January 1823, Gloucester embodied what historian Manisha Sinha has described as "an alternative tradition of political radicalism."[56] Standing before a church congregation, Jeremiah spoke on the abolition of the slave trade, criticized African American emigration to Africa, and denounced slaveholders' vapid conceptions of republicanism.[57] Like Absalom Jones and many Black orators before him, Gloucester describes the long history of free and enslaved people of African descent "striving to unloose every fetter" and calls for renewed efforts to realize the words of the Declaration of Independence and the Constitution.[58] Such criticisms and calls for action echo decades of appeals by Black voices.[59] While Reverend Gloucester stresses multiple threats to Black people, he points to the hopefulness embodied in the gradual emancipation laws passed in several northern states and praises the Haitian Revolution. From the pulpit and in the school that he founded to educate Black children in Philadelphia, Reverend Gloucester practiced and shared his faith as a means to end African Americans' time of need.

Different from his father however, Jeremiah Gloucester's portrait seizes on a different kind of institutionalization. His portrait became a means to memorialize the minister's death and raise funds soon after his passing. Gloucester died at the age of twenty-eight, in January of 1828. By this time, the first African American-edited and operated newspaper, *Freedom's Journal*, had begun operations and assisted in the circulation of Gloucester's portrait. Jeremiah's brother, Stephen Gloucester, learned that members of the public would gladly purchase an engraving of his deceased brother to "render some assistance to [Jeremiah's] widow and children."[60] Stephen solicited subscriptions for this image from individuals in Philadelphia and in New York City via a traveling agent like those who secured subscriptions for literary texts. This business strategy at once signaled the close connections between Black urban communities throughout the northeast as well as the reputation of Jeremiah Gloucester beyond Philadelphia's city limits. *Freedom's Journal* enabled a broad audience connected by the common desire to aid the causes of Black people in the United States. This public extended well beyond the Rev. Gloucester's congregation to include any Christian who read, or caught wind of, the philanthropic cause. This would include those who knew Gloucester from his time in New Jersey and his time delivering orations in several Philadelphia churches. Reported to be an "excellent" likeness of Jeremiah Gloucester modeled after a painted portrait before the Reverend's death, the image cost one dollar, a not insignificant sum.[61] The resulting image bears numerous similarities to an engraving of Jeremiah's father, the Reverend John Gloucester, because "some of [Jeremiah Gloucester's] friends" intimated that a similarly sized engraving "would meet with ready sale."[62] Published in Philadelphia on the Fourth of July, the print was offered for sale in New York City soon thereafter.[63] The transition marked by the founding of the first African American newspaper enabled a stronger connection between honorific images of African Americans and the communities served by *Freedom's Journal.* Its establishment represented the growing strength and resources of Black institutions and their ability to control the means of print production because, as editors John Russwurm and the Rev. Samuel Cornish wrote "[t]oo long have others spoken for us."[64] Their decision "to come boldly before an enlightened publick" was, in part, possible due to the educational campaigns of the early Black ministers of Philadelphia and the cumulative decades of institution-building that they undertook.[65]

Like the publication of *Freedom's Journal*, Jeremiah Gloucester's published oration and portrait embodied the transformative possibilities of education for those of African descent. His references to histories of Portuguese slave traders, the philosophies of Homer and Tacitus, and the political writings of Thomas Jefferson established Gloucester as a learned Black man, an idea that clashed with the stereotypes visible in racial caricatures like Edward Williams Clay's "Life in Philadelphia" prints that appeared in 1828, the same year as Gloucester's portrait. Similar to Phillis Wheatley and other Black intellectuals before him, Jeremiah Gloucester argued for the natural rights of Black Americans, and asserted the incongruity of slavery with the ideas of the Declaration of Independence that, "all men are created equal, endowed by the creator of the universe with certain unalienable rights, such as life, liberty, and the pursuit of happiness."[66] Gloucester addresses his Black audience in Bethel Church, and later readers of his oration, as "fellow citizens" thereby using a rhetorical intervention to correct the failings of the nation state and to incorporate Black people into the body politic. Gloucester's emphasis on citizenship echoes the making of "good citizens" and "countrymen" that Reverend Allen and Reverend Jones detail in previous sermons, but Reverend Gloucester makes explicit connections to the natural rights that people of African descent deserved and demanded.

Jeremiah Gloucester's engagement with the debates over the expansion of slavery in Missouri further underscores his critiques of the nation state and its marginalization of Black people. Much like the Bible verse above Gloucester's portrait, which instructs viewers to practice their faith to discover grace and mercy during trying times, Gloucester urges readers of his oration to scrutinize the rationale for colonization and the simultaneous expansion of slavery westward. He points out that "if they [supporters of colonization] wished slavery entirely abolished, why would they have opened a new avenue in Missouri, for the admission of slaves?"[67] These words illuminate the attacks that, according to Gloucester, people of African descent suffered at the hands of the government. Furthermore, he espouses the idea that the plan for colonization "militates against the liberation of my brethren who are in bondage."[68] In other words, colonization schemes trafficked in empty promises for freedom, in part because Black Americans would be removed from the land of their birth where, in Gloucester's eyes, all were entitled to the "imprescribable rights of man" that enslaved Haitians claimed only a few decades prior.[69] His comparison of the developments that determined the futures of many Black Americans laid bare the treatment of these people by state governments, political organizations, and the federal government.

In addition to his criticisms of contemporary law and social practice regarding Black Americans, Jeremiah Gloucester used religious teachings to argue for racial equality. In his oration, he asks his audience at Mother Bethel a rhetorical question: "But it is said we are not of the same flesh and blood; but I would ask if it is not said in the scripture that God hath made of one blood all nations of men for to dwell on all the face of the earth?" Indeed, the biblical verse present on his portrait both references these challenges faced by African Americans but also evokes Gloucester's own rejoinders to them through his religious leadership and his social activism. His insistence that slavery was a sin, a "horrid crime" that God would judge accordingly, ensured a biblically derived moral standard of accountability familiar to his audience and readers.[70] Preaching about the widespread recognition by unnamed "champions of emancipation"[71] from the moral and religious ills of slavery, Gloucester offers his listeners and readers hope for their future. In triumphant language near the end of his oration, Gloucester proclaims that "the blissful period is just at hand, when we shall be elevated to an equal stand!"[72] Through devout faith, the avoidance of sinful thoughts and activities, and the practice of virtuous acts, Gloucester taught that Providence and government alike would intercede on their behalf.

Less restrained was the optimism Reverend Jeremiah Gloucester exhibited in a January 1820 speech that celebrated an imminent transformation on the horizon for people of African descent. His address to the African Association of New Brunswick, New Jersey, testifies not only to his fervent desire for the spread of Christianity to the continent of Africa, but also that "we soon shall be the heirs of private, public and social benfits [*sic*], and on us beam the sun of science, with ceaseless splendor."[73] Gloucester's words reflect his belief that the organization of Black societies by Black men and women signaled their readiness and worthiness for full participation within the body politic. Such study of the arts, sciences, and rhetoric provided the foundation for Black clergy who Gloucester charged with converting Africans to Christianity. This process would result in Africa "becom[ing] *the* empire of reason and virtue," presumably surpassing all other continents.[74] His optimism was rooted in the campaigns and activists that secured the congressional ban on importing enslaved people into the United States. He pointed to the funding of African societies, the establishment of schools and seminaries for Black youth, and the antislavery campaigns of William Wilberforce, Granville Sharp, and Anthony Benezet, among others as evidence of rapidly approaching opportunity.[75]

The publication and circulation of Reverend Jeremiah Gloucester's 1823 oration served as both a commemoration of the ban on the international slave trade as well as a site of struggle and activism. Familiar with the doubts concerning Black authorship and ability that accompanied early Black publications,[76] Gloucester begins his Philadelphia oration with a preface that lays out the stakes of his speech, writing that "this address is likely to come out to public view." Gloucester attempts to ensure that his words would "be felt as well as heard" and that his publication would not be discounted if "one truth in this be falsified because it is written by me a person of colour."[77] Crafting his literary image as an author humbly communicating "what I have believed to be truth in my secret soul," Gloucester then formulates arguments against the many forms of race prejudice using forceful language that marks his pamphlet as a site of activism.[78] His oration reiterates the representational philosophies of Gloucester's portrait by bearing witness to the power of religious belief and the activism growing in nascent and established Black institutions. The commemorations of the end of the international slave trade and the production of portraits signaled the high values and stakes of Black education, African American political engagement, and visual representation.

Conclusion

The portraits of early Black Philadelphian ministers represent the transformations taking place as African Americans insisted on the actualization of the ideals of the American Revolution. These images represent Black male leaders committed to political inclusion based on values such as education and morality. The portraits presented some of the most respectable individuals as representative of the possibilities of freedom. All formerly enslaved men, the Revs. Absalom Jones, Richard Allen, John Gloucester, and Jeremiah Gloucester displayed the external characteristics that signified internal values marking them as prime candidates for belonging and for full inclusion within the nation. Their educational, religious, and antislavery campaigns lived on in the work that they undertook with none of them experiencing the passage of the Thirteenth Amendment. Yet, the institutions that they built and sustained over the course of decades did. Their portraits underscore the power of commemoration in much the same way that these Black leaders commemorated the ban on the importation of enslaved people into the United States during their tenure as pastors at their churches. Overlaying images of early Black ministers with their speeches and published writings renders a fuller picture of the ways that Black leaders sought to carve out space for themselves and their communities within the United States. The portraits of these early Black religious leaders were key sites to shape and reshape assumptions concerning Black leadership, Black political engagement, and Black religions. Projecting both the interior and exterior characteristics of those depicted, the images served many purposes that included religious education, commemoration, and fundraising. Celebrating freedom, bearing witness to the power of religion, and supporting a subversive racial order, these portraits testify to the power of print and visual culture for African Americans during the first decades of the nineteenth century.

Notes

1 See Erica Armstrong Dunbar, *A Fragile Freedom: African American Women and Emancipation in the Antebellum City* (New Haven: Yale University Press, 2008).

2 Sarah Barringer Gordon highlights the legal rights enabled by incorporation which solidified Black independence from white control during the early years of the African Methodist Episcopal Church in Sarah Barringer Gordon, "The African Supplement: Religion, Race, and Corporate Law in Early National America," *The William and Mary Quarterly* 72, no. 3 (July 2015): 385–422.

3 See Jasmine Nichole Cobb, *Picture Freedom: Remaking Black Visuality in the Early Nineteenth Century* (New York: New York University Press, 2015); John Stauffer, Zoe Trodd, Celeste-Marie Bernier, eds. *Picturing Frederick Douglass: An Illustrated Biography of the Nineteenth Century's Most Photographed American* (New York: W.W. Norton, 2015); Gwendolyn DuBois Shaw, *Portraits of a People: Picturing African Americans in the Nineteenth Century* (Washington, DC: Addison Gallery of American Art, 2006); Joycelyn K.

Moody, "Tactical Lines in Three Black Women's Visual Portraits, 1773–1849," *a/b: Auto/Biography Studies* 30, no. 1 (2015): 67–98.

4 Moody, "Tactical Lines," 74.

5 David Waldstreicher, *In the Midst of Perpetual Fetes: The Making of American Nationalism, 1776–1820* (Chapel Hill: University of North Carolina Press, 1997), 331–345 and John Wood Sweet, *Bodies Politic: Negotiating Race in the American North, 1730–1830* (Philadelphia: University of Pennsylvania Press, 2004), 378–390. On "public blackness," see Corey Capers, "Black Voices, White Print: Racial Practice, Print Publicity, and Order in the Early American Republic," in *Early African American Print Culture*, eds. Lara Langer Cohen and Jordan Alexander Stein (Philadelphia: University of Pennsylvania Press, 2012), 111.

6 Waldstreicher, *In the Midst*, 329–330.

7 Richard S. Newman, *Freedom's Prophet: Bishop Richard Allen, the AME Church, and the Black Founding Fathers* (New York: New York University Press, 2008), 11.

8 Ibid., 51.

9 For more on Allen's wealth, which grew from property acquisition and small business enterprises, see Gary B. Nash, *Forging Freedom; The Formation of Philadelphia's Black Community, 1740–1820* (Cambridge, MA: Harvard University Press, 1988), 153–159.

10 "Rev. Richard Allen, founder of the American Methodist Episcopal Church, in the United States of America, 1779." Watson's Annals Manuscript [Yi2 1069.F.276]. Library Company of Philadelphia. Emphasis original.

11 Moody, "Tactical Lines," 73–75.

12 Philip Sheldon Foner and Robert J. Branham, eds., *Lift Every Voice: African American Oratory, 1787–1900* (Tuscaloosa: University of Alabama Press, 1998), 57–58.

13 Ibid., 57–58.

14 Ibid., 57–58.

15 For more about Allen's guiding principles of Christian moralism and liberation theology, see Newman, *Freedom's Prophet*, 9.

16 David McNeely Stauffer, *American Engravers upon Copper and Steel: Part II, Check-list of the Works of the Earlier Engravers* (New York City: The Grolier Club, 1907), 48.

17 For a very thorough description of the secession and reunification plans, along with Tudas and Allen's printed assaults on one another, see Newman, *Freedom's Prophet*, 211–227.

18 Sojourner Truth and Frederick Douglass are later examples of African Americans' pointed and self-conscious creation of multiple portraits to shape public perception of themselves. See Darcy Grimaldo Grigsby, *Enduring Truths: Sojourner's Shadows and Substance* (Chicago: University of Chicago Press, 2015) and Stauffer et al., *Picturing Frederick Douglass*.

19 "The Society of Free People of Colour," *Poulson's American Daily Advertiser* (Philadelphia, PA), September 18, 1804, 3.

20 Ibid.
21 "Education.," *Poulson's American Daily Advertiser* (Philadelphia, PA), October 22, 1804, 4.
22 "We the Subscribers," *Philadelphia Gazette and University Daily Advertiser* (Philadelphia, PA), March 8, 1794, Supplement, 2.
23 "Extract," *Relf's Philadelphia Gazette* (Philadelphia, PA), Aug. 1, 1810: 2.
24 "All Persons Indebted," *Philadelphia Gazette and Universal Daily Advertiser* (Philadelphia, PA), February 24, 1798, 3 and "Notice," *United States Gazette* (Philadelphia, PA), November 4, 1806, 4.
25 "A charity sermon," *Claypoole's American Daily Advertiser* (Philadelphia, PA), October 5, 1797, 3.
26 For more about the speeches given to commemorate the outlawing of the importation of slaves into the United States, see Mitch Kachun, *Festivals of Freedom: Memory and Meaning in African American Emancipation Celebrations, 1808–1915* (Amherst, MA: University of Massachusetts Press, 2003) and for their place within a growing literature of the early Black Atlantic, see Joseph Rezek, "The Orations on the Abolition of the Slave Trade and the Uses of Print in the Early Black Atlantic," *Early American Literature* 45, no. 3 (2010): 655–682.
27 Absalom Jones, *A Thanksgiving Sermon* (Philadelphia, PA: Fry and Kammerer, 1808), 8.
28 Ibid., 11.
29 Ibid., 16.
30 Ibid., 21.
31 Ibid., 20.
32 Ibid., 18.
33 Ibid., 19.
34 Ibid., 16.
35 Ibid., 17.
36 "At a numerous and respectable meeting," *Poulson's American Daily Advertiser* (Philadelphia, PA), January 1, 1808, 3.
37 Jones, *Thanksgiving*, 21.
38 Absalom Jones and Richard Allen, *A Narrative of the Proceedings of the Black People, during the Late Awful Calamity in Philadelphia, in the Year 1793: And a Refutation of Some Censures, Thrown upon Them in Some Late Publications* (Philadelphia, PA: William W. Woodward, 1794).
39 Jacqueline Bacon, "Rhetoric and Identity in Absalom Jones and Richard Allen's 'Narrative of the Proceedings of the Black People, during the Late Awful Calamity in Philadelphia,'" *Pennsylvania Magazine of History and Biography* 125, no. 1/2 (January–April 2001): 61–90 and Newman, *Freedom's Prophet*, 123–126.
40 Stauffer, *American Engravers*, 254–255.
41 "Just Published," *Western Star* (Lebanon, OH), August 19, 1813, 8.

42 Bible Society of Philadelphia, *The Eighth Report of the Bible Society of Philadelphia. Read before the Society, May 1st, A.D. 1816* (Philadelphia, PA: William Fry, 1816), 18.
43 "The anniversary celebration of the abolition of the Slave Trade," *Gazette* (Philadelphia, PA), December 31, 1817, 3.
44 "African Meeting," *Gazette* (Salem, MA), August 28, 1812, 3.
45 Ibid.
46 "Circular," *Relfs Philadelphia Gazette* (Philadelphia, PA), July 13, 1816, 2.
47 Sojourner Truth, Robert Douglass Jr., and Patrick Henry Reason among many other nineteenth-century African American activists sold images as a means to support themselves and their activism. See Grigsby, *Enduring Truths* and Aston Gonzalez, "The Art of Racial Politics: The Work of Robert Douglass Jr., 1833–46," *Pennsylvania Magazine of History and Biography* 138, no. 1 (January 2014): 5–37.
48 "Circular," *Relfs Philadelphia Gazette* (Philadelphia, PA), July 13, 1816, 2.
49 Ibid.
50 "At a numerous meeting," *National Advocate* (New York, NY), August 15, 1817, 1.
51 Ibid.
52 Ibid.
53 Ibid.
54 Edward Dorr Griffin, *A Plea for Africa. A sermon preached October 26, 1817, in the First Presbyterian Church in the City of New-York* (New York: Gould, 1819), 68–69.
55 William T. Catto, *A Semi-Centenary Discourse, Delivered in the First African Presbyterian Church, Philadelphia, on the Fourth Sabbath of May, 1857* (Philadelphia, PA: Joseph M. Wilson, 1857), 68–81.
56 Manisha Sinha, "To 'Cast Just Obliquy' on Oppressors: Black Radicalism in the Age of Revolution," *The William and Mary Quarterly* 64, no. 1 (January 2007): 160.
57 Jeremiah Gloucester, *An Oration, Delivered on January 1, 1823 in Bethel Church: On the Abolition of the Slave Trade* (Philadelphia, PA: John Young, 1823).
58 Ibid., 10.
59 Sinha, "To 'Cast Just Obliquy,'" 149–160.
60 "To the Christian Public," *Freedom's Journal*, March 14, 1828, 3.
61 Ibid.
62 Ibid.
63 "Late Rev. Mr. Gloucester," *Freedom's Journal*, July 18, 1828, 6.
64 "To Our Patrons," *Freedom's Journal*, March 16, 1827, 1.
65 Ibid.
66 Jeremiah Gloucester, *An Oration, Delivered on January 1, 1823 in Bethel Church: On the Abolition of the Slave Trade* (Philadelphia, PA: John Young, 1823), 13.
67 Ibid., 14.

68 Ibid.
69 Ibid.,10.
70 Ibid.,11.
71 Ibid., 8.
72 Ibid.,15.
73 Jeremiah Gloucester, "Address, 1820 January 1, to the African Association of New Brunswick, New Jersey," 3. Mss. 09517b. Connecticut Historical Society.
74 Ibid.
75 Ibid., 1.
76 This was certainly true of Phillis Wheatley and the tribunal before which she was subjected in order to prove her ability to conceive of and write her *Poems on Various Subjects.*
77 Jeremiah Gloucester, *An Oration, Delivered on January 1, 1823 in Bethel Church: On the Abolition of the Slave Trade* (Philadelphia, PA: John Young, 1823), iv.
78 Ibid.

CHAPTER 12

Visual Insubordination within Early African American Portraiture and Illustrated Books

Martha J. Cutter

In early nineteenth-century visual history of the United States, African Americans were rarely represented as empowered. As Simon Gikandi and others have noted, they have often been shunted to the margins of visual culture in order to represent the ways in which white individuals attain civility.[1] Following Toni Morrison, we might say that in such an imaging, African Americans form the pictorial ground upon which the free, civilized white man establishes his identity.[2] African Americans most often have been depicted as objects in transatlantic visual culture, represented by both abolitionists and non-abolitionists as tortured bodies or as formulaic individuals with little particularity, such as in the ubiquitous reward posters for runaway slaves that repeated the image of the fugitive with his knapsack on his shoulder over and over again throughout the seventeenth, eighteenth, and nineteenth centuries. Even in freedom, as Jasmine Nichole Cobb and Marcus Wood have noted, African Americans have often been depicted in a mocking and caricatured way to imply that they are not fit or worthy subjects of democracy.[3] One such example of this mocking mode is Edward W. Clay's popular *Life in Philadelphia* series of racist caricature cartoons, such as the *Grand Celebration ob De Bobalition ob African Slabery* (1833), which ridicules the pretensions of free African Americans who copy and exaggerate the manners and dress of upper-class whites.[4] The import of Clay's cartoon series is to suggest that African Americans can never rise out of slavery and take their place as responsible citizens.

Given a pervasive derogatory historical context in which African Americans were portrayed as stereotyped, abject, or on the margins of society, we might wonder where we can locate in early American visual culture images that represent African Americans (whether free or enslaved) as agentive in and of themselves and central to US culture. After tracing the objectification of the enslaved within the dominant tradition of Anglo-European visual representations from 1780 to 1840, this chapter examines an early insubordinate mode of visual production within illustrated African

American materials. It first scrutinizes frontispieces contained within books by enslaved or formerly enslaved individuals such as Phillis Wheatley and Olaudah Equiano and compares and contrasts these frontispieces with less-known portraits and illustrations of African Americans such as Elizabeth Freeman (also known as MumBet, who was one of the first enslaved African Americans to win a freedom suit in Massachusetts) and Peter Wheeler (whose 1839 memoir *Chains and Freedom* details his history in slavery, escape, travels to the West Indies and Europe, and conversion to Christianity). Next, this chapter examines the illustrated antislavery books of activists Moses Roper and Henry Bibb (both of which also contain frontispieces as well as other types of illustrations). Although Roper's book was published in 1837 and Bibb's in 1849, this chapter argues that both men (being born in 1815 and having participated in the antislavery movement) were responding to and revising the abject treatment of African Americans in earlier visual materials.

In works such as frontispieces and illustrated books, this chapter locates what Michael Chaney has termed "the subtle but meaningful trace of a visual field contrary to the one established by the twin hegemonies of abolition and slavery"[5] and an argument made by the interaction between words and pictures. The words of the text interact with its pictures or drawings to interpellate or hail the reader and envision a figurative mode of agency and self-possession for the enslaved or free African American. In so doing, these materials visually begin to counter the trauma of slavery. As *revenants* (individuals who have returned from the social death of slavery and are now living in freedom) these authors present a mobile, living, and complex image of African American identity.[6] If we read carefully between the lines of the texts, then, we see an assertion of resistance that subverts the dominant codes governing African American visuality and the creation of new visual technologies in which African Americans are portrayed as gaining agency and equality. The defiant mode of visual technology in these early nineteenth-century texts may enable the more spectacular and well-known acts of visual insubordination that we find in mid-nineteenth-century individuals such as Frederick Douglass and Sojourner Truth, discussed briefly at the end of this chapter.

African Americans in the Dominant Visual Rhetoric of the US and England, 1780–1840

Pier Gabrielle Foreman argues that images of enslaved and free Africans and African Americans often attempted to "codify racial difference . . .

[and] resolve tensions between ontology and epistemology" through a visual-biological determinism.[7] To put this even more plainly, African Americans were visualized as abject, inferior, brutalized bodies, criminals, and hermits; or, they were exiled to the peripheries of social space.

Marginalization of African Americans is evident in some of the most famous portraits of the United States' founding fathers. For example, a celebrated 1780 painting of George Washington by John Trumbull includes his slave, William Lee, whom Washington had purchased in 1786 and did not free until Washington's death in 1799. Lee was the only one of Washington's 124 slaves freed outright in his will; the remaining slaves owned by Washington were to be freed upon the death of Martha Washington.[8] In Trumbull's portrait of Washington, Lee is just visible in the painting as a bright red turbaned figure in the back right corner. Lee's presence there – he stands in the margin of the painting – is meant to foreground Washington's heroic and larger than life status; Washington appears to stand (quite literally) on higher ground, and his huge size makes Lee look all the more diminutive. Lee is in the painting, but not the subject of the painting, and the expression on his face is hard to read; he appears to look at Washington with something bordering on reverence and awe. By this mechanism, Lee's status as the enslaved not-quite-subject shores up Washington's position as a heroic, aristocratic, and civilized man. Lee's existence in the perimeter of the portrait is an example of what Gikandi has called "the presence/absence of the slave in the American world picture."[9] Interestingly, this painting was the first authoritative representation of Washington that Europeans saw, and it was soon copied throughout the Continent.

Often, African Americans were represented in portraits, paintings, and other forms of visual iconography as degraded and wretched bodies or tortured objects. Famous broadsides such as *Description of a Slave Ship* (1789) depict African Americans as little more than matchstick bodies inside the confining hold of a slave ship.[10] The scientific precision of this famous copper engraving and the careful lines in it do little to inculcate a sense that *human beings* are trafficked by slavers. Yet the engraving was an incredibly popular document in the abolition movement, both in England and the United States; *Description of A Slave Ship* was reprinted in various forms more than 10,000 times between March and April of 1789 in the United States, the United Kingdom, and other locations.[11]

The enslaved were also frequently represented in graphic ways as tortured bodies, as Marcus Wood has extensively documented.[12] For example, one infamous 1792 painting by Isaac Cruikshank depicts an incident in which an enslaved African girl was beaten to death for refusing to dance naked on the deck of a slave ship with the ironic name *Recovery*. The renowned British abolitionist William Wilberforce denounced the captain of this ship, John Kimber, before the House of Commons over the incident. Kimber was brought up on charges before the High Court of Admiralty in June 1792 but was ultimately acquitted of all charges.[13] This painting – titled *The Abolition of the Slave Trade Or the Inhumanity of Dealers in Human Flesh Exemplified in Captn. Kimber's Treatment of a Young Negro Girl of 15 for her Virjen [sic.] Modesty* – was part of the attack made on Kimber's practices and on the inhumanity and barbarism of slavery, yet how does it formulate its attack from a visual standpoint? On the one hand, the woman depicted is clearly suffering. Yet the painting is almost pornographic, as a viewer can gaze on a whipped yet comely young woman. Her protruding nipples and buttocks might become focal points for an observer's gaze. In the illustration we see not only the tortured naked woman but also three other naked women who sit in the background looking on, and who even appear to be laughing at the shy virgin's modesty and pain. At least five people in the picture stare at the woman, and the implication is that they are scrutinizing her scantily clothed genitalia. While the painting is meant to protest the treatment of this woman, it replicates familiar divisions common in British and US visual culture concerning slavery in which tortured, passive, African American bodies are the object of the (white) empowered viewer's gaze.[14] The woman herself is portrayed in this image as being only a mute cipher, which silently reflects back the effects of the master's power on the subjugated body.

Some of these pieces of visual culture would become famous, and clearly they evoke pity at a spectacle of torture. Yet perhaps they fail to promote empathy, defined in its most basic form as "the power of understanding and imaginatively entering into another person's feelings."[15] As many critics have noted, in the nineteenth century the spectacle of enslaved torture – of what was termed "sentimental wounding" – often positioned the enslaved as "erotic objects of sympathy rather than subjects in their own right"[16] and fueled an "allure of bondage" which replicated physical enslavement.[17] We can see the way abolitionists deployed sentimental wounding in a painting such as *The Abolition of the Slave Trade Or the Inhumanity of Dealers in Human Flesh.* Some viewers may have found this painting of a tortured yet attractive young girl more pleasurable than painful to look upon; moreover, because the woman is given no voice or gaze, it may be difficult to unite with her on a human level, and difficult to imaginatively enter into her emotional state.

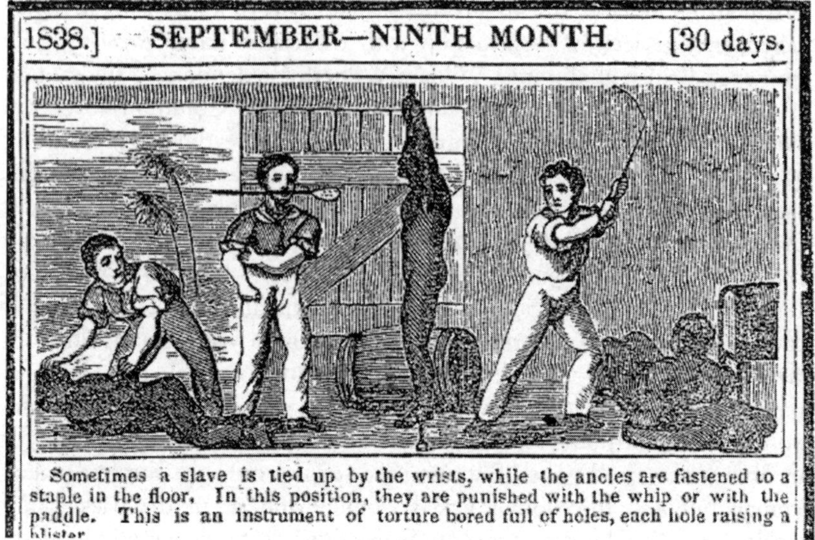

Figure 12.1 *Slave Torture* in *The Anti-Slavery Almanac* vol. 1.3 (1838); N. page. Wood engraving. *The Public Domain Review*. https://publicdomainreview.org/collections/the-american-anti-slavery-almanac-for-1838/. Public Domain

Like British abolitionists, US abolitionists often portrayed the enslaved as tortured bodies lacking agency and objects of the gaze; in so doing they replicated what Cobb refers to as the "peculiarly ocular institution" of slavery by entwining the racial and the visual.[18] For example, in an illustration from the 1838 issue of *The Anti-Slavery Almanac*, the nude enslaved man who is hung up and tortured is barely recognizable as a human being. The two enslaved individuals on the ground appear to be supine and powerless (see Figure 12.1).

The caption of the illustration speaks for the tortured, debased individual: "Sometimes a slave is tied up by the wrists, while the ancles [*sic*] are fastened to a staple in the floor." The enslaved man lacks a name and a voice; neither protest, nor lamentation, nor words of the enslaved are represented. Again, an almost scientific or educational tone seems to override the fact that *human beings* are being tortured: "In this position, they are punished with the whip or with the paddle. This is an instrument of torture bored full of holes, each hole raising a blister." Such an illustration replicates the notion of abasement and makes the enslaved the center of surveillance for the reader and three white onlookers who gaze on the body. While documenting abuse, this abolitionist illustration appears to evade the subjectivity of the enslaved and to call for knowledge of, rather than empathy for, the slave's plight.

Moreover, at work in the larger abolition movement, on both sides of the Atlantic, was a persistent strand of visual imaging which asked white men and women to create the humanity of the enslaved; in so doing, this imagery implied that African Americans lacked an a priori identity (as men or women), and that it was up to white men and women to enact it. A famous 1787 antislavery medallion created by Josiah Wedgwood, a pottery crafter and nonconformist, for instance, featured an enslaved man on his knees with the phrase, "Am I Not a Man and a Brother?"; this image was incredibly popular in the eighteenth and nineteenth centuries, adorning a variety of objects such as sugar bowls, patch boxes, aprons, and even hair pins.[19] In this visual formation, the slave is always down on his or her knees, begging that a white viewer recognize or even grant his or her human identity.

The image was also remodeled for the specific purpose of US state abolition societies. In 1800 the New-Jersey Society Promoting the Abolition of Slavery created a membership certificate in which a well-dressed white man gestures towards a naked and chained supplicant slave while holding a Bible opened to Isaiah 63.1, which reads, "He came to proclaim liberty to the captives, and the opening of the prison to them that are bound" (see Figure 12.2). As if to bless this example of white benevolence towards the enslaved, beams from Heaven shine down upon the pair through an aperture in the clouds; quite literally, the civilized, religious white man is here enlightening the primitive and apparently heathen African American, who appears in little but a loin cloth and chains.

The supplicant slave image was popular with other abolition societies in the United States. As Sharon Patton notes, the New York Anti-Slavery Society sponsored the African American engraver Patrick Reason to study engraving techniques in London. In 1839, Reason copied Wedgwood's image in a copper engraving but modified its composition (see Figure 12.3). The pleading, supplicant slave now has more clothing on his figure, but he is still down on his knees and in chains, with his hands clasped in prayer in front of him. He appears to look "off-screen" to someone (presumably a white viewer) who can answer the question "Am I Not a Man and Brother" affirmatively and grant his full humanity. Patrick Reason would go on to construct images of African Americans as tasteful, dignified, literate subjects (such as his 1849 portrait of Henry

Figure 12.2 Membership Certificate from the New-Jersey Society Promoting the Abolition of Slavery. Ca. 1800. Stipple Engraving. Library Company of Philadelphia. Used with permission

Figure 12.3 Patrick Reason, *Am I Not a Man and a Brother* (1839). Copper engraving. Collection of the Moorland-Spingarn Center, Howard University, Washington, DC. Used with permission

Bibb, discussed later in this chapter).[20] Yet the enslaved man depicted in this 1839 image reflects what Mikhail Bakhtin might call a grotesque or low body, "unfinished" and "open to the outside world."[21] Peter Stallybrass and Allon White argue for a reading of the body in which "high discourses" of the classical, finished, closed body are "structured in relation to the debasements and degradations" of low discourse and bodies,[22] and we may view such a politics of the body at work in Reason's image. The viewer's perspective is directed at the slave, an object of exchange within cultural discourse, who pleads for a granting of his unfinished subjectivity and in so doing affirms a viewer's status as someone who is complete and not debased or commodified.

As a group, enslaved Africans Americans also entered US visual culture via their rebellions and revolts. Here their criminality and brutality were often emphasized, rather than their heroism, and they often became objects to be looked at rather than authors or speakers in their own right. Most famously, Nat Turner, who led a successful slave uprising in 1831 in Virginia, was depicted within US visual culture as either a savage or a coward.[23] And the Amistad individuals, who were falsely enslaved, and who rebelled on board the slave ship *Amistad* in 1839, were depicted in a variety of ways within the text of John Barber's *History of the Amistad Captives* (1840); however, a famous colored illustration of them that was published within Barber's text circulated independently and mainly emphasized their savagery and violence.[24] The Amistad rebels do not author this text or control its illustrations, so they remain the object of a white person's gaze, rather than gazers, speakers, or authors in their own right.

Yet it was not only the enslaved who were portrayed as debased within early transatlantic visual culture. African Americans also entered visual culture as criminals, murders, and hermits. For instance, in *Dying Confession of Pomp, A Negro Man, Who Was Executed at Ipswich, on the 6th August, 1795, for Murdering Capt. Charles Furbush, of Andover, Taken from the Mouth of the Prisoner, and Penned by Jonathan Plummer* (1795), Pomp is portrayed just after his execution in a crude illustration where he hangs from hastily built gallows; this is the only image of Pomp that a viewer sees, and he is already a dead and convicted criminal.[25]

Another unflattering imaging of African Americans occurs in the story of Robert the Hermit, also known as Robert Voorhis, a man who had escaped from slavery and lived in the woods of Massachusetts as a recluse for many years. In the frontispiece to Voorhis's *Life and Adventures of*

Figure 12.4 Frontispiece of *Life and Adventures of Robert, the Hermit of Massachusetts: Who Has Lived 14 Years in a Cave, Secluded from Human Society: Comprising, an Account of his Birth, Parentage, Sufferings, and Providential Escape from Unjust and Cruel Bondage in Early Life, and His Reasons for Becoming a Recluse* (Providence: Printed for H. Trumbull, 1829). *Documenting the American South*. https://docsouth.unc.edu/neh/robert/robert.html. Public Domain

Robert, the Hermit of Massachusetts: Who Has Lived 14 Years in a Cave, Secluded from Human Society: Comprising, an Account of his Birth, Parentage, Sufferings, and Providential Escape from Unjust and Cruel Bondage in Early Life, and His Reasons for Becoming a Recluse (1829), Voorhis is foregrounded in the center of the picture, but he looks away from a viewer with a distraught expression on his face.[26] His clothing is shabby and his abode in the background is diminutive, looking more like a kennel for an animal than a home for a human being (see Figure 12.4).

In the narrative, Voorhis comes across as eccentric and depressed, defined by the trauma of enslavement, even though he has been free for many years. Henry Trumbull, who took down the narrative, describes Voorhis as living in a "gloomy cell" that has "but one or two apertures or loopholes, for the admission of lights which in winter are completely closed (as is every crack and crevice) with seaweed–this renders the apartment still more dark and gloomy than it otherwise would be, as when the door is closed to expel the cold, Voorhis remains within, day and night, in almost total darkness."[27] Symbolically, we might read this passage as implying that Voorhis has shut himself up in mental darkness, and this again emphasizes the abject quality of his depiction on both a visual and textual level.

Unlike Voorhis, Potter Jackson was never a slave, but he was cruelly beaten while onboard a British ship and wrote about it in graphic detail in a pamphlet titled *The Remarkable Case of Potter Jackson, (formerly steward of the Echo sloop of war): Giving an Account of the Most Cruel Treatment, he Received from Captain Lively, (commander of the Lord Stanly slave-ship) and his chief mate, by assaulting, imprisoning, putting in irons, and cruelly flogging him . . Written by Himself* (1806).[28] The title of Jackson's narrative asserts a type of linguistic opposition to the cruel flogging, insisting that Jackson refuses to be dehumanized by it, but instead writes about it. Jackson also sued Captain Livesly in court, and was granted a judgement of 500 pounds. Yet the pamphlet focuses extensively on the torture and on the many times that the Captain calls Jackson a "black bastard" or a "black devil," which seems to be the sole reason for the torture. The frontispiece portrait also confines itself to demarcating his torture; in it Jackson looks away from the viewer and is the object of the gaze. He is defined by his scarred back and his naked, whipped body. Because no facial features are delineated and he looks away from the viewer, Jackson, like the woman tortured by Kimber in *The Abolition of the Slave Trade*, becomes more of an *object* arguing for a cause than a person in his own right. The images define him solely as a tortured and flayed body.

As the above illustrations make evident, in the transatlantic imagination and in the early history of the United States, African Americans – whether enslaved or free – are often portrayed through images of torture, abjection, criminality, debasement, and marginalization. Within both pro- and antislavery discourses, moreover, they are often silent or spoken about rather than speaking themselves. They lack the power to gaze and often (it seems) to define themselves as fully human. Many of these drawings did have the goal of ending slavery, but at what cost to African American identity? Messages were overlaid onto the bodies being depicted, and these messages rarely granted agency, humanity, or subjectivity to African Americans.

Resistance to the Dominant Visual Rhetoric of Abjection in African American Portraits and Frontispieces

Even before the middle nineteenth century, however, scholars can locate nodes of visual resistance to the abjection present in the dominant imaging of African Americans. There were four primary modes of defiance present in African American visual culture before 1840: textual visual resistance, portraits, frontispieces, and illustrated books. Textual visual resistance is comprised of words, letters, and unusual typography that visually "scream" at the reader, interpellating him or her forcibly and even with a degree of violence. Such a visual scream is evident, for example, in David Walker's incendiary *Appeal* (1829), which uses pointing fingers, exclamation points, brackets, and capital letters to shout at the reader and compel rebellion, as Marcy J. Dinius has shown.[29]

More commonly, visual resistance echoes forth from the frontispieces of antislavery texts and portraits associated with (sometimes formerly) enslaved authors. Formal portraits of these authors were often crafted with dignity and taste to emphasize their literacy, freedom, and decorum. Such frontispieces have a long pedigree, going back at least to a famous 1768 oil painting by Thomas Gainsborough of Ignatius Sancho, a former British slave who became a composer, actor, and writer. Gainsborough was perhaps the most well-known painter of the eighteenth century, so a portrait by him was a mark of the subject's cultural significance. Gainsborough's portrait of Sancho shows him in elegant clothing comprised of rich fabric and bright colors. Sancho looks away from the viewer, off to the viewer's left, but his gaze is not abject, and he does not seem to be an object of either pity or commercial exchange. The portrait was used to create the frontispiece for Sancho's volume, *The Letters of the Late Ignatius Sancho, an African*, which appeared in 1782 and in 1803 and was engraved by Francesco Bartolozzi.[30]

Gainsborough's portrait of Sancho may have set a precedent because from this date forward it became more common to have frontispieces in works by African Americans that featured them not as objects of exchange, but as individuals with taste, intelligence, and (often) literacy. The frontispiece portrait of *The Interesting Narrative of the Life of Olaudah Equiano, Or Gustavus Vassa, the African, Written by Himself* (first published in 1789) pictures the author as a literate and tasteful subject.[31] The title of this work never calls Equiano a slave and insists that the piece is "written by himself," pointing to Equiano's control of both his literacy and his representation. In this famous portrait, Equiano holds the Bible in his hand, turned to the book of Acts, suggesting both his literacy and his ability to *act* for himself. He is elegantly dressed and he looks out of the portrait, regarding the reader evenly and patiently. He avoids the downcast gaze present in so many other eighteenth- and nineteenth-century images of African Americans, and he is not being tortured or whipped. This is an image of a man who has fashioned himself according to his own dictates, rather than being fashioned by his enslaver. He is a subject capable of reading and writing rather than an object who is merely written into the master's discourse or marked upon by the master's whip.[32] Equiano's *Narrative* went through nine editions in his lifetime and was widely read in England, Russia, Germany, Holland, and the United States. Equiano's portrait was also popular and reused as late as 1829, in Abigail Field Mott's edited, illustrated, and substantively rewritten abridgment of *The Interesting Narrative of the Life of Olaudah Equiano; or, Gustavus Vassa, the African, Written by Himself.*[33]

Phillis Wheatley's frontispiece portrait in *Poems on Various Subjects, Religious and Moral by Phillis Wheatley, Negro Servant to Mr. John Wheatley, of Boston, in New England* (1773)[34] was also extremely popular and reproduced into the 1830s in books that she authored.[35] At times attributed to an African American artist, Scipio Moorhead, this illustration shows Wheatley in a stylish dress (possibly a maid's uniform) with a neat cap on her head and a thin necklace. She engages in the activity of thinking (with her hand on her cheek) and writing (with a quill pen in her hand); a book also sits on the desk in front of her, possibly a Bible, as if she has been consulting it (another symbol of her literacy). Wheatley does not look directly at the viewer, but neither does she look down or away, as in many depictions of slave torture or in the famous icon of the supplicant slave. Rather, she seems lost in her own world of thought, perhaps imagining her own poetry. It is a peculiarly private portrait in that the viewer goes unacknowledged. In a society that viewed African Americans as innately inferior to whites and routinely denied literacy and education to African Americans (whether free or enslaved), such imaging of Wheatley and Equiano as writers would have had a huge visual impact.[36] In taking control of the pen, Equiano and Wheatley took power over their own destinies and fates; more symbolically, they also insist in their texts on their right to be understood and visualized as fully human, literate subjects, equal to Anglo-Americans in every way.

Beyond literacy, there were other ways in which the enslaved or formerly enslaved counteracted the social death that was slavery and insisted on their full humanity. In some portraits African Americans return the gaze of the viewer, refusing to be only looked at, the objects of the gaze, but also *looking back*. Elizabeth Freeman, or "MumBet," successfully sued for her freedom in Massachusetts in 1780, and her suit was a key factor in outlawing slavery in this state.[37] More than thirty years after her successful suit, in 1812, when she was 70, she sat for her portrait, a beautiful miniature watercolor on ivory painted by Susan Anne Livingston Ridley Sedgwick.[38] Freeman, now a free woman, wears a necklace with gold beads in it. Her decision to sit for a portrait with this sign of wealth on her body represents, as Cobb argues, a "conscious invocation of the visual on her part, a moment in which she applied her sense of self-possession to the terms of looking and being seen that, in part, defined chattel slavery."[39] She is well dressed, in a sumptuous blue and a white silk headdress. Her expression is difficult to read, but it most definitely is *not* patient or calming; eyes wide open, she seems to defy a viewer, asking not for empathy but equality, which was the case in her own life. Nicholas Mirzoeff argues that modern ways of seeing emerged out of slavery: "The ordering of slavery was a combination of violent enforcement and visualized surveillance that sustained a new colonial order of things." This "plantation complex" (1660–1860) granted the right to look to the overseer and his representatives, while literally or symbolically blinding the enslaved; slavery functions in part through the "removal of the right to look," and the insistence that the tortured object is always the object of the gaze.[40] So it is crucial that Freeman's portrait asserts the right to look.

A similar right to look is manifested in the frontispiece of Peter Wheeler's *Chains and Freedom: Or, The Life and Adventures of Peter Wheeler, a Colored Man Yet Living. A Slave in Chains, a Sailor on the Deep, and a Sinner at the Cross* (1839).[41] Wheeler's text depicts his birth in slavery in New Jersey, his promised freedom upon his mistress's death, and then his illegal sale in New York State, where he grew into adulthood in slavery. His memoir demonstrates that slavery was not merely a southern phenomenon. Wheeler went on to become a mariner, a domestic servant, and an author, although his emancipation from slavery is never clear.[42]

Wheeler's text has some unusual typographical features such as those used in Walker's *Appeal* – pointing hands, italics, asterisks, and exclamation points. Most daringly, the text exerts visual defiance (as Harriet Jacobs will also do in her 1861 autobiography, *Incidents in the Life of a Slave Girl*)[43] by reproducing a version of the illegal sale of his own person (Wheeler was freed on his mistress's death, but then taken illegally back into slavery). In his rewritten version of this advertisement for his sale, he appends these comments: "You see they put me on the stock-list!! Well,

Figure 12.5 Frontispiece of Charles Edwards Lester and Peter Wheeler, *Chains and Freedom; or, The Life and Adventures of Peter Wheeler, a Colored Man Yet Living* (1839). *Internet Archive.* https://archive.org/details/chainsfreedomorloolest/page/n7. Public Domain

when the day came that I was to be sold, oh! how I felt! I knew it warn't *right*, but what could *I* do? *I was a black boy*." We can hear Wheeler's indignation at being put on the "stock-list !!" and pointing hands in the text draw emphasis to his illegal sale.[44] Reading between the lines, we can locate a type of visual textual resistance that (like Walker's *Appeal*) creates an unusual typographical scream.

Defiance of the abjection of slavery is also evident in the frontispiece to the narrative, which is unlike any other discussed so far (see Figure 12.5). Even more than Elizabeth Freeman (whose head is tilted slightly to the left), Wheeler looks directly at the observer, and his stare is candid and unnerving. In discussing photographs in which the individual looks at the viewer, Ariella Azoulay argues that such images may formulate a series of questions for the viewer: "Why are these men, women, children, and families looking at me? . . . At whom, precisely, did they seek to look– was it truly at me? And why? What am I supposed to do with their look? What is the foundation of the gaze I might turn back toward them?" She argues as well that this looking back may gesture towards a realm in which relationships between the viewed and the viewer are not mediated by the dominant power but instead by a type of civil contract which presupposes or imagines a new conceptual framework of partnership and solidarity between the oppressed and the witness.[45] This may be a virtual or symbolic partnership (rather than an actual and localized one), but it is possible that Wheeler's glance here is gesturing to a hypothetical community of readers who can understand the political content of his gaze and respond to it with something like solidarity with an African American and antislavery readership.

Equiano, Wheatley, Freeman, and Wheeler transgress the ocular structure of slavery by portraying themselves not as marginal, abject, or tortured objects, but as subjects in full possession of their bodies and psyches, subjects who can in various ways manipulate visual culture for their own purposes and goals. They are agents who can gaze, read, or write, and who possess full personhood, despite the dominant socio-historical visual matrix that envisions them only as brutalized, gazed-upon objects.

Opposition to the Dominant Visual Culture in African American Illustrated Books: The *Revenant*

Illustrated books written by African Americans also strongly possess the power of the gaze, creating visual resistance by using an interaction between words and images.[46] It is often necessary to closely examine the relationship between words and text to locate this defiance because these works employ images, captions, and narrative to move a reader towards interrelationship with the enslaved. In a discussion of Frederick Douglass's use of photography, Laura Wexler writes: "Douglass believed that the formerly enslaved could reverse the social death that defined slavery with another objectivizing flash: this time creating a positive image of the social life of freedom and proving that African American consciousness had been there all along." Moreover, Wexler argues that as "an avatar of social progress, the photographic *revenant* enlivened the present and hails a better world."[47] Yet this objectivizing flash – and this hailing of a better world – may also be present in non-photographic visual texts. The objectivizing flash that Wexler speaks of might be created in these illustrated books by images of light within the text, or (more metaphorically) by a visual flash that illuminates a world of enlightenment that lies outside the text proper but can be envisioned by an empathetic reader.[48]

One space for this envisioning of a world of interrelationship between the viewer and the viewed is Moses Roper's *A Narrative of the Adventures*

FROM SLAVERY. 43

then called upon me to stop, more than three times, and I not doing so, they fired after me, but the pistol only snapped.

MR. ANDERSON ATTEMPTING TO SHOOT THE AUTHOR, AFTER TELLING HIM TO STOP THREE TIMES, ACCORDING TO THE LAW.

This is according to law; after three calls, they may shoot a run-a-way slave. Soon after, the one on the horse came up with me, and, catching hold of the bridle of my horse, pushed the pistol to my side, the other soon came up; and, breaking off several stout branches from the trees,

Figure 12.6 Illustration from Moses Roper, *A Narrative of the Adventures and Escape* (1838 British ed.), 43. Wood engraving. *Google Books*. https://books.google.com/. Public Domain

and Escape of Moses Roper, from American Slavery (1837, 1838).[49] Roper wrote what is probably the first illustrated slave narrative, published in 1837 with two images, in 1838 with four images, and in 1840 with five. The 1840 edition includes a frontispiece portrait of Roper, which all later editions carried. On the one hand, Roper's text does contain images of enslaved torture. On the other hand, many of the images (when read in conjunction with the text that surrounds them) tend to focus on the dignity, resilience, and higher humanity of the enslaved. Moreover, many of the images in the text portray Roper as active, rather than passive, and as writing his own destiny. In this way he counteracts the social death of slavery (see Figure 12.6).

In the scene depicted in Figure 12.6, Roper flees on a horse while his owner, Mr. Anderson, attempts to shoot "the author." By insisting on his status in the caption as "the author" (which he has not yet achieved in the moment that the picture illustrates) and by claiming his heroism and strength as he flees on horseback, Roper moves away from the abjection and passivity commonly found in illustrations of the enslaved.[50] Unlike many other texts from this time period, Roper is not caught in a web of surveillance and torture. A viewer's eyes might follow Roper's movement off stage and out of the picture – and a viewer might imagine the space of freedom Roper (eventually) moves into, which in this particular illustration is a non-diegetic space outside of the drawing that can only be *envisioned by a reader*. Ultimately, Roper is taken back into slavery after this flight, but what may remain with the reader is this picture of a heroic, empowered man, rather than a passive or brutalized slave.

It is also crucial that Roper wrote his own text. Moreover, because Roper achieved some renown as an antislavery orator and writer, he seems to have had some control over the images in later editions, as I discuss elsewhere.[51] In particular, he seems to have had control over the first image in the text (after 1840) – the frontispiece portrait – which works to instate his status as a man, rather than chattel, and as an agent of change who is in charge of his own destiny. Visual contestation of abjection clearly inheres in the frontispiece portrait, which greets readers on the first page of the text (see Figure 12.7). This fine, accurate, and precise engraving shows Roper regarding the reader patiently, without anger. He is well dressed, central to the portrait, and appears wise, intelligent, and humane. He is not the tortured slave of the narrative but the mature man who will transcend this torture and write about it, as well as sit for a drawing of himself. As an emblem of his literacy, his signature resides below his image and emphasizes that he has achieved authorship. This image stands in contrast to the social death of slavery, to the specular objectification typically enacted on the body of the enslaved; the portrait indicates that Roper has survived this social death to become a free subject. He is a *revenant*, flashing out a light for a better world. Roper also uses imagery to create this flash of light, contrasting his past situation with his current one. For example, on one harrowing voyage towards freedom he comments (using present tense subjectivity) "I shall never forget the journey that night. The thunder was one continued roar, and the lightning blazing all around."[52] The lightning is an image within the text for the flash of truth he hopes to create, for the light he hopes to shed not only on the predicament and tortures of slavery, but on his return from this social death into authorship and a present tense identity as the free man of the frontispiece.

Like Roper's narrative, Henry Bibb's heavily illustrated *Narrative of the Life and Adventures of Henry Bibb, An American Slave, Written by Himself*

Figure 12.7 Frontispiece portrait from Moses Roper, *A Narrative of the Adventures and Escape of Moses Roper from American Slavery, with a Portrait.* London: Darton, Harvey, and Darton, 1840. Copper engraving. *Google Books*. Public Domain. https://books.google.com/

(1849) also visually and metaphorically flashes forth something like the literal illumination of a camera; these flashes elucidate the author's survival beyond the social death of slavery and his return into living subjectivity. Bibb states at one point that he has "undertaken to write the following sketch [his narrative], that *light and truth* might be spread on the sin and evils of slavery as far as possible."[53] Bibb's text attempts to light up the darkness and misery that is slavery, as far as this is possible, but also to create the flash of truth that signals the *revenant*, the return from social death. Moreover, both Bibb and Roper exert some power in the writing of the text and in the manipulation and placement of its illustrations. They each use their influence to create alternatives to the ocular structure of slavery.[54]

Of course, Bibb's text, like Roper's, does contain images of enslaved torture, and sometimes these images are simply lifted from other abolitionist publications.[55] But often, as I have argued elsewhere, they are

Figure 12.8 "My Heart is Almost Broken," from Henry Bibb's *Narrative* (1849, 2nd edition). *Google Books*. https://books.google.com/. Public Domain

repurposed and repackaged to create new significations.[56] Bibb's text also works to undermine the visual structure of enslavement, in which both men and women often were portrayed as lacking agency. Using illustrations, dialogue, and narrative, the text portrays both Bibb and his enslaved wife Malinda as dynamic and fluid characters, rather than submissive and static ones. For example, when Bibb is sold away from his wife Malinda, her grieving is loud and long and ends with these words: "'Oh! how shall I give my husband the parting hand never to meet again? This will surely break my heart.'" The illustration that accompanies her question also reproduces her forceful words, giving her a mode of voice.[57]

Bibb's text also grants outspoken and direct voice to Malinda in another significant picture: the representation that embellishes the front and back covers of some editions but also is duplicated within the text with a caption ("My heart is almost broken"), set between pages 81 and 82 (see Figure 12.8). As Wood has noted, many of the engravings in Bibb's text appear to be somewhat formulaic reproductions of enslaved torture,[58] yet this engraving is intensely intimate and specific to Bibb's text. It grants the nearest approach to the horror of slavery in the text as a whole, and it is an entirely personal one – the psychological trauma of leaving wife and child, which marks these individuals as fully human. In the text accompanying this scene, a reader is also given partial access to Bibb's consciousness as a way of incompletely apprehending knowledge about enslavement. "This was *almost* like tearing off the limbs from my body," writes Bibb about these experiences; *almost* but not quite.[59] Reading between the lines and assessing the picture and its surrounding text, we can see the existence of a visual field contrary to the one established by abolition and slavery – a visual field in which the enslaved are fully humanized subjects.

This oppositional visual field is also present in images of Bibb himself, both while he is in slavery and after he has escaped. For example, while in slavery he tries to protect his wife and child during one escape attempt, and Thomas Strong's illustration of this scene pictures Bibb standing up in a manly way to the wolves that surround the family in a forest.[60] Yet Bibb is retaken, and ultimately he must escape alone. It is therefore only in the frontispiece to the text that Bibb escapes from the social death of slavery and flashes forth as a *revenant* (see Figure 12.9). This engraving at the top of the page by Patrick Henry Reason depicts Bibb as a serious young man. It is a tasteful and carefully constructed image of Bibb, with his hand resting on a book that symbolizes his literacy, authorship, and control over the technologies of printing and image-making; a well-dressed Bibb confronts a viewer in a direct look through eyes that appear wise but also saddened. This frontispiece is like many of the others discussed in this chapter, in that Bibb is configured as a free man in possession of his own voice, person, and subjectivity.

Yet what makes this frontispiece unusual is the small cartoon image below Reason's engraving of Bibb; in this image Bibb is fleeing recapture with his hands in the air. Surrounding this cartoon is an ironic caption, given that Bibb does escape: "Stop the runaway! Where is he!" The cartoon image also gives the information that Bibb turned the corner too quickly for his master and escaped. Bibb here hollows out the discourse of the slave reward poster, in itself a visual mode confining African Americans throughout the seventeenth, eighteenth, and nineteenth centuries, as previously mentioned. The sarcastic "Stop the runaway! Where is he!" underneath Bibb's portrait, and his flowing signature with its elliptical line, seem to indicate that "he" (that is, the escaped slave) cannot be contained by the master's discourse. At one point Bibb comments that no one would buy him because "they saw the devil in my eye; I would run away, &c."[61] "He" is ultimately a trickster-like figure who remedies the breach between his status as chattel and man, and through ambiguous and mutating identities narrows the gap between the signifier "slave" and his present-tense identity as Henry Bibb.

As Lynn Casmier-Paz has noted, author portraits often operate as paratextual elements that validate racial identity: "The author portraits of slave narratives struggle to evidence multiple icons of realistic, biographical representation available to the period."[62] Augusta Rohrbach similarly

Figure 12.9 Frontispiece and title page to some versions of Henry Bibb's *Narrative* (1849, 2nd edition) with double portrait. Top portrait: copper engraving by Patrick Henry Reason. Bottom drawing: wood engraving (artist unknown). *Google Books*. Public Domain

argues that such portraits "locate the physical body" for a readership and to some degree guarantee it a "textual authenticity."[63] Yet Bibb's frontispiece double portrait both grants his authenticity – he seems real and stable in the top image – and undermines it by mocking that assumption that "he" (Bibb) can really be found in the text at all. Bibb both is and is not a *revenant* – he both has and has not come back from the social death that is slavery. Ultimately this double portrait speaks to the ways Bibb subverts the dominant visual mode of slavery and to the lasting trauma that is slavery itself – a trauma within which many still resided.

Spectacular Acts of Insubordination

In individuals such as Wheeler, Wheatley, Equiano, Freeman, Roper, and Bibb there is therefore a persistent use of illustrations that resist the abjection of enslavement and its visual politics, in which the enslaved were pitiful objects of the gaze. The individuals pictured often return the gaze of the viewer and show whole, unbeaten, literate selves. Moving forward by just a few years, beginning in the late 1840s, individuals such as Frederick Douglass and later (in the 1850s) Sojourner Truth utilized photographs of themselves in spectacular ways, building on the defiant visual work found in portraits, frontispieces, and illustrated books. This was in part due to technological transformations that occurred. In particular, the worldwide introduction of the daguerreotype – an early type of photograph – in 1839 led to a proliferation of photographic images. By 1853, as many as three million daguerreotypes per year were being produced in the United States.[64] By 1860 the daguerreotype had been replaced with less expensive processes of photography, but during the time period of 1840–1865 abolitionists such as Frederick Douglass and others quickly seized on these new technologies as instruments in the antislavery crusade.

From 1840 to the end of his life, Douglass, who escaped from slavery in 1838, manipulated his image in drawings and photographs, refusing to be portrayed as abject or servile. For example, in a striking half-plate daguerreotype by Samuel J. Miller created in 1852, Douglas is elegantly dressed but he stares at the viewer defiantly, returning the viewer's gaze.[65] Indeed, in the vast bulk of his photographs he refuses to smile for a viewer, or look down or away. In this way, Douglass builds on the legacy of Wheeler, Roper, Freeman, and Bibb, portraying himself as a fully human subject with emotions, such as anger, that cannot be contained by the simple catch phrase "Am I Not a Man and a Brother?" or by the icon of the runaway, with his bundle of rags on his shoulder. Douglass was not always in control of his image, but when he was, he used it in powerful ways that extend and expand the work of African Americans within earlier visual culture. Douglass spoke about photography in at least three speeches, and he was also the most photographed US man of the nineteenth century. He also carefully selected his photographers and the objects that would appear in the visual field of the photograph. All this suggests that he full well knew the value of the image and of photography's ability to counteract abjection.

Sojourner Truth – who escaped from slavery in 1826 – also used the power of the image to counteract the social death of slavery. Like Bibb, Truth's images of herself often contain a subversive subtext – in this case a motto that was printed on her *cartes de visite* below her image and reads: "I sell the shadow to support the substance."[66] Under slavery, Sojourner Truth was property, bought and sold, but now she sells her image (the shadow of herself, on the *carte de visite*) to support the substance (perhaps her soul). This ironic use of the iconography of slavery the *cartes de visite* could be bought, sold, and traded, as slaves themselves were also turns the rhetoric on its head. Like Bibb, Truth visually and verbally hollows out the discourse of slavery, suggesting that she both is and is not within it, and that the flash of light that the *revenant* brings may elucidate the darkness of an enslavement that refuses to disappear from the psyche of the formerly enslaved person or from the nation as a whole.

Douglass and Truth build on earlier subversive visual work by African Americans that was present in the culture at large. During the time period of 1800–1840, the portraits and paintings of individuals like Freeman and Wheeler and the illustrated texts of Roper and Bibb may have fostered this later spectacular utilization of visual-verbal rhetoric. By recasting the visual figuration of the fugitive slave him/herself into a more agentive mode and by subverting the optical regime of enslavement, these earlier illustrations encode a mode of visual *insubordination*. In so doing they signify not the social death of the enslaved but the physical and visual propulsion of the *revenant* into freedom – into a world of both visual and psychological self-fashioning and self-control.

Notes

1 See Simon Gikandi, *Slavery and the Culture of Taste* (Princeton: Princeton University Press, 2014) (especially chapter 3) and Marcus Wood, *Blind Memory: Visual Representation of Slavery in England and America, 1780–1865* (New York: Routledge, 2000).

2 Toni Morrison, *Playing in the Dark: Whiteness and the Literary Imagination* (New York: Vintage, 1993).

3 See Jasmine Nichole Cobb, *Picture Freedom: Remaking Black Visuality in the Early Nineteenth Century* (New York: New York University Press, 2015) and Marcus Wood, *The Horrible Gift of Freedom: Atlantic Slavery and the Representation of Emancipation* (Athens, GA: University of Georgia Press, 2010).

4 *Grand celebration ob de bobalition ob African slabery*, in Edward W. Clay's *Life in Philadelphia* Series (1833), Library Company of Philadelphia.

5 Michael A. Chaney, *Fugitive Vision: Slave Image and Black Identity in Antebellum Narrative* (Bloomington: Indiana University Press, 2008), 9.

6 See Orlando Patterson, *Slavery and Social Death: A Comparative Study* (Cambridge: Harvard University Press, 1985). Patterson argues that enslaved individuals were denied an autonomous social structure and were not even considered to be fully human (see pages 55–72).

7 Pier Gabrielle Foreman, "Who's Your Mama? 'White' Mulatta Genealogies, Early Photography, and Anti-Passing Narratives of Slavery and Freedom," *American Literary History* 14 (Autumn 2002): 505–539, 527.

8 This painting can be seen at: https://en.wikipedia.org/wiki/George_Washington_(Trumbull)#/media/File: George_Washington_MET_DT2823.jpg.

9 Gikandi, *Slavery*, 150.

10 *Description of a Slave Ship* (London: James Philips, 1789), Harvard University Library (Houghton). This image can be viewed here: https://i0.wp.com/blogs.princeton.edu/rarebooks/1789_LBrooks.jpg.

11 The image of the slave ship *Brooks* first appeared in Plymouth in 1788, and was republished quickly in Bristol, London, and Philadelphia. For a discussion of the differences between the various broadsides, see Marcus Rediker, *The Slave Ship: A Human History* (New York: Penguin, 2007) and Stephen Ferguson, "219 Years Ago: *Description of a Slave Ship*," *Rare Book Collections @ Princeton* [blog], last modified May 3, 2008, https://blogs.princeton.edu/rarebooks/2008/05/219-years-ago-description-of-a/.

12 See Wood, *Blind Memory*, especially chapter 5.

13 This painting can be viewed here: loc.gov/pictures/resource/cph.3g06204/.

14 See also Mary A. Favret's reading of this image, "Flogging: The Anti-Slavery Movement Writes Pornography," in *Romanticism and Gender*, ed. Anne Janowitz (Cambridge: Brewer, 1998), 19–41.

15 "Empathy," *Collins English Dictionary* (2017), www.collinsdictionary.com/us/dictionary/english.

16 Marianne Noble, "The Ecstasies of Sentimental Wounding in *Uncle Tom's Cabin*," *Yale Journal of Criticism* 10, no. 2 (1997): 295–320, 296.

17 Karen Sánchez-Eppler, *Touching Liberty: Abolition, Feminism, and the Politics of the Body* (Berkeley: University of California Press, 1993), 25.

18 Cobb, *Picture Freedom*, 31.

19 For more on the Wedgewood antislavery medallion, see Martha J. Cutter, *The Illustrated Slave: Empathy, Graphic Narrative, and the Visual Culture of the*

Transatlantic Abolition Movement, 1800–1852 (Athens: University of Georgia Press, 2017) and Mary Guyatt, "The Wedgwood Slave Medallion: Values in Eighteenth-Century Design," *Journal of Design History* 13, no. 2 (2000): 93–105.

20 For more on how portraiture was used to undermine the objectification of enslaved or formerly enslaved individuals, see Gwendolyn DuBois Shaw, *Portraits of a People: Picturing African Americans in the Nineteenth Century* (Andover: Addison Gallery of American Art, 2006).

21 Mikhail M. Bakhtin, *Rabelais and His World*, trans. Hélène Iswolsky (1965; Bloomington: Indiana University Press, 1984), 26.

22 Peter Stallybrass and Allon White, *The Politics and Poetics of Transgression* (Ithaca: Cornell University Press, 1986), 3.

23 See the frontispiece woodcut depicting Turner's attack, *c.*1831, *Horrid Massacre in Virginia*, in the book *Authentic and Impartial Narrative of the Tragical Scene Which Was Witnessed in Southampton County* (New York: Warner and West, 1831), https://digitalcollections.nypl.org/items/29666e80-51c2-0134-a964-00505686a51c.

24 See the colored foldout illustration, *Death of Captain Ferrer, the Captain of the Amistad, 1839*, in John Warner Barber, *History of the Amistad Captives* (New Haven: E.L. & J.W. Barber, 1840), https://digitalcollections.nypl.org/items/510d47e3-1a6d-a3d9-e040-e00a18064a99.

25 *Dying Confession of Pomp, A Negro Man, Who Was Executed at Ipswich, on the 6th August, 1795, for Murdering Capt. Charles Furbush, of Andover, Taken from the Mouth of the Prisoner, and Penned by Jonathan Plummer* (Newburyport: Jonathan Plummer; Blunt and March, 1795), http://docsouth.unc.edu/neh/pomp/menu.html.

26 Robert Voorhis and Henry Trumbull, *Life and Adventures of Robert, the Hermit of Massachusetts: Who Has Lived 14 Years in a Cave, Secluded from Human Society: Comprising, an Account of his Birth, Parentage, Sufferings, and Providential Escape from Unjust and Cruel Bondage in Early Life, and His Reasons for Becoming a Recluse* (Providence: Printed for H. Trumbull, 1829), http://docsouth.unc.edu/neh/robert/menu.html.

27 Ibid., 29.

28 *The Remarkable Case of Potter Jackson, (formerly steward of the Echo sloop of war) Giving an Account of the Most Cruel Treatment, he received from Captain Lively, (commander of the Lord Stanly slave-ship) and his Chief Mate, by Assaulting, Imprisoning, Putting in irons, and Cruelly flogging him . . . Written by himself; with the Trial, before the Right Hon. Lord Ellenborough, in the Court of King's Bench, Guildhall, London, on Thursday, July 10, 1806, when the jury returned a verdict, five hundred pounds damages!!* (London: printed for the author, R. Butters, 1806), www.loc.gov/resource/llst.065.

29 For more on the textual-visual radicalism of Walker's *Appeal*, see Marcy J. Dinius "'Look!! Look!!! At This!!!!': The Radical Typography of David Walker's 'Appeal,'" *PMLA* 126, no. 1 (2011): 55–72.

30 Ignatius Sancho and Joseph Jekyll, *Letters of the Late Ignatius Sancho, an African: To Which Are Prefixed, Memoirs of His Life by Joseph Jekyll* (London: Printed for W. Sancho, 1802, 1803), https://.books.google.com.

31 Olaudah Equiano, *The Interesting Narrative of the Life of Olaudah Equiano, or Gustavus Vassa, the African. Written by Himself* (1789; first US edition, New York: W. Durell, 1791), Eighteenth Century Collections Online, Gale Cengage.

32 Of course, not all of these images moved beyond abjection; Charles Ball's *Slavery in the United States: A Narrative of the Life and Adventures of Charles Ball* (1837), for example, has an image of the enchained supplicant slave as its frontispiece. See Ball, *Slavery in the United States: A Narrative of the Life and Adventures of Charles Ball, a Black Man, Who Lived Forty Years in Maryland, South Carolina and Georgia, as a Slave Under Various Masters, and was One Year in the Navy with Commodore Barney, During the Late War* (New York: Published by John S. Taylor, 1837), https://docsouth.unc.edu/neh/ballslavery/ball.htm.

33 See Olaudah Equiano, *The Life and Adventures of Olaudah Equiano; or, Gustavus Vassa, the African: From an Account Written by Himself*, ed. A[bigail] Mott (Philadelphia: Samuel Wood, 1829), https://books.google.com/books. For a discussion of Mott's use of the frontispiece image of Equiano and other images, see Martha J. Cutter, "The Child's Illustrated Talking Book: Abigail Mott's Abridgment of Olaudah Equiano's *Interesting Narrative* for African American Children," in *Who Writes for Black Children?: African American Children's Literature before 1900*, ed. Katharine Capshaw and Anna Mae Duane (Minneapolis: University of Minnesota Press, 2017), 117–144.

34 Phillis Wheatley, *Poems on Various Subjects, Religious and Moral* (1773; Denver: W. H. Lawrence, 1887), https://books.google.com. The Frontispiece can be viewed here: www.loc.gov/pictures/resource/cph.3g05316/.

35 See Phillis Wheatley and Margaretta Matilda Odell, *Memoir and Poems of Phillis Wheatley: A Native African and a Slave* (Boston, MA: Geo. W. Light, 1834).

36 Views of African Americans' inherent mental inferiority, though always present in the United States, appear to have crystallized in the time period of the American Revolutionary era in order to justify a permanent class of nonfree (African American) laborers. See Barbara Jeanne Fields, "Slavery, Race, and Ideology in the United States of America," *New Left Review* 1, no. 181 (May–June 1990): 95–118. Hilary Moss extensively examines hostility toward African American education in the antebellum period. See *Schooling Citizens: The Struggle for African American Education in Antebellum America* (Chicago: University of Chicago Press, 2009).

37 Two slaves sued for their freedom. *Brom and Bett v. Ashley* was argued before a county court. The jury ruled in favor of Bett and Brom, making them the first enslaved African Americans to be freed under the Massachusetts constitution of 1780. The municipal case set a precedent affirmed by the state courts in later cases and ultimately led to the abolition of slavery in Massachusetts. See

Dorothy A. Mays, "Elizabeth Freeman Case (1781)," in *Women's Rights in the United States: A Comprehensive Encyclopedia of Issues, Events, and People*, vol. 1, ed. Tiffany K. Wayne (Santa Barbara: ABC-CLIO, 2014), 56.

38 Freeman's portrait can be seen here: www.masshist.org/database/23.

39 Cobb, *Picture Freedom*, 29.

40 Nicholas Mirzoeff, *The Right to Look: A Counterhistory of Visuality* (Durham, NC: Duke University Press, 2011), 49–50, 7.

41 Charles Edwards Lester and Peter Wheeler, *Chains and Freedom: Or, The Life and Adventures of Peter Wheeler, a Colored Man Yet Living. A Slave in Chains, a Sailor on the Deep, and a Sinner at the Cross* (New York: E. S. Arnold, 1839), 37, https://archive.org/details/chainsfreedomorloolest.

42 Graham R. Hodges "Wheeler, Peter," in *Encyclopedia of African American History, 1619–1895: From the Colonial Period to the Age of Frederick Douglass*, ed. Paul Finkelman (New York: Oxford University Press, 2006), www.oxfordaasc.com/article/opr/t0004/e0598.

43 Harriet A. Jacobs and John S. Jacobs, *Incidents in the Life of a Slave Girl: Written by Herself, with "A True Tale of Slavery" by John S. Jacobs*, 3rd ed., ed. Jean Fagan Yellin (Cambridge, MA: Harvard University Press, 2009), 51.

44 See p. 37 of Charles Edwards Lester and Peter Wheeler, *Chains and Freedom*.

45 Ariella Azoulay, *The Civil Contract of Photography* (New York: Zone, 2008), 18, 23.

46 Portions of this section appear in a different format in my book, *The Illustrated Slave*.

47 Laura Wexler, "'A More Perfect Likeness: Frederick Douglass and the Image of the Nation," in *Pictures and Progress: Early Photography and the Making of African American Identity*, ed. Maurice O. Wallace and Shawn Michelle Smith (Durham, NC: Duke University Press, 2012), 19–20.

48 It is possible that Roper and Bibb knew of the invention of photography and modeled it in their texts rhetorically in some way, through flashes of light and objectifying truth. The earliest known surviving photograph made by a camera was taken by Joseph Nicéphore Niépce in 1826 or 1827. However, the daguerreotype was the first publicly available photographic process; it was offered for use in 1839 by its inventor Louis-Jacques-Mandé Daguerre. Mentions of this process circulated in journals as early 1835; see Paul-Louis Roubert, "Hubert, ou l'honneur de Daguerre," *Études Photographiques* 16 (2005): 41–49, http://etudesphotographiques.revues.org/717.

49 Moses Roper, *A Narrative of the Adventures and Escape of Moses Roper, from American Slavery*, British Edition (1837; London: Harvey and Dutton, 1838). Google Books.

50 For a longer discussion of Roper's use of images, see Cutter, *The Illustrated Slave*, chapter 3.

51 See Cutter, *The Illustrated Slave*, 111.

52 Roper, *A Narrative of the Adventures and Escape*, 22.

53 Henry Bibb, *Narrative of the Life and Adventures of Henry Bibb, an American Slave, Written by* Himself, 2nd ed. (New York: Published by the Author, 1849), xii. Emphasis added. Google Books.

54 Roper revised his manuscript throughout his life and published it himself in 1840, with no introductory documents. Bibb was a printer who printed his own text.

55 For a full discussion of Bibb's use of abolitionist print culture materials, see Marcus Wood, "Seeing Is Believing, or Finding 'Truth' in Slave Narrative: *The Narrative of Henry Bibb* as Perfect Misrepresentation," *Slavery and Abolition* 18, no. 3 (1997): 174–211.

56 See chapter 4 of Cutter, *The Illustrated Slave.*

57 Bibb, *Narrative of the Life and Adventures of Henry Bibb*, 147–148.

58 Wood, "Seeing," 182.

59 Bibb, *Narrative of the Life and Adventures of Henry Bibb*, 80, emphasis added.

60 Ibid., 124.

61 Ibid., 102.

62 Lynn Casmier-Paz, "Slave Narratives and the Rhetoric of Author Portraiture," *New Literary History* 34, no. 1 (2003): 91–116, 92.

63 Augusta Rohrbach, *Truth Stranger than Fiction: Race, Realism, and the U.S. Literary Marketplace* (New York: Palgrave, 2002), 127.

64 See Frederick S. Lane, *Obscene Profits: The Entrepreneurs of Pornography in the Cyber Age* (New York: Routledge, 2001), 42.

65 This portrait can be seen here: www.artic.edu/artworks/145681/frederick-douglass.

66 This image can be viewed here: www.loc.gov/pictures/resource/ppmsca.08978/.

Index

AAFIS, 185–189
AAS, 7, 128
Abolition of the Slave Trade, The, 318–319
abolitionist writing, 101, 103, 107, 122, 140, 167, 173
ACS
  motives of, 7, 56, 86
  policies of, 110, 204
  reaction to, 30, 86–87, 110, 136
Act for the Abolition of the Slave Trade, 6
Act for the Gradual Abolition of Slavery, 1, 288
advertisements. *See* newspaper advertisements
Afric-American Female Intelligence Society, 174, 185
African American Female Intelligence Society. *See* AAFIS
African Dorcas Associations, The, 174–175
African School, 73–76, 78, 84
Afro-Native identity, 127
Allen, Richard
  about, 288, 290–296
  influence of, 6, 22, 80
  work of, 168, 239–240, 294–295
  writings of, 5, 29, 301–302
amanuensis, 154, 159, 259
American Anti-Slavery Society. *See* AAS
American Colonization Society. *See* ACS
anti-colonization, 85–87, 139, *See also* colonization
antislavery activism, 7, 28–29, 44, 220–221, 300–302
antislavery texts, genre of, 213–214
autobiographers, 146, 159, 230
autobiographies, black, 147, 169, 229–230, 240
autobiographies, dream. *See* autobiographies, spiritual
autobiographies, slave, 75, 229, 242
autobiographies, spiritual, 146, 151, 153, 159

Banneker, Benjamin, 45–46, 48–49
Bell, Phillip, 175, 191, 196
benevolent societies, 139, 175, 186, 189–191, 193, *See also* literary societies
Bibb, Henry, 184, See also *Narrative of the Life and Adventures of Henry Bibb*
Bibb, Mary, 184
Black church, 21–23, 27–28, 31, 289
Black Codes, 4–5
Black Jacobins, The, 206
Black liberationism, 27, 29
black narratives, 122, 227, *See also* slave narratives
Black public sphere, 1
Black Women's Association of Philadelphia, 190
Blind African Slave, The, 155–156, 259–260, 262–268, 280–282
bobalition print, 85–86, 289–290
Brace, Jeffrey. *See* Brinch, Boyrereau
Brief Account of the Life, Experience, Travels, and Gospel Labours of George White, an African, A, 239–240
Brinch, Boyrereau, 5, 155–156, 158, 262–268, *See also The Blind African Slave*
British abolitionists, 97–100
Brooklyn
  labor market, 71–73
  print opportunities in, 71–72, 74, 83–85
  social reform movement, 82
Brooklyn African Woolman Benevolent Society, 78–81
Brown, Christian, 74, 85
Brown, John, 184
Brown, William Henry, 5
Burrell, John, 156

Canada, emigration to, 3, 96, 111, 183–184
Cary, Mary Ann Shadd, 176, 184
Cassey, Amy Matilda, 177
Cassey, Joseph, 196
census records, 2
Chains and Freedom, 328–330
Child, Lydia Maria, 136

Coker, Daniel
  about, 56
  critique of, 52–54
  influence of, 48–49
  writings of, 5, 44, 47–52
  writins of, 55
colonization, 54, 57, 61, 85, 182–186
Colored American, The, 78, 174–175, 182
Colored School No. 1. *See* African School
Columbian Orator, The, 46
Confession of John Joyce, 168
convention movement, Black, 171, 178, 198
cookbooks, 142, *See also* recipes
Cook's Oracle, The, 137, 144
Cooper, Anna Julia, 176
Cornish, Samuel, 5, 168, 175, 308
Cotton Kingdom, 124
cotton production, 124–125
Cowper, William, 99–100
Craft, Ellen, 203–211, See also *Running A Thousand Miles to Freedom*
Craft, William, 210–211, See also *Running A Thousand Miles to Freedom*
Crandall, Prudence, 15, 198
Croger, Benjamin, 71, 73, 80, 83–85
Croger, Peter, 71, 73, 75–76, 78–80, 83–85
Cruikshank, Isaac, 318
Cuffee, Paul, 22, 29, 109–110
Cugoano, Ottobah, 24, 45

daguerreotype, 255–256, 337
Declaration of Independence, 62, 308
Delany, Martin, 190
Delany, Samuel, 184
depersonalization, 136–137
de-racialization, 136
Description of a Slave Ship, 318
Douglass, Frederick, 46–47, 184, 228, 243, 249, 256–257, 330, 337, See also *Narrative of the Life of Frederick Douglass*
Douglass, Grace Bustill, 174
Douglass, Sarah Mapps, 7–8, 176, 181–186, 190
dream visions, 146–147, 149, 154, 159–162
Dunbar, Paul Laurence, 21

Easton, Hosea, 122–124, 127, 140–141, See also *Treatise on the Intellectural Character, and Civil and Political Condition of the Colored People of the United States*
education
  impediments to, 4, 77, 85
  importance of, 167, 176–182, 294, 298
  resistance to, 15
Edwards, Jonathan, 151
Elevator, 191
emancipation
  calls for, 47, 49, 54
  laws, 28, 80, 307
  resistance to, 48, 55, 105
  routes to, 2
emigration, 183
Emma Van Name, 270, 280, 286
equalitarianism, 50
Equiano, Olaudah, 45–46, 147, See also *The Interesting Narrative of the Life of Olaudah Equiano*

Female Dorcas Societies, 174
Female Literary Society, The, 167
Female Minervian Literary Association, 174
females, Black
  bias against, 128, 153, 198
  contributions of, 7–8, 15, 171–172
  influence of, 176–182
  roles of, 133, 139
First Great Awakening, 20
Forten, Charlotte, 8
Forten, Sarah, 174, 176, 181
Freedom's Journal
  about, 5, 44, 84, 168, 307–308
  influence of, 30, 173, 175–176, 192, 220–222
  works printed in, 174, 177, 179, 204–206, 213–216
Freeman, Elizabeth, 327–328
friendship albums, 255
Fugitive Slave Acts, 2, 91

Gainsborough, Thomas, 326
Garrison, William Lloyd, 87, 168, 179, 181–182, 186, 188, 228
  about, 198
General Colored Association, 33
Genius of Universal Emancipation, 168, 174
Gilbert, Olive, 159
Gloucester, Jeremiah, 296–310
Gore, Christopher, 134, 136
Gradual Emancipation Act, 76
Granville, Jonathan, 184
Grimes, William, 3, 46
Grimké, Charlotte Forten, 176
Gronniosaw, James Albert Ukawsaw, 45

Haiti, 6, 56, 98, 183–184, 204
Haitian Emigration Society, 184
Haitian Revolution, 32, 206–207, 209–210, 222
Harlem Renaissance, 161
Harper, Frances, 176
Haynes, Lemuel, 22, 101
Heade, Martin Johnson, 278
heroines, mixed race, 204, 207–217, 219–222

Hopkins, Pauline, 176
Hopkins, Samuel, 46
Horton, George Moses, 29
House Servant's Directory, The, 127–140

immigration, 108–109, 183–184, 204
Incidents in the Life of a Slave Girl, 160
Interesting Narrative of the Life of Olaudah Equiano, The, 147–149, 326–327
interracial dialogues, 67
interracial marriages, 55, 61–62

Jackson, Andrew, 134
Jackson, Potter, 325, See also *The Remarkable Case of Potter Jackson*
Jacobs, Harriet, 91, 159, See also *Incidents in the Life of a Slave Girl*
James, C.L.R., 206
Jea, John, 23–27, 239, 243–249, See also *The Life, History, and Unparalled Sufferings of John Jea*
Jefferson, Thomas, 4, 45–46, 48–49, 53–55, 68, 266, See also *Notes on the State of Virginia*
Jennings, Elizabeth, 176–177, 196
Johnson, Henry, 102
Johnson, Joshua, 5, 261–262, 270–277, 281–282, See also *Emma Van Name, The McCormick Family, Mrs. Thomas Everette and Her Children*
Jones, Absalom
  influence of, 6, 22, 296–300
  work of, 45, 239, 290, 302
  writings of, 5, 75, 97, 299–302
Joyce, John, 168
Judge, Ona, 91

Kirk, Thomas, 74, 76–77, 80–81
Kitchiner, William, 137–138, See also *The Cook's Oracle*
Knapp, Isaac, 128, 198

labor, black, 127–131
labor, domestic, 133–135
labor, wage, 125–126
lace, 271–274, 286
Larsen, Nella, 161
lectures, printed, 188
Lee, Jarena, 153, See also *The Life and Religious Experience of Jarena Lee, Religious Experience and Journal of Mrs. Jarena Lee*
letters to the editor, 178
Liberator
  about, 168, 180
  influence of, 7, 78, 99
  works printed in, 174, 178–179, 184–186, 188
Liberia, colony of, 110, 184
Life and Adventures of Robert, the Hermit of Massachusetts, 323–325
Life and Religious Experience of Jarena Lee, The, 153–154, 230
Life, History, and Unparalled Sufferings of John Jea, The, 239–240, 243, 247–248
literacy, importance of, 15
literary societies, 171–176, 184–186, 189–192, 194, 196
lithography, 256
L'Ouverture, Touissant, 211
Lundy, Benjamin, 168
Lynchburg Virginian, 137, 139
Lyons, Maritcha, 176, 196

Madison, James, 56
Marly, 213–216
masculinist perspective, 36
McCormick Family, The, 274, 276
McHenry, Elizabeth, 10
Methodism
  antislavery and, 28, 39
  influence of, 16, 20, 22, 40, 126, 239
Miller, William, 97, 100, 103–104, 108
Morrison, Toni, 161
Mother Bethel AME, 6, 16
Mrs. Thomas Everette and Her Children, 275, 277
mutual aid societies, 6, 79, 82, 125, 180

Narrative of Sojourner Truth, The, 159
Narrative of the Adventures and Escape of Moses Roper, A, 330–332
Narrative of the Life and Adventures of Henry Bibb, 332–337
Narrative of the Life and Adventures of Venture, 231–237
Narrative of the Life of Frederick Douglass, 243
narratives. *See* Black narratives, slave narratives
Nat Turner's Uprising, 131
National Convention of Free People of Color, 139
nationalism, Black, 22, 172, 182–183, 187–190
Native Americans, 126–127, 135, 138
New York African Society for Mutual Relief, 78–79
newspaper advertisements, 75, 77–78, 107, 255
newspapers, Black, 168, 190–191, See also *Freedom's Journal*
newspapers, importance of, 76–78, 173, 181–182, 198
Notes on the State of Virginia, 58–60
Nugent, Richard Bruce, 161

Our Nig, 128, 130

pamphleteers, 5, 82
pamphlets
  examples of, 140
  importance of, 81–82
  influence of, 44–45, 81
  literary dialogues and, 66
  purpose of, 5, 16, 71, 255
Parrish, John, 54–55
Parrott, Russell, 5, 101, 303
Peale, Raphaelle, 278, 297
PFLA, 174, 181–183
Philadelphia Female Literary Association. *See* PFLA
Plato, Ann, 127
Poems on Various Subjects, 192, 327
politics, black, 119, 173, 187
politics, Black women's, 173, 178, 189–191
portraiture, 260, 268–269, 281, 288–290, 295–297, 311
Prentiss, Benjamin Franklin, 154–155, 259, 263
press, Black, 167–168, 171–172, 176, 178, 182, 190
Prince, Lucy Terry, 135
Prince, Mary, 229
Pringle, Thomas, 106
print, importance of, 77–78, 171–176, *See also* letters to the editor, newspapers, newspaper advertisements, pamphlets
Purvis, Harriett Forten, 174

race-mixing, 55–56
Ray, Charles, 175, 196
Ray, Henrietta Green Regulas, 175
Reading Room Society, 174
recipes, 132, 135
recirculation, 188–189, 193
redemption, 228–229, 233–240, 244, 248–250
Religion and the Pure Principles of Morality, 186, 188
religion, importance of, 16
Religious Experience and Journal of Mrs. Jarena Lee, 256
Remarkable Case of Potter Jackson, The, 325
Repository of Religion and Literature, and of Science and Art, 189
revenant, 330–338
revivalist movement, 20–21
Rights of All, 168
Roberts, Benjamin Franklin, 129
Roberts, Robert, 119–122, 131, 136, See also *The House Servant's Directory*
Roper, Moses, 330, See also *A Narrative of the Adventures and Escape of Moses Roper*
Ruffin, Josephine St. Pierre, 8
Running A Thousand Miles to Freedom, 210
Russwurm, John, 5, 168, 308

sailors, Black, 29, 126, 139, 238
Sancho, Ignatius, 326
Sansay, Leonora, 216, See also *Zelica the Creole*
Saunders, Prince, 5, 98, 204
Second Great Awakening, 24, 37, 228
self-publication, 160
sexual exploitation, 128
Sierra Leone Company, 108, 117
Sierra Leone, emigration to, 21–22, 96, 108–110
slave narratives
  examples of, 3, 259
  genre of, 3–4, 45–46, 260, 264, 277, 280
slave society, Caribbean, 103–107, 116
Slave Trade Act of 1807, 124
slavery, Jamaica. *See* slave society, Caribbean
slavery, West Indies. *See* slave society, Caribbean
Smibert, John, 277–278
Smith, James McCune, 204
Smith, Venture, 24, 45–46, 230–231, 238, 249
Spooner, Alden, 77
Stewart, Maria
  influence of, 174, 176–178, 185–190
  writings of, 99–101, 229, See also *Religion and the Pure Principles of Morality*

Terrell, Mary Church, 176, 191, 196
Thompson, Henry C., 71, 73, 84
Treatise on the Intellectual Character, and Civil and Political Condition of the Colored People of the United States, 127–128
Troy Female Benevolent Society, 174–175
Trumbull, John, 318
Truth, Sojourner, 337–338, See also *The Narrative of Sojourner Truth*
Tryon, Thomas, 46
Tudas, Jonathan, 295
Turner, Nat, 9, 323, *See also* Nat Turner's Uprising

Underground Railroad, 2–3
US Act Prohibiting the Importation of Slaves, 6
Vesey, Denmark, 30, 140
Voorhis, Robert, 323–325, See also *Life and Adventures of Rober, the Hermit of Massachusetts*

Walker, David
  about, 30–31
  critique of, 57–61

Walker, David (cont.)
  influence of, 9, 34–35, 61–65
  writings of, 4, 30–34, 36, 57, 98–99, 105
Washington, Erastus, 77
Washington, George, 318
Wedgwood, Josiah, 321
Weekly Anglo-African Reading Room, 190
Weekly Anglo-African, The, 190
Weeksville, 73
Wheatley, Phillis, 4, 21, 29, 33, See also *Poems on Various Subjects*
Wheeler, Peter, 328, See also *Chains and Freedom*
Whipper, William, 101–102
White, George
  about, 40, 149–153, 238–242
  writings of, 3, 27, 152–153, 249, See also *A Brief Account of the Life, Experience, Travels, and Gospel Labours of George White, an African*
Whitney, Harry, 154
Wilberforce settlement, 110–111
Wilberforce, William, 95, 310, 319
Williams, Jr., Peter, 28, 109–111
Williams, Sr., Peter, 28
Wilson, Harriet, See also *Our Nig*
Woman of Colour, The, 219
Worthington, Erastus, 74, 81

Young, Edward, 102–103

Zelica the Creole, 216–218